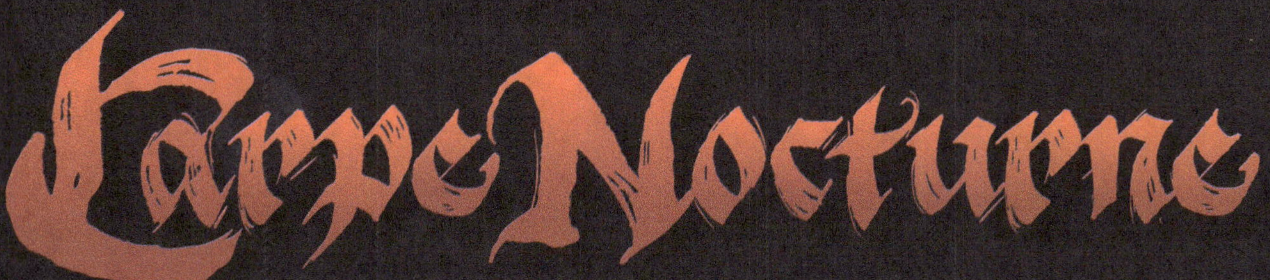

CREDITS

Publisher
Visual Adjectives

Editor in Chief
Paula Andrews Powles

Managing Editor
Michael Jack

Amy Townsend
Annabella Rios
Asylum Attendant
Bella Blitz
Chirality
Dawn Wood
Ethicus
FairlyInnocent

Hyde Falkenstein
J. David Howard
Jezibell Anat
Jesse Orr
Joseph A. Zuchowski
Isolde de Mortimer
K.A. Morris
Kathleen Sharkey

LinnieSarah Helpern
Michele Combs
Omen
Sergio Manghina
Sonnett57
XXX Zombieboy XXX
Zahara
Zannie

*Carpe Nocturne Magazine is available
in Digital and Print Edition!
Available in print at
www.barnesandnoble.com*

SUBSCRIBING IS EASY!

*Never miss an issue.
Have Carpe Nocturne Magazine
delivered directly to your front door or
office 4 times a year.
Email: subscribe@carpenocturne.net*

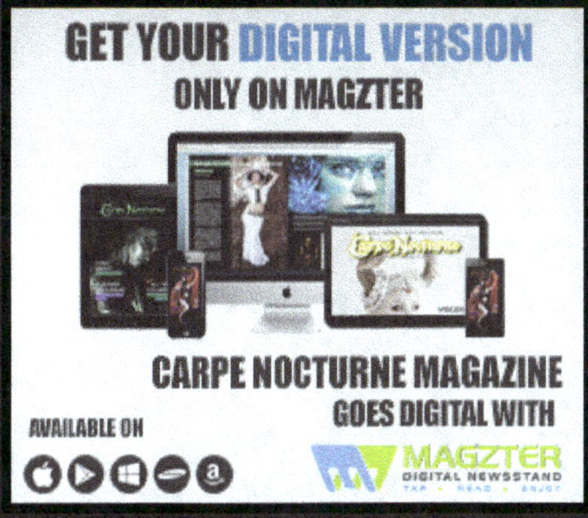

VOLUME X
FALL 2015

Carpe Nocturne Magazine Volume X • Fall 2015
is a publication of Visual Adjectives, LLC and published four times a year.
All reviews and coverage expressed in this publication are the opinions of the writer
and/or those being interviewed and may not be shared by Visual Adjectives.
Copyright © 2015 by Visual Adjectives, LLC. All rights reserved. October 2015.
14280 Military Trail, #7501, Delray Beach, FL 33482, USA.
No work may be copied or reproduced without the express permission of the editor or publisher.

E-mail: editor@carpenocturnemagazine.com
www.carpenocturnemagazine.com
p: 561-809-3834 • f: 904-701-6272

CORRESPONDENCES SHOULD
BE ADDRESSED TO:

Carpe Nocturne Magazine
14280 Military Trail, #7501
Delray Beach, FL 33482, USA

Carpe Nocturne

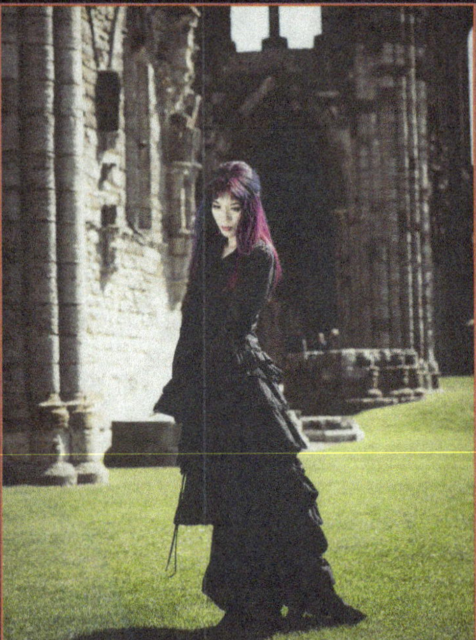

ON OUR COVER
LaCarmina
Read more on page 12 .

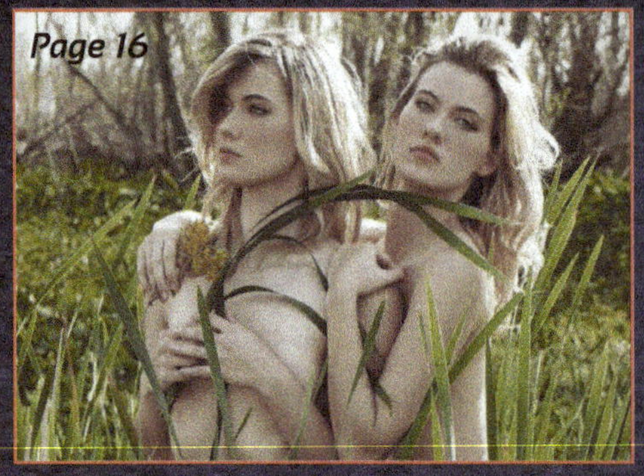
Page 16

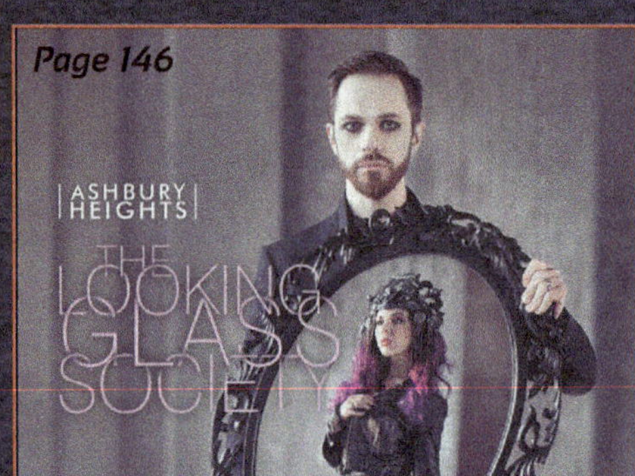
Page 146

INTERVIEWS

FEATURES

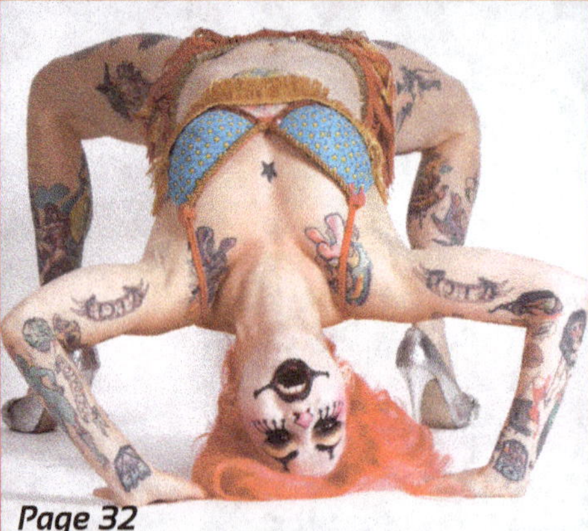
Page 32

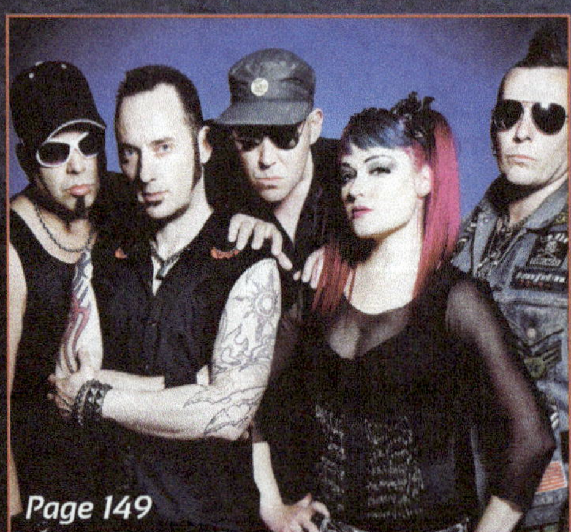
Page 149

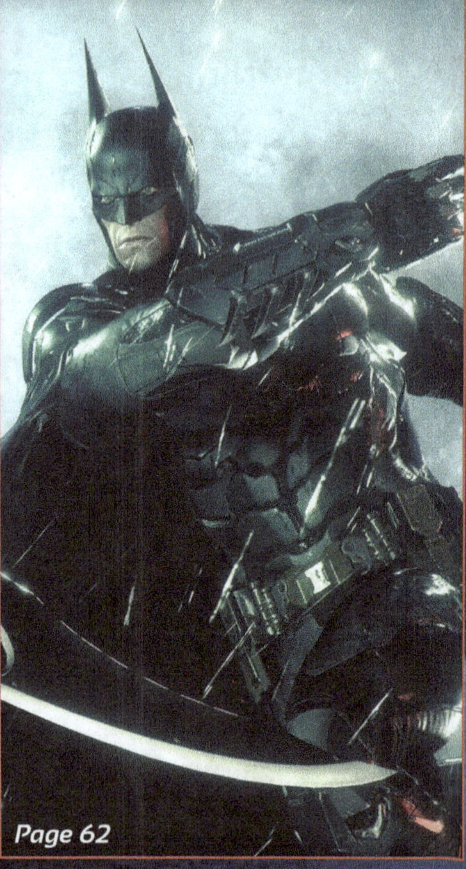
Page 62

OTHER THAN THE NORM

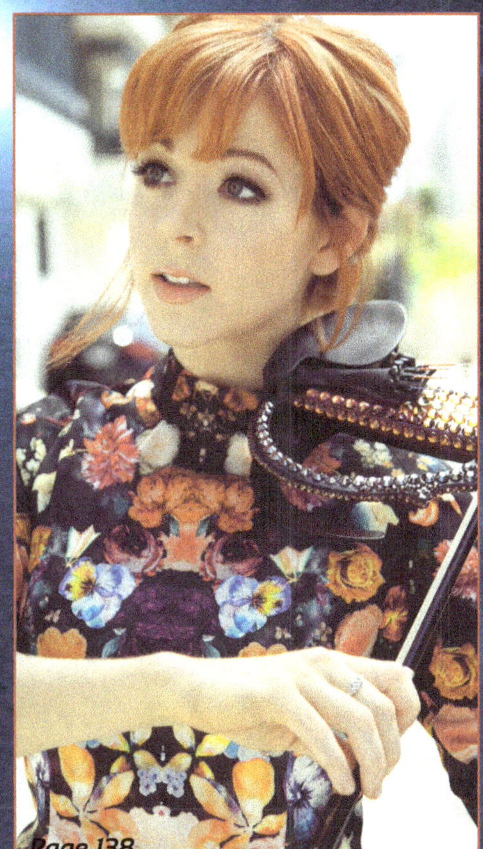
Page 138

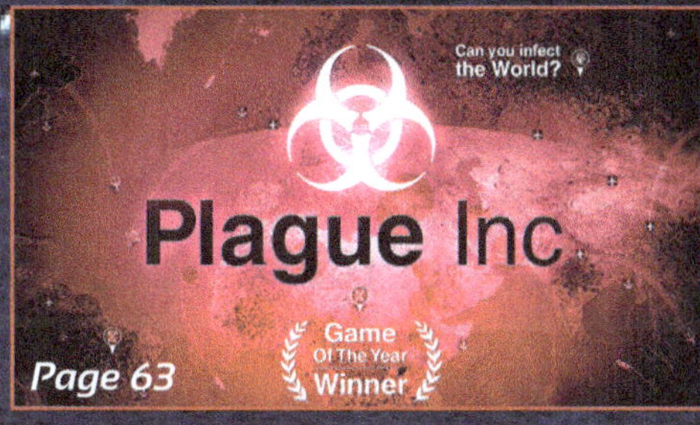

Page 63

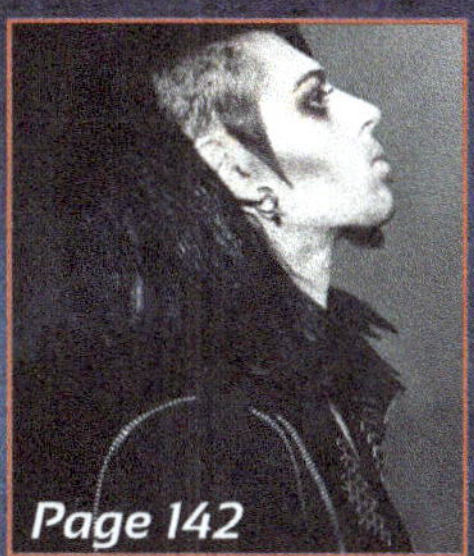
Page 142

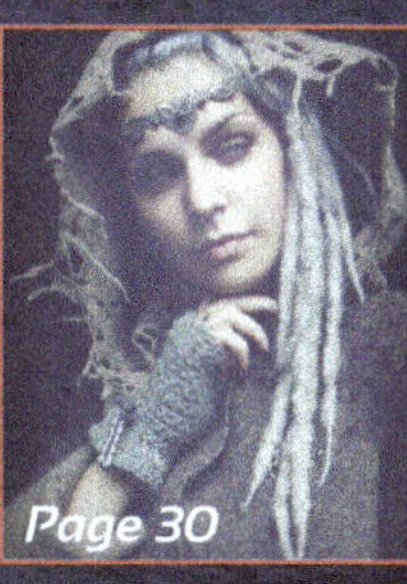
Page 30

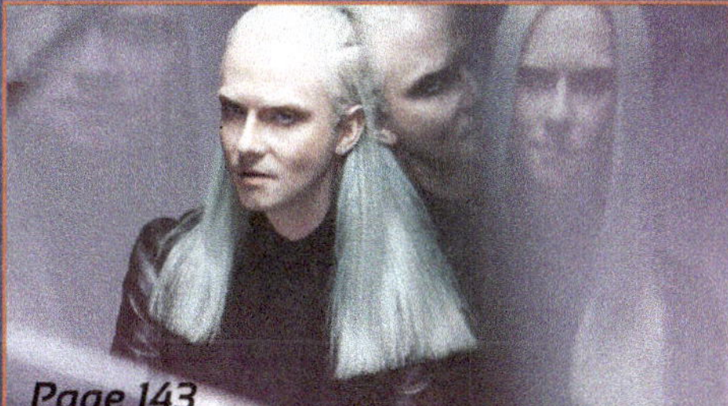
Page 143

REGULARS

REVIEWS

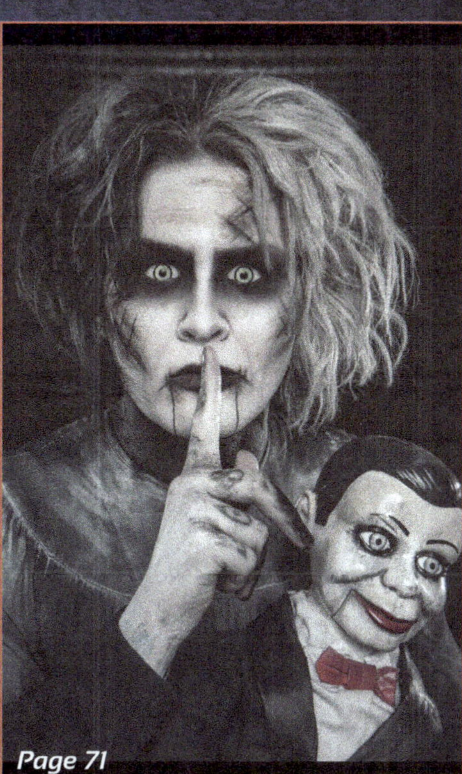
Page 71

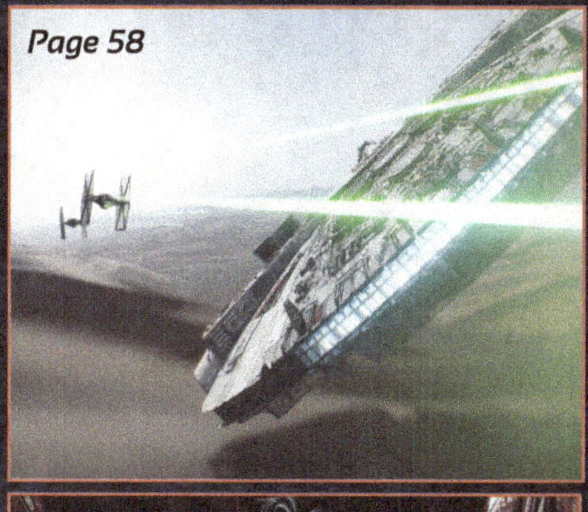
Page 58

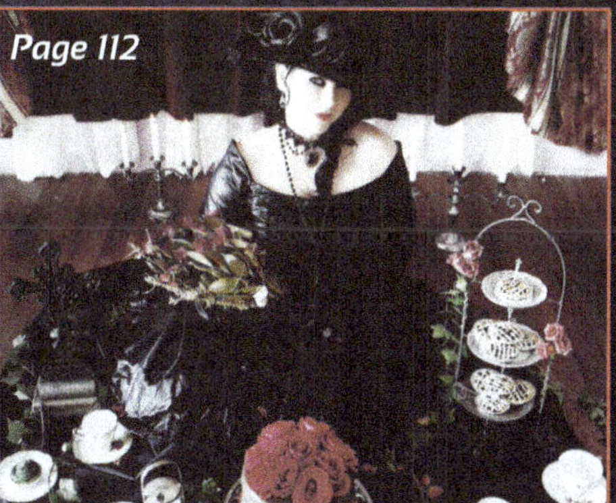
Page 112

SPOTLIGHT FEATURE

There are a lot of truly talented people out there, especially in our culture. Some use this talent simply for passing the time and personal growth, while others develop their talent to create services, works and objects for others to enjoy. Some post their creations on their website and never try to sell their works, while others use their talents to supplement or create their income. Carpe Nocturne Magazine admires, respects, and supports YOUR TALENT!

Whether you are creating to sell or only for personal enjoyment, LET THE WORLD SEE WHAT YOU'VE GOT!
There is NEVER A CHARGE to be Spotlighted or Featured!

The feature within Carpe Nocturne Magazine spotlights artists, designers, photographers, crafters and others with a creative side.

Does your work relate to the subject matter of this publication. Whether you do what you do for self-enjoyment or to sell your craft, we support you.

Contact: art@CarpeNocturne.net
Subject Line: Spotlight Feature

ARTISTS • COSPLAYERS • CRAFTERS • DESIGNERS • MODELS • MUSICIAN • PHOTOGRAPHER

When Reality Hits

By Chirality

This article will not be pretty, it will not use big words or adjectives. It is going to get to the point. It may anger some and make others relieved. Let me say first that I love this scene, this culture. I am lucky to live in the NYC area where I am not hassled or bothered by my choices. I am not really called names or made fun of. I know some kids in small towns who are yearning to get out.

That being said, I need to address something that has been pressing on my mind for a while, which is life and the scene. We work, we get married, and maybe have kids. We get sick, we get busy. When I hear people say, "the scene is dead," I want to claw my eyes out. Does new life need to come into it? Maybe. All I know is you cannot fault people for working, living and doing what they need.

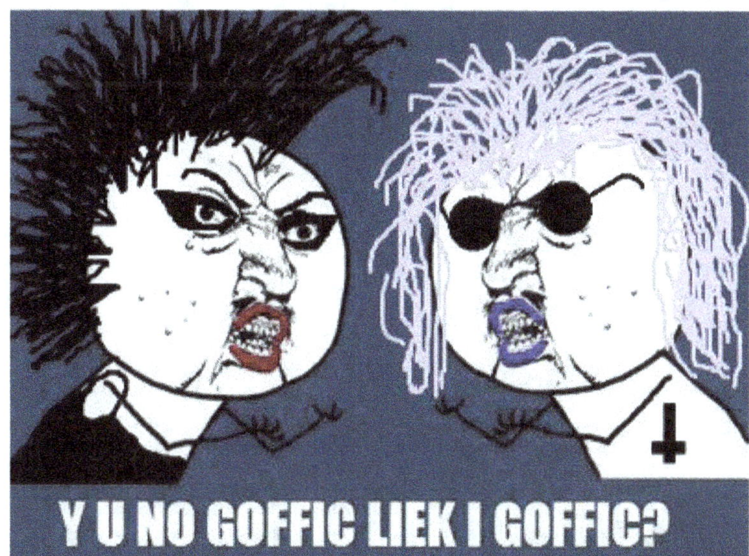

I will share a personal story. I have worked very closely with the clubs. I was a frequent face. I started to have various health issues. I also work 12 hour days. I remember coming into the club one night and someone asking where I had been. I told her work has been insane. She looked at me funny so I felt like I needed to defend myself. "I have also been having some health issues." "Oh!" She replied. "I was going to say, work is not an excuse. I work two jobs and I am here". Well congrats sporto, but you are not everyone. I am not exactly 18 and I am not exactly the pinnacle of health. What really got me upset though was that this person never texted, called, Facebooked me... ANYTHING, and yet you think you have the right to question not only my loyalties but my whereabouts? SCREW YOU. We are allowed to have boyfriends, marriages, babies and shouldn't have to fear the "YOU SO SOLD OUT!" What are you, five?

For serious, if you do not want the scene to die then make the people in it want to stay in it! After all this, I am not too keen on the club or the scene friends. I realized that if I am not there I basically have no friends and well. I would rather have zero then thirty fake ones.

You want to bitch about a dead scene and make people feel bad for growing up? Why don't you plan hang out days or dinners out? Last I checked, the world is much more than drinking and dancing. It used to make me sad, and I guess I still am, otherwise I wouldn't be writing this. My illness is my own, but I will be DAMNED if I am made to feel bad about it. I lost many said "friends," but screw them. I need to look out not only for my job, but my health as well. I need my health to keep my job.

Bottom line: REACH OUT. That is all. You want the scene to thrive? Then help and befriend the ones who need it the most. THAT makes people want to come out.

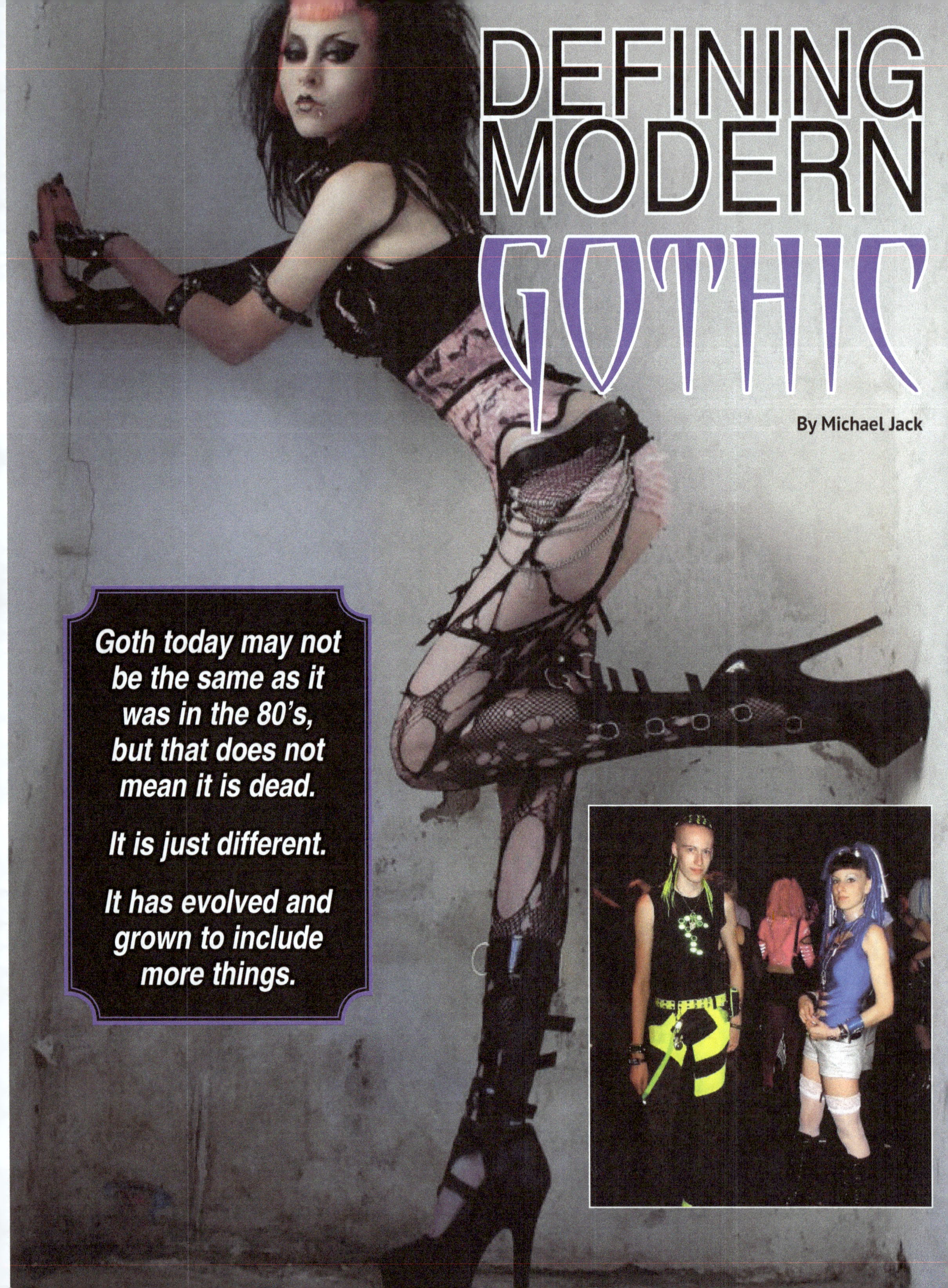

DEFINING MODERN GOTHIC

By Michael Jack

> Goth today may not be the same as it was in the 80's, but that does not mean it is dead.
>
> It is just different.
>
> It has evolved and grown to include more things.

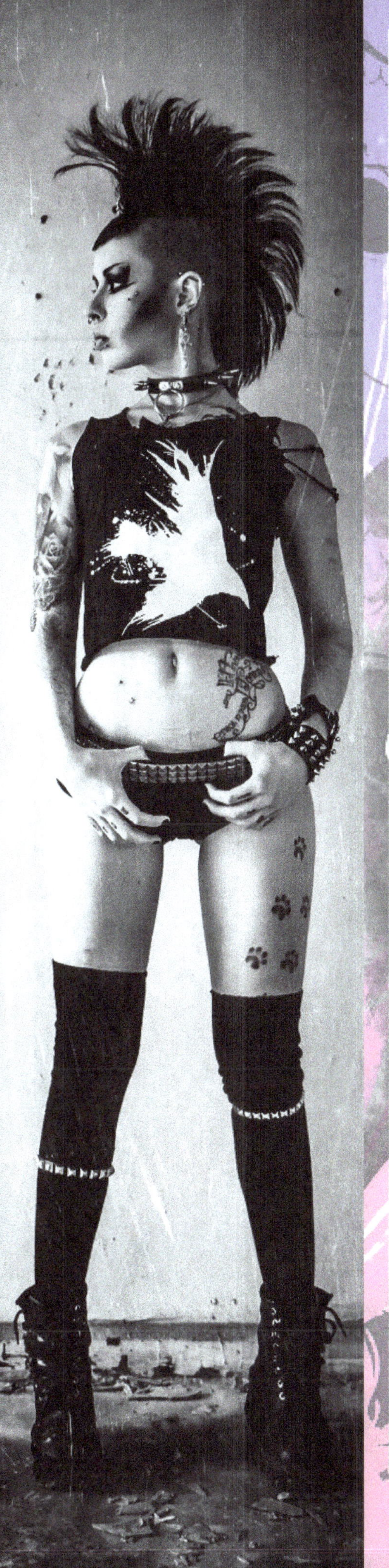

I think it is safe to say the word "Goth" has become an umbrella term used to describe a lot of different things and people of darker tastes and lifestyles. Is the general use of the word correct, and does it really matter? It matters to some people, and not at all to others. I have learned this. In fact, I have learned a lot of things by simply reading and doing research for Carpe Nocturne.

I love blogs. I am extremely interested when people write, "For the last time, this is the definition of Goth." It is actually their definition, because there is no generally accepted definition. I'm also curious when people write, "Do not label me Goth. I hate labels." Although, I think most people would agree if that person had to be labeled, Goth would be the correct one to use, including themselves. The one statement I generally don't like to see is, "Goth is dead. What you see today is not Goth." I think that opinion is very narrow minded. Goth today may not be the same as it was in the 80's, but that does not mean it is dead. It is just different. It has evolved and grown to include more things. I think a more accurate statement would be, "Goth today isn't the same as it was when it began." I can accept that statement, and we can have a conversation about our opinions of why it is better or worse and how exactly it has changed.

I love to read when people outside of the culture study Goths, and try to explain who we are. Amusingly, these are usually people in the psychology and sociology fields. Honestly, most of them do a fairly decent job, and I personally enjoy when they admit how surprised they were at their findings. Goths do not generally fit the popular stereotypical mold. We all know this. We are very social, friendly, and generally outgoing. It is the love of the macabre and the bizarre that tie us together. Yes, yes, again we know this. The only thing I would comment to the so-called experts is we are not a tolerant culture. I see this statement a lot. We are an accepting culture. It is very different. I do not tolerate that a person is bisexual because I am heterosexual, or a person is Jewish because I am Catholic. I accept them as they are. Those kind of differences in people don't matter to me, just as they don't with most Goths. At least the people who take time to really research us are on the right path.

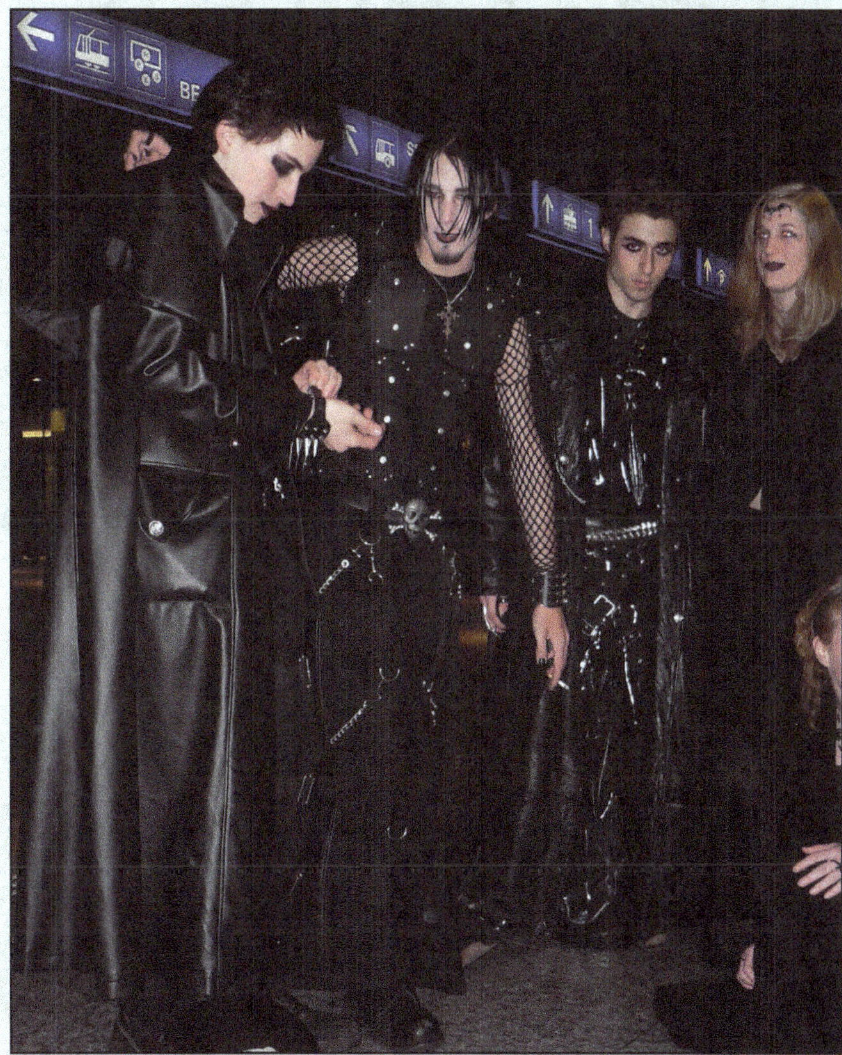

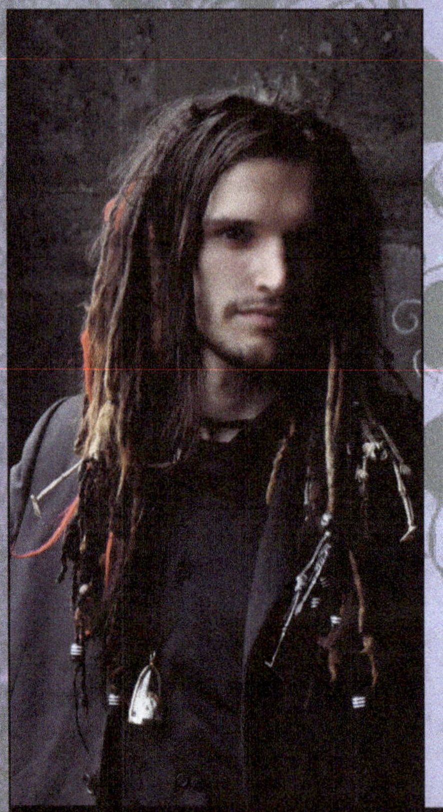

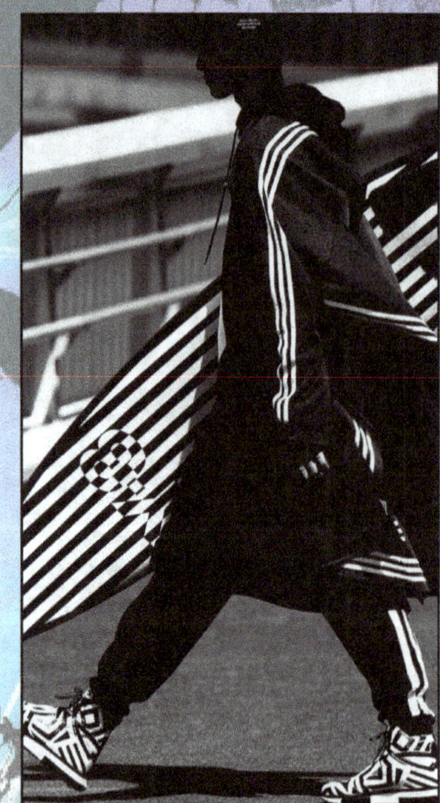

Another thing that fascinates me about the growing Gothic culture is the sub-classes. This is where the debates get really heated. Is CyberGoth really Goth? What about the Punk Goths, Hippie Goths, and RomantiGoths? One new offshoot are the Pastel Goths. People get particularly up in arms about them because they break a lot of the accepted aesthetics. We all admit that Goth is a culture, not a fashion or trend. Therefore, you would think if these groups adhere to the core beliefs of Goths, then they are Goths. Yet, you have the fundamentalist Goths saying CyberGoths are not Goths, and the CyberGoths saying the Pastel Goths are not Goths, and it goes on and on. I think the basic assumption I can make is Goths are protective of our culture even though we can't agree what exactly that culture includes. I also believe there is huge difference between being Goth and being active in the scene. However, the people who are just being active in the scene are helping to keep our culture alive. Therefore, I don't see a problem with it or a reason to call them out as some people do.

The newest sub-class I have seen pop up lately is the Health Goth. From what I can tell, this is a fashion style, and has nothing to do with the Gothic Culture. The term Goth is being used to describe

We all admit that Goth is a culture, not a fashion or trend.

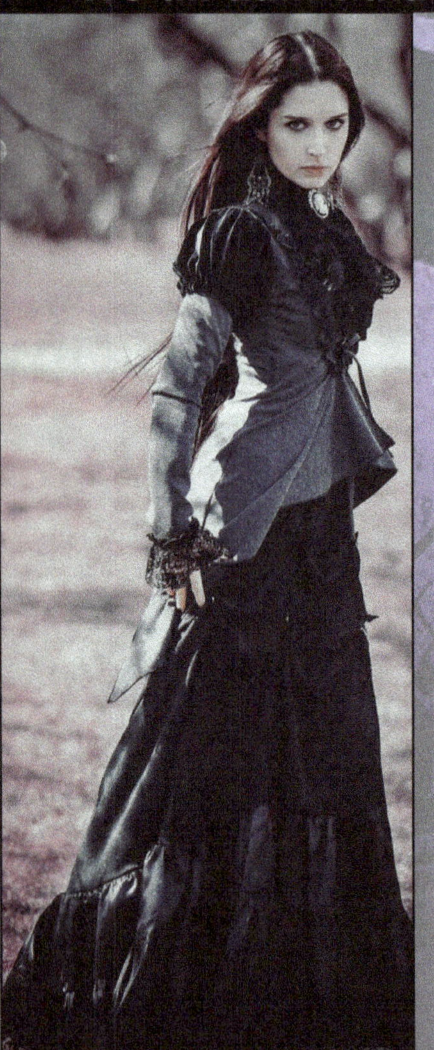

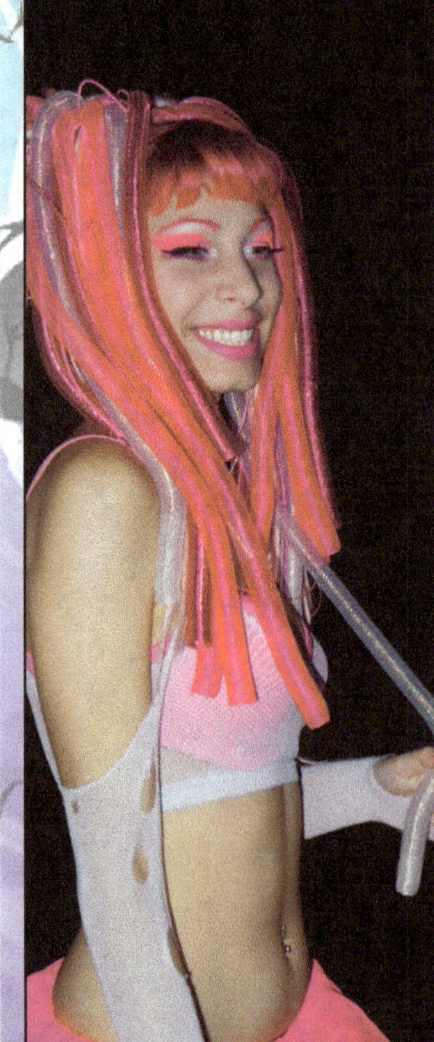

a darker fashion sense, and brands like Nike are jumping on board. Already Health Goth is evolving, and has expanded to include a belief in a healthy body and mind. This still doesn't make it anywhere near the proper use of the term, but it is interesting. The second someone uses the almighty G word, there will be people of the darker cultures jumping in and voicing their opinion. Interestingly, there doesn't seem to be a lot of negativity being thrown at the Health Goth community. Instead, there seems to be a mission to bring them more in line with the beliefs and preferences of the darker cultures. I am very curious to see where this thing goes. It is very possible in the future I may be interviewing the very first Health Goth band. Then again, this trend, for that's what it appears to be, may die, and I've just wasted a paragraph of this article.

I think the thing that intrigues me most out of everything I research is how incredibly powerful the word Goth has become. It instantly evokes a reaction from within the culture and from without. It inspires fashions, fuels debates, and peaks curiosities enough for people to study us. We are almost taboo to a lot of people because our styles and tastes are so far outside of the accepted norms. Yet, people want to know more, see more, and incorporate part of us into part of what they do. Perhaps some of them are Closet Goths? That very well could be a new sub-class. When dealing from within our culture, I'm not sure there will ever be a universally accepted term of what Goth truly is. What I do believe is the struggle to define ourselves and to protect our culture are traits of what I consider to be the Modern Goth.

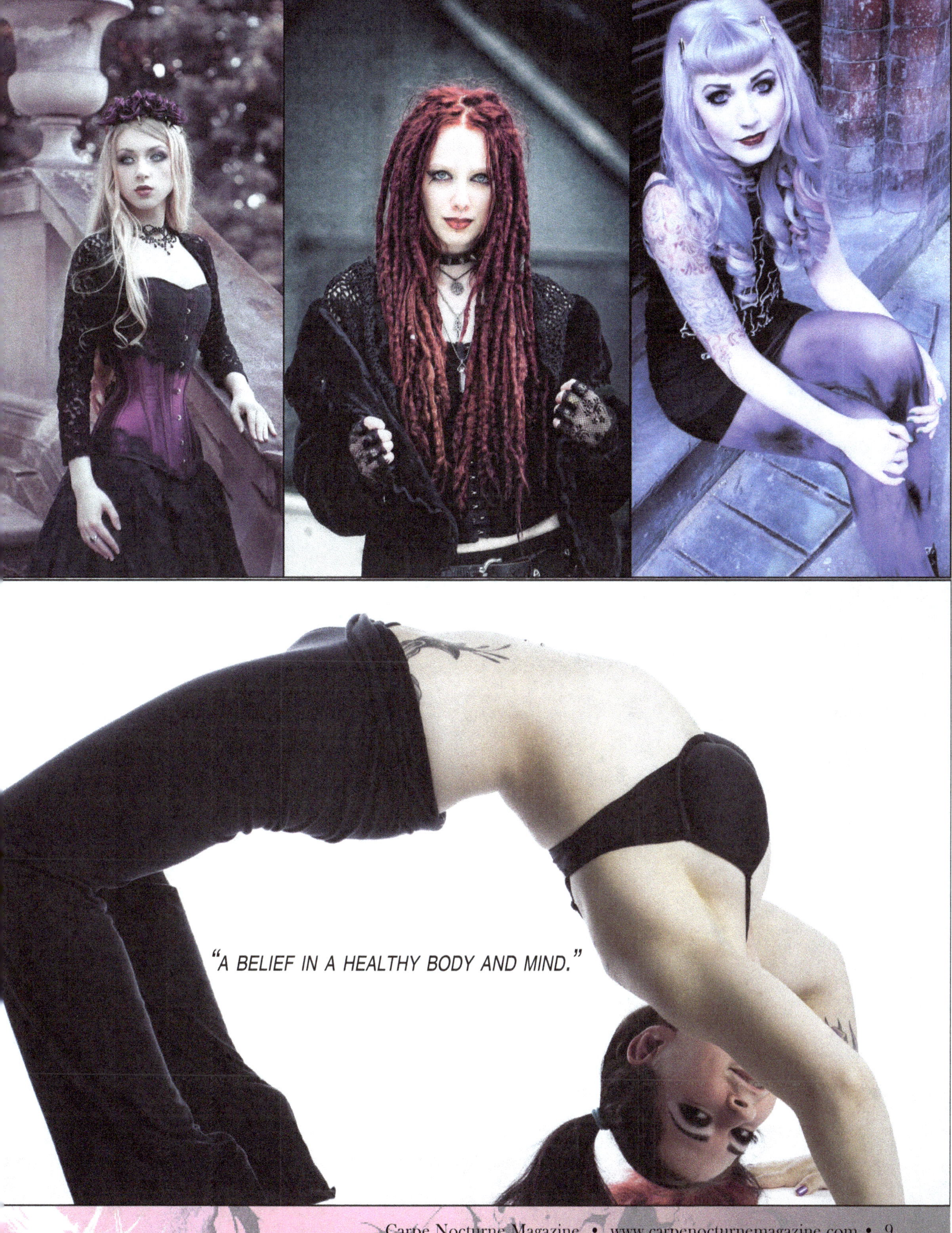
"A BELIEF IN A HEALTHY BODY AND MIND."

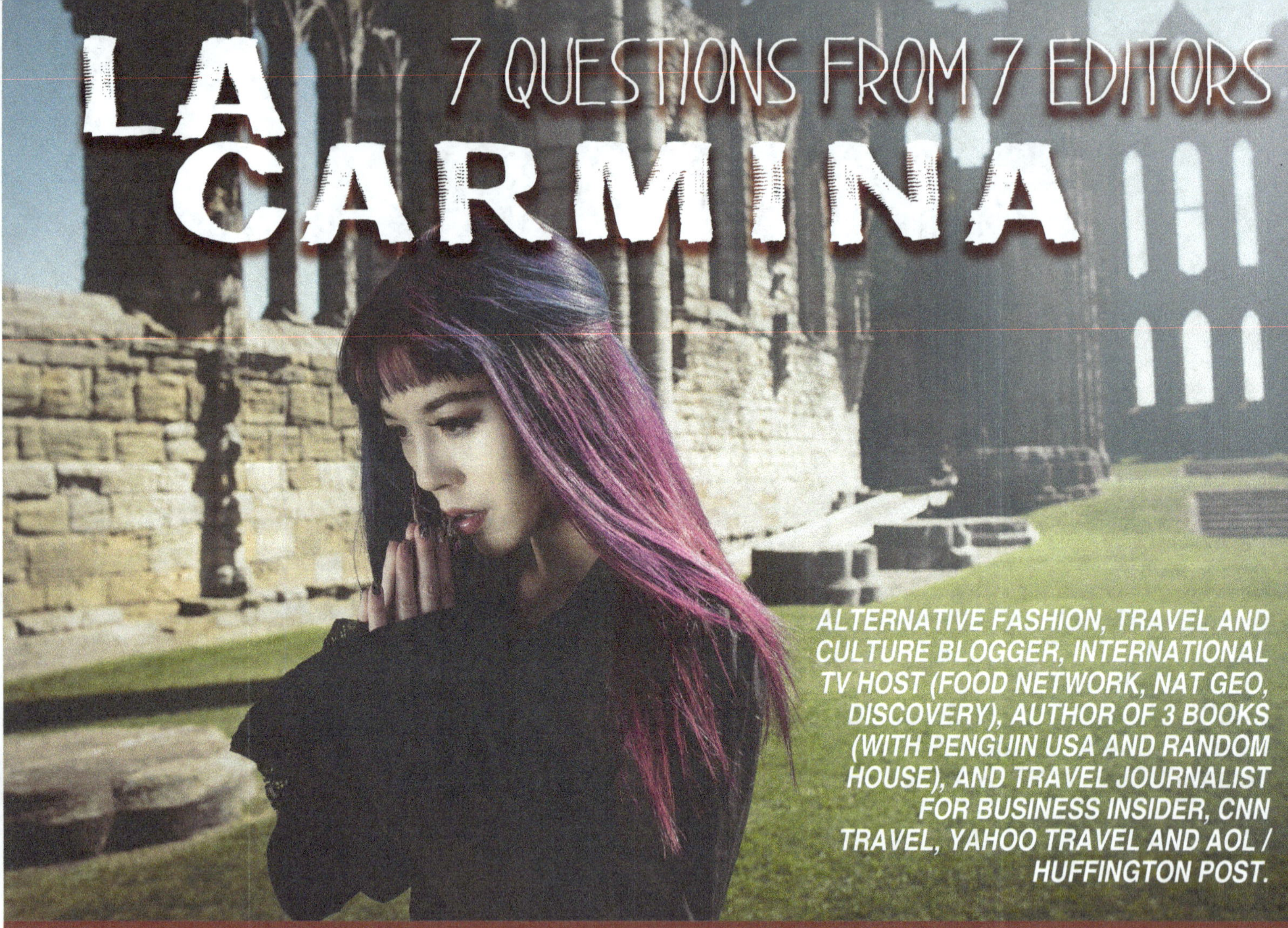

ALTERNATIVE FASHION, TRAVEL AND CULTURE BLOGGER, INTERNATIONAL TV HOST (FOOD NETWORK, NAT GEO, DISCOVERY), AUTHOR OF 3 BOOKS (WITH PENGUIN USA AND RANDOM HOUSE), AND TRAVEL JOURNALIST FOR BUSINESS INSIDER, CNN TRAVEL, YAHOO TRAVEL AND AOL / HUFFINGTON POST.

[Zombieboy, LifeStyle]: *Steampunk tends to follow a trend of colors based on daguerreotypes aged photographs from the subject era. Thus, a trend of browns, yellows, gold, brass, burnt umber and black have emerged. Yet, these are not the true colors of the period. Would you lend your thoughts to this trend and how it relates to popular fashion?*

[La Carmina]: I think Steampunk is a wonderful interpretation of the Jules Verne aesthetic. The colors and styles convey this feeling of experimentation and adventure, in a modern-meets-historical way. I feel Steampunk pays homage to the fashions and attitudes of this era, without attempting to replicate it exactly - so it's exciting to see different people's interpretations through their outfits.

[Kathy Sharkey, Fashion]: *How do your variety of occupations, and variety of cultural interests, affect the way you perceive scene fashion, music, performance, etc.? Have you found that you can see more of the minute changes, and are there some interesting changes coming up you think the world would love to know about?"*

[LC]: I am very lucky to be able to take part in subcultures worldwide, thanks to my work. Over the past years, I've been all around Asia, North America, Africa, the Middle East and Europe, and attended major Goth music festivals like Wave Gotik Treffen and Kinetik. I've read about these places, but it's so different to be there in the flesh, interacting with locals and witnessing things with my own eyes. All these experiences have definitely made me more attuned. Initially, my La Carmina blog was quite Japan-focused, but traveling has opened my eyes to the extraordinary variety of underground fashion and lifestyles in the most surprising of places. I'm intrigued by the burgeoning youth scene in Eastern European countries like Serbia, and loved seeing drag queens perform in Cape Town, Israel and Iceland. I encourage people to be open to all destinations, rather than sticking to the major cities that are best known for alt culture.

[Michael Jack, Music]: *It is extremely difficult for a musician in the underground genres like Goth and Industrial to make money with their music. Do you ever foresee these genres expanding to a wider and more popular market? If they do, how will it affect the music itself?*

[LC]: I just got back from Whitby Goth Weekend in the UK, where I saw bands who have been performing for decades to an underground Goth audience: including Andi Sex Gang, Sigue Sigue Sputnik, The Last Dance and Cruxshadows. It's fantastic to see that these artists are continuing to connect with fans old and new, and getting such a warm reception. However, the reality of the music business is that it is always challenging for Goth/Industrial bands to make a good living. This is not necessarily a negative. I recently went on a music tour of Manchester with Craig Gill of Inspiral Carpets, who tell me his band is happiest working part-time on their music. They are able to perform worldwide and record, but don't have the pressure of touring nonstop and depending on income from album sales. I think it's most important that musicians are happy with their lifestyle and the music they are creating, rather than factors like mainstream recognition.

[Fairly Innocent, Entertainment]: *Of all the interviews you have done with people in the entertainment industry, who was the most challenging? Who made you feel the most nervous, starstruck and why?*

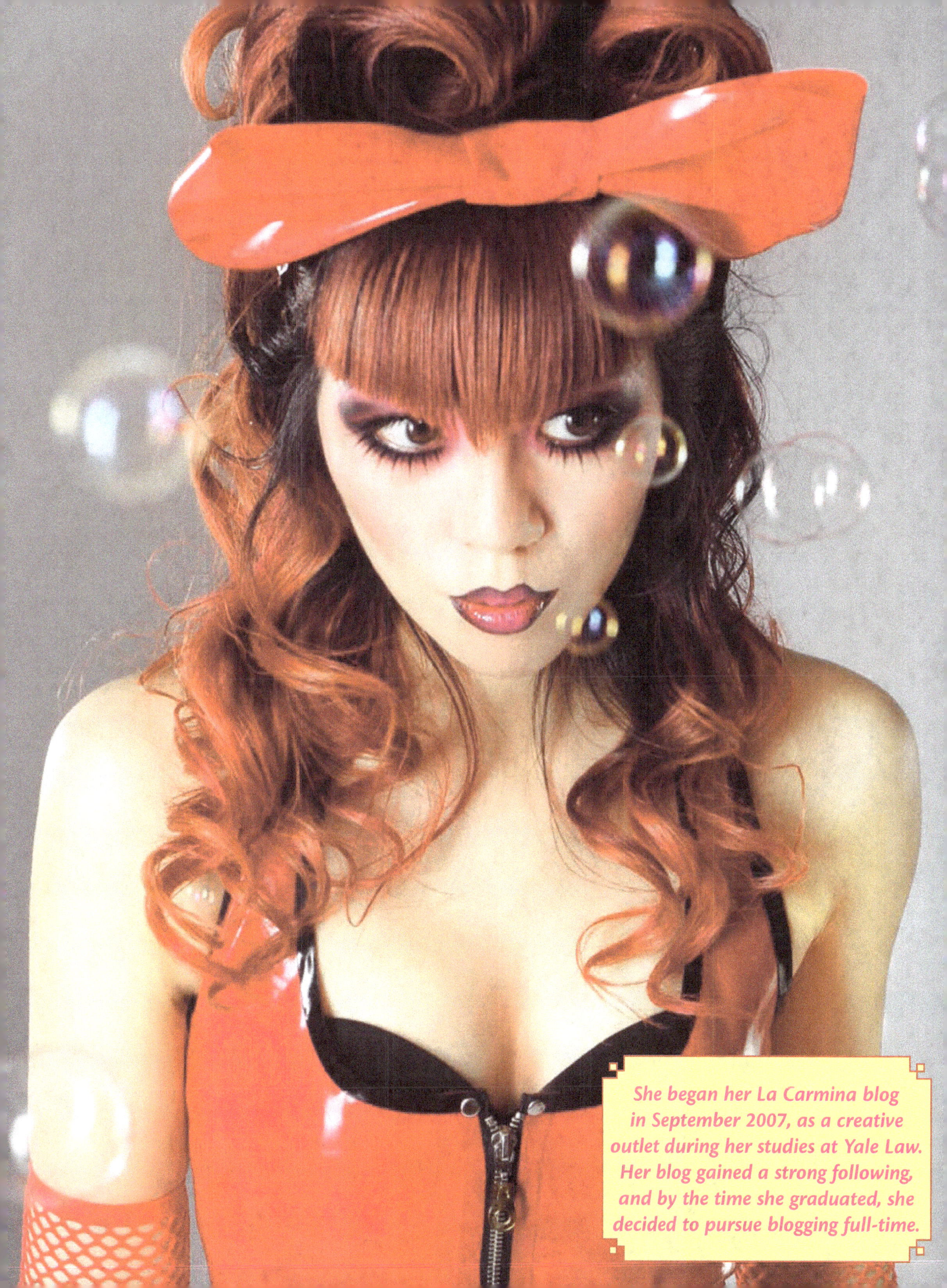
She began her La Carmina blog in September 2007, as a creative outlet during her studies at Yale Law. Her blog gained a strong following, and by the time she graduated, she decided to pursue blogging full-time.

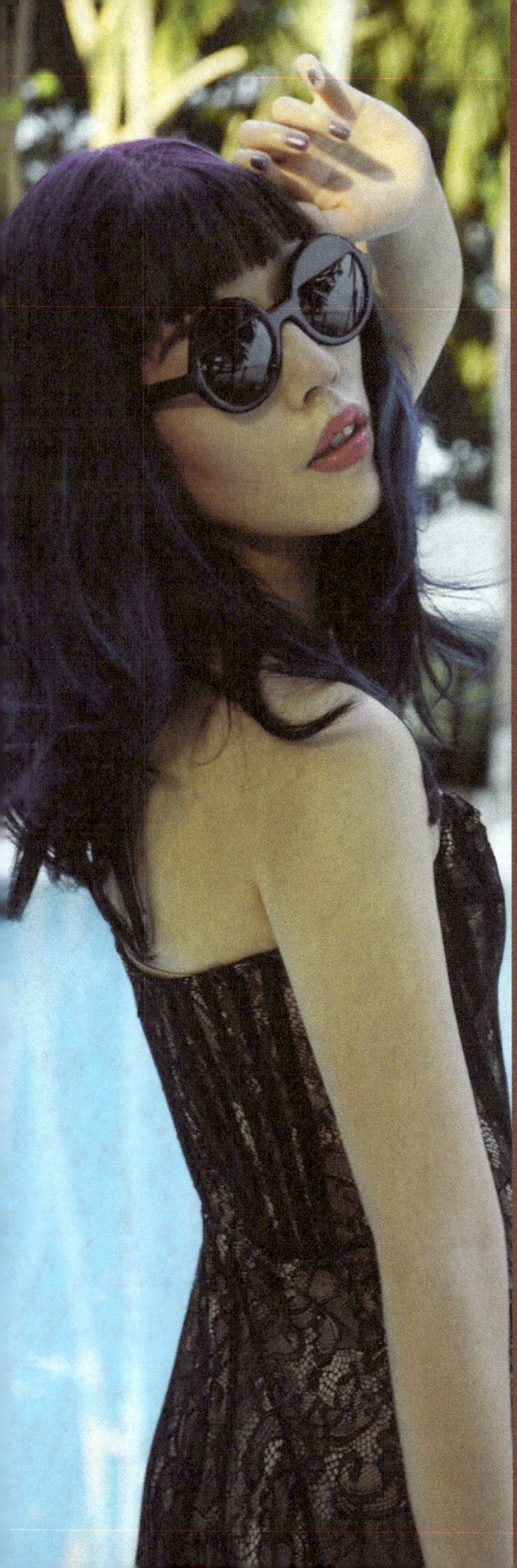

[LC]: I can't really say I've been starstruck - I don't have that type of reaction to public figures, even if I admire them greatly. Perhaps this comes from age and experiences, since I might have replied differently if you asked me this 10 years ago. Today, I'd be most excited to have deep conversations with Buddhist leaders, as opposed to entertainment celebrities.

[Zahara, Art]: *I see references to your look when I'm scanning various belly dance blogs and sites. Have you ever tried belly dancing and/or been to any belly dancing shows? I would imagine the Dark Fusion or Gothic forms would be very appealing to you.*

[LC]: My friends tell me that no matter what you Google, La Carmina shows up! I suppose it's the case for Gothic bellydancing too. I have a friend in Toronto who leads a troupe, and I've enjoyed watching performances in Portland, NYC and other cities. While I appreciate the art of belly dancing, it's not something I feel compelled to do -- just as I've never felt a strong urge to get a tattoo, or fly a plane. However it's wonderful to see how fellow creatives express themselves in such different ways.

[Linnie Helpern, Film & Lit]: *Because fashion tends to be cyclical, what genre of pop culture do you think will be the next to inform the fashion world? We recently saw 20s and 90s style make a comeback... What do you think it is about past decades that leads designers to return to older looks?*

[LC]: I can foresee a fashion throwback to the 2000s, particularly the frosted lips and layered hair: think Buffy the Vampire Slayer. Designers seem to get inspired by what was "in" around two decades ago, since that era tends to be their childhood, and far enough away to conjure up warm feelings of nostalgia. I'd personally love to see people re-interpret the neon cyber rave looks of the early 2000s, as epitomized by Cyberdog.

[Michael Jack, Technology (Yes, I get two questions)]: *You basically rule the social media world. How important have these platforms been in establishing your career, and what part do you see these mediums play in the future of marketing and promotion?*

[LC]: Social media is a fantastic way to interact, respond, and share ideas with people around the world with similar interests. However, it can also be a time-waster, and people tend to get too obsessed with follower numbers. I see social media as merely one part of the bigger picture, which is my mission to share stories about alternative culture and innovators worldwide. The "meat" and focus of my work remains the writing, photos, video and TV... you simply can't encapsulate a meaningful experience within 140 characters. I think social networks will keep growing in importance, but I hope people don't get stuck on these externals (marketing, promotion, followers) at the expense of what's truly important.

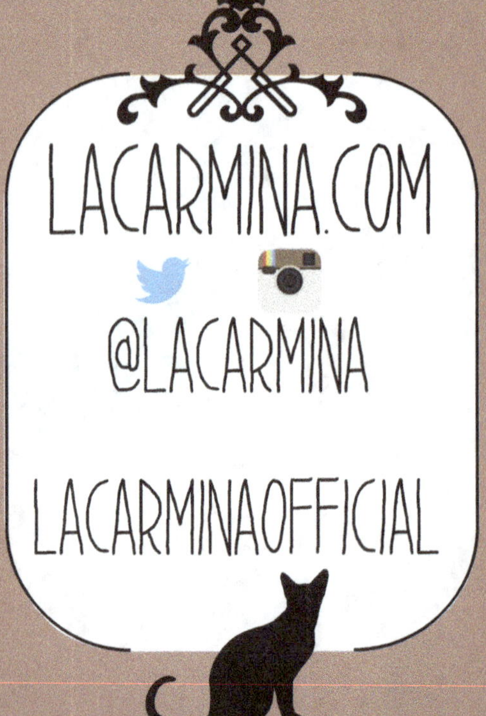

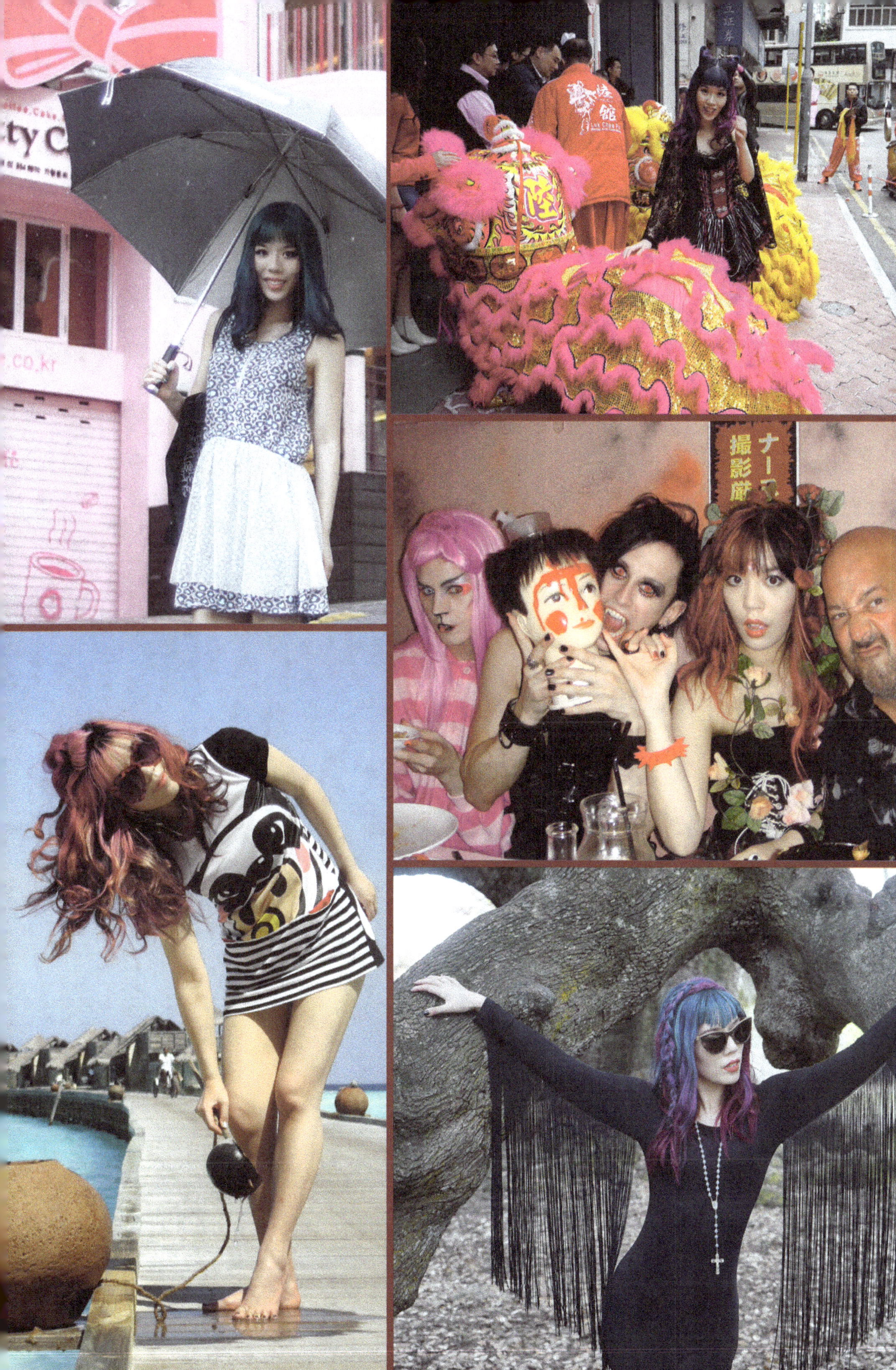

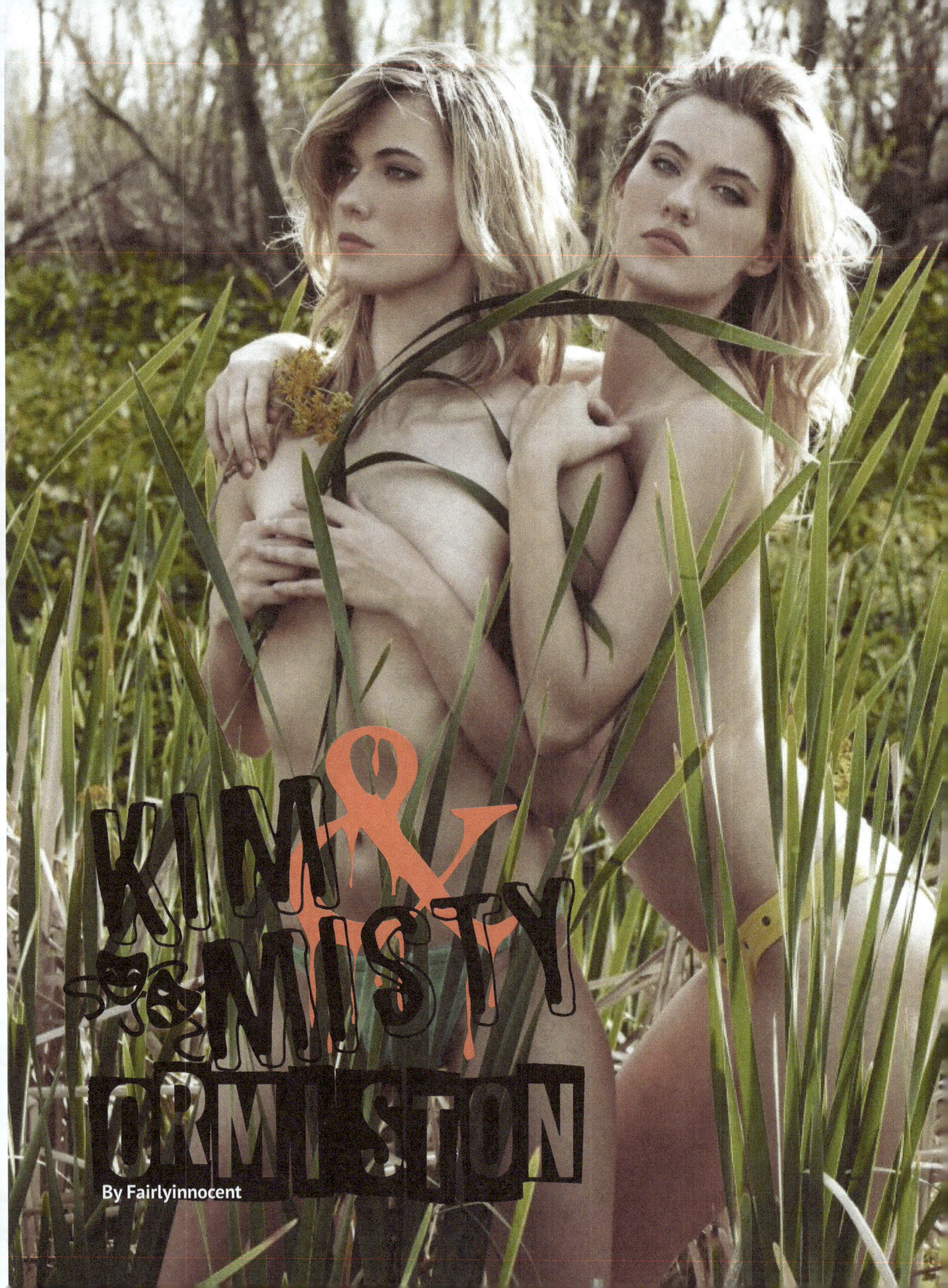

KIM & MISTY
ORMISTON
By Fairlyinnocent

[Carpe Nocturne] *First let me say thank you for doing this interview with us as we know you both are very busy with your acting and modeling career.*

[KIM & MISTY] You're very welcome, Angie. We're very excited to be interviewed by Carpe Nocturne!

[CN] *Tell us, what age did you start your modeling/acting careers?*

[KIM] Hard to say exactly, it was a slow climb of inspiration, commitment, support, and passion. We started falling in love with the camera since age 6. Our brothers would film us and after a while we started picking up the camera ourselves and our favorite pass time became playing on camera. They made homemade videos that inspired and fascinated us and so we started making actual homemade music videos and videos with storylines at about age 8. Our dad always inspired us and made performing fun as he would give us lines to perform and both of our parents would always watch performances that we would put on in our living room. Our dad always showed us great films with great acting since we were at least age 8. He would show us full films, or great scenes. At age 8, we were in a beauty contest and dancing competition and because they couldn't decide on just one of us to win-we both tied!

[MISTY] They loved the idea of working with twins because you can only work child actors for a certain period of time, and they were considering us switching to keep the filming process going!

[KIM] But we were too tall for the role (which I guess kind of inspired us to get into modeling, given our height). Our mom put us in modeling school at age 14 and we got a modeling agent which started our modeling careers. All through high school we were blessed to have to amazing and incredibly inspiring acting teachers, Mr. Rene` Piazza and Mrs. Ferne "Broadway" Kistner. Our high school plays were so much fun. It was then that we knew for sure that we

wanted to do it for a career after high school.

At age 17, we went on a modeling competition and Misty and I were honorably noted in having over 15 modeling agencies interested in us in the competition. Soon after high school, our parents sent us to New York and helped back our funding to stay up there for a couple of years while we pursued our modeling and acting career where we landed the "Maxim" magazine gig from our modeling agency "Click" at the time and also were cast in our first film role in, "The Last Request" (comedy as Siamese twins attached on the back as prospective dates) from our acting managers, twins agency, Debbie and Lisa Ganz with Twins Talent. We were also called to be on "The Ananda Lewis Show" for a personal Interview which was pretty neat. This is pretty much how our career gradually built itself.

[CN] *Who/what inspired you to get into modeling/acting?*

[MISTY] Our brothers really kind of inspired us since age six because we saw them making the coolest home videos! It made us want to pick up the camera and start making videos too. We've just continued to make home videos and get into acting ever since! We started putting on our own plays and making our own videos which our dad and mom completely supported and encouraged. Also our dad always showed us the great classics which made us love great acting and be inspired by the impact of what great movies can do!

We did an audition when we were nine for "Interview with the Vampire" and got a callback, which was awesome. It turned out we were too tall for the role, so that's when our mom got us into modeling. We started with photoshoots, but our modeling career really took off when we went to New York and landed a two-page story and spread in Maxim Magazine. It was a very artistic and beautiful shoot, sort of had a Yin Yang quality to it. As far as acting, our mom got us in the acting program at school and we qualified.

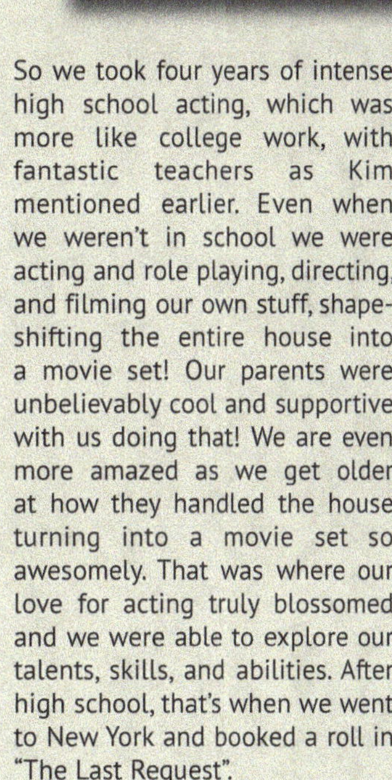

So we took four years of intense high school acting, which was more like college work, with fantastic teachers as Kim mentioned earlier. Even when we weren't in school we were acting and role playing, directing, and filming our own stuff, shape-shifting the entire house into a movie set! Our parents were unbelievably cool and supportive with us doing that! We are even more amazed as we get older at how they handled the house turning into a movie set so awesomely. That was where our love for acting truly blossomed and we were able to explore our talents, skills, and abilities. After high school, that's when we went to New York and booked a roll in "The Last Request".

[KIM] We would get a new costume box full of costumes from our aunts since we were 4 and would do runway shows for our family in them to show them the new costumes. Our family also always danced together, so performing came natural to us.

[CN] *Was your family supportive of your desire to be involved in this line of work?*

[KIM] Extremely! From putting us in plays, film auditions, watching our performances and videos that we made, and sending us to New York. What our mom and dad put up with amazes us to this day just to support what we loved and our passions. They would put earplugs in their ears at night because we would be inspired and awake all night writing then acting out scenes for weeks or months on end and sometimes the scene called for a passionate call out like "Stella!!!!", a bloodcurdling scream or a loud and heated debated argument. They would fly into the room sometimes saying, "Are you' all alright?!" and we would smile and say, "Yeah! Just doing an acting scene"! We would change the whole house around like it was a movie set. One time we had coffins and a huge man-sized wooden cross up in the kitchen for the 'set' and our parents were so awesome about it, it was around Halloween, and

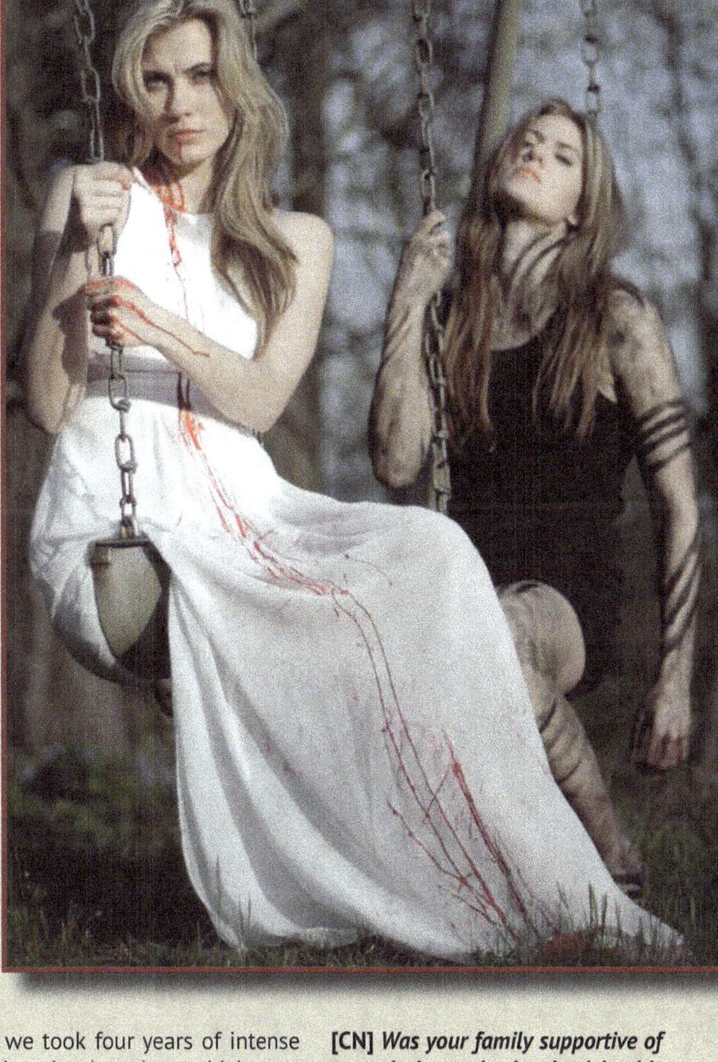

they said, "Well, the place will look great for Halloween!" and we kept it up, and it was a hit for the party decor.

After New York, we made short films in New Orleans and asked them if we could borrow the house and change/move all of the house and furniture around for the vision of the project. Our mom stayed at our apartment and our dad stayed at a hotel for three days. I mean, their support blows us away. They are dream parents and their support continues to this day just as adamantly and remains such an incredible support system in uncountable ways. Our entire family (brothers, aunts, uncles, cousins, nieces, and nephews) and friends have always been a strong, encouraging support system which we're so thankful for. They all are excited about the next video that we make and give us constructive criticisms or encouragement that helps or inspires us for the next project we do. They always keep our career moves in their minds and ask us when they see us what acting we are doing lately. (Smiles)

Also, one of our absolutely best support groups for our acting careers as well were our high school play directors, Mrs. Kistner and Mr. Piazza! They let us "spread our wings" to play all types of roles (comedy, drama and from Greek Goddesses to male roles-and even goblins!) They made acting SO MUCH fun but also taught us how to take it seriously as a profession and taught us the discipline involved. They're awesome!

[MISTY] Extremely! Our dad would always encourage our plays that we would put together and perform and our mom always helped us out on gathering any outlandish things that we needed for our acting videos and plays. They have been behind us 101% the entire way!! Our mom and dad paid for rent and food while we were in New York until we were able to book work and pay for it ourselves. They never stopped believing in us and do whatever they can for us. They have been unbelievably, amazingly supportive!!

[CN] *Were you encouraged to pursue further education and not solely rely on acting? If so what was your major or degree if any?*

[MISTY] Yeah, we were encouraged to pursue education as well, while fully continuing to pursue acting and modeling in New York, New Orleans, and California. With education we could have a side job that we enjoyed to make income while we also continued to pursue and focus on acting. While in New York we took a Screenwriting class at HB Studios, as well as attended a class with a teacher that taught Robert De

Niro. In New Orleans, we took an Advanced Screenwriting class and Acting for the Camera class at college at the University of New Orleans. We also graduated in Massage Therapy, which was a great suggestion from our brothers (and inspired from our aunts) because we can set our own hours based around random auditions and shoots, as well as travel, while continuing to have a source of income.

[CN] *Are there any other actors in your family?*

[KIM] Our mother can act. They actually almost wanted her for a role in "Interview with the Vampire" when she was only there for us! She must have that actress aura about her. We've always seen her dance and draw everybody in! She has magnetism.

Our dad has done classic black and white 8mm acting with us in a silent film project we had to do in college. He also gave us really good directing advice. Our dad is an English Major and has a talent for writing, as well as majored in film history. We would be the first in the theater (and audition) if he were to write and sell a screenplay (which he has mentioned an interest in) we enjoy scriptwriting as well.

Our brothers, Scott and Keith, could be actors if they wanted to easily! They made home movies, acting, and film look so cool, fun, and hilarious!! They can also do some awesome voiceover work! They read books to us playing out the different character voices and read the dialogue in video games we played together. One time our brother read aloud l8 hours straight from the anime" Sailor Moon" 5th series, Japanese version – we couldn't get enough of it!

[CN] *Are there any actors/models that inspire you?*

[MISTY] James Deane is one for sure. He set a whole new level of acting. Our dad showed us some of his movies and pointed out the little things that James Deane that made him flow so intricately into his characters and make them come to life! Also, Jennifer Lawrence has been a more recent inspiration, and we can see why she won an Academy Award. It was a true pleasure working with someone who is inspiring to us as actors. To top it off, Jennifer complimented our acting after we finished shooting one of our scenes, which was very cool!

[KIM] Yeah they are usually the first ones to come to mind.

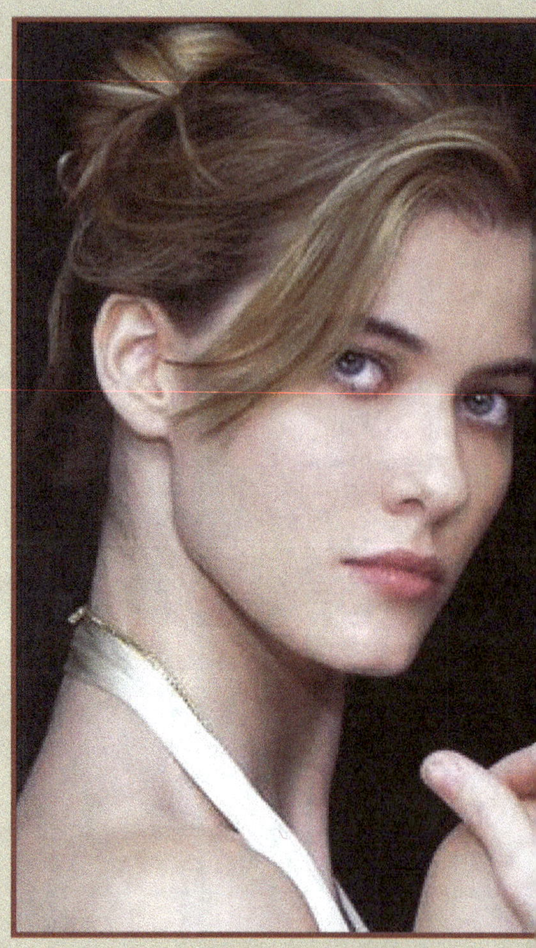

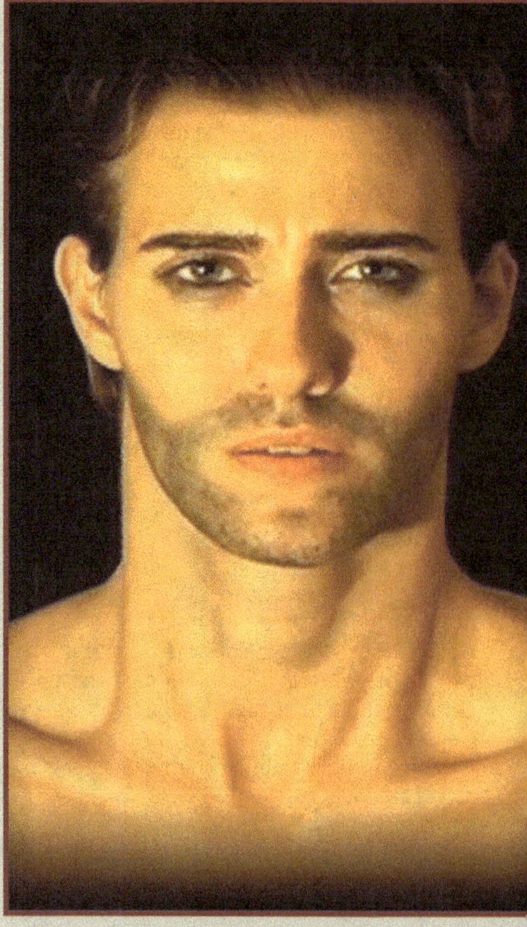

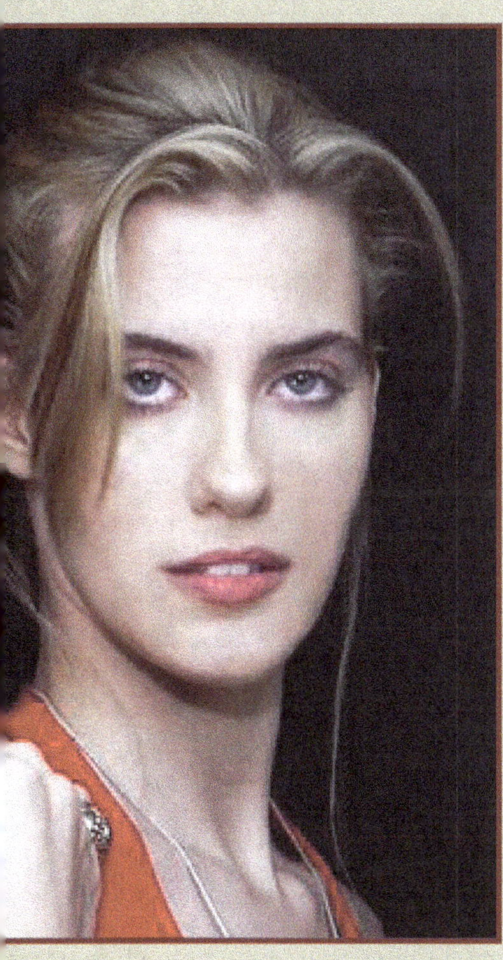

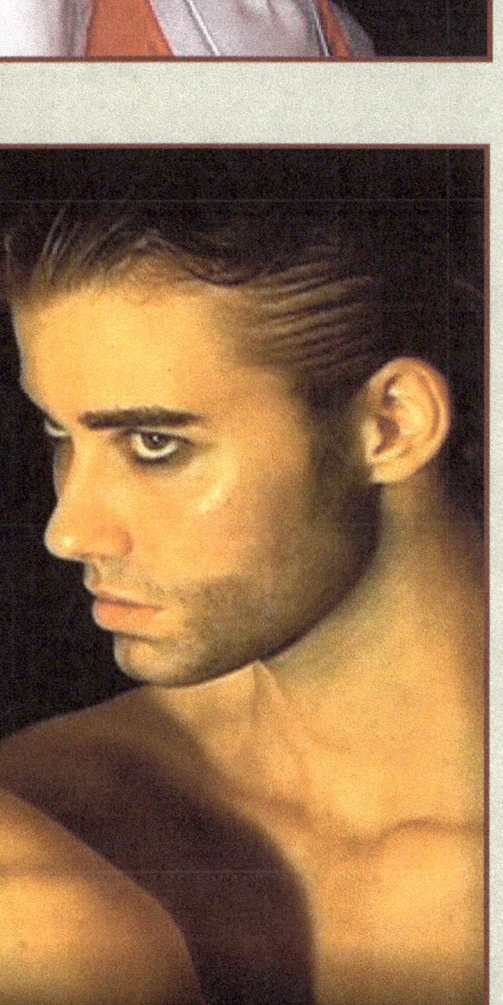

[CN] *Let me cover one of your modeling jobs, the Maxim magazine photoshoot. That was amazing and beautiful. Was this the biggest print/publication that you have been photographed for?*

[KIM] Thank you very, very much, Angie. Yes, to this date, we would say that "Maxim" was the biggest print/publication that we have been photographed for. We also did a shoot for "Wrangler", but never saw the final product. We also did our first cover shoot (twice) and had an eight page spread for "Cue" magazine, "Bride" Magazine, and "Cycle Dreams" on a motorcycle.

[CN] *You both have a lot of acting credits under your belts such as The Loft, Scream of the Banshee, Blood Out, Meet the Spartans, and many more. How do you choose what movies to do?*

[MISTY] Interesting question! Um...usually we're drawn to character roles that we believe in or have something unique or interesting about them. Usually we're drawn to gothic characters and period pieces! Or characters that revolve around a storyline that we believe in. But mainly, if the characters "speak to us" in some way, then we go for it!

[KIM] We also just did a shoot that was for a TV series coming up called "The Magicians" where we play gothic characters that have a simultaneous reaction for special reason. That was a lot of fun, and we loved the cool, interesting, Goth aspect of the characters! Sometimes if the characters are just fun and cool, we'll be down to rock them.

[CN] *You have done TV and movies but which do you prefer? Or is both equally fun and challenging?*

[KIM] We enjoy both! With TV series, we learn the character in a protracted manner and secrets and inner experience is learned over time. With film, it's all uncovered in the length of that film. So it's a somewhat different acting experience (just as watching them is a different experience for the audience). But we find that we can appreciate both.

[CN] *Of all the jobs you have done they all include the both of you with the exception of one episode of a TV show "Treme" in 2010 that Kim was in without Misty. Do you pick your parts based on the two of you doing the jobs together? And if not will you turn down a part if it can't be cast in that manner?*

[MISTY] We were actually both in that series as well! Haha I played "Cowgirl" and Kim played "Pony Girl" and kissed the actor, Michiel Huisman ("Game of Thrones") in the scene! That was a really fun shoot. Our agent usually offers roles that are single and with twins, but usually the casting directors love us both and hire us both, which is awesome! In high school we did a couple plays that each other were not in, however. We wouldn't turn down a part if we weren't cast as twins. We're very supportive of each other for any roles that we each believe in or want to do.

[CN] *You have done Steampunk, Gothic, and dark characters as well as males. It is fantastic to see all the costuming you wear and how well executed, especially when dressed as men (Jim and Mickey). You are absolutely unrecognizable as females. Have you learned to do all the make-up techniques on your own or do you generally have make-up artists?*

[KIM] Wow, so awesome, thanks! We actually taught ourselves the techniques. We've done the "transformation process" since we were probably 5 years old. But we hadn't started playing with facial techniques until we were about 9. Our first attempt was a bluntly painted on mustache using regular art paint, and our brothers said, "if you want it to look real, paint ain't gonna cut it, ha-ha Since then we've worked on improving upon the desired look that was in our minds. We just kept working with techniques until the vision in our minds came to life! And we continue to be open to any new ideas! Interestingly, we noticed that quite a few people have followed us on our technique since we'd brought it into effect, which was totally awesome to see! We kind of blushed when we came face-to-face with local friends sporting the new techniques! Sometimes we'll look at a picture that attracts us and work from looking at the picture for inspiration for the desired look.

[CN] *Have you done any acting/modeling as Jim and Mickey?*

[MISTY] We have! We went on several auditions as males and for male roles, and have made a lot of our own music videos as males. Since a lot of the characters in the scripts we're writing are males as well, we'll sometimes role-play as male characters to get ideas of where to take the script. We're also setting up a male photoshoot in the near future which we're pretty excited about.

[CN] *Do you get to keep any of the costuming/ clothing you two get for sets or is it based on each situation/job?*

[KIM] For a gothic shoot we particularly liked the many wardrobe options. They end up using our Goth attire for the shoot but we expressed much interest in the wardrobe attire options that they had available. At the end of the day's shoot, wardrobe surprised us by giving us these awesome (not to mention expensive) articles of clothing as a present to go! We thought that was so incredibly awesome of her!

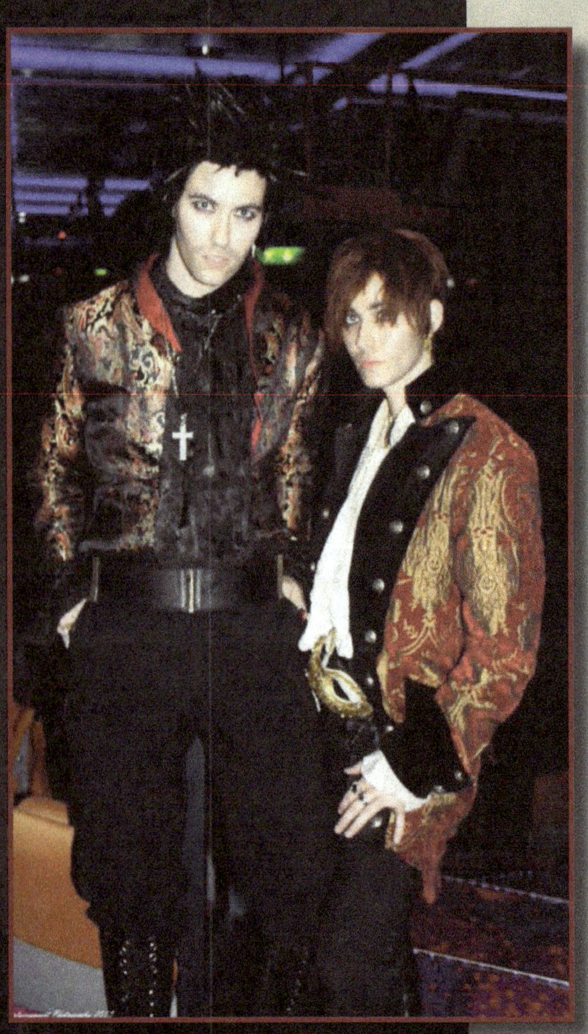

[MISTY] Not usually, but the one time that we really, really loved a hoody shirt that was the film's wardrobe, and the wardrobe lady surprised us at the end of the shoot and gave it to us!! And these were no cheap clothes either! We remember having just received a text that we could keep the clothes, then we saw her from a distance and started running full speed towards her and gave her a huge hug jumping up and down! It was an awesome moment.

[CN] *Who are your most favorite actors dead or alive?*

[MISTY] Oh, so many good ones to choose from...James Deane, Johnny Depp, Jennifer Lawrence, Brandon Lee, Cate Blanchett, James Franco, Daniel Day Louis, Leonardo DiCaprio, Hilary Swank, Jim Carrey, Jack Nicholson, Heath Ledger....to name some. Most of the people we named have a few things in common....they are either character chameleons (literally seem to become different people when they act), have an inspiring energy about them, or are very original in the way that they act and portray their characters. These are all qualities that we love!

[KIM] Yes, each actor has their own techniques and style so it's so cool to appreciate each of them.

[CN] *Let's switch gears for a bit. Something you have done recently was being the leads in Bella Morte's newest music video "Exorcisms" from Metropolis Records and directed by Marshall Camden. You both were absolutely brilliant in the video. How was it working with such a great group of musicians as well as part of such a deep and emotional song?*

[KIM] Thank you!! It means a lot to us that it reached you and that you enjoyed it. That's one of the main reasons that we act, is to reach people emotionally, mentally, or even spiritually. It was an absolute privilege to work with people that we've admired the most since high school.

Andy's alluringly and almost tragically beautiful, emotional, and heartbreaking voice has captivated, mesmerized, and entranced us and deeply touched our soul with emotion as we were introduced to the gothic genre of music for the first time (aside from awesome 80's Goth bands such as "Depeche Mode", "The Cure", and "Gary Numan" whom we LOVE)!

The group is hilarious to goof off with and so chill to hang around. We had a blast with them and they are inspiringly beautiful souls to be around, carefree, humorous, and cool. They are so loose to do a shoot with which makes it so much fun, yet at the same time are passionate and focused about the projects at hand.

When Marshall and Andy asked us to be in their next music video (and throughout the whole shoot), we kept thinking, "this is a dream come true." It was something that we dreamed of doing for such a long time. The entire "Exorcisms" album is so incredibly, deeply touching to the soul and to emotions. It draws us in when we listen to it like a current from rhythmic ocean waves under a dark night lit only by moonlight...You see what Bella Morte does to us? Haha Yeah, we were totally excited about it! "Exorcisms" and what the video had to express was something we connected with, believed in, and were super excited to be a part of....we felt completely in unison with the vision, the lyrics, the song, and the storyline. It was an honor to be part of such an intense video with such a powerful and inspiring meaning...and we hope we have brought to the screen, the portrayal of the lyrics through visual art. We felt it was meant to be expressed and felt also, somehow, an emotional release by the end of the project.

[MISTY] Thank you very much! It was a super awesome experience. Those guys had us constantly laughing on set! They were all so awesomely humble and down-to-earth to work with as well. Andy asked us several times if WE needed anything, and here he is the lead singer of the video! The whole experience felt like fun teamwork and creative collaboration! Being that we had been listening

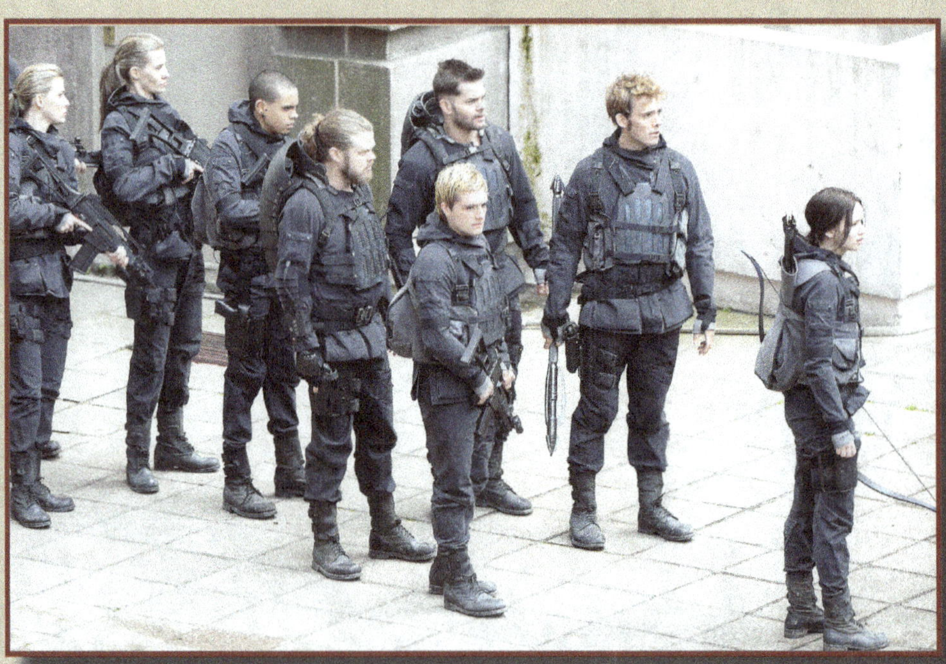

to Bella Morte for about 15 years and absolutely love their music and what they stand for, it was truly an honor to be in their video. The video itself was brilliantly written and directed by Marshall, who worked amazingly with us, and allowed us a lot of character freedom. Andy, Tony, Marshall, and Brandon made us feel at home. Listening to Andy's passionate and well written music during a lot of the takes immediately drew us into our characters, which was fun and awesome! The lyrics in combination with the story of the video made a creation that we feel is truly unique and are proud to be a part of.

[CN] *How long did it take to do the music video? And was this a lot different from other acting gigs?*

[MISTY] The longest shoot started around 6am and ended around 8pm. This is actually a usual day's work on set usually. It took two days to shoot and one day for the 'Bella Morte knights of the round table' to get together for the creative planning process! We admire Bella Morte's openness to ideas and joining creative forces. It's very cool.

[CN] *Was this video shoot more fun to do since you already knew the band?*

[KIM] Definitely!!!! Every step of the process to make the dream shoot into a reality was a blast with the band!!! They are so fun and full of energy to work with! From the planning stages in the beginning, through the shoot, and the after parties and hangouts, we had a fantastic time that we hold as a treasure in our memory keepsakes. We all are so naturally comfortable hanging out together that the project seems like a passionate project among good friends (which is I guess exactly what it was)

[MISTY] We know that if we didn't know the band, we would have still had so much fun working with them, because they always give everyone an awesome time! But knowing them and their work made us have a flowing, trusting, familiar chemistry with each of them that was really cool! We knew that anything we were doing with them was going to be awesome because we believe in their music and writings!

[CN] *Would you like to do more music videos in the future? If so what bands would you like to work with?*

[MISTY] We would absolutely love to be in another Bella Morte music video and have awesomely been invited to possibly be in another one in the future which we're totally excited about! Other bands that we would like to work with would have to be "The Cruxshadows", because we've also known them for about 15 years and have always believed in what they sing about. They have a true connection to life and love, which has always been a huge inspiration in our creative works.

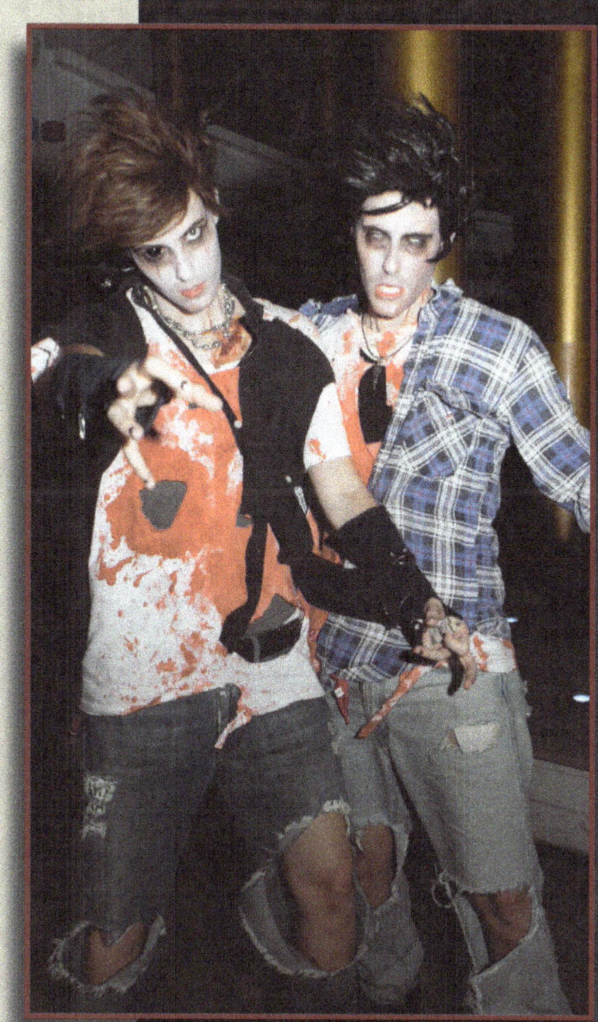

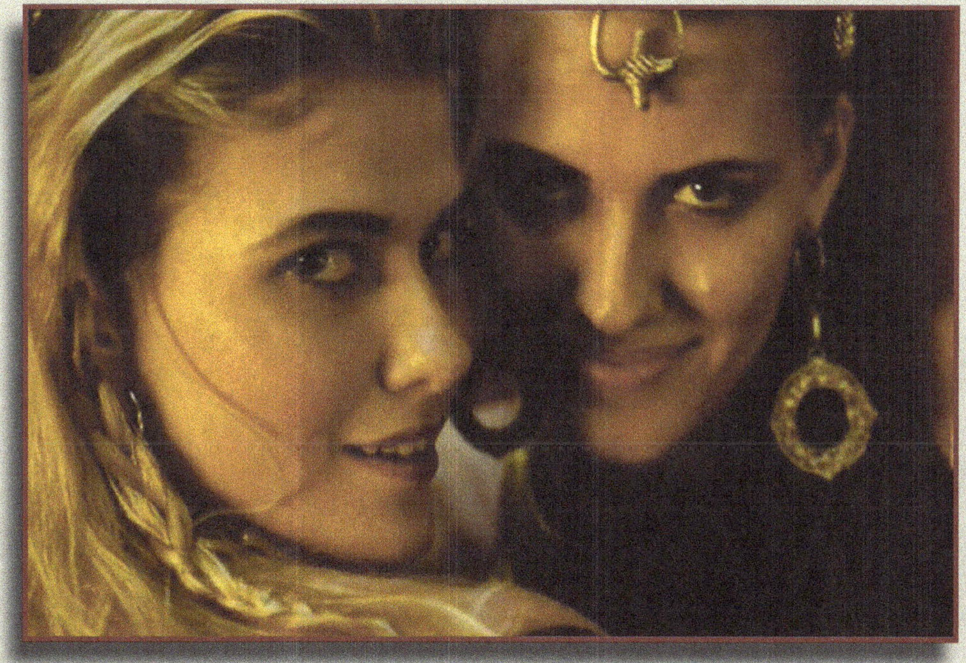

Also the band "The Absence Project", because our best friend from childhood, Richard White, is the lead singer of that band and we have always made movies together since our childhood! Other gothic/mood bands that we would also love to work with would be "Depeche Mode", "Platform One", "Behind The Scenes", "Gary Numan", "Pink Floyd", "Linkin Park", "Metallica", and "Thou Shalt Not" because we deeply feel and connect with their music. Also "Ego Likeness" would be fun and awesome too since we heard their music when we were in high school and just spent time with them on the amazing Gothic Cruise. Their vocals and sounds are incredible and enchanting!

[CN] *You got to know of Carpe Nocturne during The Gothic Cruise. How did you find out about the cruise?*

[KIM] Yes, and it was a pleasure to meet you, Angie! We LOVE all of the photos you take of the Gothic Cruise and of the moments captured that would otherwise be long missed!

The Gothic Cruise was another sort of "Dream come true" that unfolded before us! We found out about The Gothic Cruise

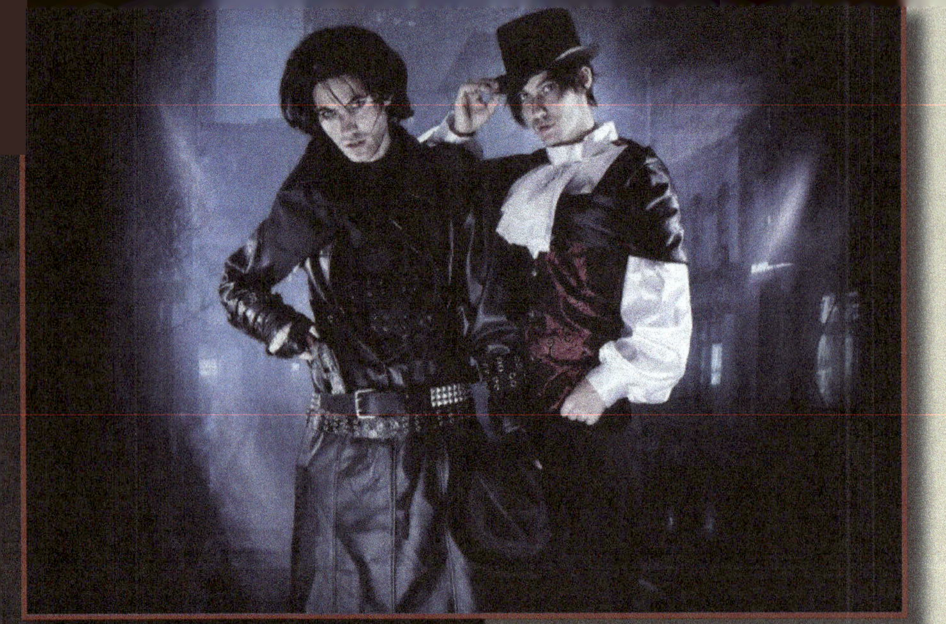

gothic expression and style. It's honest, expressive, awesome, sexy, and badass!

[CN] *What do you feel has been your biggest accomplishment/s in modeling or acting so far?*

[KIM] In our acting career so far, we would say that booking "The Hunger Games: Mockingjay Part 1" has been the biggest film accomplishment.

For modeling, we'd say that the "Maxim" magazine shoot has been our biggest accomplishment, although we've also done some runway and modeling for great designer names such as Fendi, Christian Dior, L'Oréal, Wrangler, Bebe, a Hilary Swank charity show (to name a good few). And we modeled latex clothing on runway before which was a completely new and erotic experience.

The "Exorcisms" video by Bella Morte has been our biggest acting accomplishment as far as music videos...and one of our biggest personal accomplishments.

[CN] *One thing the two of you did was an FX ad for American Horror Story's Freak Show "Back to Back". How were the two of you picked for that or is it something your agents found since it was a job involving you both?*

[KIM] Our awesome agents, Dawn and George Landrum with "Landrum Arts LA" agency got us an audition with Brent Caballero Casting for the show. Then about a few days later we got a random phone call which I picked up last second even though it was an "unknown" caller and it was a crew member interested in us flying up to Los Angeles the very next day for the promo shoot! It was the most instant notice we had received for flight/hotel arrangements, but we said YES and our mom (a miracle-worker!) worked magic to make it happen and we were on the plane by sunrise. That was a fun shoot!! The director and second AD would call out fun cue names for us to follow with identical twin movements and we fell right into it naturally and the set was extremely upbeat and excited of the "identical performing series of movements" that we did back-to-back in a row. It was quite a fun rush, and they were a fun crew! The final promo is one of the movements that we flowed into.

We also had some fun in Los Angeles and went out and explored in between shooting days! Life is all about living it up and making the most of every moment!

[MISTY] You said it!

[CN] *Is there an actor/model that you would absolutely love to work with?*

[MISTY] All of the actors that we mentioned

---

while scoping out Bella Morte's website on their upcoming tours and not only do we hear about the AWESOME Gothic Cruise filled with events and an incredible number of attendees, but we hear that one of our first and favorite Goth bands would be riding as well: Bella Morte. HELL - YEAH. The Gothic Cruise had been one of the most enchanting experiences that we've ever had or felt, and the "goth family friends" that we met have been incredibly interesting, lasting, genuine, humble/down-to-earth, and so much fun to be around!

[CN] *Do you consider yourself "Gothic" as far as your everyday life regarding music, likes, and clothing tastes or no specific genre?*

[MISTY] We definitely consider ourselves gothic at heart in our everyday lives! Goths usually feel like they stand out differently for one reason or other, and we kind of feel this way, in a good way. We don't just have

Goth dark clothes, but we do have one specific "goth closet" with purely dark, Goth clothes! And a different closet for any clothes with color, haha. As far as music, we love - literally - all types of music! We love every genre for their own great sounds of music and lyrics. We've definitely had an instant connection to gothic music, the moment we heard it when we were as young as six with" Depeche Mode".

[KIM] We allow ourselves to open up and express our deepest emotions... instead of fearing them or shying away from them, we embrace our emotions and what we are able to learn and feel from them, which we feel is a very good and healthy thing...and we do this naturally day in and day out and love the mysteries of life... In this way, we feel "goth" in our everyday life but as Misty said, as far as music, we love it all. As far as our clothing, we roll with what we feel each new day. But we have a specific excitement and desire for

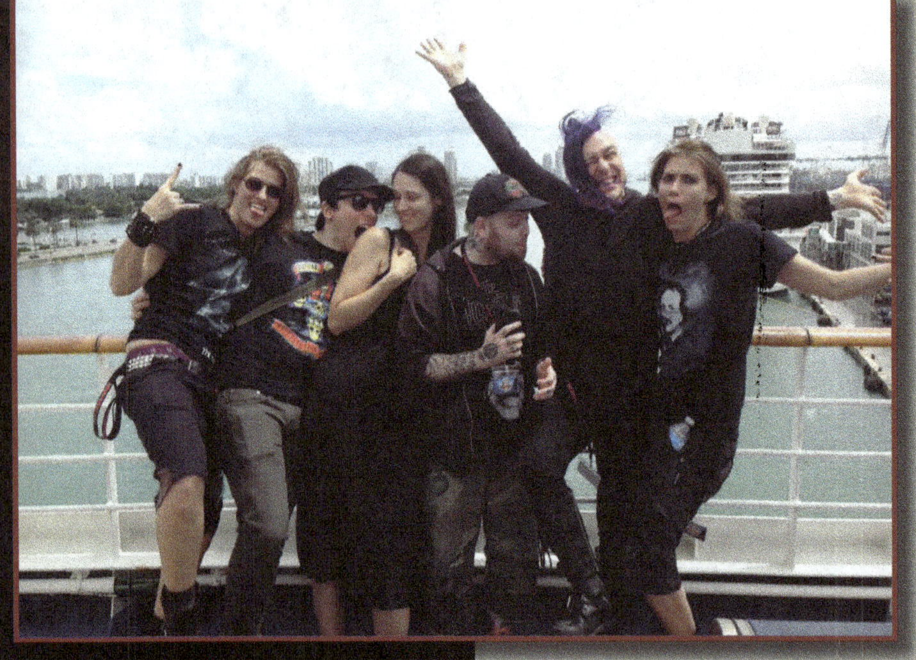

above we would absolutely love to work if ever given the opportunity! (James Deane, Johnny Depp, Jennifer Lawrence, Brandon Lee, Cate Blanchett, James Franco, Daniel Day Lewis, Leonardo DiCaprio, Jim Carrey, Hilary Swank, Jack Nicholson, Heath Ledger)

As far as models, it would be very cool to meet Gisele Bundchen. She seems to have a super cool vibe about her and her style in modeling.

[CN] *Are there any jobs that you are adamant you will not do?*

[KIM] As an actor, if the role is a good role, has a good story, good character, good plot, and has a deep or informative message to relay, then there probably isn't much that would prevent us from being interested in considering the role. We love doing our own stunt work too! If it was a role that's message we truly didn't believe in, however, then we probably wouldn't do it. For example, we probably would decline a smoking cigarettes commercial, because we're pro-health.

[CN] *Do you prefer a certain genre of movie or is it based on the appeal it has to you both and which ones do you enjoy the most?*

[MISTY] We love every genre from comedy to drama to horror to action. We love movies/TV series!! We also love "cheesy horror flicks". Some of our favorite TV series are "The Walking Dead", "Game of Thrones", "Outlander", "Archer", "Friends", "Deadwood".... Some of our favorite films are "Edward Scissorhands", "Brokeback Mountain", "Titanic", "Rubber" (about the serial killer tire!), "Evil Dead 2" (laughed our butts off!), "Braveheart", "Casablanca", "The Crow", "A Streetcar Named Desire", "The Hunger Games", "Rebel Without A Cause", "It's A Wonderful Life", (yes, we watch this every year around Christmas time, lol), "This Is The End" (we were also featured extras in this film), "Clockwork Orange", and so many more, but these are a few..

[KIM] I think it is based on the appeal… we're interested in all stories to be told and in every unique type of perspective in which it could be seen through…

[CN] *Do you take or have you taken any acting/ modeling classes or were you lucky enough to have that natural born talent?*

[KIM] We took intense acting classes in high school for 4 years, took a class for "Acting For Camera" in college as well as attended a couple of acting workshops. We were told, however, at an early age, that we have a natural born talent for it. The classes helped us fuel our talent and were a place to express and release it! We also went to an acting class in New York that also taught Robert De Niro - how cool! Our dad has always shown us great films with great actors. This is probably where some of our biggest inspiration comes from - watching and observing other great actors and allowing ourselves to be inspired by them through our admiration and appreciation for their work. Also, just watching people in everyday life has been instructional in its own way. Our dad told us before to "be observant and watch people. See what people do naturally."

[MISTY] But honestly, we've always been naturally drawn to expressing and exploring different characters, really, since we could ever remember. We role play all of the time to see where different character minds go, choices they make, what storylines unfold, choices in attire, ways of thinking, etc. - and this has always been like a natural acting class for us - and super fun!

[KIM] Career wise we definitely plan to continue acting for sure. It's a passion for us. Also, we would like to write a screenplay together and act in it together. That's a big one for us. We are open to do modeling as well, awesome imagery, and massage therapy, all of which we enjoy very much too. We plan to continue to make home videos and short films for personal projects and improvisational acting for natural screenplay storyline, and dialogue as well. We have a lot of fun with that! We also have acquired an interest in perhaps playing with music and soundtracks, and are starting to learn how to play the guitar, which has been totally awesome and rewarding. We have lots of interest in directing and have directed, produced, acted, wrote, edited, and filmed our own short film ("Confessions At Death" which won "Best Screenplay-Short" at the Queens, NY Film Festival).

Ultimately, we hope to inspire and reach people through our acting, writing, and imagery…and so that's also a goal for us. Inspiration, higher learning (emotionally, spiritually, and otherwise) is so important we feel. Having a better understanding of each other and connecting with each other keeps life real and alive.

Outside of our career, we plan to continue to meet awesome people, live life, rock out, continue to expand and gain new experiences, perspectives, and basically to just cruise, flow, jam, and have fun with it all! That's what life is all about and what makes it all count and worthwhile). Live the moment - Carpe Noctem!

[MISTY] Ditto! Live the moment - Seize the Night!
~ ~ ~

KIM & MISTY's Facebook Fan Page, search for "Kim and Misty Ormiston"!

Watch the "Bella Morte" video "Exorcisms" with Kim and Misty Ormiston on You Yube!

Bella Morte website: **http://www.bellamorte. com.**
Bella Morte stills/scene shots from "Exorcisms" video shoot were done by Brian Wimer.

All photos from "The Hunger Games: Mockingjay Part 1" from different internet sites.

© Fairlyinnocent Photography 2013

[CN] *Please elaborate on anything you would like the reader's to know about you that we may not have covered.*

[MISTY] We made our own short film which we acted in, directed, written, filmed, edited, and produced. It's called "Confessions At Death" and won "Best Screenplay-Short" at the Queens, NY Film Festival. Maybe you'll get to see it one day!

[CN] *What are your future goals and endeavors?*

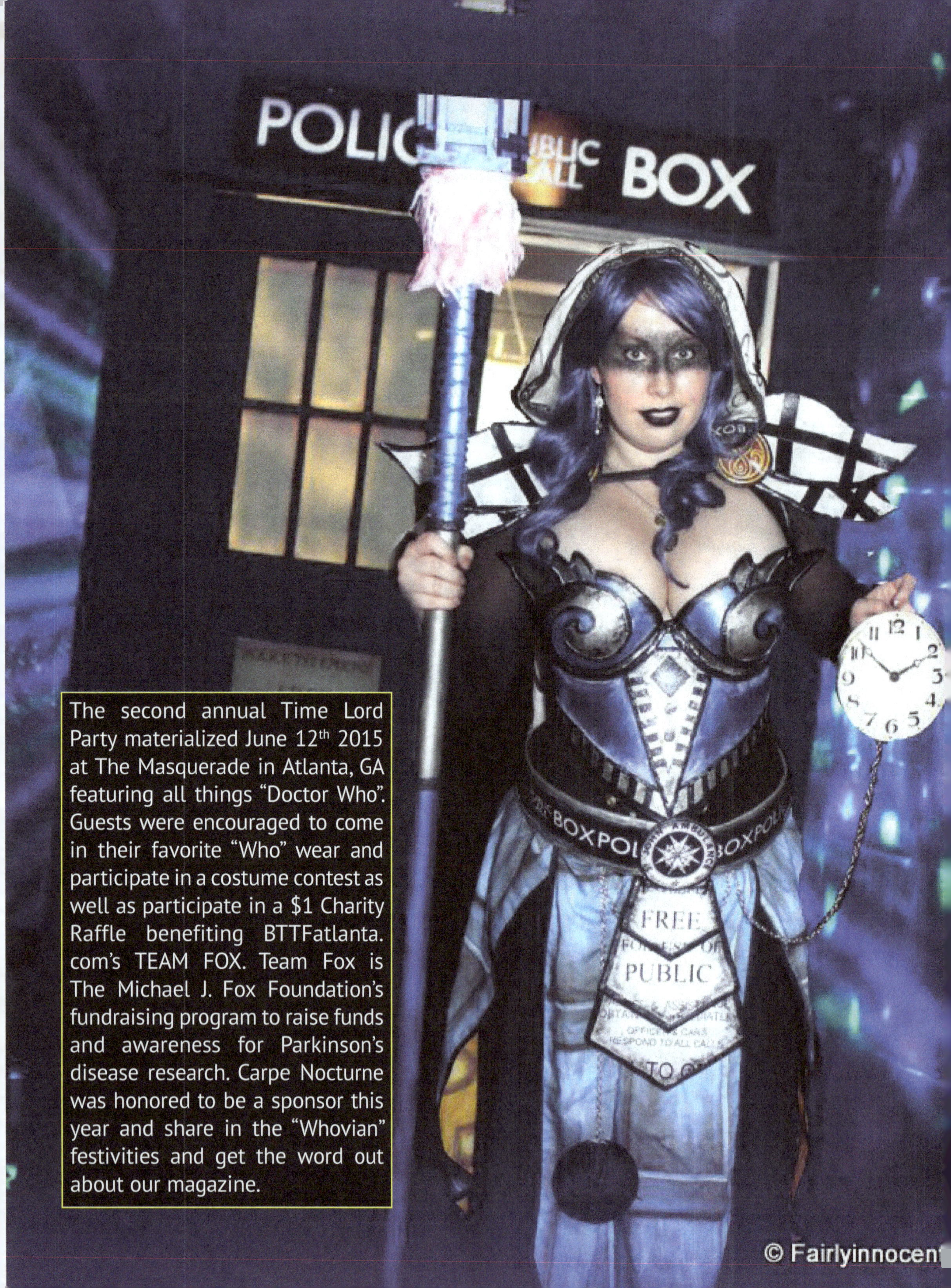

The second annual Time Lord Party materialized June 12th 2015 at The Masquerade in Atlanta, GA featuring all things "Doctor Who". Guests were encouraged to come in their favorite "Who" wear and participate in a costume contest as well as participate in a $1 Charity Raffle benefiting BTTFatlanta. com's TEAM FOX. Team Fox is The Michael J. Fox Foundation's fundraising program to raise funds and awareness for Parkinson's disease research. Carpe Nocturne was honored to be a sponsor this year and share in the "Whovian" festivities and get the word out about our magazine.

THROUGH THE WORMHOLE WITH "THE DOCTOR"

By: Fairlyinnocent

The mood came complete with a "Tardis" for photos to propel you into another dimension, and artists such as Dimitri Walker, Fresh Baked Pottery, Artist.Life.Vision, and CONjuration to entice you with their "Doctor Who" wares. DJs Seraph, resident DJ for Dragon Fire Events and Dungeon Studios and DJP, from The Shelter (now closed) and The Masquerade, were spinning a fantastic blend of music to energize you out on the dance floor all night. With dancers like Foxy Roulette, who rocked the stage "Tardis" and Judah Krypt, who wouldn't want to participate in the fun! A live performance by Atlanta band "The Extraordinary Contraptions" were belting out their quirky, steampunkish brand of music as well creating their own electricity. There was even a hooping performer, Kyo Flow, who was lighting up the room with her amazing talent.

What "Doctor Who" event would be complete without having signature drinks! There were three- The Sonic Screwdriver: Vanilla Vodka, Blue Curacao, lemon-lime soda, the Tardis: Pineapple Rum, Coconut Rum, Blue Curacao and Sprite, and Ood Juice: Black Cherry Rum, Grenadine, Cherry Pucker, Vanilla Rum and soda. It would have really been spectacular if there were waitresses dressed in "Who" costuming to hand deliver the drinks to the patrons!

Carpe Nocturne was honored to be a sponsor this year and share in the "Whovian" festivities and get the word out about our magazine. Carpe Nocturne partook in this event by doing a four ticket random giveaway to their readers to attend "The Time Lord Party II" and those winners of the drawing were Andrew Ingram, Christy Leigh Russell, Jerome Hambrick, and Taureen Cogburn. This was a very fun way to get our readers involved in the magazine and activities that we sponsor and events we support.

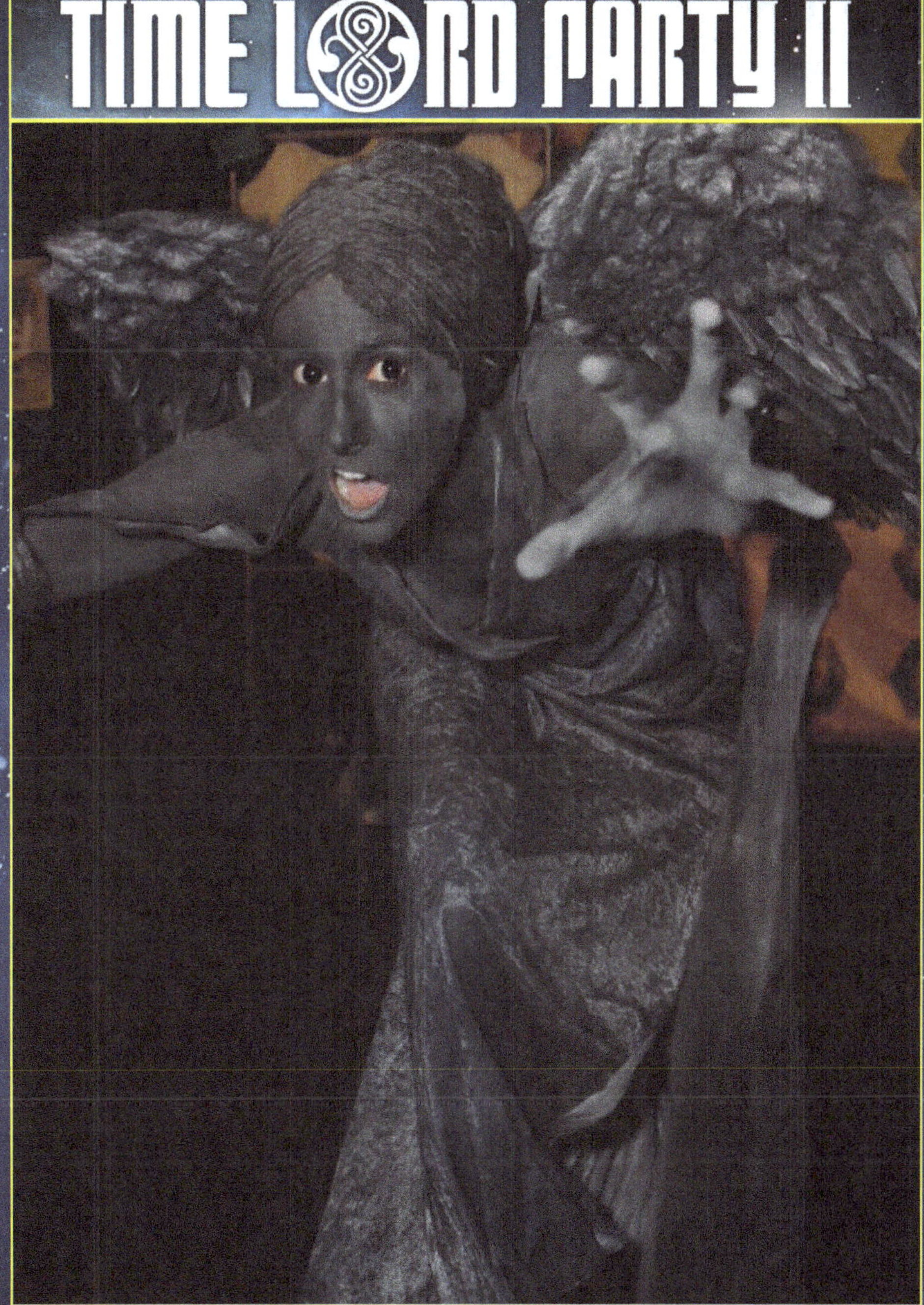

Markster Con did a phenomenal job with the "Time Lord Party II" production and is known for all the events he produces throughout the year along with Co-Host Dragon Fire Events. For more information on videos or upcoming events with Markster Con go to:

www.markstercon.con/
www.facebook.com/MarksterCon
Photography provided for this review by Fairlyinnocent Photography at: www.fairlyinnocentphotography.weebly.com

Vendors:
Dimitri Walker: http://www.walkerdesignconsultants.comyr.com
Fresh Baked Pottery: https://www.etsy.com/shop/FreshBakedPottery
Artist.Life.Vision: http://www.artistlifevision.com/More/What-Is-Time
CONjuration: https://www.facebook.com/CONjurationcon
Drop Dead Bizarre: https://www.facebook.com/dropdead.bizarre
Ritual Club Wear: http://www.ritualoni.com
The Extraordinary Contraptions: https://www.facebook.com/theextraordinarycontraptions
Foxy Roulette: http://www.facebook.com/FoxyRoulette
Kyo Flow: http://www.kyoflow.com

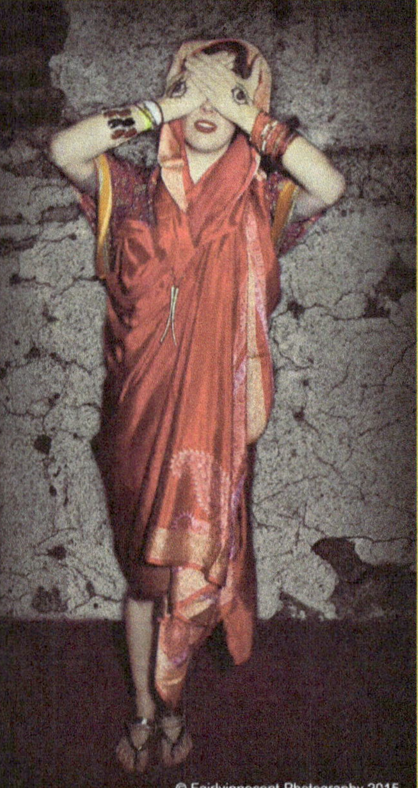

© Fairlyinnocent Photography 2015

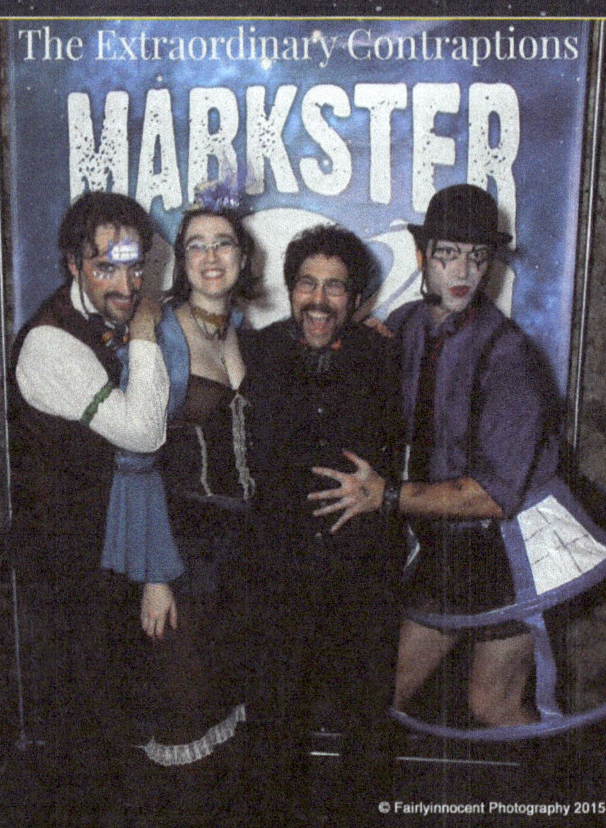

© Fairlyinnocent Photography 2015

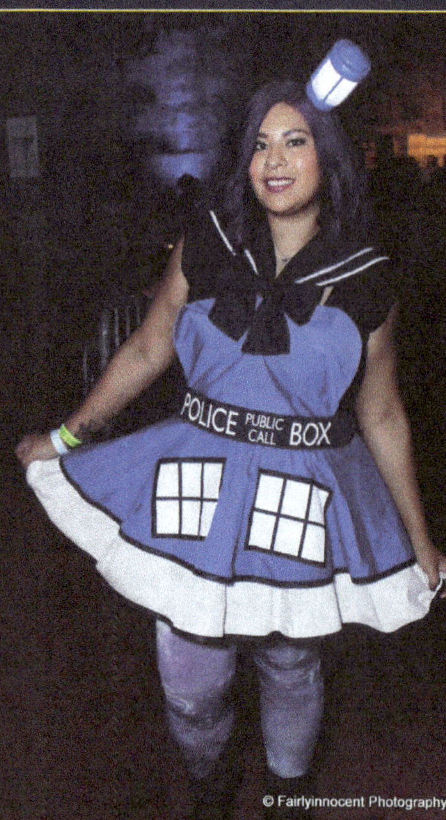

© Fairlyinnocent Photography

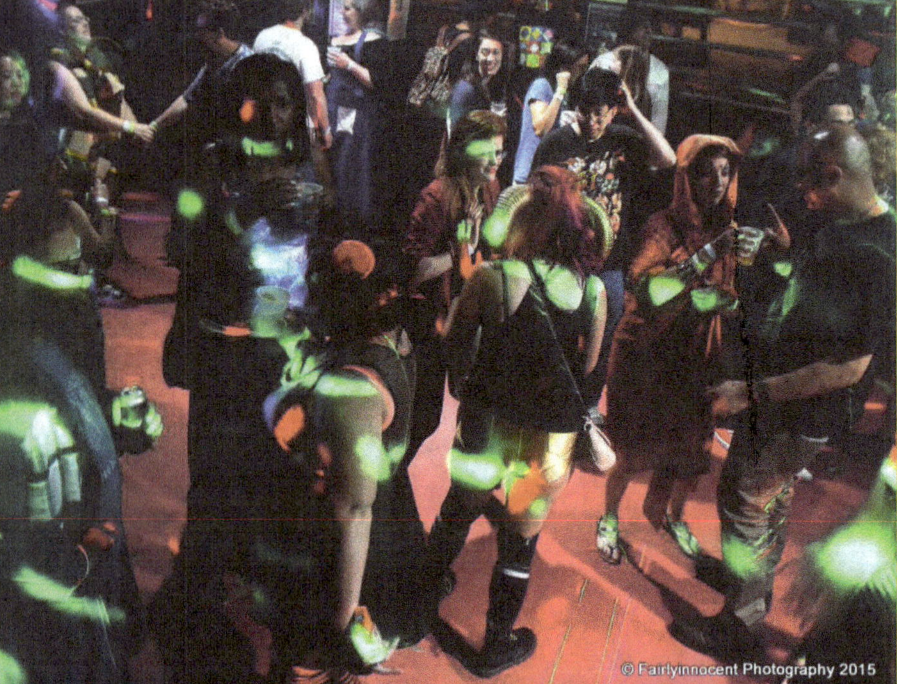

© Fairlyinnocent Photography 2015

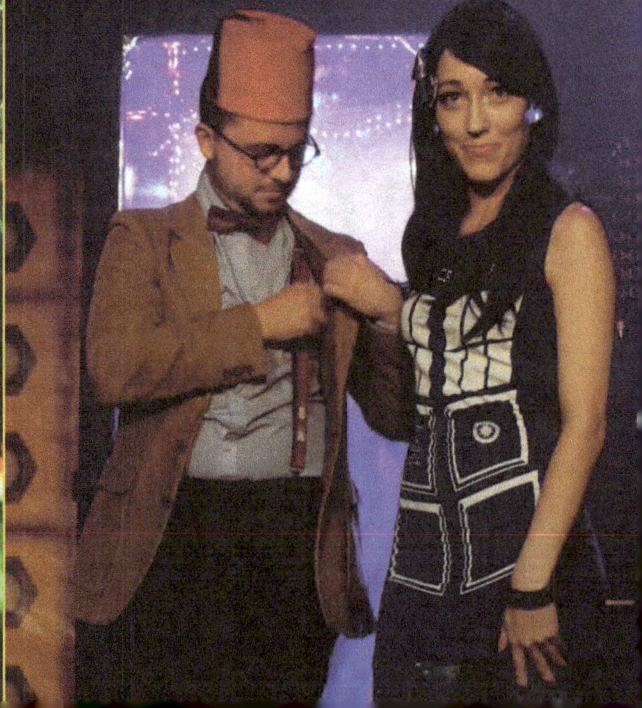

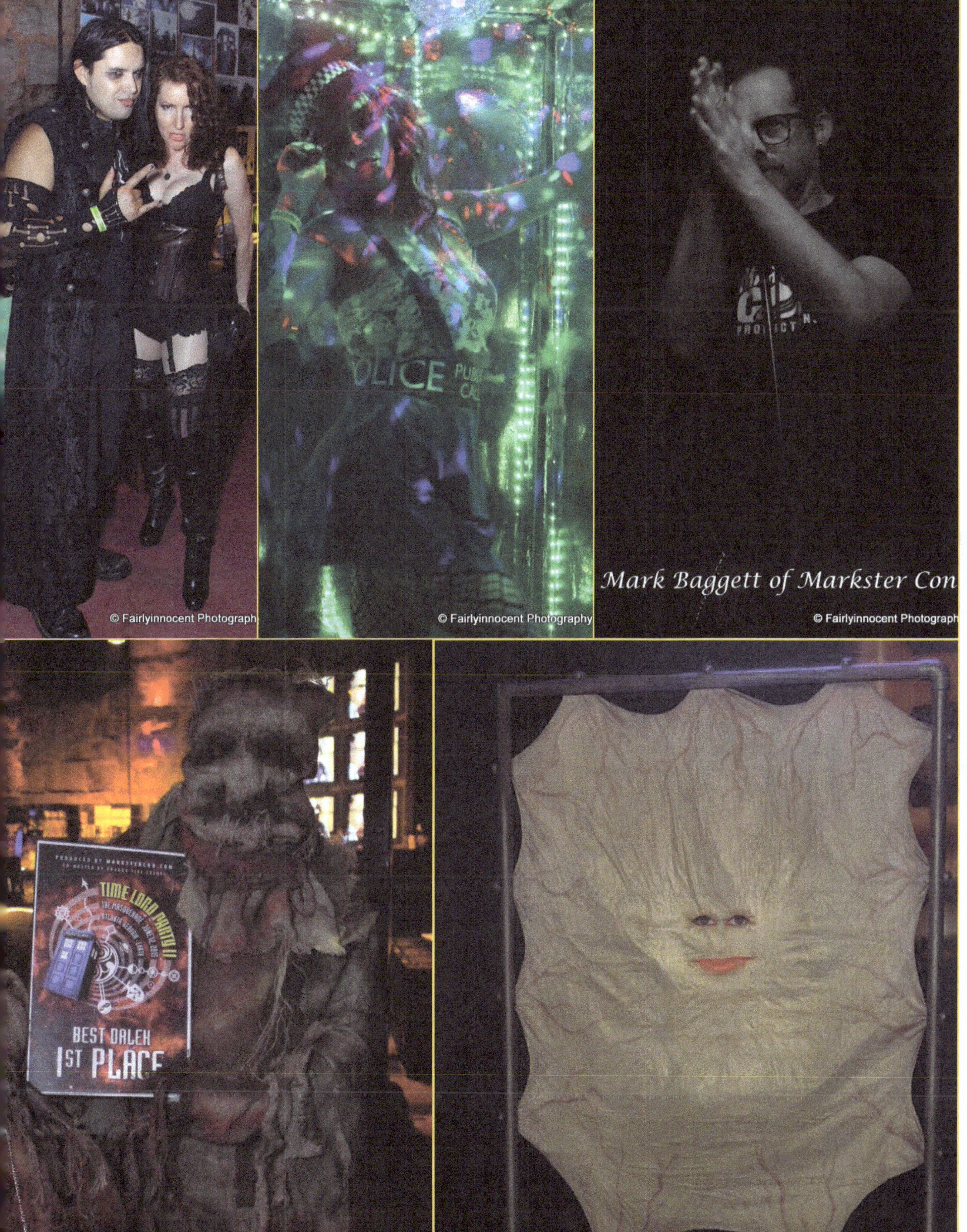
Mark Baggett of Markster Con
© Fairlyinnocent Photography
© Fairlyinnocent Photography
© Fairlyinnocent Photograph
POLICE PUBLIC CALL
TIME LORD PARTY II
THE MASQUERADE
PRODUCED BY MARKSTERCON.COM
BEST DALEK
1ST PLACE
© Fairlyinnocent Photography 20

MORTICIA ADDAMS

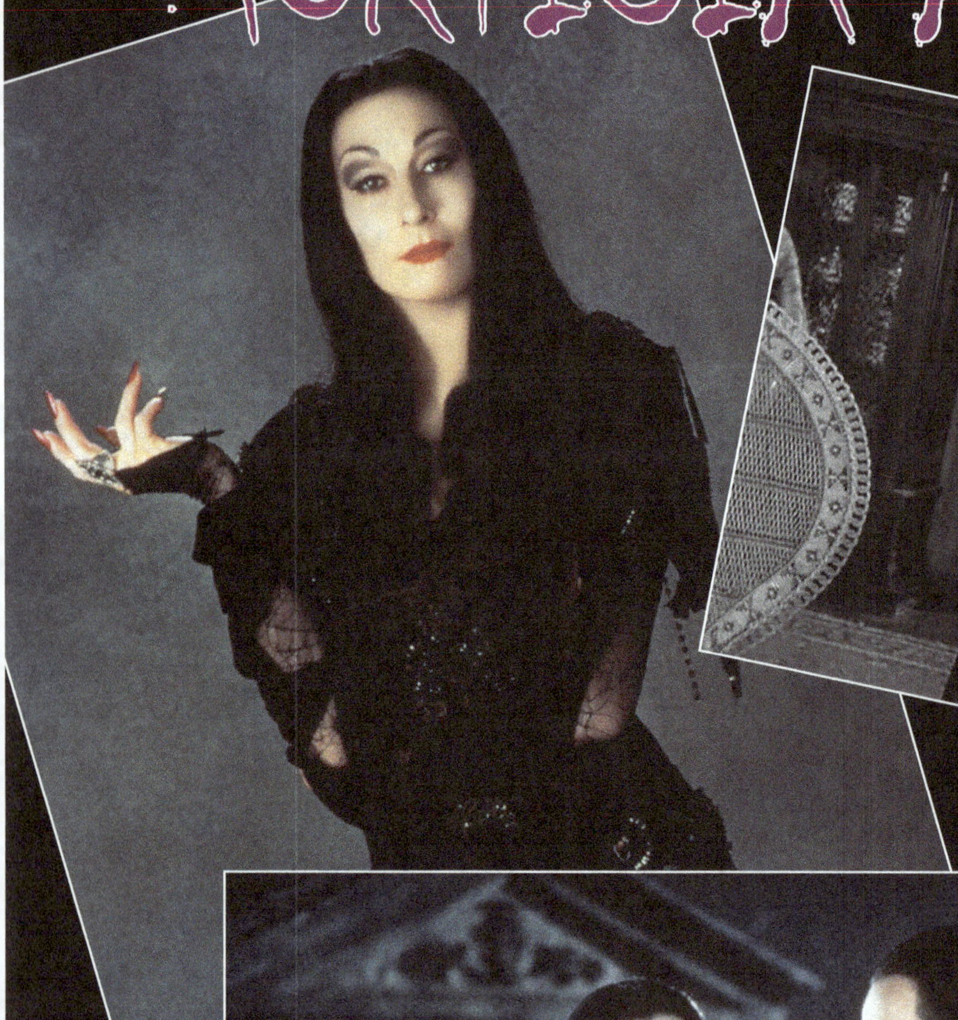

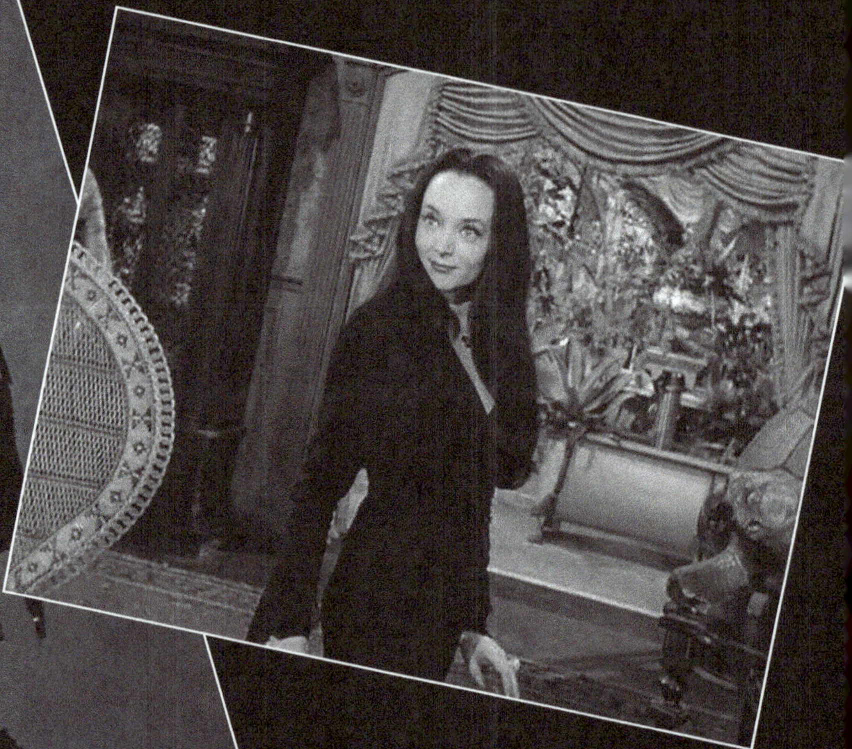

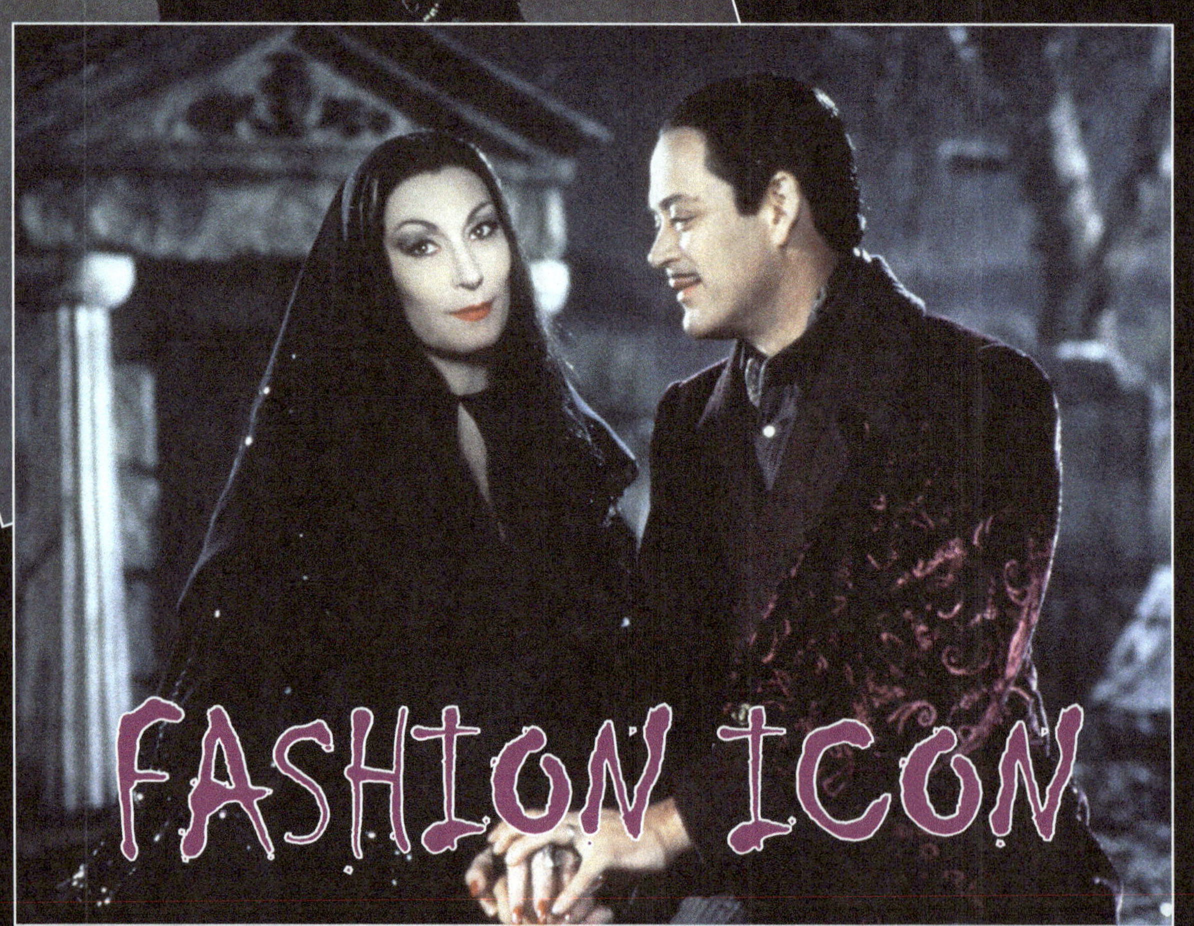

FASHION ICON

By Kathleen Sharkey

Long sheets of black hair falling over pale white skin, charcoal grey eyeshadow under perfectly shaped eyebrows, deep cheekbones and perfect dark shaped cupid bow lips, floor length black hobble dress with tentacled hemline and tattered sleeves. This description may be synonymous with the fashion of some of the early gothic fashionistas, but this particular description actually comes from a femme fatale from the 1930s. Created by Charles Addams for the New Yorker Magazine, the mother of a macabre family began her black and white life with no name. She appeared in over 100 single celled comics and was based off of Addams' second wife.

It would not be until the 1960's that Morticia Addams would have a name, her name seems to have come from the Latin "mort" meaning death and perhaps the fact that Morticia sounds so much like mortician. Carolyn Jones, the actress who played Morticia in the Television series, became the first physical manifestation of

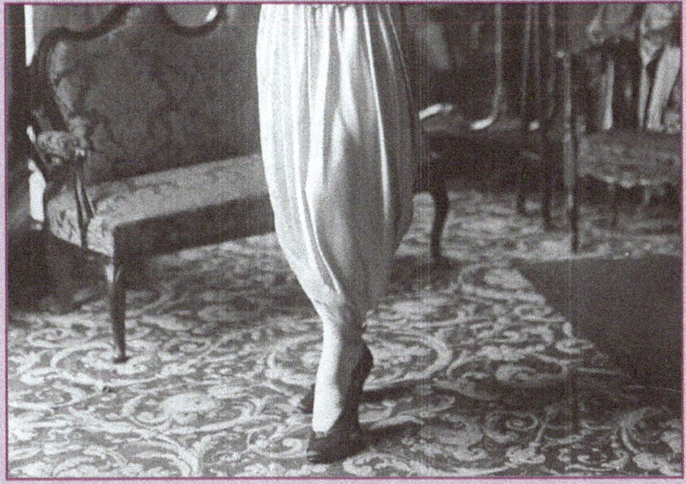

this eccentric mother. Her hobbled hem followed the comic strip as did the octopus like hemline. The sleeves were dark, long and tattered and her long dark tresses fell over powdered pale skin, dark painted lips and Jones' own perfect high cheek bones. Jones portrayed Morticia with an ease and grace while breathing life into the towering waifish comic caricature.

In 1991 the remake of the Addams family brought the elegant and beautiful Angelica Huston into the matriarcle familial position. Though they had similar dresses Huston's gown was a little bit more elaborate. Her sleeves have spider webbed lace, her bodice is more ornate. Huston's costumes changed from scene to scene, probably because of colorization of videos. Huston brought more of a sensual sexuality to Morticia's character and made the famous smoky eye sexier by having special effects which focused light specifically on her powerful eyes. Huston's long elegant face makes her own cheekbones even more pronounced. Where Jones gave life to a 60s version of Morticia, Huston gave her sensuality and modernized Morticia's look and personality.

Morticia Addams is always in the list of people and characters that helped to start the Gothic Fashion movement of the 1970s. With over 5 decades in the public eye and an ever evolving costume arena brought about by different portrayals (Carolyn Jones, Angelica Huston, Darryl Hannah and, most recently, Bebe Neuwirth, on Broadway) it is not hard to see why this dark macabre beauty would impress upon any fashion culture. The pieces that make up her iconic beauty have a great deal to do with the history of fashion and beauty.

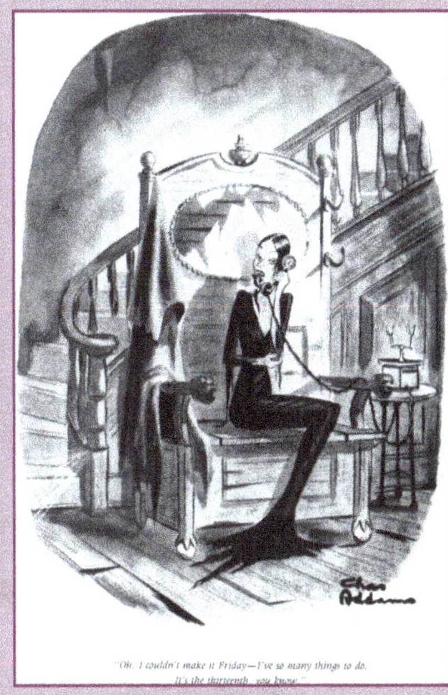

Starting with the 1930's when the Addams family first appeared in the New Yorker Magazine. Less than 20 years before the comics' initial appearance the hobble skirt/dress appeared on the American streets. The design came originally from France and gave women a little freedom by displacing the heavy petticoats of the time. It also gave women more of a defined femininity by better defining their lower bodies; ankles once left to the imagination now appeared below the tight hemline. On the other hand it decreased mobility from a glide to a shuffle and created a great scandal in the American papers. The fashion was far too disgraceful for the American streets and those who wore the fashion were publically shamed in the papers. This may be the reason the fashion only lasted from 1910-1913, though the beginning of World War 1 and fabric rationing may have also had a part in the end of this fashion.

Morticia's smoky eye has an even longer background in history. From 3,500 B.C. the smoky eye was used to keep away optical ailments in ancient Egypt. More recently the smoky eye has been thought to represent the look in the female eye during the height of passion. As for the pale skin it has a Morticia-esque background. Back in the Elizabethan times the pallor of women's skin was very chique with

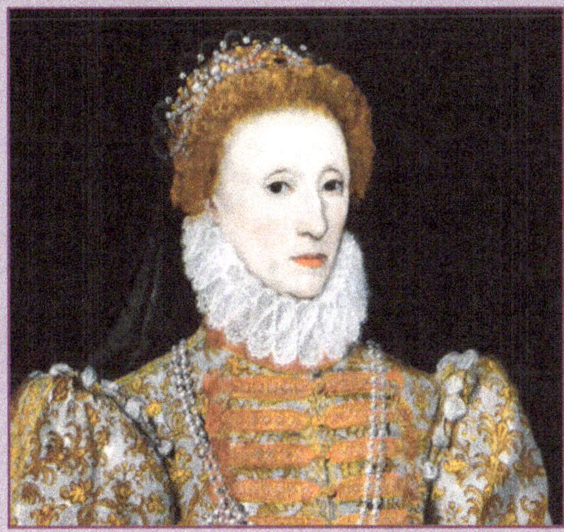

the use of lead, tin and sometimes alum, all poisonous ingredients and definitely Morticia approved methods of beauty.

So was the physical manifestation of Morticia on both the TV and Silver Screen the beginning and reinforcement of the Goth movement or was this beauty pattern merely a cyclical reoccurrence? Considering the bright conceited era of the 70s and the cynicism of the 80s it would make sense that the television watchers of the mid 60s might find solace in the dark beauty of the gothic movement. So perhaps the dark beauty of Morticia Addams and the reinvention of her historical beauty really was a spur for the Goth movement.

Strega Fashion

By Amy Townsend

Photos by Jordan Kelsey

Once upon a time, alternative subcultures thrived underground. They arose from nebulous origins in backstreet clubs, each enthusiast crediting a different journalist, a different band, with starting it all. Now we live in the age of social media, and whilst some in the alternative scenes remain offline, enjoying the mystery of relative anonymity, many have taken to the web with great delight to share music and fashion with friends all across the globe. We can now document new tattoos, winklepickers and growing eyeliner skills in the blink of a mascaraed eye, creating a network of oddballs, geeks, witches and darklings knitted together by WiFi.

Perhaps strangely, the rise of the internet has led to what could be called a growth in the Old Ways. The net is a haven for witchery and the occult. Tumblr and Instagram are used to share dozens upon dozens of oracle card spreads, altar photographs, haunting and beautiful images of faeries and forests in the moonlight. There is a hankering for myth and magic still, and whilst an interest in folklore and fairytale might be considered a little eccentric amongst one's contemporaries in a small town, online we can cheerily and freely talk about everything, from Tarot to trolls, with people who share our interest.

Mai Agerlin, a 22 year old artist from Copenhagen, is one such internet user. Mai's dress sense was inspired by fairy tales from a young age, and now under her Tumblr handle 'shortcuttothestars', Mai posts dark and unusual fashion images, including her own daily outfits running the gamut from Lolita to post-apocalyptic. Mai's interest in witchcraft and folklore has lent itself to the growing popularity of a new subcultural style, and its accompanying hashtag, #stregafashion.

Unlike Goth, for example, with its numerous contradictory origin stories, strega was born on picture-sharing social network Tumblr, and dozens of people, excited about dark fashion and otherworldly aesthetics, have recognised the community as a place where they might feel at home. As of now there are strega Pinterest boards, blogs and shops, and new offshoots such as 'celestial strega', 'urban strega' and 'swamp strega' already emerging.

So what is strega fashion? Strega is a visual interpretation of witchcraft and folkloric themes; its aesthetic roots are in Goth, boho style and Mori Kei, a whimsical Japanese fashion subculture whose adherents like to dress as though they live in a cottage in the forest. Mori, and its spookier sister, Black Forest or Dark Mori, incorporate layers upon layers of clothes in rustic styles (usually brown, cream and earth tones for Mori; black and grey for Dark Mori).

The name 'strega', in fact, comes from the Italian word for 'witch'. Mai says, 'Strega was a rather random choice, any word for witch in any European language could have been picked (like heks, for example).' Some have objected to the use of the term, suggesting alternative names such as 'dark fairytale', but strega blogger Rae, aka 'c4tbus' on Tumblr, points out, 'Honestly almost every person I know in the strega fashion community practices some sort of craft. Like it wasn't just a name. It was really like a bunch of "witches" came together to make our own fashion subculture.'

Dutch Goth/alternative model Psychara posts many of her daily outfits under the strega hashtag, and she says, 'I've always been interested in anything witchy, because of the relationship witches have with nature and my grandmother who was interested in witches too. The magic, spells, herbs, way of life is so inspiring!' Mai's mother describes herself as a witch, and thus, Mai says, 'it's always been a positive thing for me. A witch is a strong, feminine woman and a force to be reckoned with. A witch cares about nature and her surroundings and the welfare of other people.'

Several bloggers have been influential in the development of the style, such as Pandora, whose blog Strega Forest curates inspiration for an audience of over a thousand followers. Pandora's 2012 Dark Mori 'Style and Lifestyle' checklist (with bullet points such as 'strangeness over prettiness', 'believes in fairies' and 'old

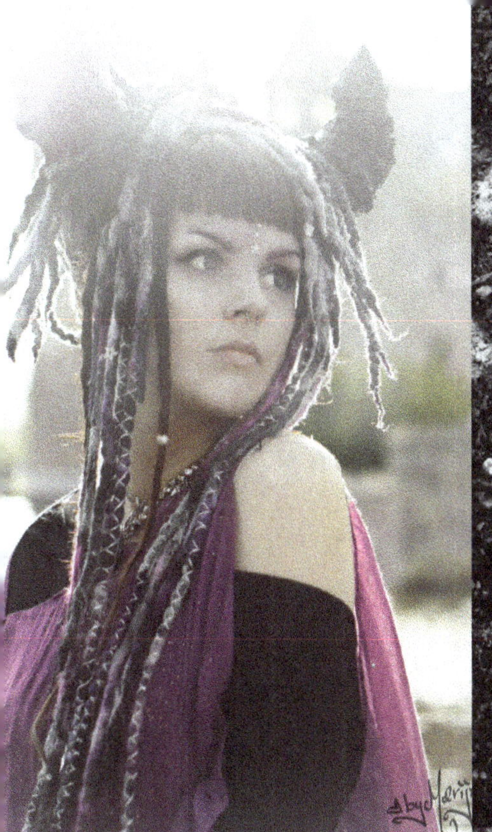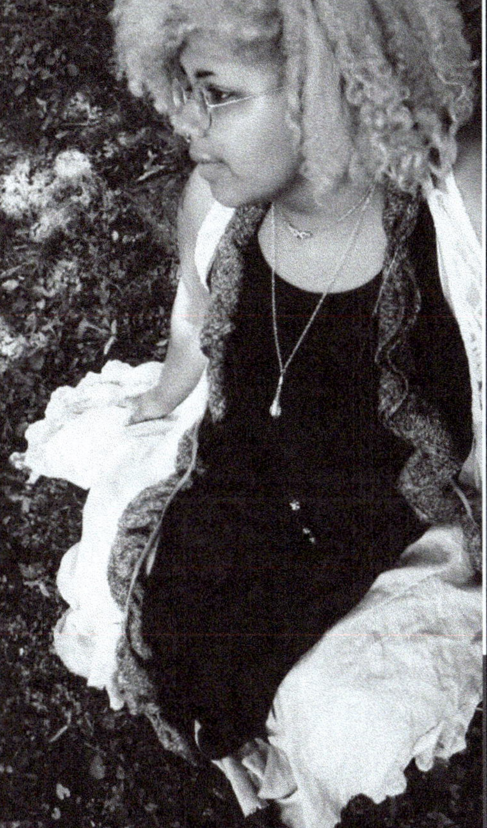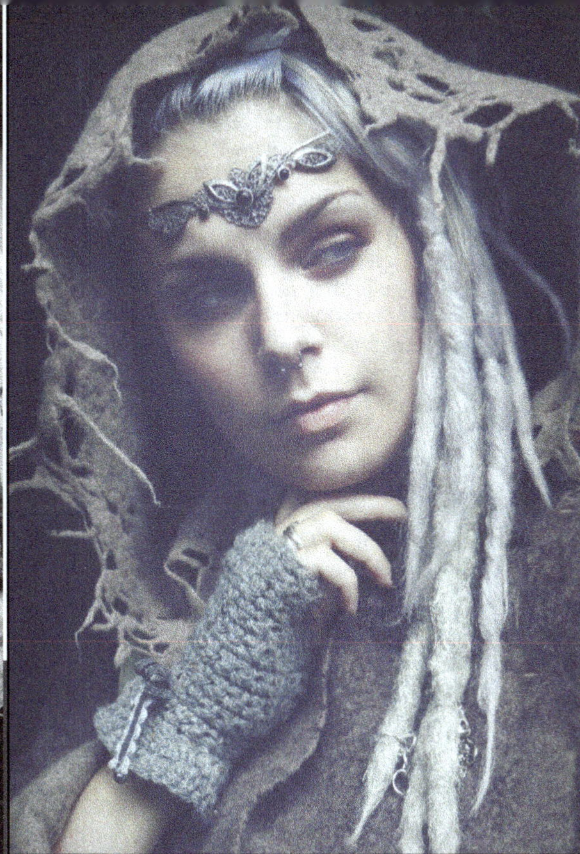

bookstores are a favourite place') captured the imagination of many internet users interested in esotericism and dark fashion. Mai's Tumblr post, 'Strega Fashion Manifest', also gave those interested in the style a set of guidelines to help them express their inner witch.

In strega, there are no definite rules, unlike the Japanese fashion subcultures which it draws from. Whilst Dark Mori and strega have similarities in terms of colour schemes and a fondness for layering, Mai draws a distinction between the two: 'Strega fashion has European roots and inspiration, whereas Mori has Japanese. Strega fashion has no other rules than that it has to be witch inspired. Mori has stricter rules about silhouette and colors, whereas strega has only this one. We came together to create strega because we felt that Mori was too limiting.' She explains, 'Strega started when people started pointing out how far I'd strayed from the mori aesthetic and I realized I didn't wanna fit back into it. I was way more drawn to this European-inspired boho/witch look, and thus Strega was born.'

Indeed, this freedom of expression is a large part of the appeal for other strega enthusiasts. Psychara says, 'Styles and communities with rules are often too intimidating, while strega is very openminded about everyone's opinion about what is witchy! I think that plays the biggest part in its growing popularity!'

Accordingly, every strega has their own take on the style. Goths, Mori girls (and boys), fans of fairy fashion and practicing witches have all been attracted to the new community, and while some wear strega occasionally; some, like Rae, adopt the look as their everyday wear. Rae says, 'I know others might see my outfit and say well I don't think that's very witchy but the whole point of strega fashion is that it's what YOU think a witch would dress like. And since I consider myself a witch I would think I could dress any way I want and it be considered strega fashion.'

Another element of strega is its emphasis, intentional or otherwise, on low-budget, eco-friendly fashion. Mai, Pandora and Rae source a large proportion of their wardrobes from thrift stores, and many stregas are selling second-hand clothes and handmade jewellery online. Rae has even set up a thrift-based service, 6rimoire: '6rimoire is my personal stylist service that I created all myself to help others achieve the look they want in an affordable way. When I have spots available a customer will have a "dressing room" on the blog/website and we'll discuss what they really like fashion wise, and what they're comfortable with, and then with their measurements and a set budget I will go out thrift shopping for their perfect outfit. So it's very eco-friendly! And I also have a thrift shop that is connected with the company where if you just want to find the one perfect piece for an outfit you

already own you can purchase something from there.'

The growing strega community is already very close-knit. Rae describes it as 'a family': 'We're all diverse people, genders, races, sizes. It's very warm and welcoming and I think it's a rare thing to have in a fashion community.' As such, #stregafashion is a welcome addition to the darker side of the web; not just a style but a supportive online community for the spooky, the magical and the Crafty to enjoy.

Strega Resources

tumblr.com/search/strega+fashion

shortcuttothestars.tumblr.com/post/96018512650/strega-fashion-manifest

stregaforest.tumblr.com/post/16855814273/my-dark-mori-style-and-lifestyle-checklist

shortcuttothestars.tumblr.com

psychara.tumblr.com

c4tbus.tumblr.com

6rimoire.tumblr.com

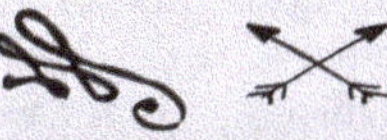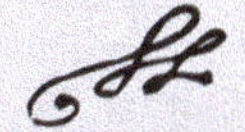

Scarlett Storm may very well be the strangest performer you may ever get the chance to witness. Burlesque dancer, tattoo model, movie actress, and circus freak are just a few of the talents she lists on her decade long resume. No matter what she does, you can expect it to be raunchy, or at the very least...different. She is known for pushing the limits with her performances and photo shoots, with the intended purpose of evoking a reaction. Sometimes it is fear, sometimes lust, sometimes hilarity, but usually it is a combination of many emotions Scarlett Storm draws out of her audience. She is here to entertain, but her methods can be borderline madness.

Recently I had the pleasure of interviewing Scarlett Storm. Catching her in between shows and tours proved difficult. She is a busy woman, and is always on the go. I wasn't sure what to expect when I sat down to interview her. I assumed Scarlett's answers would make me laugh a little, blush a little, and maybe I'd actually learn something in the process. Scarlett definitely did not disappoint. She was everything I had hoped for and more. Here is my interview with the tremendously talented, highly provocative, and downright filthy...Scarlett Storm. Parents, cover your children's eyes.

Scarlett Storm now resides in my nearby hometown of Philadelphia. The arrangement to meet wasn't overly difficult. I would like to say our meeting happened at some dive bar where we tossed back shot after shot of whiskey as we delved into Scarlett's history, but the truth was much less entertaining. Maybe next time. We met at a local coffee shop around noon. Scarlett was easy to spot with her bright red hair and body full of tattoos. I was most interested to see the patrons' reaction to her, and it was mixed. Most people simply paid no attention to the naughty burlesque dancer slash everything whom I was about to meet. I obviously did. She was the entire reason I was here. With a warm smile Scarlett greeted me. We made a bit of small talk about nothing very important, and then we sat down before I dove into my questions.

Although we were here in Philly, Scarlett was actually raised in Oregon. It isn't a place I would naturally associate with burlesque, which prompted me to ask my first question, "What was it about burlesque that drew you in?" Her answer, in many more words, was the spectacular oddity of it all. Scarlett described the only burlesque in her west coast hometown. "It was very DIY, punk rock, no fucks given vibe. One of the performers smashed a big old box tv with an ax. There were clouds of glass dust in the air so everyone had to move back before the act. Another act involved a girl covering

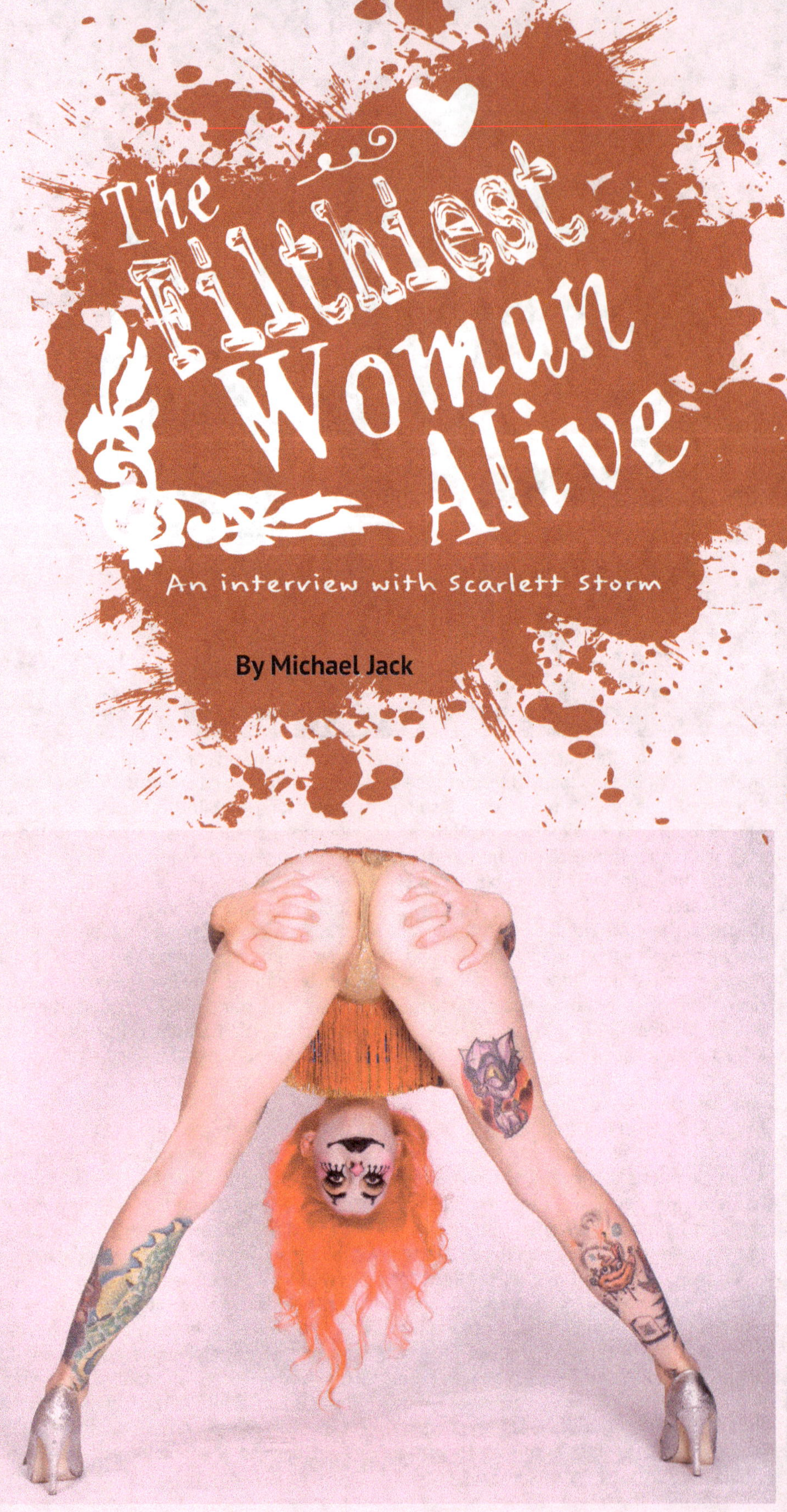

another girl in blacklight paint to a creepy Bob Ross parody voice over. There was a guy juggling machetes on top of the bar. The show lived up to its "Classy as fuck" tagline. It was pasties-optional, raunchy, hilarious and everything I wanted to be about! I had done theater and every kind of dance I could find in high school and college, but this was different. This was my intro to performance art for sexy weirdos."

Sexy weirdos...she stated it with so much pride. I guess that is part of the charismatic charm of Ms. Storm. She wears her unconventionality like a badge of honor. Her shows, her live shows, can be downright outrageous. Expect to cringe, to laugh, and perhaps be embarrassed. This is something I would come to learn all too well. When I asked her to describe her show, she stated, "Oh boy! Well...ahem...It's gonna be a little 'touch-funny' and hopefully inspire some Fear Boners." Fear-boners, that was a completely new term to me, but I had a feeling it was probably strangely accurate. She expanded upon her answer and described, "There will probably be at least one dick in the show. Not an actual dick...but who knows, that has happened too. Sometimes there is a prop-vagina that bugs and pee come out of. But then again sometimes it a very clowny silly show...or very sparkly and classy. I want to try to be as versatile of a performer as I can be and that means I can't be weird all the time...but I'll take it to newer, creepier levels whenever I have the chance!" Then to my chagrin, Scarlett asked me the next question. "Are you blushing?"

"Sorry," I half laughed and half cringed, "I guess I just didn't expect to be talking about pissing vaginas and dicks."

"You asked the question," she reminded. I nodded my acknowledgment, and stared down at the next one I had on the list. I took a very long sip of my coffee and prayed my face wouldn't reach the color of Scarlett's hair. After a seemingly forever amount of time stalling, I finally asked, "You are obviously comfortable with nudity. Was this always the case, or were there any mental obstacles you needed to overcome?"

Scarlett immediately shook her head back and forth. She answered, "I don't ever remember being uncomfortable with the nudity aspect of it. When I first started performing I had terrible stage fright. Naked or clothed, I was just a little ball of nerves. I still get those flutters every now and then before shows, but mostly from the excitement of, 'wow,' we are about to do something really special."

Ok, that one wasn't so bad. Feeling a little more confident again, I dove into question number four. "You perform so many different types of acts. Do you have a particular favorite?"

"That's hard...like asking me to pick a favorite cat!" That is another one of Scarlett's

many faceted personas...crazy cat lady. She continued, "I have a Metalocalypse inspired Dr. Rockzo Act that is pretty fun. I do a bunch of 'fauxcaine' and climb a machete ladder. I also have a King Diamond/Golden Girls act where I come out as a little old lady in a shawl with a wrinkly half-mask...which I remove to reveal full KD face makeup and leather to King Diamond's high pitched metal scream of Grandmaaaaaaaaa."

I sat, and listened, and was astounded by the sheer number of different acts Scarlett would describe. Then again, she has been doing this for ten years. Finally, and with relative certainty, she finally stated, "My very favorite is probably the Beetlejuice act. It's one of my oldest acts. I just keep adding more and more to it. I now have a giant sand worm who joins me onstage and a tiny sandworm who lives in my underwear!"

I almost spit out my coffee. "A sandworm?" The question was more of a what-the-hell reflex. "How the heck does that tie in with Beetlejuice, and why in your underwear?"

"You'll just have to come to my show and find out," Scarlett winked.

I shook my head yes, but really I was thinking about me trying to explain to my wife what kind of show I was going to go see. I'm not so sure she would understand the concept of fear-boner. She is not a prude or anything. She is just a little more...conventional. Trying to clear the sandworms and pissing vaginas from my head, I asked my most enthusiastic guest, "Clowns...a lot of people fear them more than zombies. You portray both. Ever get any memorable reactions from your zanier/scarier costumes?"

"It always makes me so happy when someone will come up to me after a show or send me a message saying, 'I was always scared of clowns, but now I think I have a bit of a clown fetish' or 'I should be creeped out, but instead I'm turned on,' but that's not always the case." Scarlett almost glowed with excitement as she answered. "Sometimes at shows people will ask us to mess with their friends who have a clown fear. I think the clown business has gotten much more fear out of people than anything I ever did as a zombie or horror character."

"I think I would be more afraid of a clown as well," I admitted. "So, what inspires you?"

"Most of my ideas for acts come from some inside joke or drunken brain storm," Scarlett laughed. "I'm also really lucky to work with some of the most amazing performers around. They are a constant source of inspiration."

"I know you pride yourself on pushing the envelope with photo shoots," I continued on, "the stranger the idea, the better. Was there ever a concept suggested that was even too strange by your standards?" My gut told me the answer was no, but I thought just maybe I would be surprised.

Scarlett thought for a moment. Slowly, she replied, "Not really too strange, but I don't like the idea of doing anything that involves killing bugs or little critters. It's pretty brutal and too touch funny in the bad way. I've been covered in real cows intestines and all kinds of gross questionable things, but for some reason killing bugs makes me squeamish."

Of course, I thought...being covered with real cow intestines, no problem. Squash a centipede, off limits. Made sense. Yet, as I

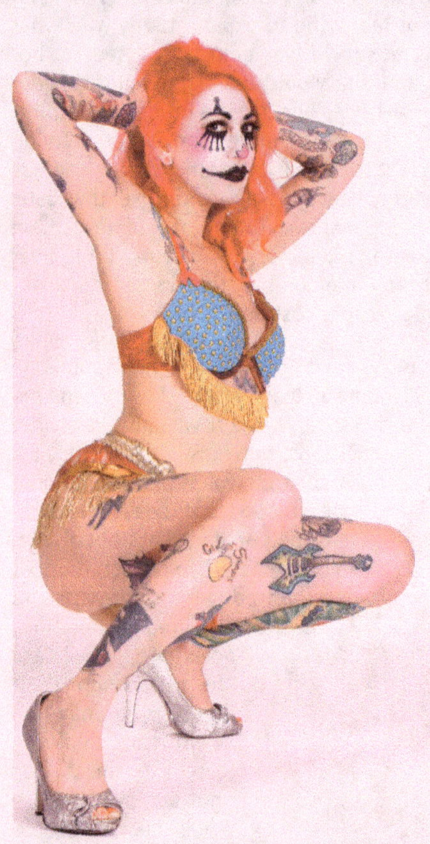

sat there and looked at this woman I had tracked down and requested this interview with, I guess it kinda did. She defies most accepted norms. I shouldn't expect her to say what the average person would say. If she did, then my reasoning for interviewing would have been somewhat invalid. One of the things I enjoy most about Scarlett Storm is how outrageous and different she truly is.

"So how the heck did you learn to walk on machetes and broken glass?"

Scarlett leaned forward and almost whispered, "I don't know if I'll get in trouble with the others for giving this away, but everyone does it a little differently. Before I attempt glass walking or machete ladder climbing, I apply a generous helping of glitter to the exposed areas. Oddly enough, glitter protection can be used for sexual situations as well." Scarlett smiled and stated, "You're turning red again." I just laughed, shrugged my shoulders, tried not to think of how to apply glitter protection sexually, and asked the next question. "You are also an actress. Any big roles coming up we should know about? What has been your favorite to date?"

"I have been talking to a few indie directors about shooting a few things this Fall, so that's pretty exciting. The screening party for my latest Bill Zebub movie, Nightmare on Elmo St was in late August. I'm excited to work on another project of his, 'Dickshark' later this year as well. I'm also going to be involved with a horror film called Asylum by 2365 films which will be shooting in late 2015. So far my favorite project was for a live action video game called Camdrome. I play an eccentric interpretive dance cam character who mock jerks a rubber chicken and proudly strips to reveal one werewolf titty! The project was filmed over two years ago, but has yet to be released. I guess the world isn't ready for werewolf titty. I don't know if they ever will be."

"Let's hope they are more ready for Dickshark," I added.

"It's going to make a big splash," Scarlett beamed.

Speechless. I just smiled, looked down at my notes, and was relieved to see the final question. It is not that I wanted the interview to be over, it's just that I wasn't fully prepared for the answers she gave. In retrospect, I'm glad Scarlett was as blunt as she was. At the time, I was just uncomfortable. How exactly do you respond to wolf-titty or fear-boner, which was still stuck in my head? My coffee had been finished at least twenty minutes prior because I used it as a means to not respond. Smile, sip, pray she does not see me squirm. With a long deep breath, I asked one of the most poignant questions on my list. "What are the biggest misconceptions about what you do?"

"It's a lot of fun," Scarlett explained, "but it's also a lot of work. Between booking, costuming, training, and traveling, it's a full time job. And that's just performing! Somehow everything else fits in there too, but I'm always busy working on something or getting ready or planning. People also think I do a lot more adult work than I have ever actually done. Apparently my filth is legendary. Just another step in my Mink Stole Life Goal of being the filthiest woman alive!"

There you have it...Scarlett Storm. Yes she has made adult films. Yes I have seen them. I research thoroughly. From what I have seen, from what I have heard from her lips, from the enthusiasm she spoke about it, cow intestines, crazy burlesque shows, tiny worms in her underwear, vaginas with bugs exiting, I can go on, I have to say...Scarlett, I think you already are the filthiest woman alive. I do mean that in the most sincere way possible. I hope you keep it up for decades more. The world can use a heavy dose of your insanity.

If you want to catch her act, Scarlett will be touring the country with Thunder Snow Cone and Cut Throat Freak Show. I guarantee you haven't seen anything like it, but don't say I didn't warn you.

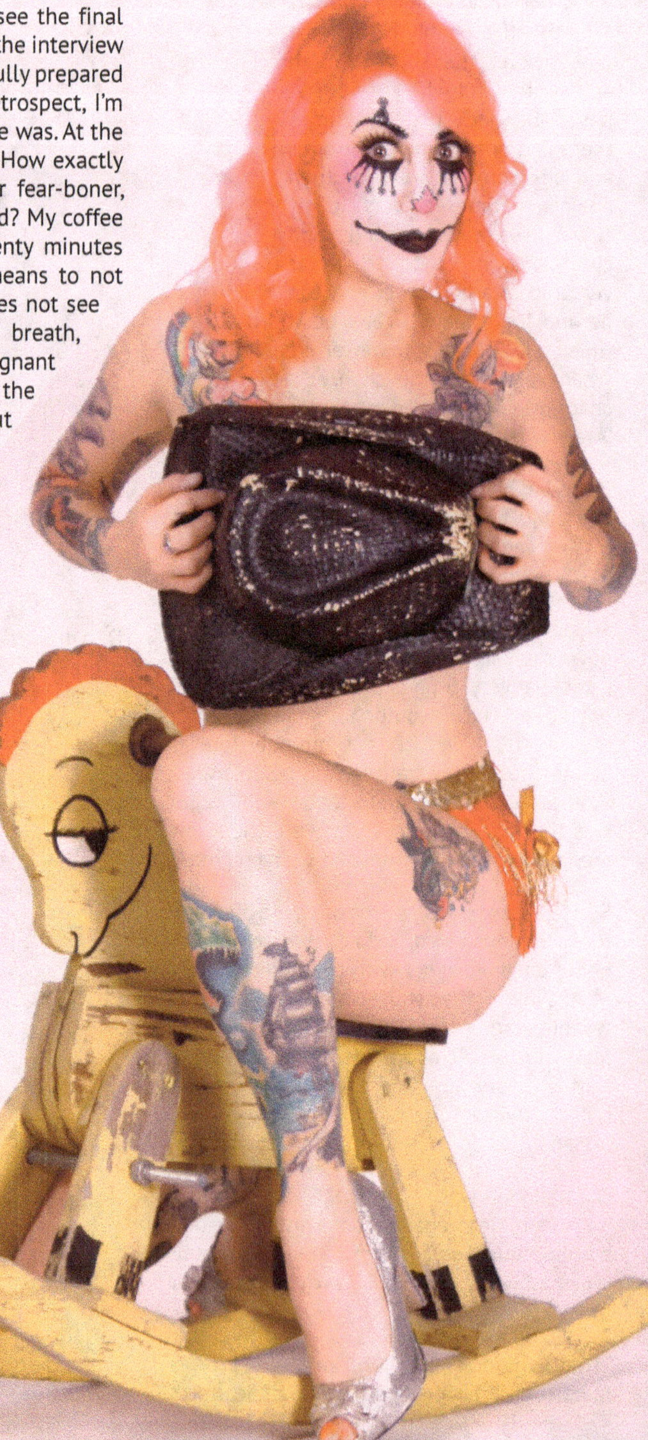

Photos By Strettography

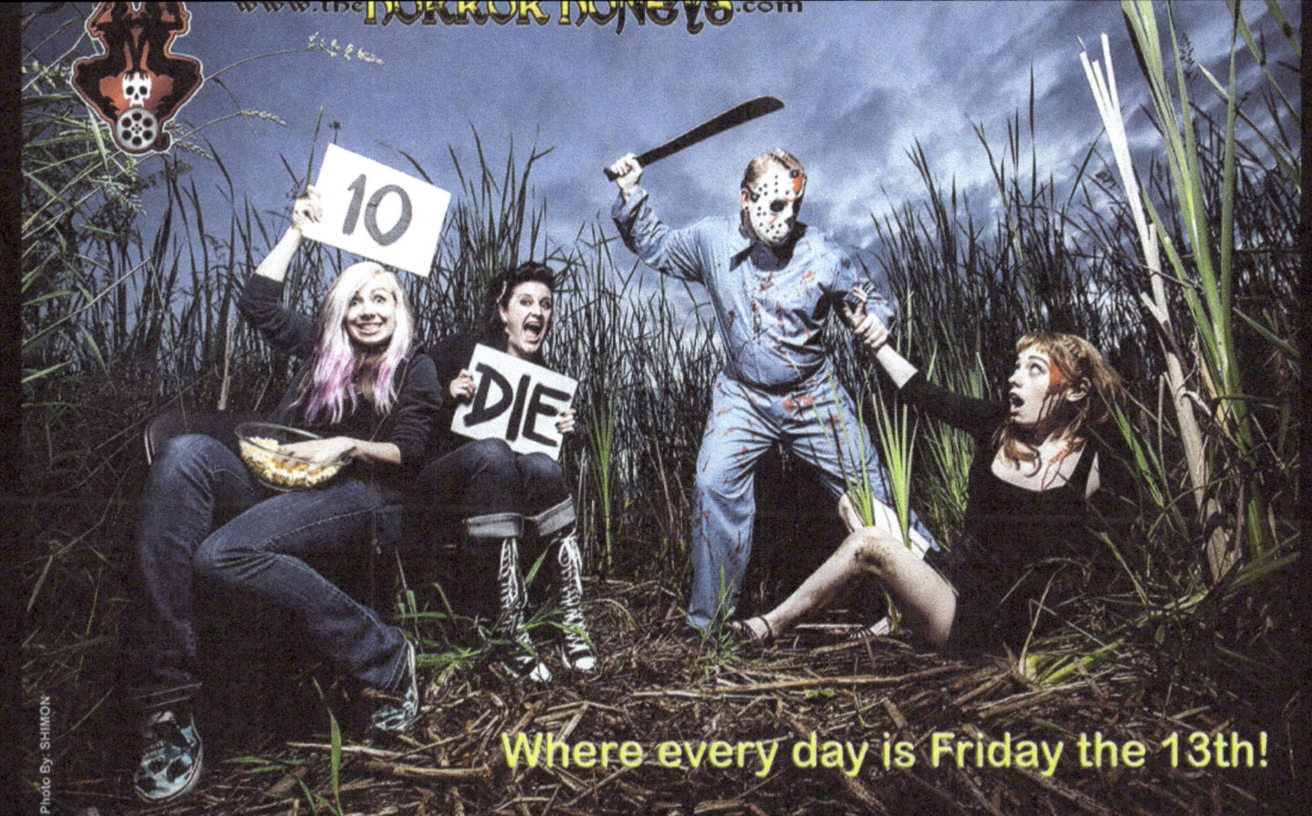

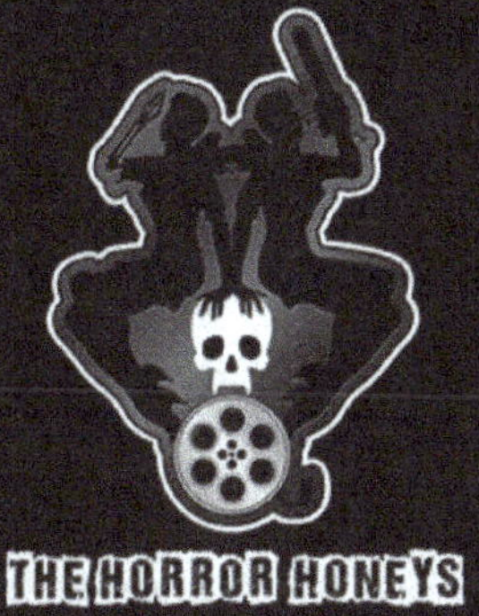

The Best in Horror

News | Reviews | Podcast | Attitude

www.thehorrorhoneys.com

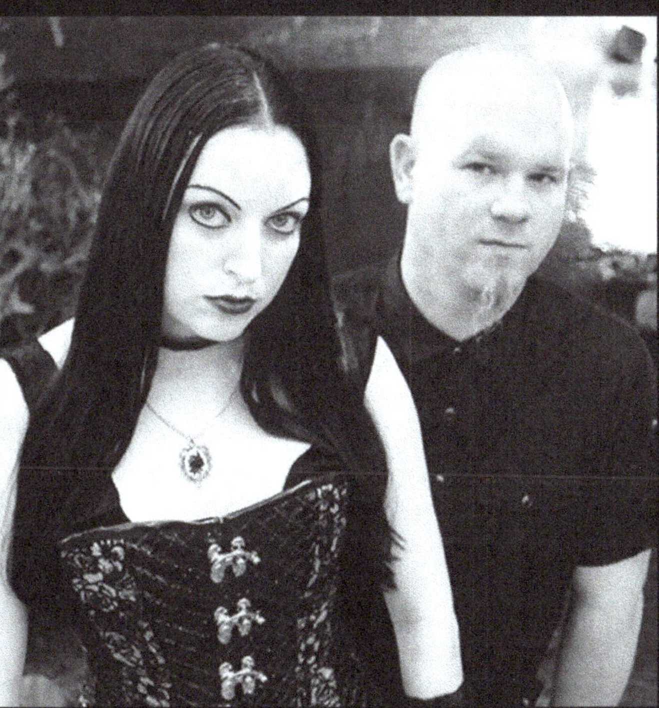

Petals And Thorns

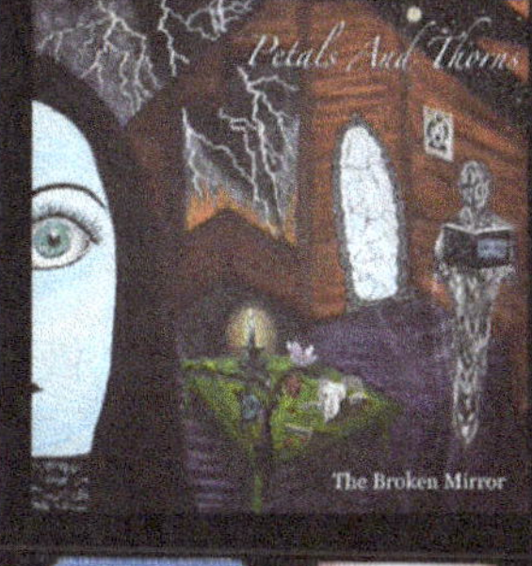

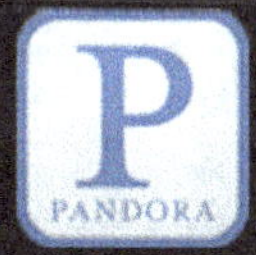

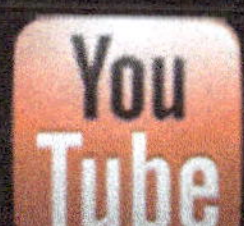

www.petalsandthorns.net

a creepy & cute life:
An Interview with Hello Batty

By Hyde Falkenstein

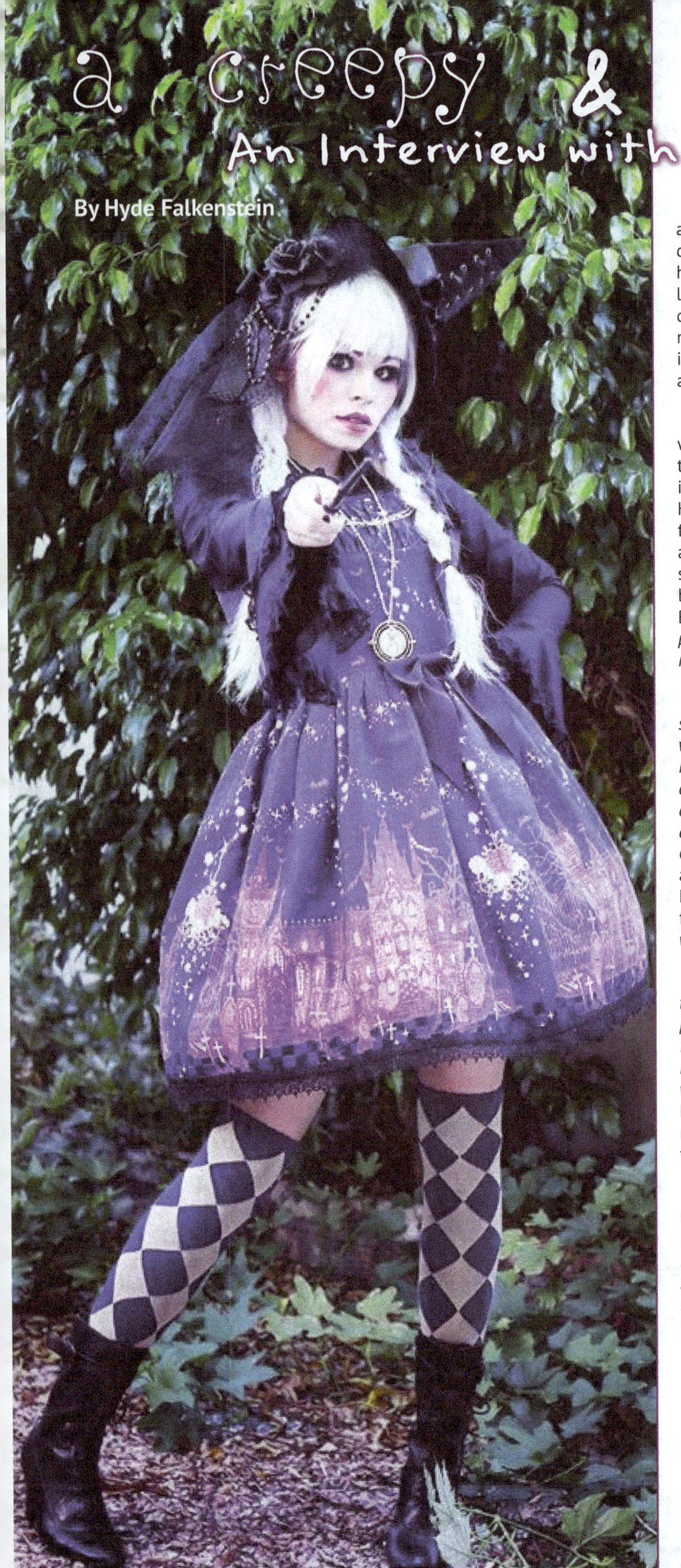

Hello Batty, whose name is Kathryn, is a 25 year-old Fashion and Cosplay Youtuber that also covers Gothic and Japanese culture. She has had her Youtube account for a few years and has gained thousands of fans. I started watching her videos last year and was ecstatic to find an alternative Youtuber that covered some of my favorite interests and had great style. Her most popular video, "You Are Not a Real Goth! – Discrimination in The Subculture," explained to others that Goth does not have a strict guide and showed us other sides of the subculture.

While Kathryn was growing up in Arizona, she would always watch shows like Sailor Moon and Card Captor Sakura. She tells me one day she picked up a comic called Othello, which is about a school girl who on weekends spends her time in Harajuku as a Gothic Lolita. Kathryn believes that that was the first time she heard the term Lolita used and quickly started to add lace and frills to her already Gothic wardrobe. Eventually she became addicted to a band called Malice Mizer and their beautiful member Mana. She discovered the Gothic & Lolita Bibles through him and his brand Moi-meme-Moitie. *"It all pretty much went downhill from there"*, she tells me, *" I have never recovered from my addiction to the fashion and lifestyle."*

She continues,*"It wasn't really till Jr High till I met my first school friend that liked anime. I met quite a few actually and it was really awesome to go to comic shops and swap the latest manga with each other. In High School we started an anime club and learned about conventions. We were really lucky that Arizona actually had a comic convention and anime convention we could attend. I went to my first when I was 15."* She would make costumes for her friends and they would cosplay on Halloween and at comic shop events. She says her first cosplay was in Jr High when her mom designed for her a Sailor Mercury costume for Halloween. *"I felt so awesome! I bet if I found a picture now it would be so embarrassing."*

Her fashion inspirations are constantly changing. *"I think that's why I can't really build a solid wardrobe. I am all over the place with what I like and can never focus on one thing. Right now I am stuck between a love of neons, plastics, and the idea of kawaii magical alien girls or leaning towards earthy dark and mysterious witchy vibes."* There are so many things that continue to inspire her she says. She thinks the most important are all things magical and bringing a bit of magic into everyday life through the clothes we wear and I agree with her.

Since she started her Youtube channel she tells me her life has pretty much been the same, except now she has many new friends to talk to and share her life with. *"I've met so many amazing people by breaking out of my awkward anti-social shell through videos and having my camera with me at events! It makes it so easy to start conversations and not be shy which is wonderful because I am horrible at talking to strangers."*

Where can you find Hello Batty?
Youtube.com/thehellobatty
hellobatty.com
facebook.com/thehellobatty
Instagram.com/hellobatty

COMING OF AUTUMN

By XXX Zombieboy XXX

Into cold winds grabbing
Like fingers of vitality

Bring down the stars to see a little bit closer
Their ancient light mingling with the swirling bonfire smoke

The blood boils anew with the coming cycle
The harvest reaping complete
While over the green and purple hills comes moonlight
Gateways for those so long forgotten by man in his digital setting

The very air itself smells like smoke and like frost
And there is nearly imperceptible music upon the breeze
The leaves scatter by along the roadways
And the fields are full of pumpkins that wait to greet the ghosts

Night comes full with mystery in masks
Little ghouls fulfilling rites without knowing
The bones are cast into the flames
The crofters and loomers watch with vigilance
Here in the now it is all the same
Yet it creeps through with silent and powerful knowing
All things left are never forgotten
All things returning with the inevitable wheel
Slàinte mhòr oirbh agad Ban-Druidh!
To each huddled close to the fire
When the dead don't stay dead
When the faery folk gather
Slàinte mhòr agus a h-uile beannachd duibh!
Tha gaol agam ort bithbhaun…

MASQUERADE

By Asylum Attendant

Behind the labels and technology,
Frightened eyes peer back at me.
I've now come to realize
I'm older than you'll ever be.

A human emerged from the shrine
Too late, yet much too soon.
From infatuation to contempt,
Your presence no longer makes me swoon.

Feigned compassion
Integrity is not your virtue.
I bled to death
While a scratch never appeared on you.

Desperate to garner affection,
Primping gave way to a loss of identity.
Striving for your ideal
Destroyed my originality.

Glimmers of sweetness still appear,
Taunting me from their lofty height.
Distance would heal my wounds;
The daily axe I cannot fight.

Hiding within a nonstop masquerade,
You're spinning out of control.
I tried to ride the twisted carousel,
But, the revolutions took their brutal toll.

Back in my personal asylum,
I slowly discover myself again.
Your spell over me has lifted
And another chapter now begins.

SUMMONER'S DANCE

By Zahara

The darkest forces dwell below...
Those parts of us we never show.
I summon you and set you free!
Now bring your darkest powers to me!

From my fire, I watch the wind change directions, trees do bend,
Before a mist begins to creep upon the foliage long asleep.

Lurking from a damp, dark cave gazes
He who looks for slaves.
Peering at me, all the while, with a murderous, putrid smile.

Through a crevice in the earth emerges shadows of angry mirth
Seeking to corrupt and spoil the wills of girls and all man's toils.

Demons reflect the Devil's glance,
Encircling him in their fiery dance,
Spinning orbs of lava light, with eyes of evil glowing bright.

Revelers want to join in, entranced by flames that gently spin.
Distracted now, they cannot tell...
And I laugh as they dance to Hell!

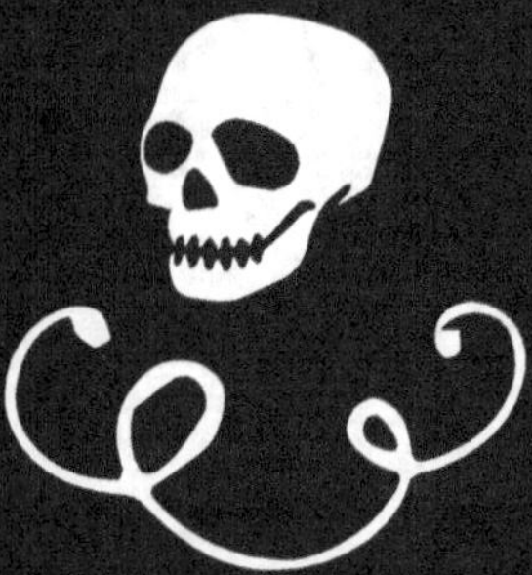

Think your poetry is good enough to
be published in Carpe Nocturne?
Send submissions to
mj@carpenocturne.net
subject line "Poetry."

All submissions must be under 250
words, and will be judged by Managing
Editor Michael Jack and Art Editor Zahara.
The best entries will be featured in our next
issue along side of our very talented staff.

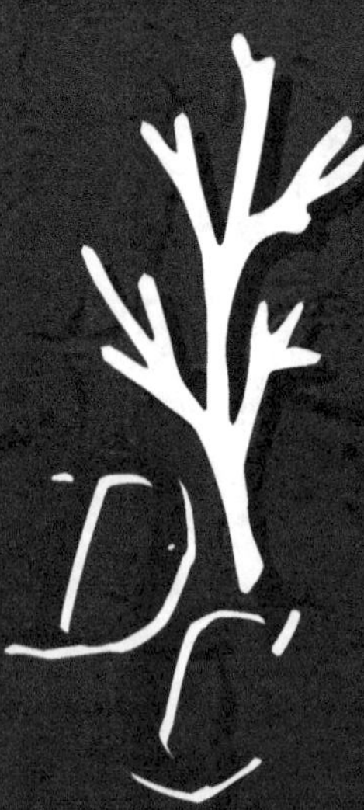

BED OF DOOM

By Jezibell Anat

All the sweet young virgins of Persia were perishing,
Not from disease or famine or war,
But by the command of their own Sultan.

Betrayed by his first wife,
He punished all women,
Deflowering a new bride each night,
Decapitating her at dawn.

She would be bathed, perfumed, hennaed,
Then escorted to the bed of doom.
She was allowed one final indulgence,
Anything she wanted to eat,
Perhaps musicians or dancers or even a visit with family,
But no sighs, no tears, no pleas for mercy.

In the morning, the guards tramped in,
Led by my father, the Grand Vizier.
One slash of his scimitar sufficed.

Persia mourned.
Some girls fled, some hid,
Some disguised themselves as boys,
But most relinquished their heads.

Father's rank granted me immunity.
I delved into our great library.
I read history, poetry, philosophy,
Lore and legends and literature from many lands.
I studied, and I absorbed.

Then I volunteered for the bed of doom.
Father did not want me to go,
But I had a plan.

For my favor, I asked to see my little sister.
She requested a story,
And the Sultan granted permission.

Thus I crafted my first tale
Of heroic adventures and fantastic creatures.
I sustained it through all the hours of that long night.
At dawn, I paused, exhausted.

The Sultan wished to know the ending,
But the guards had arrived at the bed of doom.
To their surprise, he pardoned me,
And told me to return that evening to finish it.

For a thousand more nights, my voice became my lifeline.
As I engaged my memory and my imagination,
Developing characters and intrigues,
Directing each narrative to the height of suspense
Just as the sun rose.

By the time I had no more tales,
He was in love with me,
And I, Shahrazad, was the Sultana.

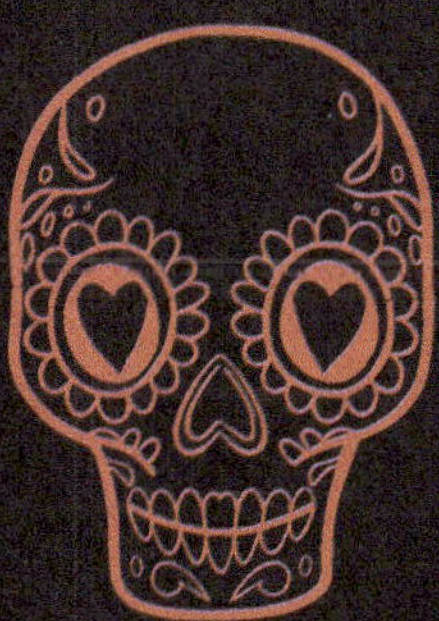

THE LITERARY ROOTS OF GOTH

By Michele Combs

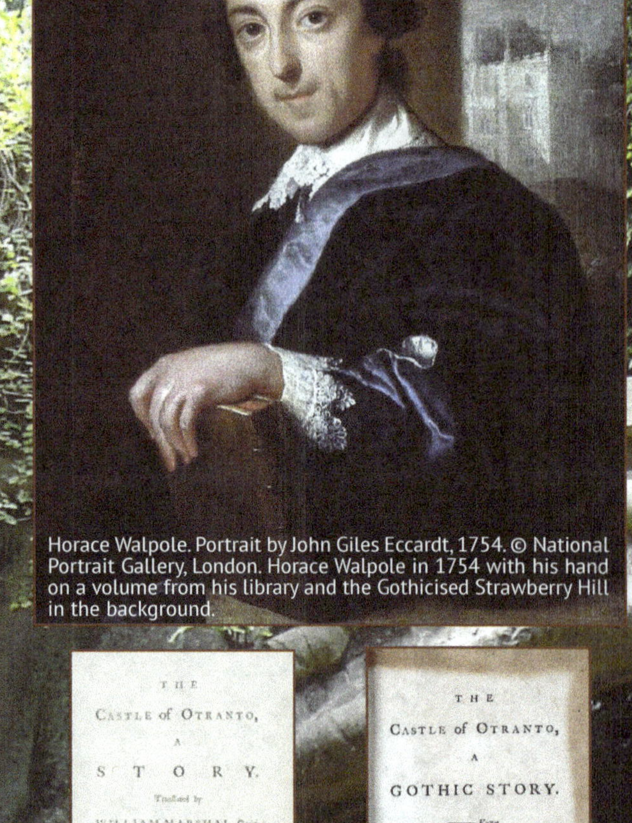

Horace Walpole. Portrait by John Giles Eccardt, 1754. © National Portrait Gallery, London. Horace Walpole in 1754 with his hand on a volume from his library and the Gothicised Strawberry Hill in the background.

Goth culture, which arose in the late 1970s and early 1980s, is today most strongly associated with music and fashion, but its aesthetic roots go back much further, to late 18th and early 19th century literature. Mary Shelley's *Frankenstein* (1818) and Bram Stoker's *Dracula* (1897) and are perhaps the best-known Gothic novels, although they are more often today classed as horror, but they built on tropes and themes established nearly a century earlier.

Gothic architecture, which peaked during the High and Late middle ages, was an ornate style typified by massive castles, manors, cathedrals and abbeys, often perched high above the surrounding town or landscape, built of stone with vaulted ceilings, pointed archways and lancet windows, and soaring towers or spires.[1] Neo-Gothic, a somewhat exaggerated and fantasized version of Gothic, enjoyed a renewed popularity in the late 18th century, and it is during this period that Gothic literature was born.

Gothic literature was so named because the stories are set in exaggeratedly Gothic or pseudo-medieval settings: huge ancestral homes, monasteries, or convents with foot-thick stone walls, stone staircases climbing up to long-deserted towers, mysterious ill-lit passages, creaking doors, dank crypts draped in shadow. Emphasizing their setting, many of these novels contain the building's name in their title, and/or incorporate the building as a central part of the plot – e.g. *The Horrors of Oakendale Abbey* (Carver, 1797), *The Children of the Abbey* (Roche, 1800).

To this gloomy and brooding physical atmosphere, the Romantics added their belief that "the complexity of human experience could not be explained by an inhuman rationalism… [More important were] the inner worlds of the emotions and the imagination," particularly the powerful emotions of horror and suspense.[2]

Unsurprisingly, the stories that resulted from this baroque mental and physical collaboration were dark, apprehensive, morbid, unsettling. They challenged traditional ideas of prose and drew harsh criticism: novels were bad enough in themselves, was the general belief, but this "literature of terror threatened the social order in terrifying ways."[3]

Horace Walpole's *The Castle of Otranto* (1764) is widely recognized as the first Gothic novel and established many of the parameters of the genre. Although the title page to the first edition read simply "The Castle of Otranto : A Story," by the second edition it had become "The Castle of Otranto : A Gothic Story." Walpole was aware that in *Otranto* he was creating a new literary form, describing it as "an attempt to blend the two kinds of romance, the ancient and modern" and he hoped that "the new route he [had] struck out shall have paved a road for men of brighter talents."[4]

The novel opens with the sensational and dramatic death of young Conrad, heir to the Castle of Otranto: he is crushed to death by a giant stone helmet that falls upon him as he is en route to the his wedding, a helmet which is later found to have mysteriously disappeared from the head of a stone statue in a nearby church. Conrad's father Manfred, lord of the castle, interprets this as the workings of an ancient family curse and determines to thwart it by marrying Conrad's fiancée Isabella himself. As Manfred's machinations become more evil the castle becomes more eerie, and the plot unfolds in melodramatic fashion with villainous guardians, damsels in distress, obstructed or doomed romances, abductions and imprisonment, disputed inheritances, secret passages, long-lost fathers and sons, startling revelations, mistaken identities leading to murder, and everyone in the end getting exactly what they deserve.

A few years later Clara Reeve, daughter of an English curate, wrote *The Champion of Virtue* (1777), later retitled *The Old English Baron: A Gothic Story*. Like *Otranto*—which the Preface acknowledges as inspiration even while criticizing it as exceeding "the utmost verge of probability"—the plot revolves around a family castle which has been usurped from its rightful owners, Lord and Lady Lovel, following Lord Lovel's murder. Shortly after seeing the apparition of her dead husband, Lady Lovel falls into a "distraction" and dies:

> Soon after, it was reported that the castle was haunted, and that the ghosts of Lord and Lady Lovel had been seen by several of the servants. Whoever went into this apartment were terrified by uncommon noises, and strange appearances; at length this apartment was wholly shut up, and the servants were forbid to enter it, or to talk of anything relating to it...[5]

The solution to the mystery brings to light a long-lost heir, a ghost, and a commoner who turns out to be a nobleman.

Reeve was by no means the only woman writing Gothic novels. Other authors in the "Female Gothic" tradition include Sophia Lee (*The Recess*, 1785), Mary Robinson (*Vancenza; or, The Dangers of Credulity*, 1792), Eliza Parsons (*The Castle of Wolfenbach,* 1793), Eleanor Sleath (*The Orphan of the Rhine*, 1798), Regina Maria Roche (*Clermont*, 1798), Sarah Wilkinson (numerous short pieces such as *The Subterraneous Passage; or the Gothic Cell*, 1803, and many later novels), and of course Anne Radcliffe.

Radcliffe's *The Mysteries of Udolpho* (1794) is perhaps the most Gothic of all Gothic novels. The heroine, Emily St. Aubert, loses first her mother and then her father; separated from her lover Valancourt, she is held captive in the remote and decaying Castle Udolpho by the unscrupulous Italian husband of her aunt and guardian, who wishes her to marry his friend, an impoverished Count. After several terrifying and inexplicable events Emily escapes with the help of a fellow prisoner who is in love with her, only to find herself in the equally menacing chateau of her rescuer, which has some connection with her father. In the end Emily uncovers the mystery, inherits a fortune, and is reunited with Valancourt. In Radcliffe's later novel, *The Italian* (1797), an aristocratic woman schemes with a degenerate monk to kidnap and murder her son's lover, whom she thinks is not worthy of him. Imprisoned in a convent, the young woman finds her long-lost mother and discovers that (of course) she is nobly born after all; she marries her fiancée while the evil monk is killed by the Inquisition.

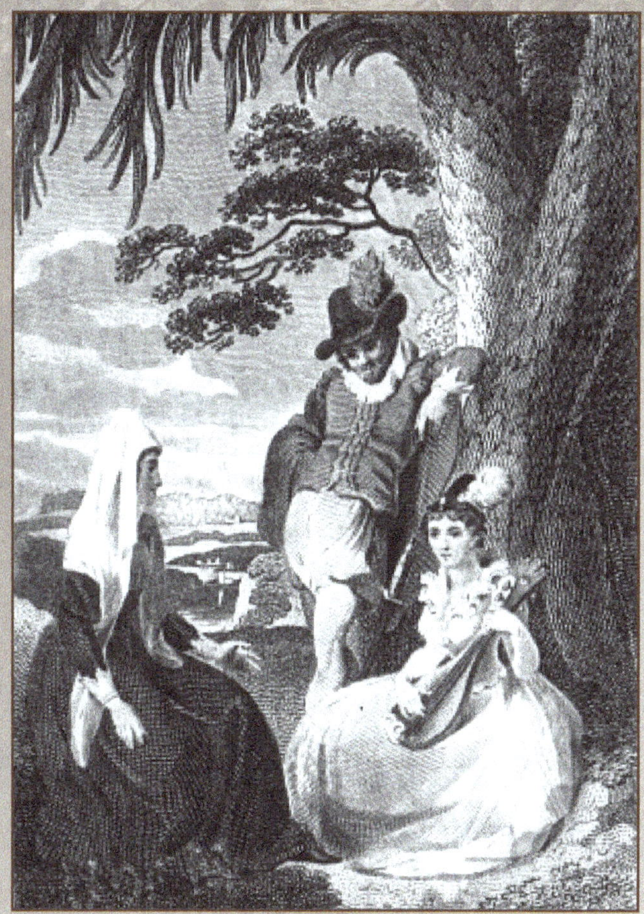

Illustrations from *The Mysteries of Udolpho*
(1806 edition)

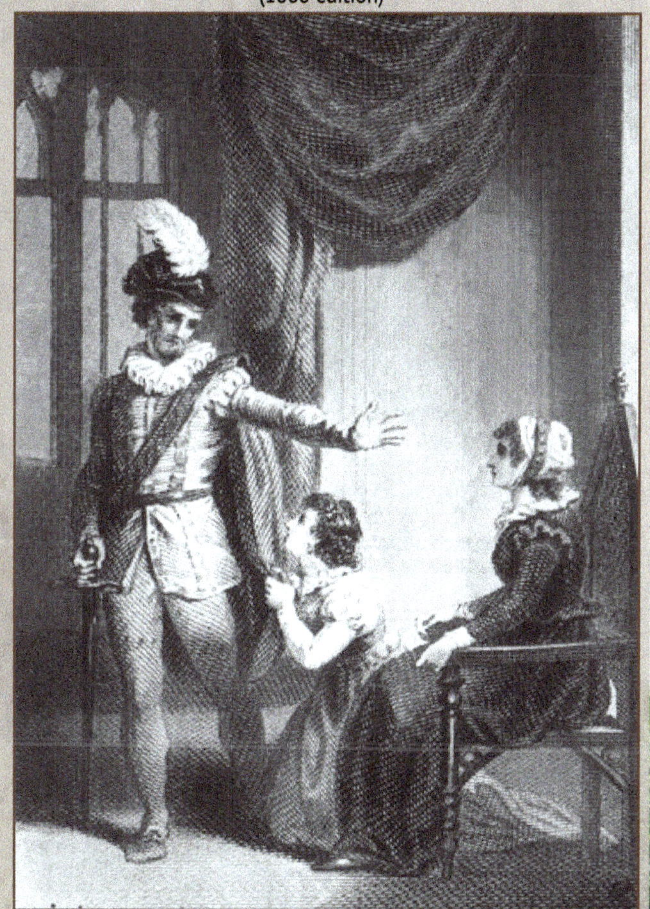

Matthew Lewis' *The Monk* (1796), another Gothic classic, tells the tale of Ambrosio, a monk who is "without reproach... [but whose] established reputation will mark him out to Seduction as an illustrious Victim." This is indeed what happens: tricked by a demon who poses for a portrait of the Virgin Mary, Ambrosio becomes the kidnapper, rapist and finally murderer of a young woman who turns out to be his long-lost sister. Subplots include a pregnant nun, the ghost of a murdered mother, and a literal deal with the devil.

Even in America, despite its lack of medieval castles or monasteries, Gothic literature took root. Charles Brockden Brown, for example, wrote *Wieland* (1798), whose Gothic elements include spontaneous combustion, a mysterious ventriloquist who creates disembodied voices, and at least one near-murder. The heroine Clara begins as one who is "not fearful of shadows. The tales of apparitions and enchantments did not possess that power over my belief which could even render them interesting" but falls under the spell of the Gothic: "My fears had pictured to themselves no precise object. It would be difficult to depict, in words, the ingredients and hues of that Phantom which haunted me" (178).

Gothic literature has proven remarkably durable. A century after *Otranto* the Brontës gave us *Wuthering Heights* (1850) with the Byronic hero Heathcliff roaming its desolate moors and *Jane Eyre* (1847) with Edward Rochester's mad wife locked in the attic. Louisa May Alcott, best known for her story of four sweet young women growing up during the Civil War (*Little Women*, 1868), also penned "blood and thunder" Gothic tales under the name A.M. Barnard, replete with opium, abduction, revenge, hidden identities, and murders (e.g., *A Long Fatal Love Chase*, 1866; *Behind a Mask, or A Woman's Power*, 1866). Still another hundred years after that, authors like Mary Stewart (*Nine Coaches Waiting*, 1958), Shirley Jackson (*The Haunting of Hill House*, 1959), Victoria Holt (*Bride of Pendorric*, 1963), and Barbara Michaels (*Greygallows*, 1972) proved the genre was alive and well, albeit with feistier and more self-reliant heroines. Arguably, Toni Morrison's *Beloved* (1987) and Thomas Harris' *Silence of the Lambs* (1988) could be considered modern Gothic novels[6], while authors like Joyce Carol Oates and Anne Rice continue to produce works in the Gothic tradition.

As many philosophers have noted, it is the journey that matters more than the destination. Perhaps this is why the Gothic genre endures: because it represents a search more than an answer. For the Gothic sensibility, "what finally matters is not finding a source of knowledge, but finding the source of mystery. The Gothic only indirectly, and by the most roundabout means, asks 'who did it?' (Committed the murder, stole the jewel). Most overtly it asks what generated the obfuscating ambiance in which the heroine is immersed...not who did this or that, but what produced the atmosphere of mystery."[7]

Note: Several of the titles mentioned above are freely available online in text form through Project Gutenberg (http://gutenberg.org) or in audio form through Librivox (http://librivox. org).

The British Library Gothic Shop

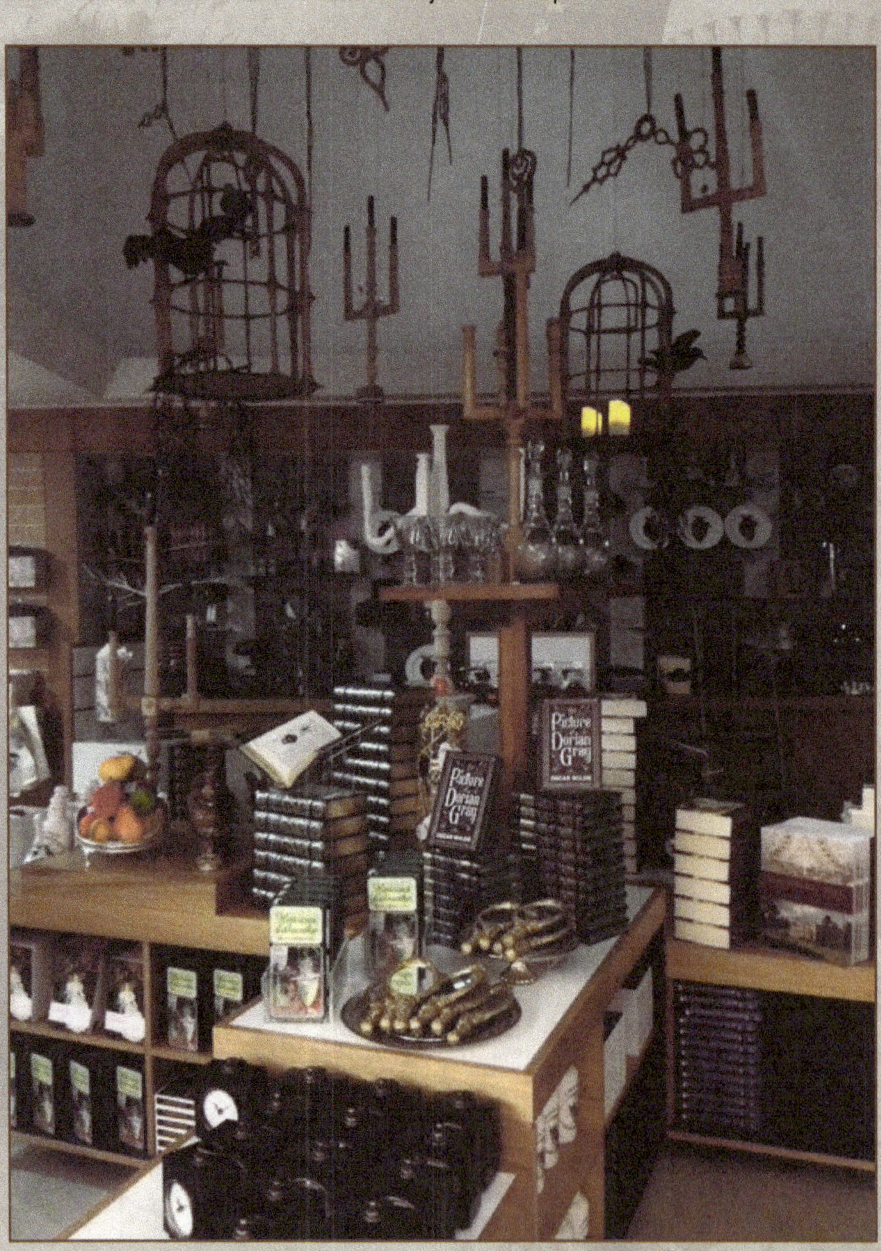

[1] Interestingly, Gothic architecture was not called Gothic architecture until a century after its heyday. Renaissance architects, who wanted their work seen as the ultimate achievement, dubbed medieval masterpieces like the cathedrals of Chartres and Reims "Gothic" as a derogatory term, referring to the Ostrogoths and Visigoths, Germanic tribes of the fourth and fifth century who were considered barbarian savages.

[2] Andrew Smith, *Gothic Literature*, Edinburgh: Edinburgh University Press, 2007, p. 2.

[3] Andrew Cooper, "Gothic threats: The role of danger in the critical evaluation of *The Monk* and *The Mysteries of Udolpho*," *Gothic Studies* 8(2), p. 18.

[4] Walpole, quoted in Smith, *Gothic Literature*, p. 19.

[5] Clara Reeve, *The Champion of Virtue*, Project Gutenberg, http://www.gutenberg.org/ files/5182/5182-h/5182-h.htm Accessed 10/12/15.

[6] Smith, *Gothic Literature*, ch. 4.

[7] Eugenia Delamotte, "'Collusions of the mystery': Ideology and the Gothic in *Hagar's Daughter*," *Gothic Studies*, 6(1).

LAYER BY LAYER

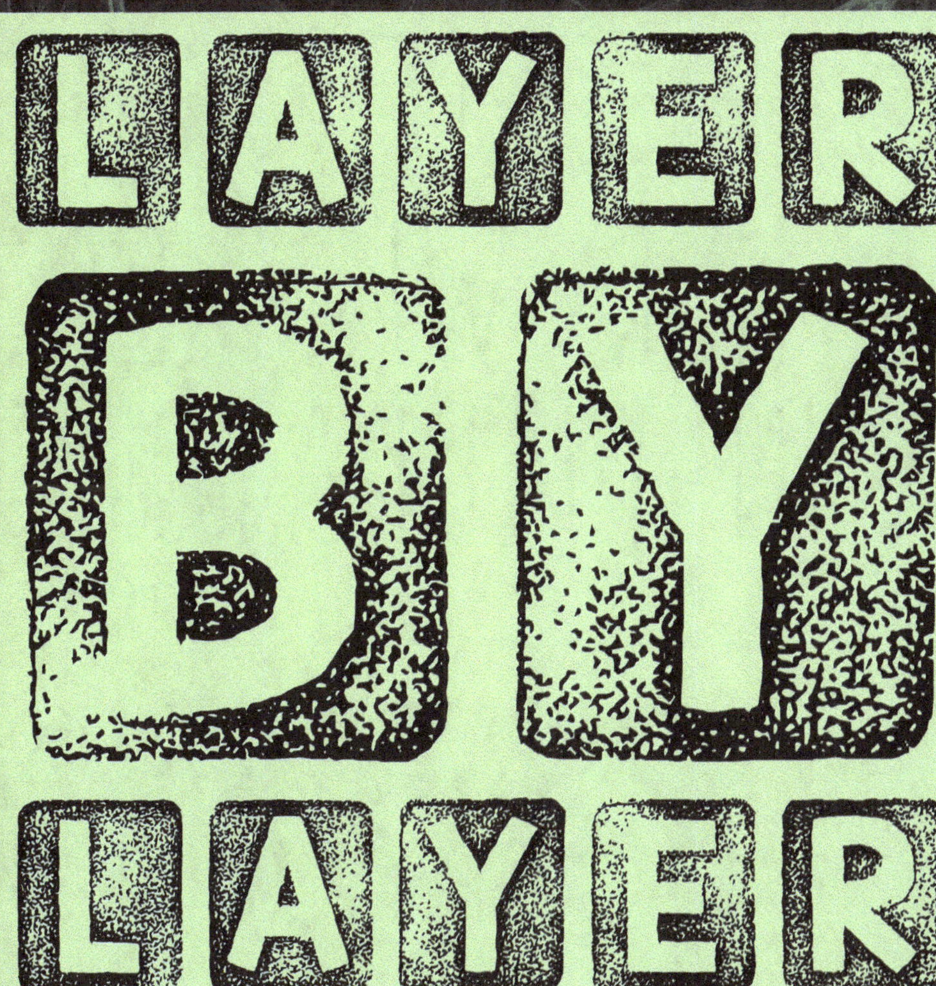

A Short Story
by Jesse Orr (@murderweapons)

Alyssa hated Brussels sprouts. Simply hated them. Her first memory of them was the noxious cloud they spread in the kitchen as her mother opened the pot lid to the steam of their boiled horror. She could not believe it when her mother expected her to actually eat the hateful things. She could not understand further why her mother continued serving them to her as she progressed in years, her reaction firm and unyielding in its convictions. Brussels sprouts were pure evil.

Therefore, she had no idea why she was eating this one, layer by layer, and with such careful precision. She started at the bottom, carefully nibbling away the fibers connecting the outer layer to the stalk, then peeling at the layer with her teeth, tearing it away in small shreds and rags. With every bite, she felt she was doing something inexorable, something that wasn't right. She couldn't think of what it could be, and chalked it up to simply eating a food she despised.

Come to think of it, why was she eating this confounded thing? And why couldn't she stop? This last question she asked herself as the outer layer was finally consumed, leaving its successor in its place, just a little greener than its predecessor. Without bothering to answer the question of why, she immediately set to work separating this new green barrier from its stalk and shredding it, just as before. Layer by layer.

The problem was that she hated cabbage, and wasn't a Brussels sprout just a tiny and intensely concentrated cabbage? Right down to the layers. Until it was cooked, anyway. Alyssa rather liked the smell of corned beef and cabbage, though she could never stand the taste of the cooked stuff. However, when her mother cooked Brussels sprouts, the entire house filled with a ghastly stench that refused to dissipate for hours, sometimes days, though her mother insisted Alyssa was guilty of being a drama queen. At any rate, as she finished the next layer and moved ever inward, the taste was the same. So why was she eating it? Layer by layer.

She couldn't even remember how she had come to be nibbling anything, let alone one of her least favorite foods of all time. It was as though she had come to find herself snacking on handfuls of caviar or munching on a beef tongue with no will to stop. Although, she reflected, a little sprout was certainly preferable to fish eggs or a cow's tongue. Still, it nagged. Why was she eating it? Why? Dimly, she could hear her mother's voice. It hooked into her ear, pulling her upwards out of her dream like a fishing lure hauling a snagged stick to the surface.

"ALYSSA!"

Her eyes flew open. Her head jerked around, her mouth still working at the sprout even as her heart jumped into it at the volume of her mother's scream. She tried to speak, but her mouth was full. Her mother was standing at the door with a ghastly look on her paper-white face, her hands over her mouth, eyes bulging. Alyssa blinked, squeezing her eyes tight together and opening them again. The world seemed more clear. Her mouth tasted coppery, not like Brussels sprouts at all.

"What have you done?"

Her mother's voice was a whisper, but carried more than enough volume to convey more horror than Alyssa thought one person could feel.

Until she removed her thumb from her mouth and saw it had been eaten down to the bone.

Layer by layer.

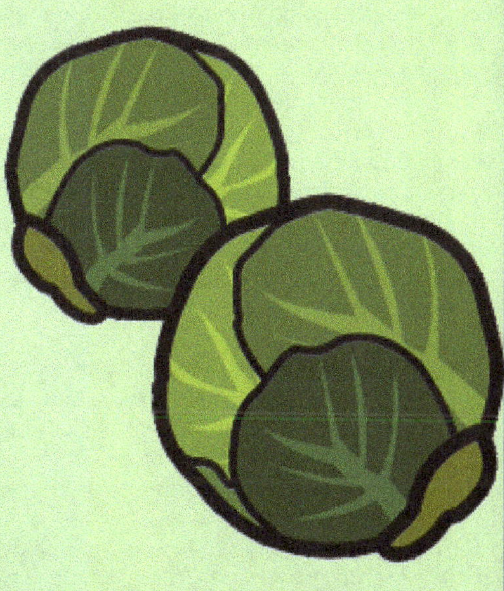

THE DARK GODDESS

HECATE AND HER WITCHES IN LITERATURE

By Jezibell Anat

The stories of ancient world religions contain many gods and goddesses of magic, divination, death, and the Underworld. These dark deities have intrigued writers and artists for centuries, and today they are gaining popularity among contemporary Pagans who honor their power and mystery.

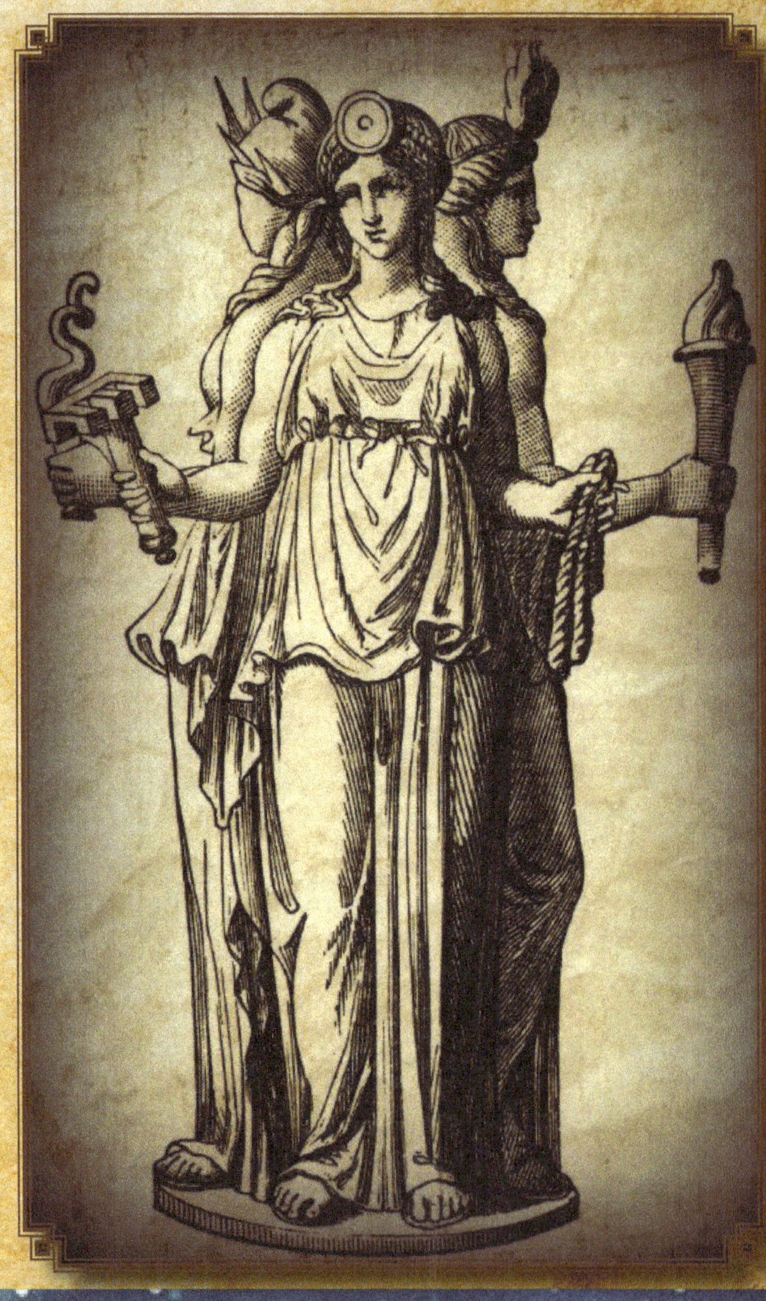

One of the most enduring of these immortals is Hecate, the Greek triple goddess who guards the thresholds of birth and death. She is a wide-ranging goddess, with a share in the realms of earth, sky, and sea. Her roles include the midwife who delivers babies and the psychopomp who carries souls to the Underworld. She engenders the chthonic force that pushes the green shoots up into the sunlight in the spring, and her meeting place is the crossroads, acknowledging her ability to walk multiple paths.

Her earliest descriptions show her as a beautiful maiden, usually carrying two torches as she lights the way for her followers, and in Neo-Platonic philosophy she appears as a savior goddess connected with the world soul. But she is most renowned for her aspects of prophecy, witchcraft, ghosts, necromancy, the dark moon, and the mysteries.

Overall, witches were viewed with suspicion in the ancient world. The Greek word for sorcery is pharmakeia, meaning the use of medicine, drugs, and spells. This is the root word of our pharmacy. Witches were expected to be proficient in the employment of plants, both to heal and to harm.

The most famous witches from Greek mythology, Circe and Medea, were associated with Hecate, but in their time they were not well-regarded. Homer's epic poem The Odyssey, describes the adventures of the cunning Greek warrior Odysseus as he returns from the Trojan War. Circe, an alluring sorceress renowned for her potions, lived on an island in the Aegean where Odysseus landed. She first turned Odysseus' men into pigs, but, with the help of the messenger god Hermes, Odysseus outwitted her, and she became his friend and lover. Odysseus lived with her for a year, then she told him how to go to the Underworld and speak to the souls of the dead to gain information that would help him on his journey home.

Euripides' tragedy *Medea* dramatizes the grim story of Medea, princess of Colchis, a city on the Black Sea. Medea was a priestess of Hecate and also Circe's niece. Defying her father, she used her spells to help the Greek hero Jason obtain the Golden Fleece, and he took her back to his home in Corinth. Though she bore him children, the Greeks regarded her as a foreigner, and later Jason abandoned her for the King's daughter. In revenge, Medea poisons her rival, and then she kills her children, claiming that they would have been executed anyway.

In her final speech, she declares, "I am resolved upon the deed; at once will I slay my children and then leave this land, without delaying long enough to hand them over to some more savage hand to butcher. Needs must they die in any case; and since they must, I will slay them-I, the mother that bare them."

Medea is often condemned for killing her children, but in other versions of the tale it is the people of Corinth are the ones who murder them. Euripides' Medea has been interpreted both as villainess and as victim, and this play has enthralled audiences for over two thousand years.

Witchcraft features prominently in the *Metamorphoses* by Lucius Apuleius, the only novel to survive in its entirety from antiquity. Written approximately 170 C.E., this book is sometimes called *The Golden Ass*, and is still an enjoyable read today. In this story, the protagonist Lucius is turned into an ass by an evil witch. After many adventures, he is returned to human form by the goddess Isis, whom the author conflates with Hecate.

Because of their alleged powers, witches became suspect, and were often blamed for poisonings, crop failures and curses. The Romans depicted Hecate as an ugly, malevolent old woman, a concept of the witch that endures into the typical green-faced warty hag of Halloween.

Early Christianity actually denied the existence of witchcraft, but by the end of the medieval era witchcraft was equated with Satan.

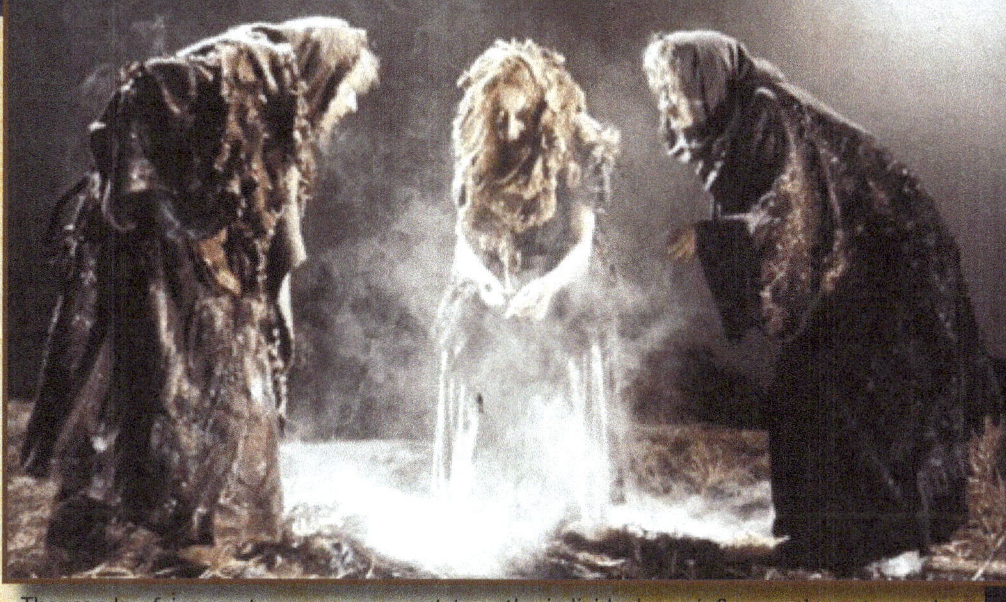

Thousands of innocent women were put to death between the fifteenth and eighteenth centuries, and the fear of witchcraft was very real in England when William Shakespeare was writing his plays.

The three witches in Shakespeare's tragedy *Macbeth* do not actually have much stage time, but they are among the most memorable of his characters. His source for them was *Holinshed's Chronicles,* an extensive description of British history published in 1587. Holinshed describes the witches as "the Weird Sisters, that is... the goddesses of destiny."

Weird in this context does not just indicate something strange or odd but refers to wyrd, meaning the course of events, or what may come to pass. Wyrd is a concept in the ancient Anglo-Saxon world view that roughly corresponds to karma. Each individual has his or her own wyrd, or personal destiny, which is interwoven with the wyrds of others in an ever-widening pattern - the belief that in today's parlance could be termed the interconnected web of life.

Specifically, the wyrd sisters refer to the Norns, Urda, Verdandi, and Skuld, the goddesses who spin, weave, and cut the threads of life, as do the Greek Moirai or Fates, with whom the Norns are often equated. In the ancient worldview, the acts of spinning and weaving were associated with magic and transformations, and we all recognize that our own thread of life can be severed at any time.

Both the Moirai and the Norns were intimidating figures in their respective mythologies, since we all want to know our future, and what, if anything, we can do to affect it. The main difference between them is that the wyrd has some flexibility. In the Greek myths, once a fate is decreed, the individual may not escape it, no matter what anyone does. Among the Teutonic peoples,

the individual can influence the outcome by his/her choices and efforts, along with the actions of others, and, in some cases, magic.

Shakespeare turns these weird sisters into horrifying witches who hail Macbeth as king. In some interpretations of Macbeth, it is the dark power of the witches who lure Macbeth to murder rather than his own ambition and the urgings of his scheming wife. Many wonder if he really would have killed Duncan if he had not met them.

Considering the beliefs of his time, it is actually quite unusual that he associated his witches with Hekate and the Norns rather than characterizing them as minions of the devil. If he somehow could have been truly consistent with the Germanic mythos, Freya, the beautiful goddess of love, fertility, and magic, would have been the queen of the witches, but in *Macbeth*, it is Hecate, and she is not pretty.

Macbeth reflects upon her on his way to murder Duncan, "Nature seems dead, and wicked dreams abuse the curtain'd sleep; witchcraft celebrates pale Hecate's offerings." Hecate was not present when the witches first met Macbeth, and later she chastises them for acting without her.

After this, the witches approach to Macbeth goes from suggestion to incitement of his destructive path in a scene where they boil a noxious potion in a cauldron to raise apparitions. For their speech, Shakespeare switches from his usual iambic pentameter to a trochaic tetrameter with rhyme, creating the iconic incantation, "Double, double, toil and trouble," with a gruesome list of ingredients such as animal and human body parts.

> *Double, double toil and trouble;*
> *Fire burn, and caldron bubble.*
> *Fillet of a fenny snake,*
> *In the caldron boil and bake;*
> *Eye of newt, and toe of frog,*
> *Wool of bat, and tongue of dog,*
> *Adder's fork, and blind-worm's sting,*
> *Lizard's leg, and owlet's wing,—*
> *For a charm of powerful trouble,*
> *Like a hell-broth boil and bubble.*

These witches have been portrayed as loathsome hags, beautiful temptresses, hippies, and Goths, and Orson Welles interpreted the witches as voodoo priestesses for a version set in Haiti.

Depending on how it's staged and performed, this speech can be terrifying or silly. Set to music, parts of it were used as the lyrics for the welcoming song at Hogwarts in the Harry Potter movies. Harry's favorite band is called The Weird Sisters, though his consists of eight males. Macbeth supposedly is J.K. Rowlings' favorite Shakespeare play. Besides Macbeth, Shakespeare calls Hecate the source of evil magic in several other plays as well. In King Lear, the mad king curses his daughters "by the sacred radiance of the sun, the mysteries of Hecate, and the night;" in Hamlet Lucianus describes poison as "thou mixture rank, of midnight weeds collected, with Hecate's ban thrice blasted, thrice infected."

Hecate is also cited in Midsummer Night's Dream, the comedy where humans encounter fairies in the woods. Part of this plot is borrowed from The Metamorphoses, as Bottom's transformation into an ass by fairy magic resembles Lucius' transformation by witch magic. Puck reminds us that these fairies are certainly not sweet elementals.

> *Now it is the time of night*
> *That the graves all gaping wide,*
> *Every one lets forth his sprite,*
> *In the church-way paths to glide:*
> *And we fairies, that do run*
> *By the triple Hecate's team,*
> *From the presence of the sun,*
> *Following darkness like a dream.*

A revival of Macbeth in 1795 inspired poet and painter William Blake to create a piece called The Triple Hecate. In a style reminiscent of Michelangelo, Blake employed the then-new technique of distemper on millboard to provide a rich, dark effect. Hecate takes a triple form as a young female, a young male, and a beautiful woman, and she is attended by an owl, a bat, and a toad, creatures associated with Macbeth's witches. There is also an ass, hearkening back to Midsummer Night's Dream and The Metamorphoses.

For the past couple of centuries, feminists have been reconsidering history's unfavorable portrayal of witches in the context of misogyny and male fear of female power. Today Hecate is circling back into popularity among contemporary Pagans. Practitioners of the modern witchcraft religion, Wicca, seek to refute the repugnant stereotype of witches as they work to reclaim and reconstruct the power and beauty of the ancient Pagan religions.

Hecate continues to inspire writers and artists in the twenty-first century. A chant by Sharon Knight and T. Thorn Coyle sums up this new view of the ancient goddess:

> *Hecate, keeper of the crossroads*
> *Hecate, holder of the flame*
> *Hecate, wisdom of the darkness,*
> *Guide our way, guide our way.*

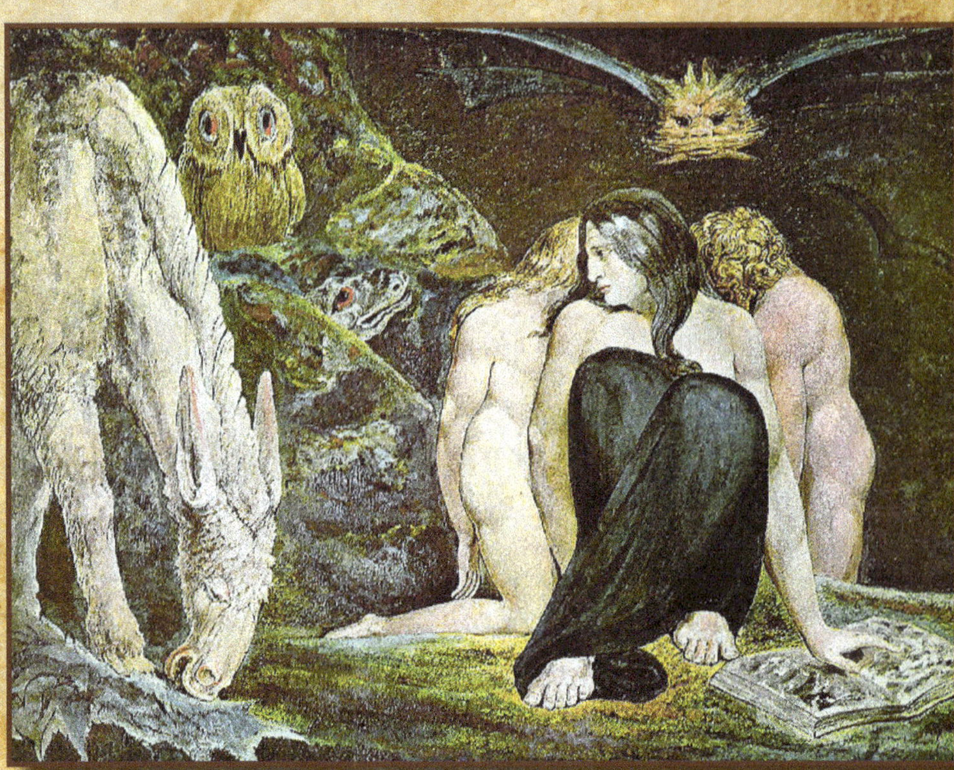

The Triple Hecate, 1795
William Blake

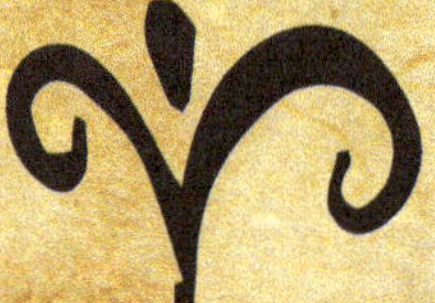

HECATE'S SUMMONS

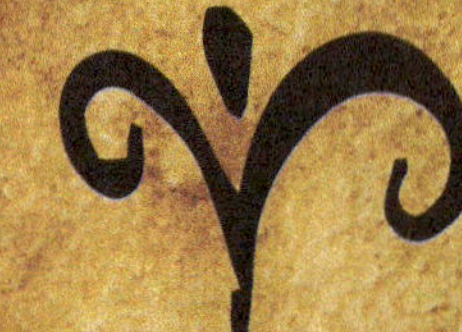

by Jezibell Anat

I roam the hidden realm.
I wander the shadow of the spirit,
Teaching the dead to dance and the living to dream.

Those who walk with me may cross the threshold of the mysteries
And enter the place of secrets.
I hold the keys to all the doors.
I set the boundaries of infinity, granting and guarding revelation.

The roots of wisdom dwell in the Underworld,
Beneath the borders of the ordinary.
Reach down, reach deep, and do not fear the decay.
In the decomposition and dissolution, your essence will be revealed.
Only in the darkness can you behold the light,
And chaos is the mother of comprehension.

Dark Desire in the Clouded Tower

Erotica with Katrina Rose

By Zahara

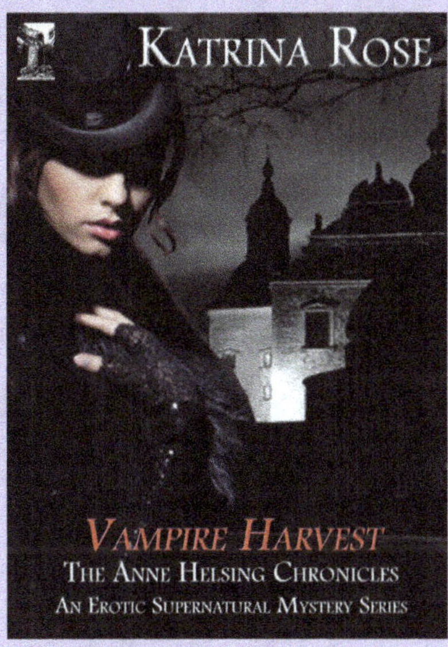

Clouded Tower Press has just launched a website catering to fans of dark erotica. Whether you long for sci-fi, goth, horror or fantasy, you're sure to find something appealing among these offerings. Many of the tales are series, and all are available digitally. Katrina Rose (Author & Owner) has several titillating topics from which to choose.

Self-publishing has opened new doors for would-be authors, and Katrina saw a way to take control of her own creative process, as well as assist other authors with a flair for geeky or horror inspired erotica. She originally started Clouded Tower Press to sell her own works, and now has three more authors in her arsenal of artists.

"CTP publishes a unique kind of erotica that I feel is an exciting niche within the sub-genre. Our brand of erotica is definitely different than what is widely available." But the works on CTP are about more than appealing to fans of sci-fi, etc. They deviate from the tried-and-true (and predictable) pattern of "alpha male/submissive female" found is most erotic literature. There's a focus on strong heroines that are relatable and realistic. Curvy, sassy, women who have jobs, are sexually experienced and 'take charge' of the situations. "There are no wilting flowers in our roster. As I mentioned before, the glut of erotica featuring strong, angry billionaires who sweep waitresses off their feet is boring, so we're trying to do something a little different."

But how does one get started in the business of writing erotica? Katrina has been a writer for years under a different name in other genres, but it seems to have been an easy transition for her to stretch into erotic writing. "I started writing erotica almost by accident, actually. I've found that it's a fun and lighthearted genre to write in, and sex and erotica are very genuine." Fans will get more than just steamy stories by reading the works on Katrina's site. "I would hope that the target audience for the work published at Clouded Tower is looking for more than what traditional erotica (and neo erotica) has to offer - something more honest and more personal."

I agree with Katrina whole-heartedly when she says that good erotica is about honesty. For those of us who like our erotica highlighted with horror or scintillating science fiction, it's exciting to have a new site devoted to our interests. Katrina feels that being able to lose yourself in a book that is not only titillating, but also makes you think and get involved in the story, is a rare thing in the genre.

Visitors to cloudedtowerpress.Wordpress.com will even find a piece written by a devout Star Wars fanatic. But "Slave to the Empire" is not a typical Star Wars inspired piece. "I think all Fan Fiction functions as an expression of what we really want to see from a series or anything related to a fandom... I'm pretty sure every fan harbors secret and not so secret fantasies about their favorite characters, and Ravyn Jade took it to a different level by creating her own storyline within the Star Wars universe. It's intensely well researched and really sensual."

I enjoyed the Sleeping Beauty series by A.N. Roquelaure (Anne Rice). It offered a lot of variety when it came to the sexual appetites described, and it was a vivid, intriguing take on the old fairy tale. I was curious what Katrina's favorite piece of erotica was, and why. Not surprisingly, she also chose an Anne Rice selection that was published close to the same time ("Exit to Eden"). "I read it when I was quite young, and it was shocking but exciting - I had never read a book that made me feel that way, and I haven't since. It blows "Fifty Shades of Grey" out of the water like a 100 megaton bomb. Another early favorite was Anäis Nin's "Little Birds". It not only opened up a world of truly literary erotica, but I fell in love with the whole ex-pat movement because of it."

Some people credit "Fifty Shades of Grey" with the widespread, renewed interest in erotic literature. However, the genre has always enjoyed a devout, expanding audience. While I found the dynamic between the leads in FSoG to be disturbing, that series did seem to bring the genre out of the shadows and into the general public (even for Target shoppers). "Sex is a basic human thing... we're hard wired for it. Erotica and sexual tension is everywhere, and what I think "Fifty Shades of Grey" (as much as I hate to admit it) did for the genre was bring it under the scrutiny of the mainstream, and made people realize that they could be vocal about the fact that they read it, and that it was OK to read it, and that it wasn't something shameful - hence the uptrend. Erotica is another form of escapism. Do I wish that a better example of the genre was the catalyst for this refocus? Obviously." After talking with some of my friends who are fans of FSoG, they've begun reading other pieces of erotic literature, including the works listed above. So if nothing else, it has encouraged readers to broaden their horizons.

Ultimately, what makes a piece of erotic literature (or any story) successful is up the reader and his or her unique palate. "Half the battle is writing an engaging storyline and creating a world that a reader can sink into, and even imagine that they themselves are participating in - whether it's the action or the sex. That takes more than being able to write decent sex scenes; being able to write good, believable, identifiable characters that a reader can root for and feel for is the most important part." This is what makes the stories available on Clouded Tower Press all the more fascinating. The writers are creating and expanding upon new worlds and landscapes, with fanciful characters who are more than just sexual beings, doing more than just having sex.

The future of Clouded Tower Press looks bright. In addition to the individual works, CTP has a new short-story anthology titled "Captive Hearts" that's available. And the website will also be featuring work from some additional writers in the coming months. As we head into winter, what could be more satisfying than curling up with a warm book that really gets your blood pumping?

cloudedtowerpress.Wordpress.com
Twitter: https://twitter.com/CloudedTower
Facebook: https://www.facebook.com/CloudedTowerPress

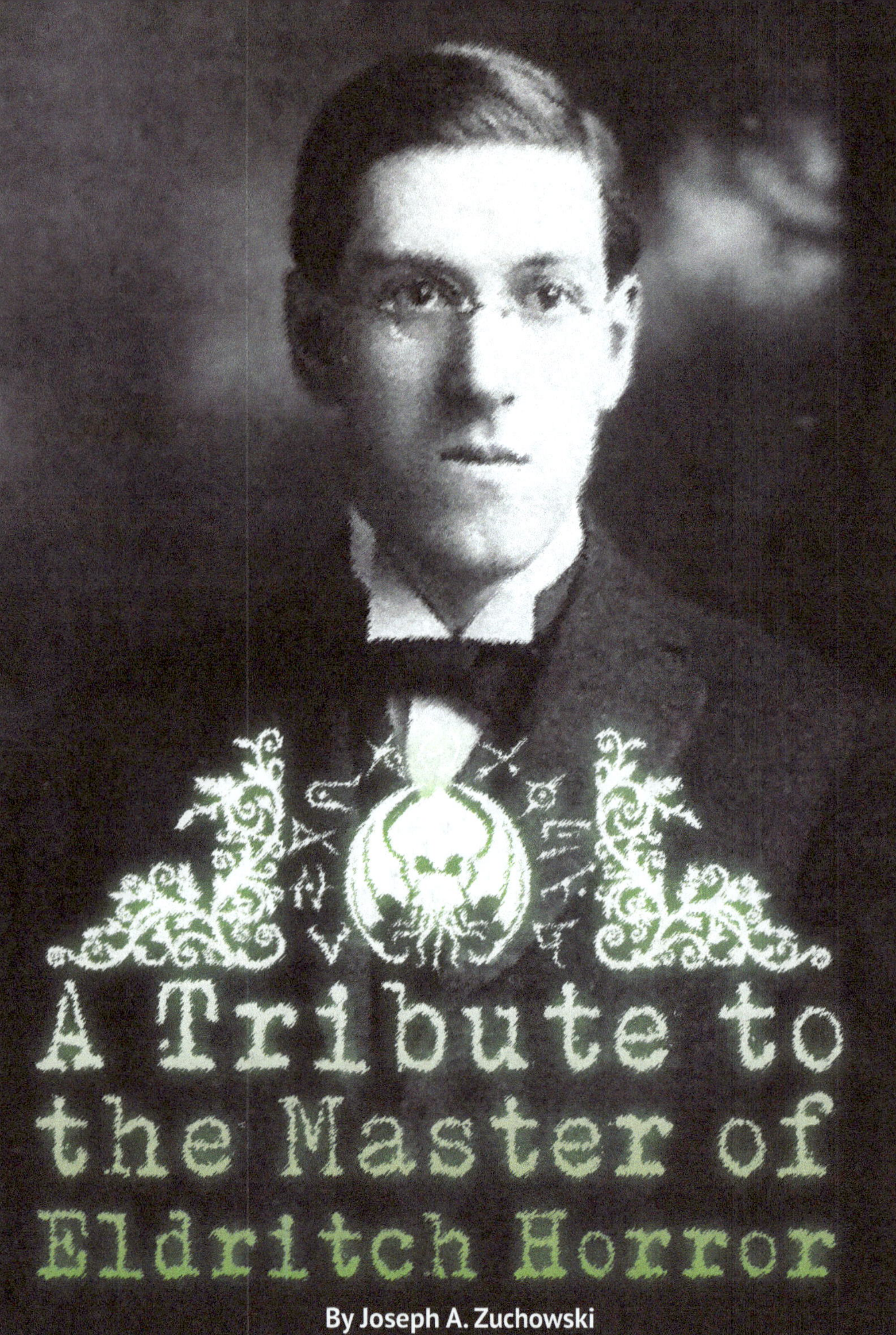

I often muse that if there is such a thing as an afterlife he must chuckling away merrily. Now his name is almost a household word. The adjective "Lovecraftian" describes a fantastic horror story full of madness, supernatural beings, death and destruction where if you are fortunate you die brutally and fiendishly, and if not you go insane and remain locked away in some lonely asylum, a gibbering idiot haunted by what you have witnessed.

This is the world of H.P. Lovecraft, modeled on his sad and troubled life. He was a rationalist and atheist. Physically he cut an outstanding figure at five feet, eleven inches, lean and sinewy, with a lantern jaw, sharp features, large ears, and a loping gait. He truly believed himself to be abominably ugly. He had a very measured way of speaking, never raising his voice, with a slight New England accent.

Lovecraft's appeal to Goth culture becomes apparent when you understand that this staunch, quiet son of New England, was, like all of us who choose an alternative lifestyle, at heart a romantic dreamer, though he would never admit it. His stories reflect his inner sorrows, his fears, his longing, his alienation - emotions that most of us know too well.

He was a troubled youth, an eternally trapped Peter Pan whose greatest fears of being alone would eventually become the reality he knew. He is someone for whom I have felt not just a fan's admiration but a friendship and in some way a mentorship, even though he died twenty years before I was born.

As a child, he was afraid of the dark but as an adult he turned into a nictophile. He would rise late in the day, draw the curtains to his room, and under lamplight he would write his stories by hand. He had few actual friends but corresponded extensively with other authors such as Robert E. Howard, creator of Conan the Barbarian; Zelia Bishop, one of the few female horror writers of the era, and Robert Bloch who wrote the script for the film Psycho. Lovecraft would often proofread, edit, and even ghostwrite some of his friends' works.

As for me, I've been a fan of horror for over fifty years. I watched every film and read every story I could see or get. The classic Universal monster movies, the works of Poe, television shows like Boris Karloff's Thriller or Rod Sterling's Twilight Zone - I still cherish all these wonderfully terrifying memories. But what does all this have to do with Lovecraft?

On the morning of March 15, 1937, Howard Phillips Lovecraft succumbed to intestinal cancer, dying in a manner similar to the way he had lived most of his short life of forty-six and a half years, quietly and alone. He was buried several days later in the family plot at Swan Point Cemetery. His funeral was sparsely attended - an elderly aunt who would join him a few weeks later, a cousin, and a couple of friends. By every standard imaginable, Lovecraft died a failure. His life could be best described as an almost self-destructive melodrama of escapism and delusion.

It should have ended there, yet, like one of his literary idols, Edgar Allan Poe, it was in death that his greatness, barely acknowledged by a few friends in life, would gradually become renowned worldwide. Some of today's best known horror writers claim him as an inspiration, including Stephen King, Joyce Carol Oates , and Brian Lumley

Lovecraft accepted the finality of death, and

This nexus is the one word, which I have already used - loneliness. Many of these monsters were trapped in horrible situations that they did not cause. Larry Talbot bravely goes out to rescue a young woman from an attack by a wolf only to find that he himself is bitten and must bear the curse of the werewolf. Frankenstein's monster was created by a scientist who wanted to force open the doors of life and death by galvanizing a creature composed of the parts of dead men to satisfy his own ego, thus creating a being that has no place in this world but can not return to the one it came from.

Dracula and the Mummy were two victims of their passion. Dracula sold his soul to the Devil to gain power to drive the Turks from his homeland, and the Mummy was buried alive for attempting to restore his deceased beloved. These stories had pathos, and the monsters were surprisingly relatable. In many ways they reminded me of the tales of ghosts, witches and faeries that got me to sit still and listen to my Polish grandmother, tales which also connected me to a land far across the ocean but was as real as the one I lived in. Those stories shaped my love of the supernatural, and in many ways I felt more akin to those beings then the flesh and blood ones i lived with.

Lovecraft was a living anachronism and an Anglophile, feeling more at home in the seventeenth and eighteenth centuries than in the America of his day. His work was based on his own life. He was the only child of Winfield Scott and Sarah Susan Lovecraft, an upper middle class family in Providence, Rhode Island. His father was the son of recent immigrants, and his mother was old New England blood. Initially he enjoyed a privileged life, but that did not last.

When Lovecraft was about two years old, his father was committed to an insane asylum where he would spend the remainder of his days. The elder Lovecraft suffered from what was then called the paresis of the brain, and some speculated that he had contracted syphilis from his days as a traveling silver salesman. But his has never been verified.

Lovecraft and his mother returned to live with her family, the patriarch Whipple Van Buren Phillips, a successful Victorian businessman. He cherished art and literature, and his personal library contained books that were centuries old, as well as original prints. Imported art from Italy graced the home, and Whipple was an indulgent grandfather.

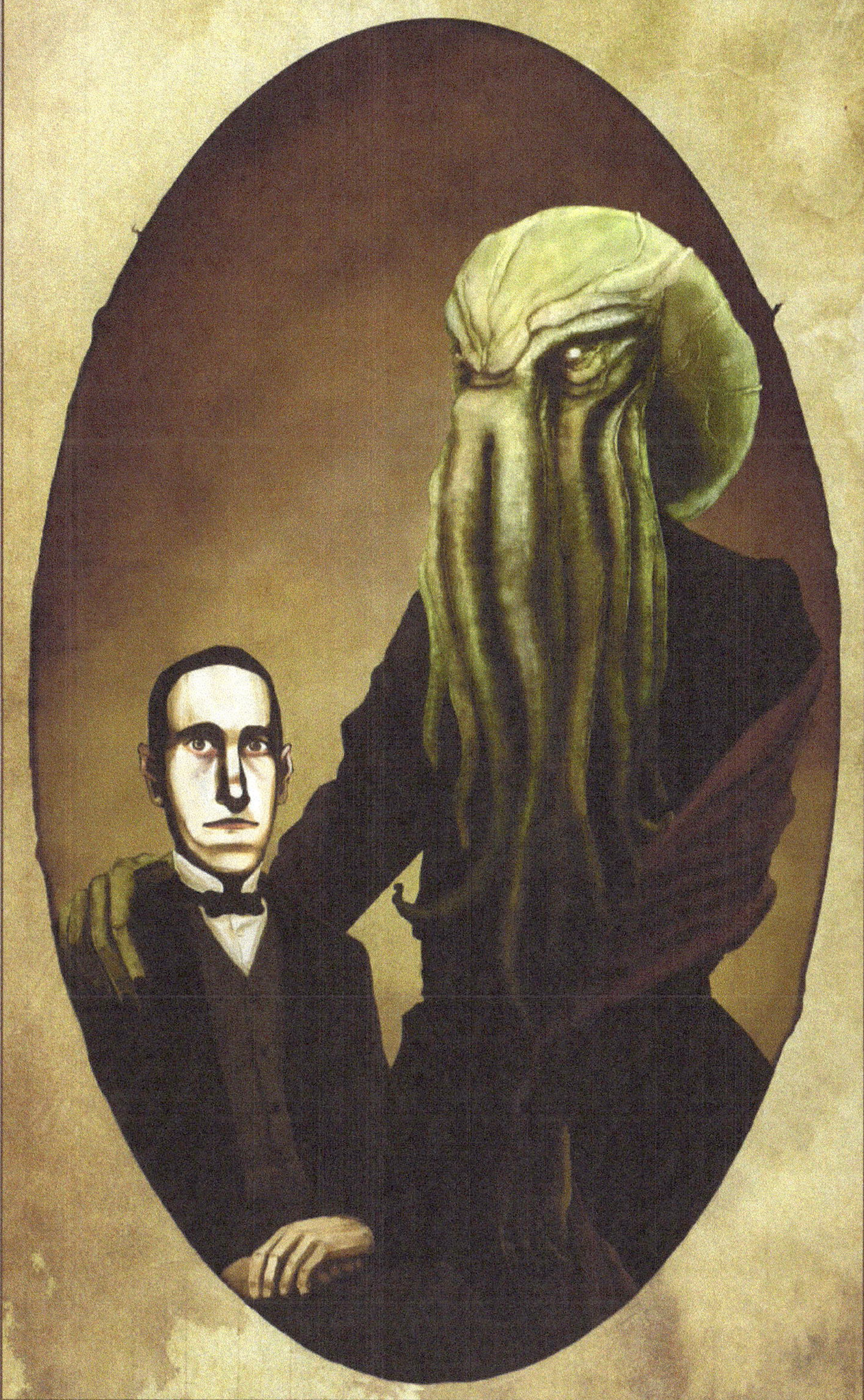

This love of Italian art influenced young Lovecraft. As a child he felt drawn to classical Greek mythology and actually constructed altars to the ancient gods and goddesses. Though raised nominally Christian, Lovecraft was removed from bible study when he said that agreed with the Romans throwing the Christians to the lions. By the time he reached his teens, he was an atheist.

In his youth Lovecraft's precocious nature began to materialize. He virtually taught himself to read, and his first love was the fantastic stories of the Arabian Nights. Whipple had Sir Richard Burton's translation in his library, where the young Lovecraft soon made himself a nest of an oriental carpet in a small pile of cushions. He insisted on being called "Abdul Alhazrad."

This idyllic childhood soon came crashing down. Several failed business ventures bankrupted Whipple, and Lovecraft saw his precious heirlooms being auctioned off. When his beloved grandfather died of a stroke, the family mansion itself had to be sold.

Lovecraft, his mother, and his aunts had to move to smaller accommodations. Lovecraft himself suffered a nervous breakdown and was unable to finish high school, which prevented him from attending college. This aborted formal education was not unique among men of his time, but it was a major blow to him, Without that diploma, he could never attain a college degree, which pained him throughout the rest of his life.

Early in his life, he discovered his passion for writing. We have no samples of his childhood endeavors, for he destroyed them later in life, calling them "trite juvenalia." Perhaps he was trying to destroy his own past in doing so.

His personal experiences provided the model for his tales. A kitten lost in childhood became the basis for his story "The Cats of Ulthar." Getting lost in a carnival mirror maze inspired his own true science fiction story, "In the Walls of Eryx." When he was in his twenties, his mother followed her husband into the same asylum, and his character of Lavinia Whately in "The Dunwich Horror" was modeled on her.

From 1920-1935 Lovecraft produced 70 short stories, a novel, and a play, which to the best of anyone's knowledge was never performed. His literary brilliance was in the development of a genre which was unlike any other in imagination. He created a lore for the twentieth century, the infamous "Cthullu mythos," though he never used that term. He regarded religion as nothing more than socially acceptable superstition, and mysticism were even below that.

Lovecraft's Great Old Ones are actually aliens who obtain their power through the use of skilled technologies which seem supernatural, almost foreshadowing Arthur C. Clarke's adage "any sufficiently advanced technology is indistinguishable from magic." These "gods" were beings unlike anything we had previously imagined. They were powerful, terrifying and amoral, seeking only their own desires. Humans to them were like ants to us. Yet in these stories humans often seek to dwell with them and suffer horrible consequences in the end.

One of his first pieces, "Dagon," appears to be referencing an ancient Philistine fish god but is actually the testimonial of a morphine addict who plans to commit suicide after a nightmarish sea journey. Lovecraft later wrote, "I dreamed that whole hideous crawl, and can yet feel the ooze sucking me down!" Interestingly for a New Englander, Lovecraft was said to become easily nauseous at the sight and smell of sea food. That is probably why he chose sea creatures for his most horrific creations.

Cthulhu is the most prominent of these aquatic beings. Debuting in the 1928 tale "The Call of Cthulhu," he is gigantic, with a bloated humanoid body, an octopoid head and great leathery dragon-like wings. He lies in suspended animation in the sunken city of R'lyeh, somewhere in the Pacific, where he is guarded by strange ichthyoid beings known as the Deep Ones.

Not all of Lovecraft's monstrosities are from the ocean. Yog Sothoth, an iridescent collection of spheres in constant motion, is the gate between our world and the trans-dimensional world of the Old Ones. Shub Nuggerath personifies chaos, a bubbling mass of eyes, mouths, and tentacles continually appearing and disappearing across itself. The most human looking is Nyarlathotep, sometimes called the Black Pharaoh, personified as a tall, slender, ebony-skinned man.

Lovecraft's other entities include the Mi-Go, bizarre crustacean beings from the frozen planet of Yuggoth (our Pluto) who steal human brains to power their equipment, and the faceless, black, winged skeletal Night Gaunts from young Lovecraft's childhood nightmares. These fiends would grab a young child, carry him to their rocky peaks and there tear open his stomach and devour his entrails. Ironically, Lovecraft died of intestinal cancer.

Along with these monsters, Lovecraft created his own community, setting his tales in dark, desolate Arkham County in Massachusetts, home of the town of Dunwich and the infamous Miskatonic University. Perhaps his most famous literary creation is a book he never wrote, the vile Necronomicon, an imaginary opus which is said to help bring the Great Old Ones from their dimension into ours.

Many of his fans are involved in the occult, myself included. Years ago I used to work at Manhattan's best known magical emporium, Enchantments. One day a very High Goth couple came into the store. The man was dressed in dark purple velvet, a tall black top hat, purple octagonal sunglasses, a skull-topped walking stick and a full-length black cape. His partner wore a Vampira dress, with the classic white makeup and deep red lipstick, but her long black hair was showing some brown roots. The man approached me and, in a staged British accent,

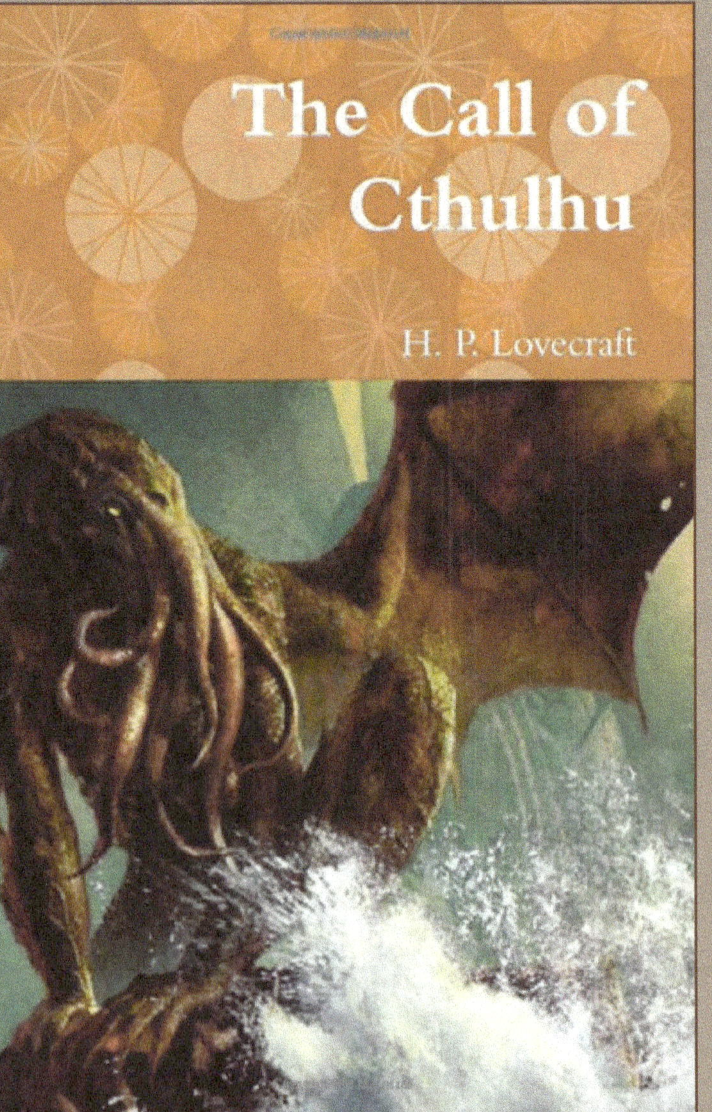

declared, "I am in need of assistance." "Sure, whatddya need" I replied in my indigenous Jersey City speech. "I am in search of the tome of most evil and blasphemous magic." he said " I seek the Necronomicon"

I told them that we didn't have it but that it could be obtained at Barnes and Noble for the princely sum of $3.99. He said he was aware of that one, but he wanted the actual Necronomicon. When I told him that it was purely fictitious, he accused me of making fun of him, and with a very theatrical flourish of his cape, he and his friend departed. At that moment I had a vision of H.P. Lovecraft and P.T. Barnum sharing a good laugh.

Many of Lovecraft's stories have been made into film, though usually the titles were changed. "The Colour Out of Space" became Die, Monster, Die with Boris Karloff and Nick Adams in 1965, and "The Case of Charles Dexter Ward" turned into The Haunted Palace with Vincent Price, Debra Paget, and Lon Cheney. The first twenty-first century film inspired by Lovecraft was Dagon, based on "The Shadow over Innesmouth," and more are on the way.

Lovecraft felt, lived and expressed a loneliness and isolation which he carried in him almost all his life. For all his failings and idiosyncrasies, Lovecraft was at heart a gentle, giving person who would often sacrifice for those he cared for, going more than the extra mile. While visiting a friend, a kitten fell asleep in Lovecraft's lap. He sat perfectly still throughout the night so as not to disturb the sleeping kitten. Some today say he could have used medication and therapy to repair his mental state, but if he had, then we would not have had his beautifully crafted horror stories.

August 20, 2015 was the 125th anniversary of his birth. This tribute is my belated birthday present to someone who has been with me longer than most living people I know. To take a line from one of my many-loved songs "Drift Away," I say, "thanks for the joy you've given me," and I'm more than certain that this is the feeling anyone who has come to know him feels about Lovecraft and his stories.

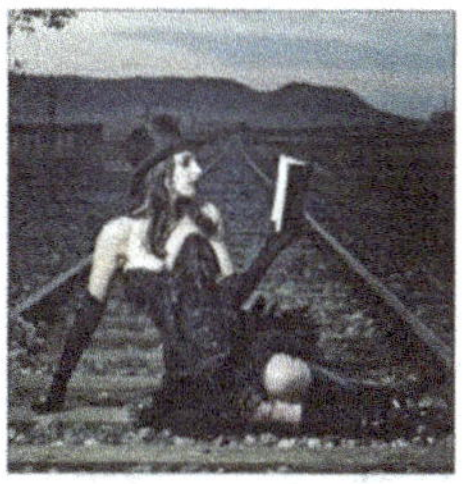

THE PRICE IS REASONABLE & THE VIEW IS TO DIE FOR: THE HAUNTED HOUSE IN GOTHIC HORROR

By: LinnieSarah (@linnieloowho)

With the October 16 release of "Crimson Peak," Guillermo Del Toro's haunted house film joins a long line of movies in the gothic tradition that focus on a home infested with the "other." That "other" may be ghosts of nefarious intentions, or they may be benevolent spirits seeking to protect a new family that have taken shelter inside a house with a grim past. From the earliest entries to the canon of gothic horror cinema, the haunted house has been an important part of what makes the genre so memorable. So let us look back at some of the most remarkable examples of "gothic haunted house horror," And always remember...

A house can be haunted by more than just ghosts!

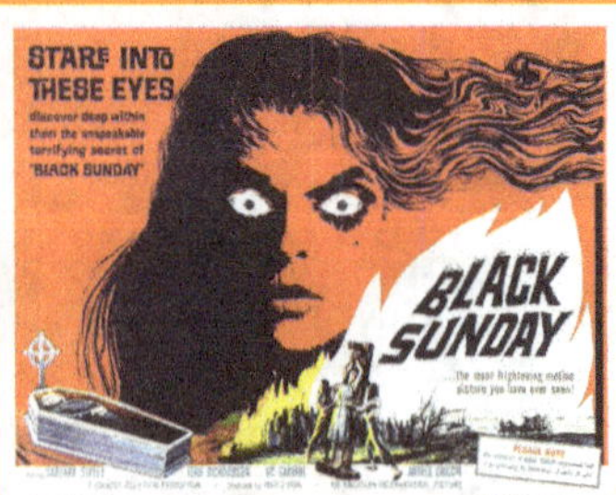

"Black Sunday" (1960)
Dir: Mario Bava

"Black Sunday" is easily one of Italian horror maestro Mario Bava's best example of gothic horror, but it is also a wonderful example of a film in which a haunted house isn't *really* a haunted house. In 1630, witch/vampire Asa Vajda is put to death in the most gruesome way imaginable. Two-hundred years later, she returns from the beyond to seek vengeance against the ancestors of her killer, her own brother. "Black Sunday" is a gothic horror film full of beautiful and horrifying imagery, and a brilliant archetype of a movie in which the house has nothing to do with haunting... only the people residing within in its walls.

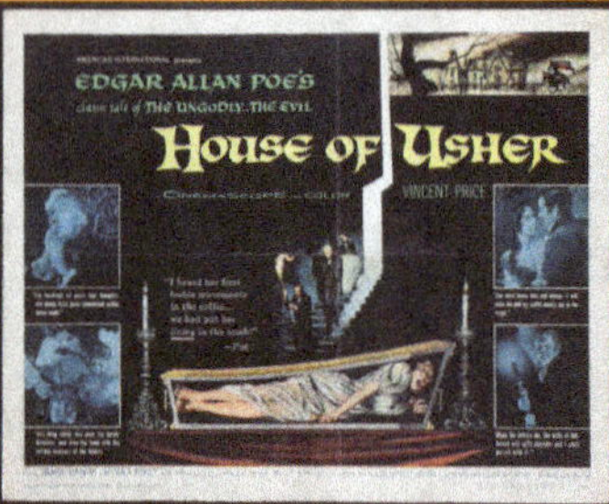

"House of Usher" (1960)
Dir: Roger Corman

Here again, we have a film in which the family is haunted, not the house, and in which "haunted" takes on a less literal meaning. Directed by the legendary Roger Corman early in his career, and based on Edgar Allen Poe's "The Fall of the House of Usher," this film focuses on the ways in which a family suffers a strange and inexplicable curse that drives them all to madness. The titular "House of Usher" becomes a metaphor for that eternal question: are we purely our genetics, or do we make our own destiny?

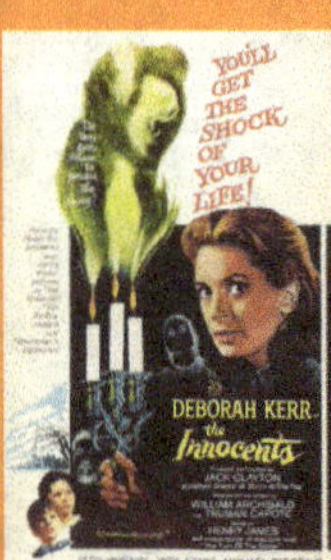

"The Innocents" (1961)
Dir: Jack Clayton

Based on the classic Henry James novella, "The Turn of the Screw," "The Innocents" is truly one of the most frightening gothic haunted house films ever created. Starring Deborah Kerr as a governess in charge of two very strange young children, "The Innocents" is one of the few films of its kind that had the courage to cast children in the roles of the aggressors. While they may have been possessed by ghosts, that made it all the more frightening, as they weren't in control of their young psyches. Few films about scary children have ever measured up to "The Innocents,", both in terms of its gothic set pieces, nor its shocking subject matter.

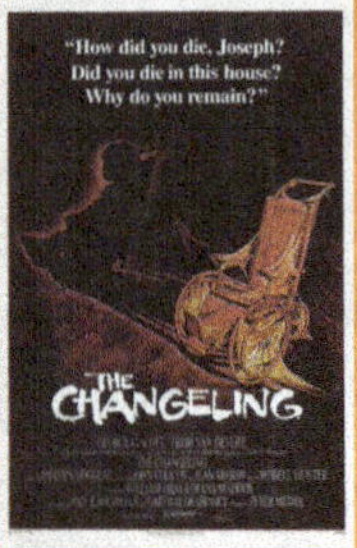

"The Changeling" (1980)
Dir: Peter Medak

"The Changeling" is probably the best horror film you've never seen, which is shame because it's a lovely example of both gothic filmmaking and the haunted house narrative. George C. Scott stars as a composer who loses his wife and daughter in a car accident. In an attempt to heal, he rents a gothic mansion where he can write, but instead finds he is sharing the house with the spirit of a murdered child. "The Changeling" is a quiet masterpiece, and the kind of gothic horror film that will haunt *you* for days after you finish it.

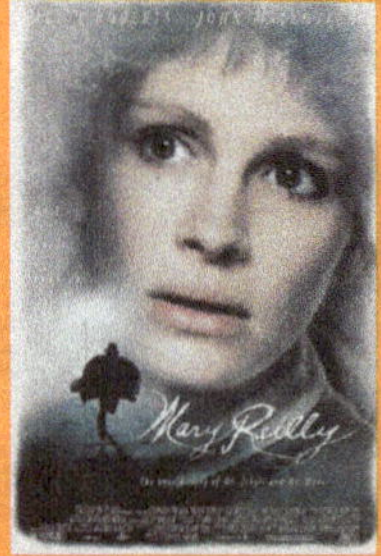

"Mary Reilly" (1996)
Dir: Stephen Frears

Listen, kids... It's time to give "Mary Reilly" a break. Directed by the amazing Stephen Frears, and starring John Malkovich as Dr. Jekyll/Mr. Hyde, I think this film suffered from a period of Julia Roberts-overload. It's not perfect, but a movie that focuses on Dr. Jekyll's smitten housemaid and *her* experience as he struggles with his alter-ego is a movie that is due a second chance. Gothic, haunting, and strangely romantic, "Mary Reilly" is a film that has earned the respect that comes with hindsight. Give it a watch, and if you hate it... Send Julia Roberts a letter. It's not my fault.

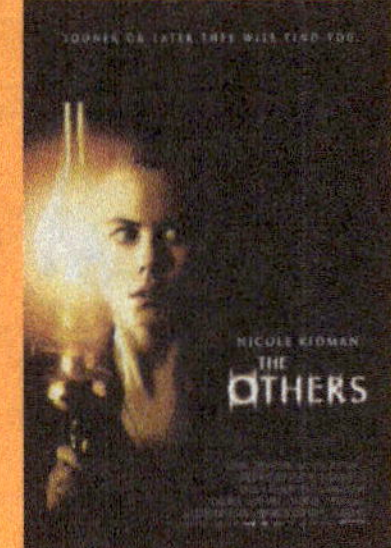

"The Others" (2001)
Dir: Alejandro Amenábar

Nicole Kidman vehicle "The Others" is one of the best recent examples of the gothic haunted house film, in which a twist ending was actually brilliant, and where we never truly know what to believe about the nature of the home until those final thrilling moments. Beautiful, terrifying, and enduringly lovely, "The Others" is a film like no other, that has aged perfectly.

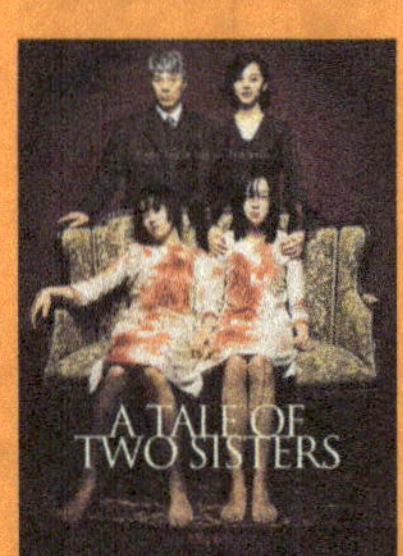

"A Tale of Two Sisters" (2003)
Dir: Kim Jee-woon

This Korean haunted house/haunted family film is one of the most recent examples of the way in which other cultures interpret gothic horror. After two sisters return home from a bout in a mental institution to face the horrors at home, they are confronted with not only a vicious stepmother, but also a ghost who seems hell-bent on sending them both running back to the institution. Dark, unsettling, with another genius twist, watch "A Tale of Two Sisters," and skip its inferior American remake, "The Uninvited."

There are obviously dozens more we could cover, but these are just a few of my favorites! Shoot me a tweet and let me know which haunted house *you'd* like to move in to!

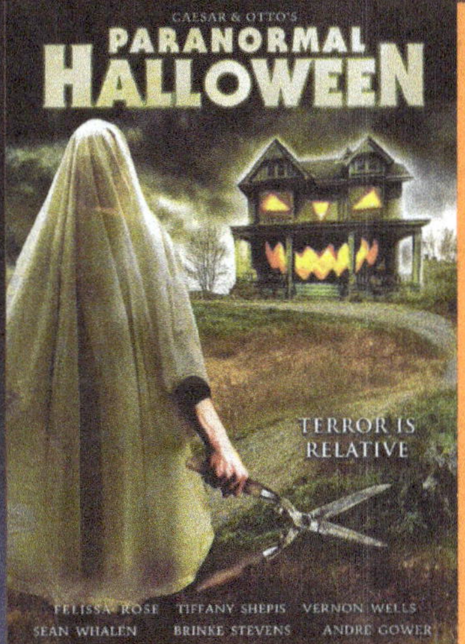

Caesar and Otto are back and they don't seem to have learned anything! Created by actors Dave Campfield and Paul Chomicki, half-brothers Caesar and Otto Dinovio have already bumbled their way through a *Summer Camp Massacre* and a *Deadly X-Mas*, but now they have returned to take on a *Paranormal Halloween*.

If you are a fan of lovingly crafted horror meta-humor and gentle ribbing at all of the campy madness that makes the horror genre what it is, then you will love *Caesar and Otto's Paranormal Halloween*, just like I did.

The Story: After accidentally killing notorious serial killer Michael Miles while babysitting, Caesar (Campfield) and Otto (Chomicki) are offered the chance to housesit at the Governor's summer home, a surprisingly modest affair that may be just a little haunted. Comely neighbors, cooks of questionable mental health, and the fellas' leech of a father are just a few of the complications they face as they try to sort out exactly what is going on in the Governor's house.

Starring, directed, written, edited, and produced by Campfield, *Paranormal Halloween* is a stellar example of low-budget filmmaking done right. Nothing is perfect, nor really, should it be. What it lacks in mind-boggling CGI or high-end production design, it makes up for in a truly clever script delivered by a cast that is having a ball. Featuring cameos from genre legends such as Felissa Rose, Vernon Wells, Debbie Rochon, Beverly Randolph, and Tiffany Shepis, the cast of *Paranormal Halloween* knows which horror tropes to mine for the best laughs, because they've been at this game for a while.

And *Paranormal Halloween is* really funny. *Halloween*, *The Amityville Horror* (original and remake), *The Shining*; even if you think you've seen these movies lampooned before, Caesar and Otto approach it with their trademark, "Laurel & Hardy" vibe and it's a real blast to watch. Previously, Caesar was always a *jazz hands* style caricature of a Hollywood wannabe, and while Campfield has toned down Caesar's rougher edges for *Paranormal Halloween*, I have to admit that I missed bitchy Caesar. Mellower Caesar aside, the camaraderie between Campfield and Chomicki is obvious, and it's only getting better with time.

As a fan of *Caesar and Otto* from way back, I am thrilled to say that *Caesar and Otto's Paranormal Halloween* is a fabulous addition to their screwball canon.

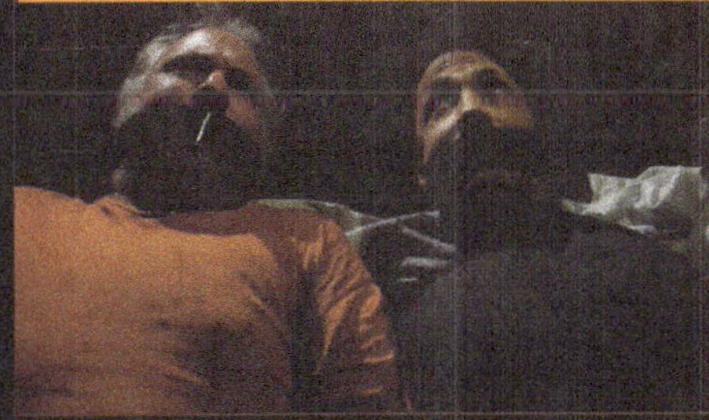

Caesar and Otto's Paranormal Halloween is available NOW on DVD!

Rating: 4 Flawless Rob Zombie Gags out of 5

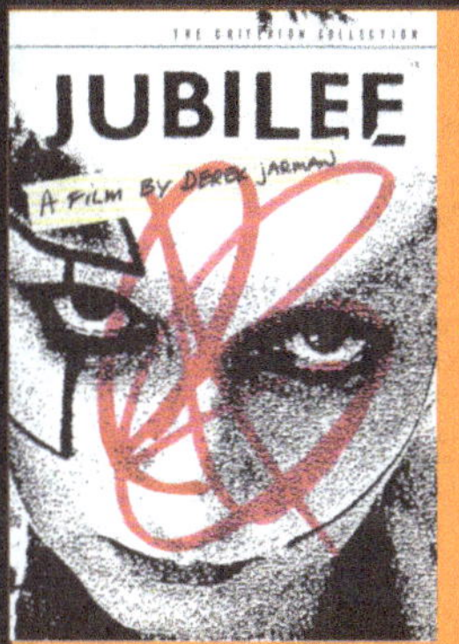

Can you even *begin* to imagine Stanley Kubrick's classic adaptation of Anthony Burgess' dystopian novel, *A Clockwork Orange*, if all of the droogs had been played by women? Crazy, right? Well, good news rhetorical question junkies: wonder no more! Because Derek Jarman's dystopian fever-dream *Jubilee*, set in a futuristic punk-rock London dominated by girl gangs, kinky sex, and ultra-violence, is precisely what a female-fronted *Clockwork* would look like.

And that is why I count it among my favorite films. So settle in, you punk rock anarchists and ballet-dancing bitches, it's time for Linnie's Lost Favorites: Derek Jarman's *Jubilee*.

"This is the generation who grew up, and forgot to lead their lives."

The Story: is insane. Queen Elizabeth I (Jenny Runacre, in a dual role) desires the ability to time travel into the future, which she is granted by her occultist, John Dee (*Rocky Horror Picture Show*'s Richard O'Brien). Led by spirit guide Ariel, the same Ariel from Shakespeare's *The Tempest*, Elizabeth I arrives in an alternate-reality 1970s London, in which Elizabeth II is dead but punk rock is alive and well. The world is ruled by music, violence, sex, and glorious combinations of all of the above. Starring punk icons such as Adam Ant, Toyah Wilcox, Jordan, and featuring performances from Siouxie and the Banshees, Wayne County, and The Stilts, *Jubilee* is anarchist musical madness of the highest order.

Once you move through the wraparound story featuring Queen Elizabeth and Riff Raff, it's impossible not to draw parallels between *Jubilee* and *A Clockwork Orange*. This isn't a bad thing. Roving gangs of criminal women lead by badass rockstars named Amyl Nitrate (Jordan) and Mad (Wilcox) prove that ladies can be just as dangerous as men. As they engage in various forms of corporate-sanctioned violence, most of the film's best moments are soundtracked by brilliantly infectious punk rock anthems. If you're able to get songs like "Rule Britannia" and "Plastic Surgery" out of your head… then you're a robot and I'm a little bit afraid of you.

What I love most about Jarman's film, and discover more of every time I watch it, is *Jubilee*'s commitment to the philosophical concept of nihilism. In Jarman's alternate 1978 England, morals are relative to your position in life, and life is generally without meaning or purpose. Once all social norms and laws have been removed, ethics are entirely objective, and pleasure becomes subjective. Do you enjoy threesomes with bisexual incestuous brothers? Have at it! Do you prefer picking up transients for sex and then suffocating them in plastic with your friends? Then do what makes you happy, says nihilism. Yes, this would likely make for a terrifying way of life, but when it comes to watching a cultural artifact of the punk rock aesthetic of the late 70s, it's a hell of a ride.

Jubilee is available on Criterion DVD and is absolutely worth adding to your collection! So do it today, before Amyl Nitrate comes for YOU!

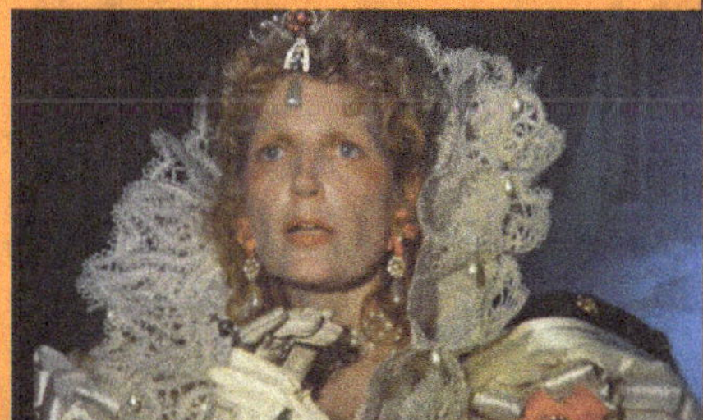

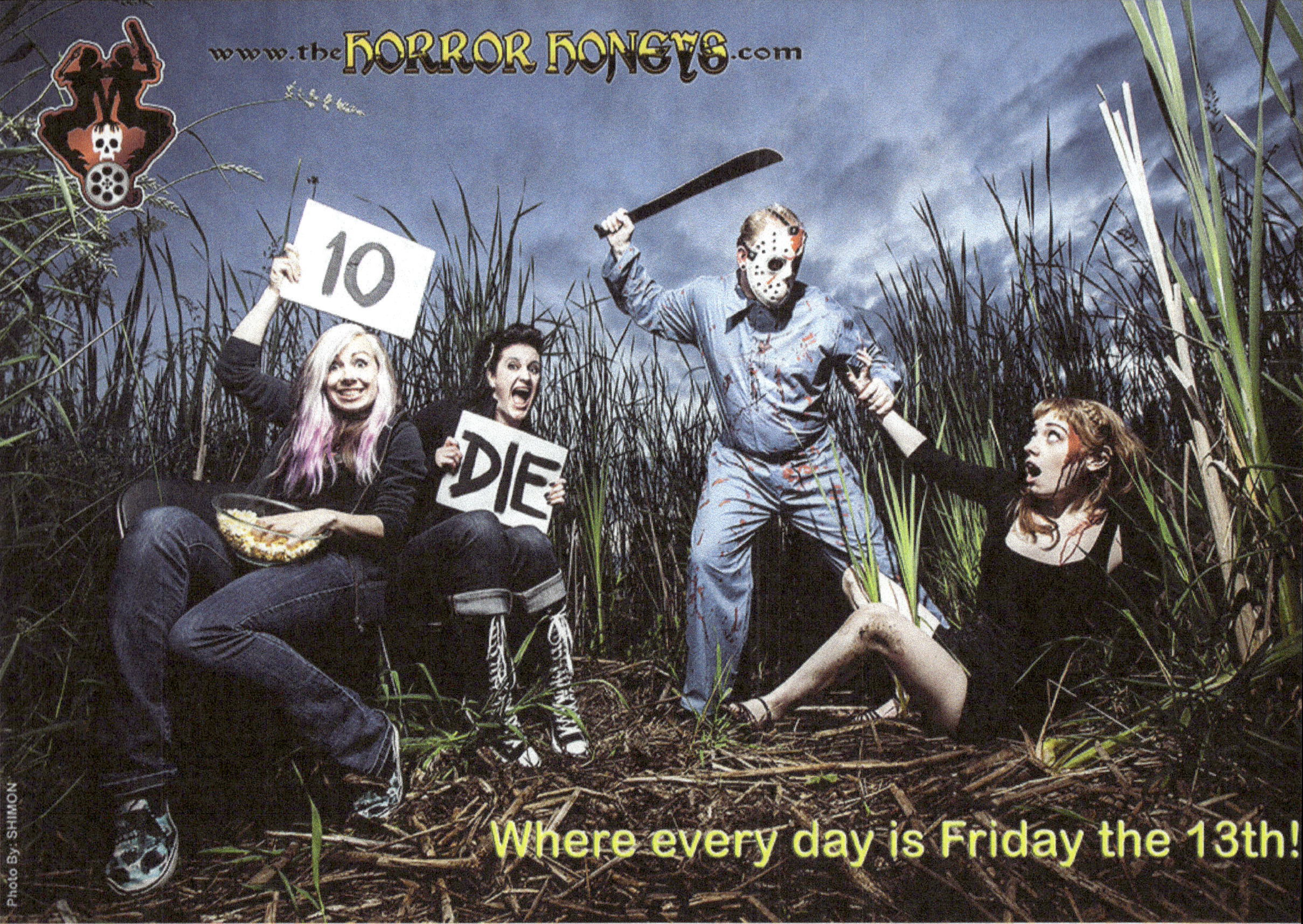

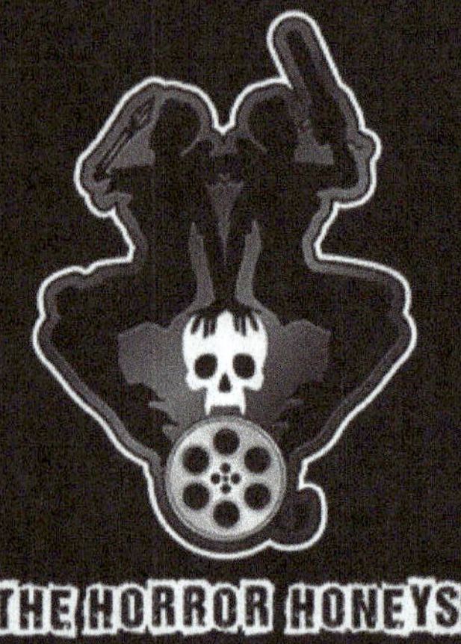

www.theHORROR HONEYS.com
10
DIE
Where every day is Friday the 13th!
Photo By: SHIMON
THE HORROR HONEYS
The Best in Horror
News | Reviews | Podcast | Attitude
www.thehorrorhoneys.com

Blurring the Lines of Revenge and Morality in "The Gift"

By Bella Blitz

"The Gift" is a 2015 psychological thriller that follows a young married couple essentially starting their lives over. Simon (Jason Bateman) and Robyn (Rebecca Hall) move back to Simon's hometown; buying a new house, entering a new job and most importantly, starting a family. While getting settled, they run into Gordo (writer/producer/director, Joel Edgerton), who is apparently an old classmate of Simon's. Gordo's social awkwardness seems quirky at first - strange conversation; harmless, but personal gifts and frequent visits - but soon enough, these quirky habits become creepy. When Simon finally puts a stop to it all, things take a turn for the worse. Soon, Robyn is digging up Simon's past, and as previous events come to light, the future is seeming less and less bright for Robyn and Simon.

Like so many thrillers that have come before it, one might expect the outcome of "The Gift" to be completely predictable. It's a formula as old as time, yeah? A happy couple starting a new life runs into old classmate holding a grudge, revenge is either carried out or squashed by the reformed classmate. The end. Except that's not the end at all. And that's not this movie's formula. For every moment you think you have figured out, there's a slight twist - one plausible enough to keep you from thinking there could be any other option.

The character outlines seem simple enough: This is who you trust, this is who you distrust, this is who you accept as a catalyst for the plot. But Edgerton doesn't make it that easy. Just like with people in real life, these characters are three-dimensional, fully formed, complex beings that you can feel multiple emotions towards. So rarely does that occur so completely in film. But, in "The Gift," it seems to occur naturally - if unsettlingly. And it's unsettling because you don't expect to have empathy for the truly bad guy, and you definitely aren't entirely comfortable feeling anger towards the seemingly good guy. And, once you get comfortable with either of these feelings you realize that everyone exists in this moral middle ground.

As per usual, Bateman manages to play the perfect everyman in Simon, an everyman with a dark, looming center. Through the volatile progression of Simon's character development, you can never quite forget how easy it is for this man to be anyone you know. Hall's Robyn, although my least favorite of the characters, was the catalyst for most of the plot progression. Without her, the audience wouldn't be able to unravel the story; but there was too much, which made it seem like Edgerton in his writing had forgotten that the audience had a brain and didn't need extra prodding to manipulate their emotions.

And what is a good psychological thriller without a little home invasion? But how can you feel invaded when you have repeatedly invited the invading someone into your home? That is the brilliance in Edgerton's writing and characterization of Gordo. It's a constant struggle to keep the rug under your feet, all while realizing that it's about to get pulled out from under you anyway. Gordo is as complex as "The Gift" itself; never quite falling fully into one characterization or another - and yet fully realizing each aspect of who Gordo was.

Despite my dislike of the use of Robyn's character in place of the audience's own ability to read contextual clues, most of "The Gift" is, much like Gordo's gifts, a nicely wrapped and tidy package. Almost all of the resolutions are hinted at throughout the movie, although some are a bit more abstract than others - leaving complete resolution up to interpretation, making the "The Gift" a most effective thriller. Just when you think you've got the solution firmly in hand, you'll find yourself grasping for a true grip. And just when you think you can sit back and enjoy the movie, you catch yourself sitting on the edge of your seat wondering where all your formulas went wrong.

Truly, "The Gift" is an amazing study in audience manipulation. I don't believe I have seen a film, this year, so thoroughly manipulate an audience's empathy, trust, and disdain as well as this one has. It's quite impressive and something I'm still considering days after having seen it. "The Gift" is uniquely intelligent in how it presents ethical situations to the audience and forces them to question how they might deal with similar conflicts, but never presumes to present a final "right or wrong" solution. Because there truly isn't one. Which feeds right back into the complexity of the characters and their moral ground.

Rating: 4 out of 5 stars

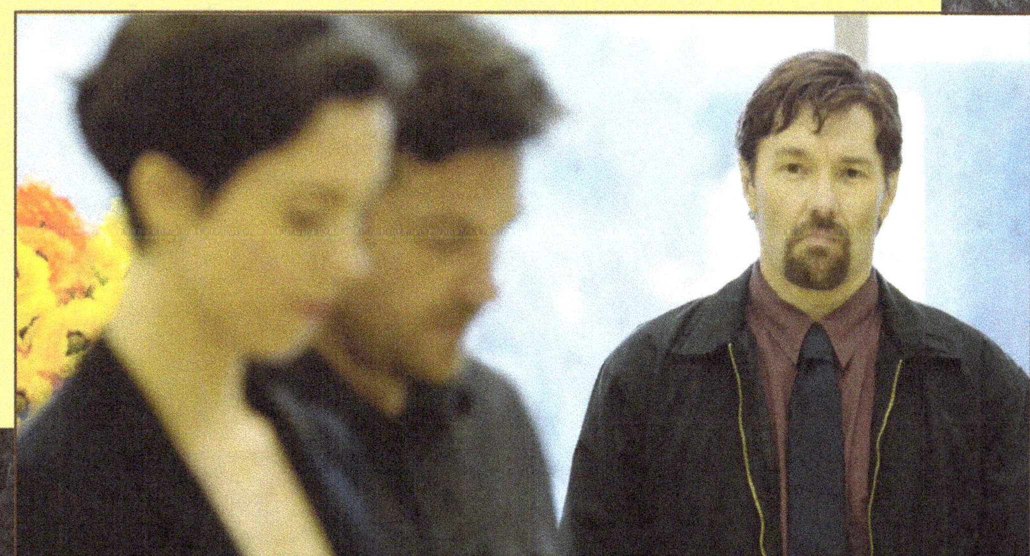

Shakespearean Sensibility Meets Gothic Horror in

"MARY SHELLY'S FRANKENSTEIN......"

- KA Morris

The early 90s were interesting years for horror film, with the rise of several memorable series origin stories, and the introduction of some amazing book adaptations. Supernatural horror films dominated the box office and straight to video releases, and films like "Bram Stoker's Dracula" and "Interview with the Vampire" turned being undead into something highly alluring, and let's not lie about it, completely romantic. In 1994, Francis Ford Coppola intended to release a companion piece to his Gothic vampire romance, but wound up producing instead. "Mary Shelly's Frankenstein" experienced trouble in its early days, and then again after shooting wrapped as Coppola publicly distanced himself from his own creation...

Wait, that sounds familiar, doesn't it?

I'm a hardcore Branagh fan from way back, and while many aren't familiar with his early Shakespearean work, I find that his directorial pieces share a similar lushness. The costuming is always rich and impeccably detailed, and Branagh has a way of bringing a poignancy out of his actors that is really more suited to stage plays - dramatic, heartfelt and unique performances that strike the viewer on a very basic level. Branagh's approach to "Frankenstein" is also an antique one, as he takes more cues from the original novel to augment those from previous film incarnations of the Monster.

The characters are obviously familiar, and like other films, Victor Frankenstein and his evolution from eager young medical student to a driven and fanatical being is the focus of the story. The action of the other characters serves only to further the progression of Victor's personality, and the problematic nature of the roles of the female characters are more a function of the time period of the original material (book and film) than anything.

Elizabeth (Helena Bonham Carter) is one of the less exciting character sketches from this film. She exists in a bubble of sorts as nothing more than a titillation, a reminder of a "normal life" that Victor knows he needs to return to, but that he can't seem to come to terms with either - Elizabeth waits... and that's about it... Waiting to marry Victor really is her only function. She also doesn't seem to have any more depth to her character other than the fact that she and Victor grew up together, always knowing that they would be married, which, while common for the time period, is by modern standards exceedingly off-putting.

However, in "Frankenstein" she does serve one very special purpose - again as a catalyst - as one of the more interesting incarnations of The Bride. We're used to James Whale's stunning presentation of Elsa Lanchester, but Branagh's horrifying Bride is far closer to what I've always imagined for her. Another sidelined female character, Josephine, also serves zero function other than to wait around to be wrongly accused of the death of a young boy (Victor's younger brother, killed by the Monster) and then hanged for the perceived crime. Josephine's corpse provides a base for Frankenstein's Bride, and as an added creepy detail, he's not only exchanged Elizabeth's head for Josephine's, but also her hands... for that familiar touch. *shudder*

Elizabeth's suicide is one of the more beautifully captured moments in the film, and my previous reference to Branagh's films being cinematic stage plays is never more evident that here. Elizabeth's tortured realization of what she has become, and what Victor intends for her, is too much to bear. Elizabeth's death is the only action her character takes in the entire film that is a decision made for herself, and not one that has been determined by a male figure in the film, and that in itself has its own poignant power.

Victor, of course, is the character we are most familiar with - and with Branagh himself taking the role of the tortured genius, it's hard not to see a correlation between his acting/directing choices, which all flow in a similar vein. Branagh's obsession with fatally flawed protagonists is something I enjoy most about his earlier film work and his Victor Frankenstein is perfectly flawed. Frankenstein's progression through medical

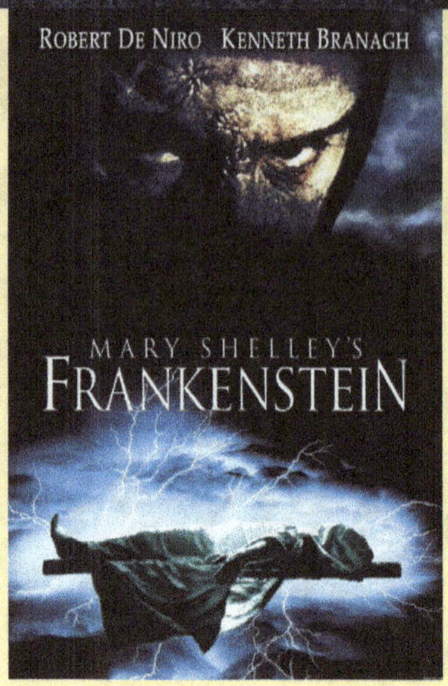

school is marked more by his interactions with his mentor than by anything he learns in his classrooms, and while the action of the film in these sequences is by no means anything new, the imagery is what makes everything resonate.

Copper wires, zapping electrodes and an almost steampunk aesthetic create a unique world where science is very close to magic, and the unexplained is attempted. Victor's obsession with being able to chase away death is what drives his research, and what gives literal birth to his creation - the Sharp Featured Man. Sadly, the less said about De Niro's role, the better, and I personally feel that his casting is one of the bigger missteps of the film – that being said, De Niro does what he can with awkward prosthetics, and maneuvering his bulk with as much grace as possible.

As far as Gothic horror is concerned, "Mary Shelly's Frankenstein" is the closest adaptation of the original source material that you will find – the costuming is rich and over the top, and the set pieces are luscious in their color and depth. Victor's laboratory is a lesson in "How to Be a Mad Scientist" from the use of period correct materials to innovative ways to mimic the birthing process; everything about these sequences is a love letter to true Gothic horror. Everything people of this time period were frightened of is sealed up within this movie, and that is the true genius of Shelley's book, and Branagh's adaptation of it.

While areas of production are problematic, just like with "Bram Stoker's Dracula," I'm willing to overlook a multitude of sins for the reward of a visual feast that while telling the same story as countless others, tells it in such a way that we can imagine Frankenstein perhaps in the way that Shelley herself did. Frankenstein was a man possessed, and then ultimately consumed by his own passion – but at the core of it, he was a deeply flawed man coming to terms with his own grief only to ultimately be crushed under the weight of it.

Rating: 3.5 stars out of 5

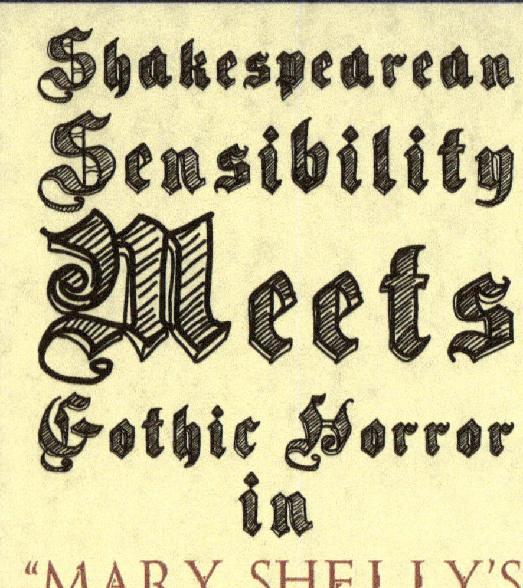

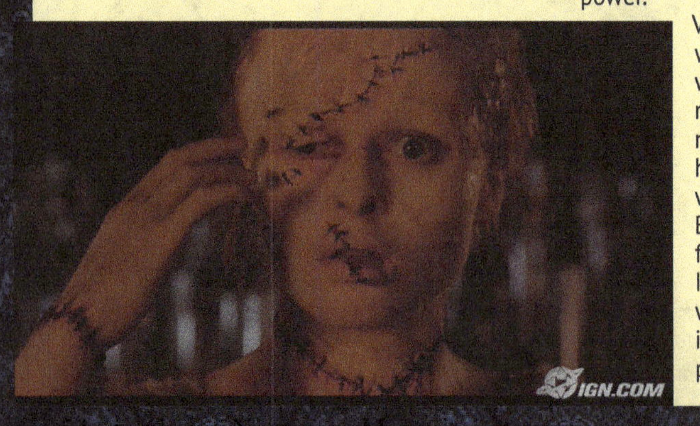

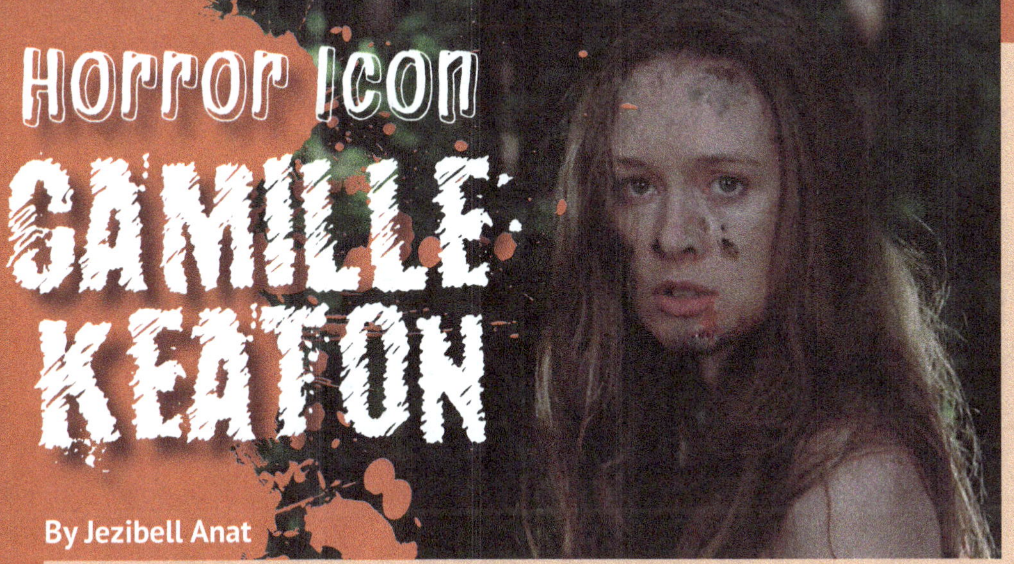

By Jezibell Anat

Actress Camille Keaton is known for her fragile, sensual appearance and is most famous for her starring role in the controversial film *I Spit on Your Grave*. Released in 1978, this film is considered one of the most violent in cinematic history and established Camille Keaton as a horror babe.

Camille was born in Pine Bluff, Arkansas, but began her acting career in the Italian *giallo* cinema in the early seventies. She explains, "I wanted to travel and learn a language, and my aunt was married to an Italian gentleman. He was a wonderful man and that's one of the reasons I chose to live in Italy. Clint Eastwood was making his spaghetti Westerns so there was a lot of film work. Franco Zeffirelli was casting for *Brother Sun, Sister Moon* so I sent in my picture."

This was when actors had to mail in original photos and wait by the telephone. Camille never heard from Zeffirelli, but another director, Massimo Dallamano, called her and said he'd gotten her picture from Zeffireli's office. To her surprise, he offered her the part of Solange in his upcoming thriller *What Have You Done to Solange?*

Camille said, "I was hesitant because he wanted me to play a sixteen year old with infantile paralysis, and I was 21 with no acting experience." She remembers his gruff voice declaring, "You can do this, I will direct you." He guided her through the role, and the film was released in 1972. Though her part was not huge, it was memorable, and it led to other roles.

She worked in Italy for four years, and also posed for men's entertainment magazines. She notes, "Italians have a much more liberal attitude towards nudity, so that was never an issue for me. I even look sweet and innocent when I'm posing naked - of course the long hair helped too!"

Despite her success in Italy, Camille became homesick. She came back to the Unites States and stayed at Manhattan's historic Barbizon Hotel for Women. (This residential hotel was part of the twentieth-century's cultural shift, as single women came to New York seeking careers but still wanted a safe home environment.)

Like all the New York actors at the time, Camille scoured *Backstage* and responded to casting calls. One was for *I Spit on Your Grave*, directed by Meir Zarchi, about Jennifer Hills, a young writer who goes to an isolated summer cottage to work on her first novel. A gang of local rednecks savagely gang rape her and leave her for dead, but Jennifer recovers, hunts down her attackers one by one and viciously slays them.

Camille auditioned several times and got the part "because Meir wanted to cast against type and go for someone who wasn't an Amazon." She was "very concerned about the level of violence and how it would be filmed, but Meir reassured me that all the sexual scenes would be simulated. We talked through all the details of the action and rehearsed everything before we filmed it. For the rock rape scene, there were about four inches of foam rubber contoured to my body between the rock and myself so that I wouldn't get hurt, and the actor wasn't making solid contact. Meir just shot the sexual scenes in a way that made them look harrowing."

When *I Spit on Your Grave* was released, It was banned in 200 theatres. Camille was "very nervous about how it would be received, and even hoped it wouldn't be distributed. Film critic Roger Ebert told people not to see it, and that was the best free marketing we could get. He claimed it was the worst movie ever made."

I Spit on Your Grave has been considered an exploitation film because of the gang rape scene. However, it has also been praised because it does not sanitize rape, but shows it in its true ugliness. This film has gained popularity among some rape victims because the rapists deserve their punishment. One of its taglines is "This woman has just cut, chopped, broken and burned four men but no jury in America would ever convict her."

As Camille explains, "It's a film about poetic justice. The film was originally titled *Day of the Woman* because Jennifer does strike back instead of being permanently traumatized by the experience." Camille won the *Medalla Sitges en Plata de Ley* Best Actress award for it at the 1978 Catalonian International Film Festival in Spain.

Because of this movie's following, Camille is a frequent guest at horror conventions, and she enjoys the diverse crowds that attend. She says, "I like talking to people and interacting with fans. It's good to hear different perspectives. Attitudes towards the film have changed since it came out, and I see it differently myself because of the people I've talked to. In the 90s I met a girl who said it had changed her life because Jennifer's survival was such an inspiration."

Camille continues to act in movies, most recently playing FBI Agent Marcia Wilson in the independent horror musical *Cabaret Diabolique*. She saw the film for the first time at Spooky Empire's May-Hem in Orlando and declared, "I love it! I am very happy with the quality of this film, and the music is great. I enjoyed working on it. I liked (director) Christopher Forbes' relaxed style. He made me look good. I think this film will be around for a long time."

She is now working on a sequel to *I Spit on Your Grave*. She says that "Meir has written the script, and it's called *I Spit on Your Grave: Deja Vu*. I play Jennifer about 35 years later, and she's a mother That's all I'm allowed to say about the story. We should be filming later in 2015."

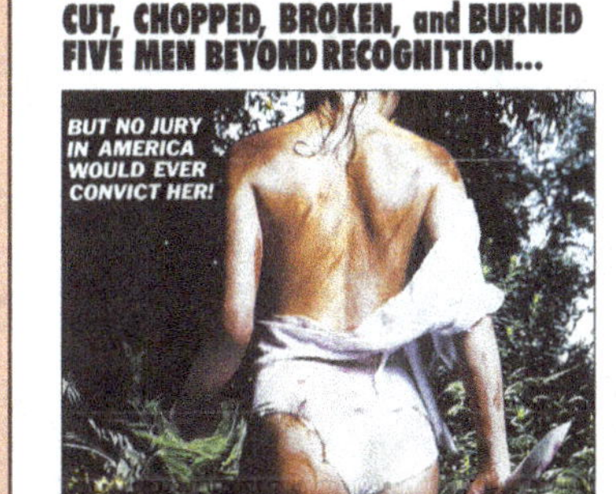

AWAKENING A FANDOM

By K.A. Morris (@horrorhoneys)

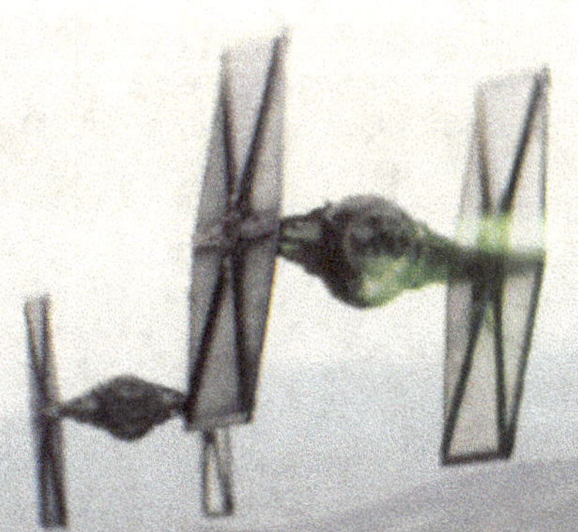

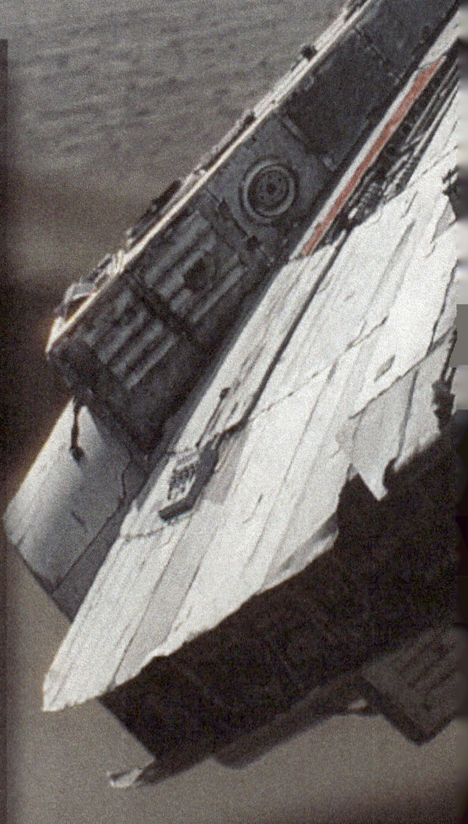

In 1999, "Star Wars" fans were divided by the Force. Some felt betrayed, and not a small percentage. A young actor's life was literally ruined by the fallout that echoed around the prequel films, and a series of films that was supposed to reignite the flames of passion in a fandom desperate for any scrap of newness may have actually ended up doing more damage than intended.

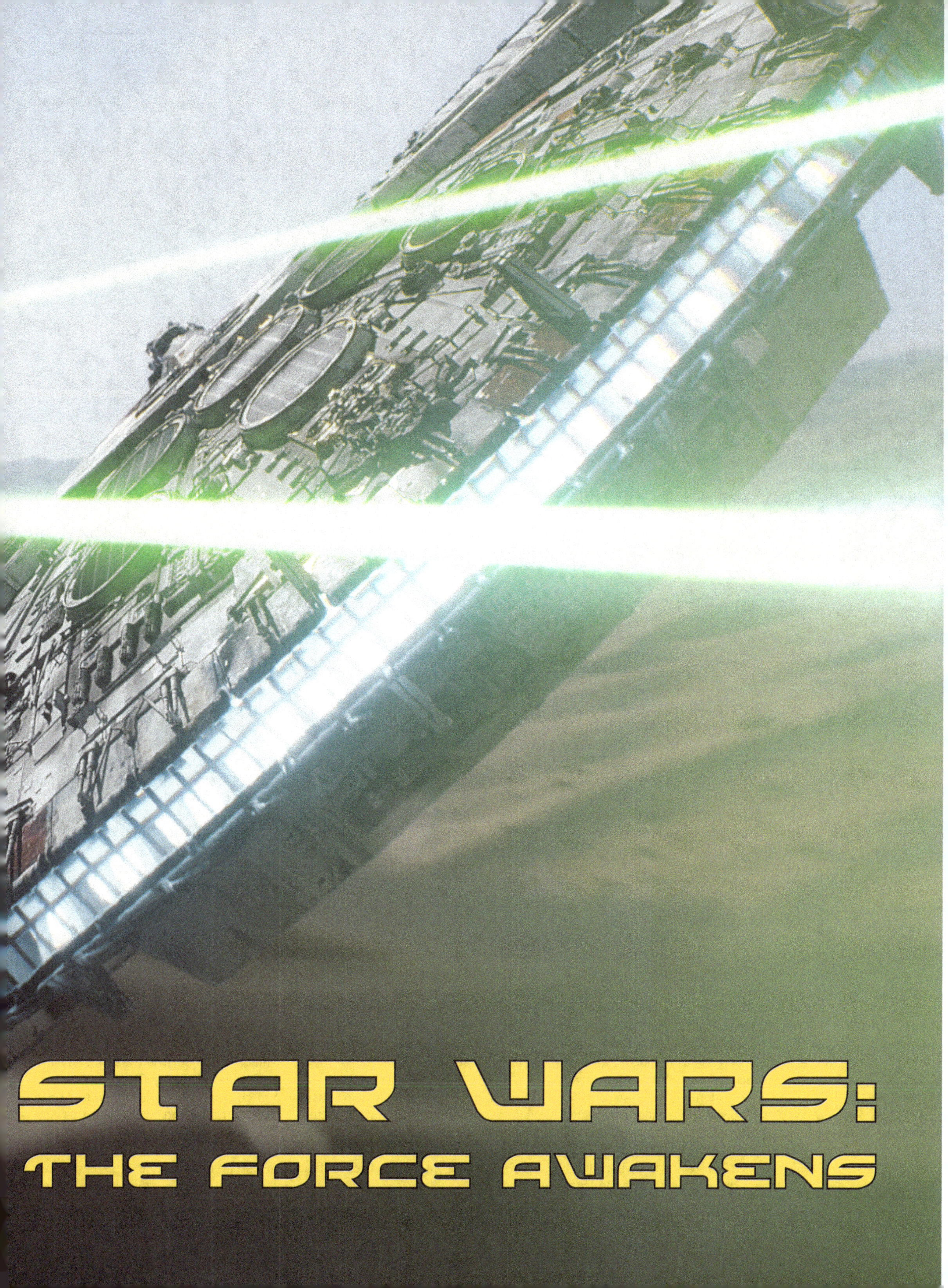

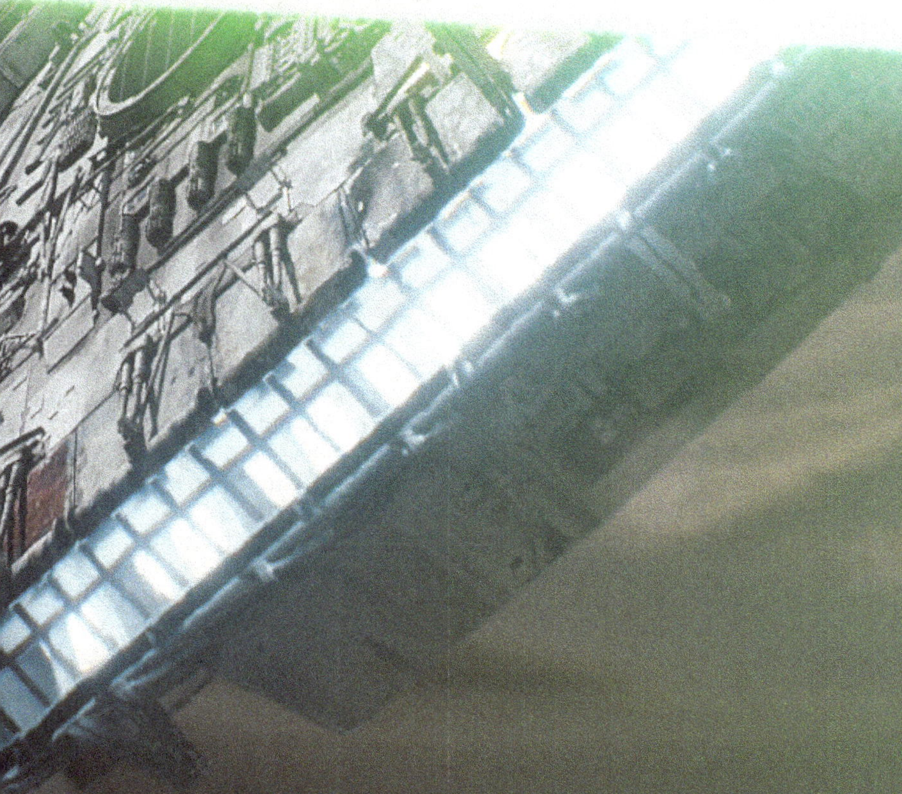

STAR WARS:
THE FORCE AWAKENS

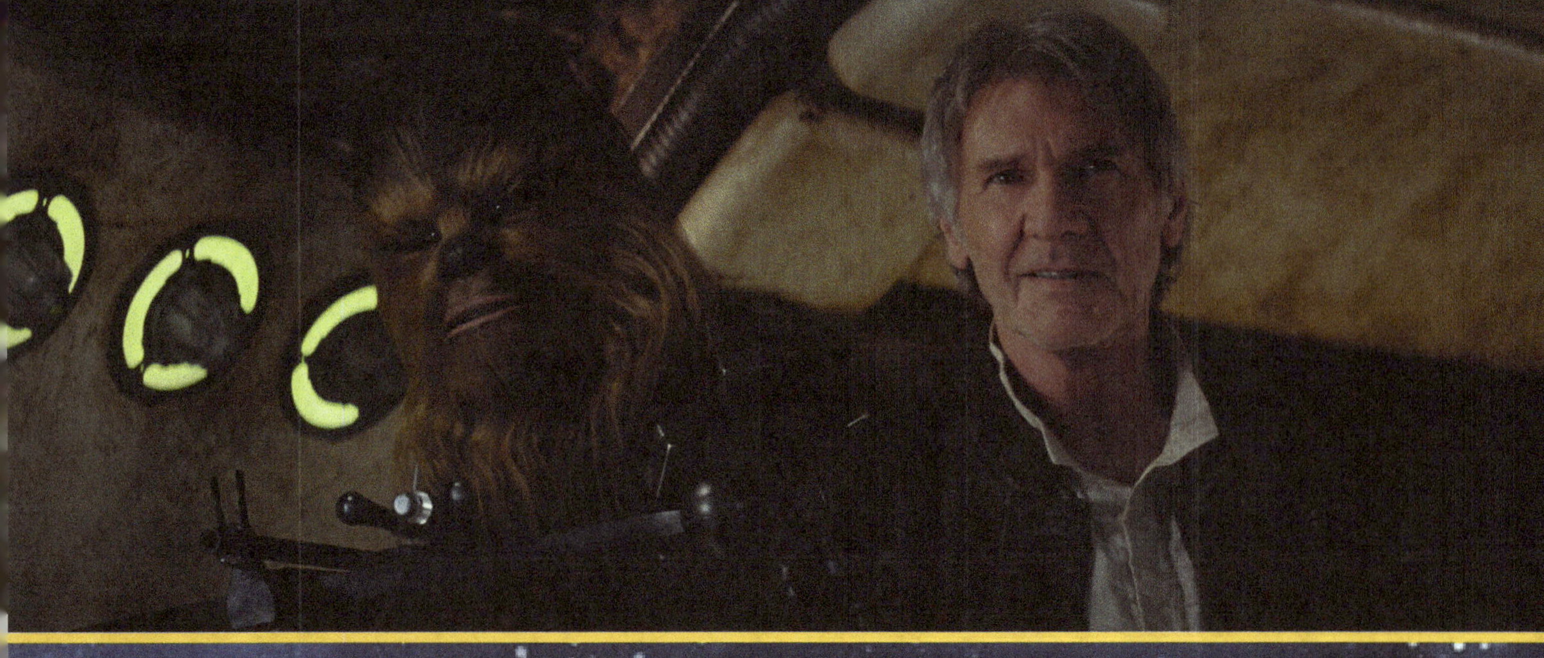

Don't even get me started on Jar-Jar, or the racial insensitivity implications that also reared up after "The Phantom Menace" was released. Barring the fact that I don't have a personal beef with the prequel films, and don't have to pretend that they don't exist so that I can sleep at night, I do know fans who are scarred in irreparable ways because of it.

As a completionist in the most honest sense of the word, my "Star Wars" universe contains a great many additions to the traditional canon. Cartoon Network's "Clone Wars" animation series is intense, and quite dark in places, and gives backstories to characters that are tragically only given lip service in the rest of the prequel trilogy. The animated feature length film of "The Clone Wars," while geared specifically (and unapologetically) towards the children of "Star Wars" fans, is another well balanced addition to the canon, and the CG animated TV series provided a sturdy support to the story arc of the Clone army - some of the episodes are extremely touching, and provide a human face to an army that didn't necessarily have one, or need one as far as any of the films seemed to be concerned. If anything, the addition of these chapters, added ostensibly for children, make the betrayal of Order 66 that much more painful. As an adult fan looking for ways to appreciate "Star Wars" in a deeper way, these canon additions are actually essential to gaining a wider perspective on the progression of the series.

As a devout "Star Wars" fan, when Disney took over the stewardship of the iconic sci-fi franchise, questions from friends (and even people I didn't know) poured in. Would Disney ruin "Star Wars"? Contrary to the worries of others, I was honestly more thrilled to see that Leia Organa was, by default, a Disney Princess and there was nothing anyone could do about it, which made it even better.

In almost the next breath, it was announced that a new addition to the "Star Wars" universe would be introduced, and that it would be directed by none other than JJ Abrams. This is where I began to get a little nervous. I had enjoyed the new imagining of "Star Trek" produced the same year as this announcement... but I was also nervous. Can you cross the streams of these two fandoms and come away unscathed?

Like every devout fan, I asked the question that seems laughable to any rational person I ask - Can a director tainted by the fiction of the far future (and an alternate retelling of that universe) really encapsulate the hopes, dreams and feels of a long time ago in a galaxy far, far, away? And what about that lens flare? Cue the nervousness. But, amidst all of this, I was hopeful. "Star Trek" was a unique undertaking, and it was not unsuccessful in its execution. Abrams could be trusted with a large scale project with a huge history and a rabid fan base.

However, my trepidation was increased again when after months of conjecture about what story from the canonical timeline the film would be following, we were stunned again to discover that, as he had with "Star Trek," Abrams was venturing away from canon to tell a new and unique story within the "Star Wars" universe. But, with established characters and familiar names returning in droves, it was hard to be skeptical without sounding like a moron. If Luke, Leia, Chewbacca, and Han were returning, why couldn't we return with our full hearts? But we'd been scarred... so scarred by that goddamn Gungan.

While I might be the only one to have read the "leaked" storyline and promptly forgotten all about it, any "Star Wars" fan worth their salt waited with baited breath for the trailer release, as more and more names were added, confirmed, or teased. New characters, unfamiliar faces, and some set photos of a desert planet that made my heart do a backflip. However... I would be remiss if I didn't mention my one failing as a fan - I still can't get behind the title. I know that the trend of the films is to follow a naming convention that is (typically) passive/aggressive/passive as the dark and light sides struggle with the balance of power. The title of "Star Wars VII" is passive to a fault. "The Force Awakens" has still not grown on me as the months have passed, and I couldn't help but hold on to some hope that when the Force finally awakened from its nap, it would be a little cranky.

Things I forgot when the first trailer was released? Aside from the fact that I forgot every single issue I would have had with anything to do with this film from word one, I'm pretty sure I forgot to breathe. And that was the least of my problems as tears streamed down my face in public while I stared open mouthed at my phone, not caring that everyone on the bus was watching me - or that I audibly lost my composure when Harrison Ford's grizzled visage appeared (I need the number of Chewie's plastic surgeon BTW, he looks like he hasn't aged a day. Damn those Wookiee genetics).

What we saw: What stood out the most of me, aside from the fact that Abrams' new "Star Wars" world is made up of starkly stunning landscapes, reflective of the years after the fall of the Emperor, and the defeat of tyranny. However, we also see that this new world is not all it's cracked up to be. The Empire still exists, and it's shiny and chrome. If the Imperial Army is taking conscripts, I'll be the first to volunteer to fall at the feet of the chromed justice of Gwendolyn Christie's Captain Phasma - but that's a different story for a different day.

The nostalgia of the original trilogy is strong in "The Force Awakens" and so is the powerful imagery that comes with it. The might of the Empire is still standing strong, and the seeds of rebellion are alive and well in the hearts of some unexpected characters. Oh, and let's not forget, a brand new robot sidekick for the kids (sigh). The Dark Side, one can assume, has always been awake - but what is the catalyst for the awakening of what I can only assume is the power of the Light Side. While I am always hopeful that I will never see a separation of the Force in this way, I suppose that it is the natural progression of the exploration of this unique religion.

Did I get involved in the lightsaber cross-guard debate? No. No I did not. And no, I don't care. Whoever this Sith Lord is, they're a stone cold badass and I can't wait to see their powers revealed.

For a starved fan base, Abrams' "Star Wars" installation has awakened more than a passing hunger for its arrival, and we're still months away from official release. In a time when high hopes are placed on the briefest of glimpses of an upcoming franchise property, "The Force Awakens" is easily the only film to be released this year (or the next few years perhaps) that has earned the moniker "highly anticipated."

May the Force be with you... I'm going to be living in the theatre once it's released.

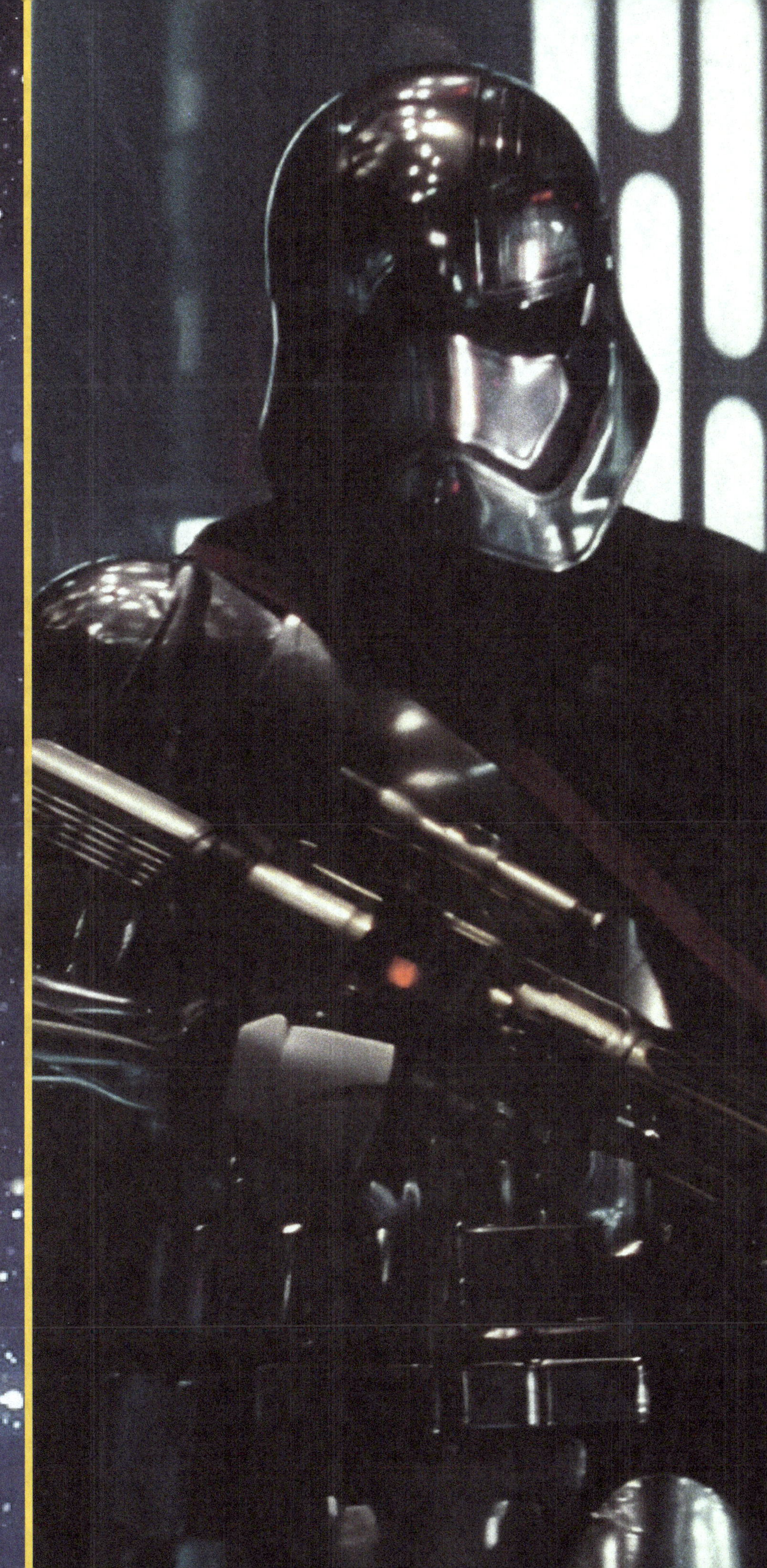

Batman: Arkham Knight

By Bella Blitz

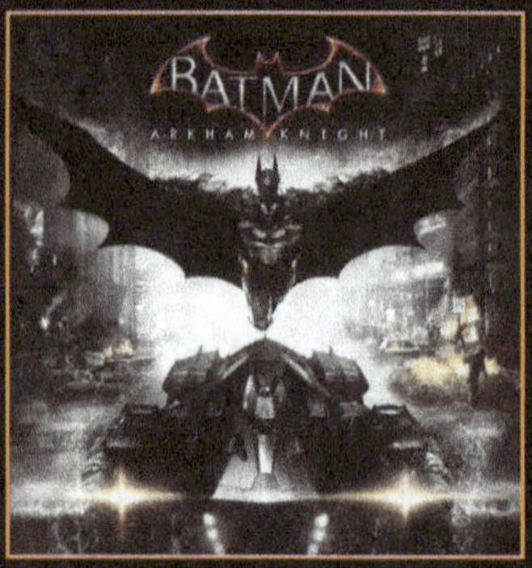

"Batman™: Arkham Knight brings the award-winning Arkham trilogy from Rocksteady Studios to its epic conclusion. Developed exclusively for New-Gen platforms, Batman: Arkham Knight introduces Rocksteady's uniquely designed version of the Batmobile. The highly anticipated addition of this legendary vehicle, combined with the acclaimed gameplay of the Arkham series, offers gamers the ultimate and complete Batman experience as they tear through the streets and soar across the skyline of the entirety of Gotham City. In this explosive finale, Batman faces the ultimate threat against the city that he is sworn to protect, as Scarecrow returns to unite the super criminals of Gotham and destroy the Batman forever."

Tired of Batman games? Well, stop, because Batman: Arkham Knight is here! Picking up in Gotham city, where the ever tumultuous relationship with The Joker has ended, Arkham Knight begins a new descent into madness with the Scarecrow. Formerly known as Dr. Crane, the Scarecrow has threatened an all out attack on Gotham city, forcing the ever-on-the-run citizens to - once again - evacuate; leaving the city open to all manner of thug.

Arkham Knight, with the evacuation of all of Gotham, has expanded the territory quite a bit. As Batman you have room to play through the entire city - not just the smaller map of Arkham City or the even smaller zone of Arkham Asylum. Although most of the gameplay remains similar: looking for clues, piecing together puzzles, hording nifty gadgets, all to the end of catching the big bad; it's never truly a grind. Plus, there's always the plethora of opportunities to beat the living… life out of all of the Scarecrow's lackeys. So that's fun.

Not that the mechanics of the Batman battle needed much upgrading, but there are a few that are going to give a +1 to fights. For instance: you can now interact with your environment by smashing your foes into buildings or taking their weapon and using it against them. Batman can now also be joined by secondary playable characters to team up for a beat down, oh, hello Catwoman.

The real star of the new show, though, is the Batmobile, Batman's ultimate companion and helpful butt-kicker. The Batmobile is an essential aspect in the Arkham Knight gameplay. Not only will it help you get from point A to point B quickly - but you can call it to attention with the press of a button. And, should you be in midair, you'll land squarely in the driver's seat. Where you belong. Just like Batman, the Batmobile has a ton of tricks up it's sleeve. It's not just any car, you see, with certain triggers the Batmobile easily transforms into a rolling tank, or even propels you into the air as though fired from a circus cannon. Robin would be proud.

Batman: Arkham Knight doesn't get lazy with the story or gameplay either. As with the previous games there is dialogue to help contextualize your missions and goals, and you're still only given just enough information to get you part of the way to your achievement. The rest is entirely up to you. You are Batman, after all. And, being Batman, you know it can only get darker from here.

Batman: Arkham Knight was developed by Rocksteady Studios and is available on Steam, PS4 and XBoxOne.

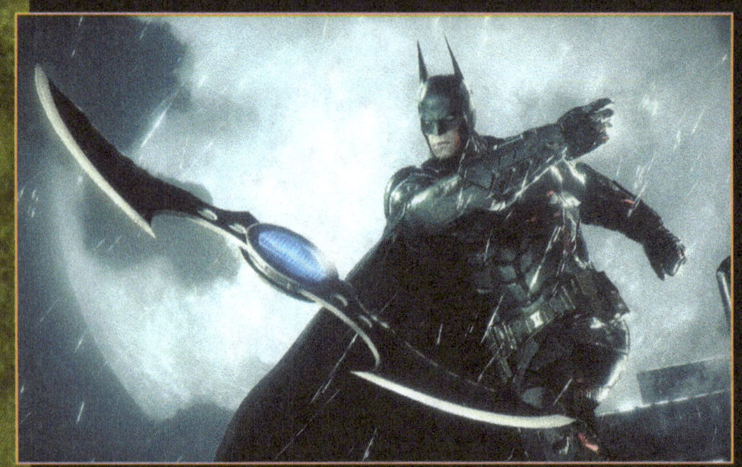

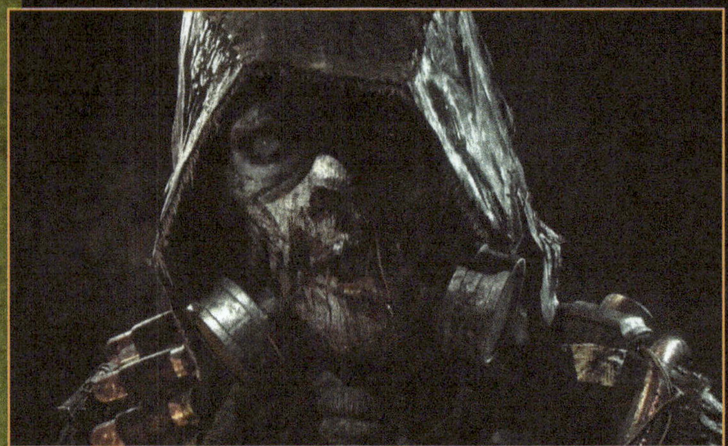

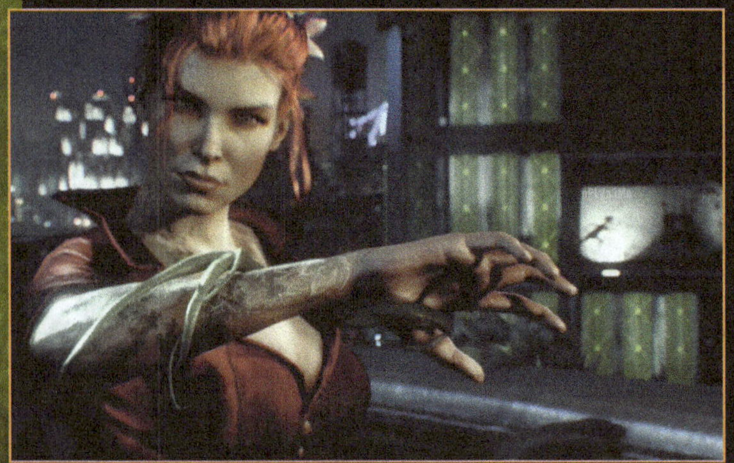

The Fun of Human Eradication
Plague

By Michael Jack

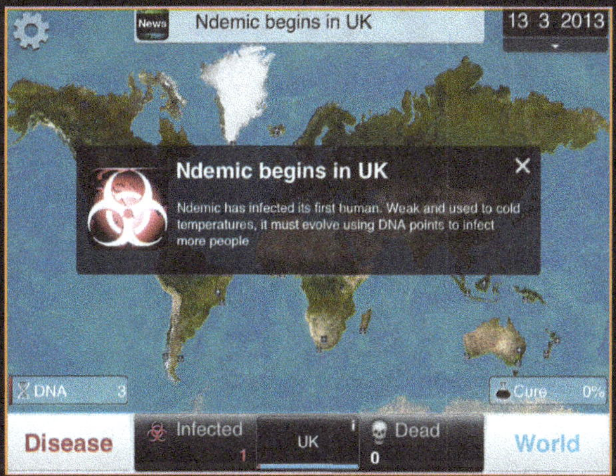

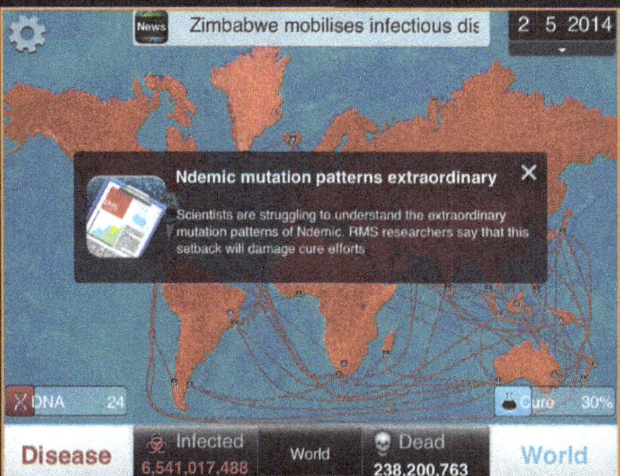

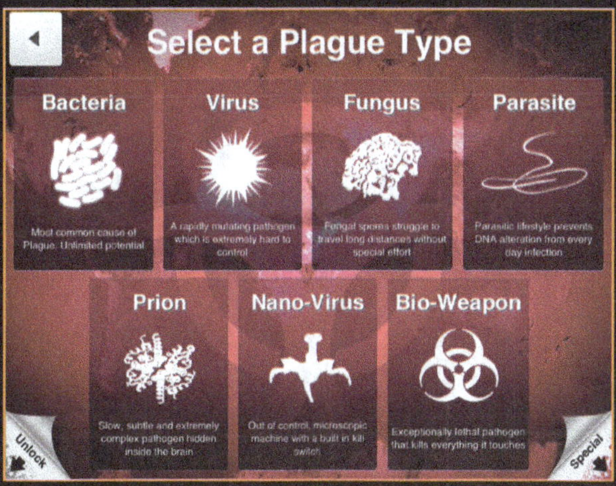

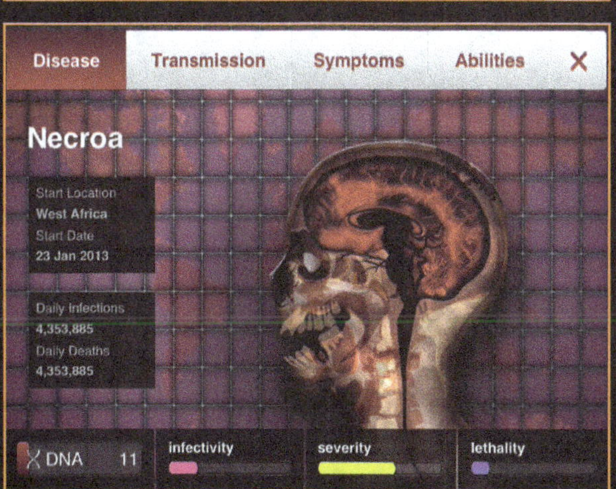

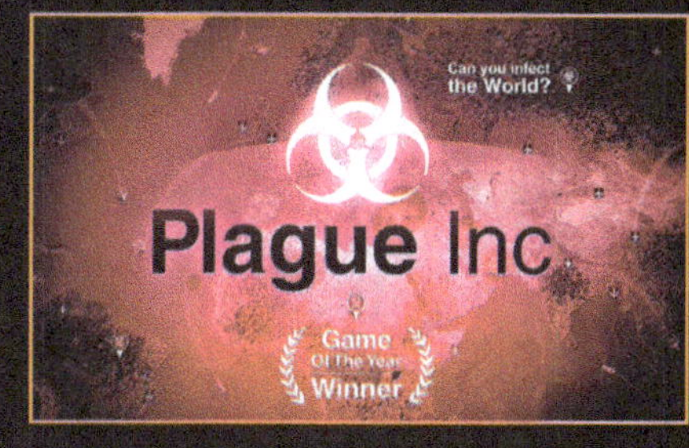

If you are like me, there has been a multitude of times you have sat on your couch secretly wishing you could wipe out the entire world with some abominable disease. Now you can, thanks to brains at Ndemic Creations. Plague is a game that has been duplicated many times, but never equaled. There is a reason it has been one of the top selling apps for the past couple of years. Available on PC, Mac, Android, and iOS, Plague is the game many people turn to when they have some free time on their hands, or just have an hour to kill. You will find me quite often with my iPad on my lap, game open, and screaming, "I am the Fungus King!" (you can insert strange looks from my wife here).

Plague is much more than a sadistically pleasing end of the world game. It is extremely complex and strategic. You begin with one person infected… patient zero, in the country of your choice. From there, you need to evolve your organism to infect the world, and ultimately bring humanity to their day of reckoning. It's not so easy, especially when the world bands together to research a cure to fight you. The game becomes a race against time, and hopefully you have done enough to outpace modern science. I also hope you have managed to infect Greenland before they shut down their seaport…it's a real challenge to infect every country.

To begin, you are given a simple bacteria, but other diseases are relatively easy to unlock (if you have skill and patience). Next is the highly mutating Virus, which seems to throw you curve balls when you least expect it. Next is the Fungus, my particular favorite. Mold and yeast are my allies. Parasite comes next, and oh what fun that is. Next is Prion, Nano-Virus, and finally…a highly lethal Bio-Weapon. All have different abilities, and different strategies are needed to win the game. What works for bacteria, will not work for Nano-Virus, or at least not as well. This game makes you constantly think and adjust.

Besides the standard diseases, Plague gives you even more to keep you occupied. First, there are the scenarios. Want to bring back the Black Death and finish the job it started in the fourteenth century? Yes, Yersenia Pestis is playable. You must evolve this ancient global killer to take on modern medicine, and wipe out the human race. What happens if the Earth meets another Ice Age? This is another playable scenario you must adapt to. There are tons.

If you are starting to think this is a game you might want to download, just wait. It gets better. There are the special plague types. First is the Neurax Worm. This is an organism that gets into the host's brain and can control their actions. Do you want to destroy humanity, or enslave them? That is an option. Next, is the Simian Flu. It is your job to bring about the virtual Planet of the Apes. Finally, there is ultimately pleasing Necroa Virus. With this little bad boy, you can unleash the Zombie Apocalypse.

Plague is not just your standard game. There is so much to do, so much to complete, and so much to keep this game from getting boring. You can spend all night destroying humanity, or kill a half hour while you are waiting for your car's oil to be changed. There are regular updates and more always being added. It keeps the game fresh. There are also four different difficulties, which the more challenging ones have a tendency to humble even the most able of mad scientists. Can you adapt? Are you strategic enough? Find out, and download the extremely enjoyable game, Plague.

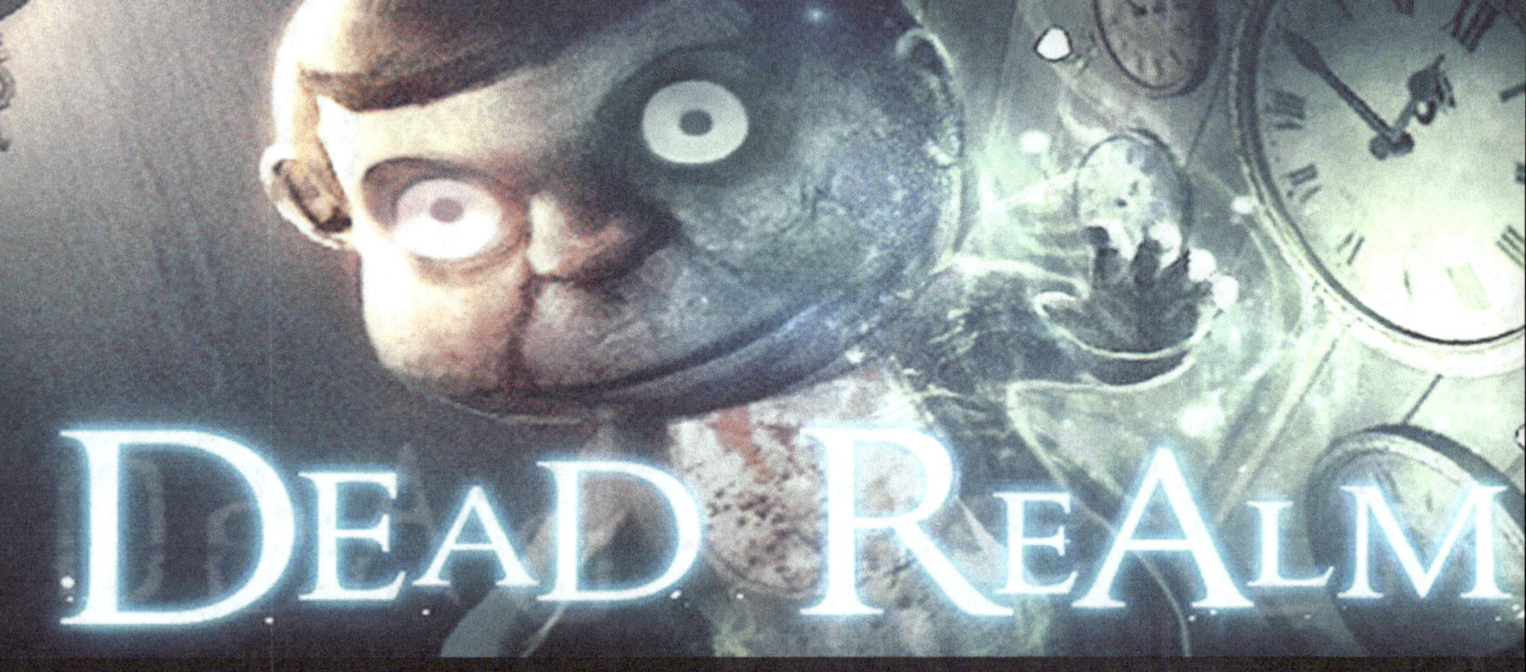

By Bella Blitz

"Ghosts prey on the living inside the haunted mansion of a long dead electricity tycoon. Dead Realm is a creepy, multiplayer action game with beautiful, immersive environments. You can play as either a Ghost or a Human character and work with your friends to run, hide, survive... or die."

The idea of adult hide and seek has always appealed to me. Couple that with horror elements like; wolves, creepy babies, and a soundtrack that makes the hair on your arm stand up, and I'm pretty much in like Flynn. This is the world of Dead Realm, a multiplayer horror game that stands out on it's own without any combat, collecting, or grinding; just hiding, fleeing - and if you're the ghost - seeking.

Dead Realm's game play breaks down as easily as the children's game it's based on. There are two gameplay modes: Bounty and Seek and Reap. At the beginning of any turn/mode there is a ghost (the seeker) and the humans (the hiders). In Bounty mode the humans must collect pocket watches. In Seek and Reap mode the humans must survive. The ghosts - they just want to find the humans and suck out their souls. As the humans are hunted and turned into soul sucking ghosts, they continue the gameplay, picking off the remainder of the surviving team, one by one.

Doesn't that just sound dreamy... err... nightmarish?

What is really going to make your gameplay for Dead Realm are the other people playing. Having lookouts and keeping each other company in the face of the creepy dead things will definitely be a perk. While the game might not keep you entertained for days and hours on end, it'll be enough to straighten your spine and engage you in some horror survival with the like-minded.

Plus, there's always the possibility of witnessing a final survivor lose their mind and taunt the ghosts, only to be sucked away to their doom. Good times.

Dead Realm was developed by Section Studios and is available on Steam.

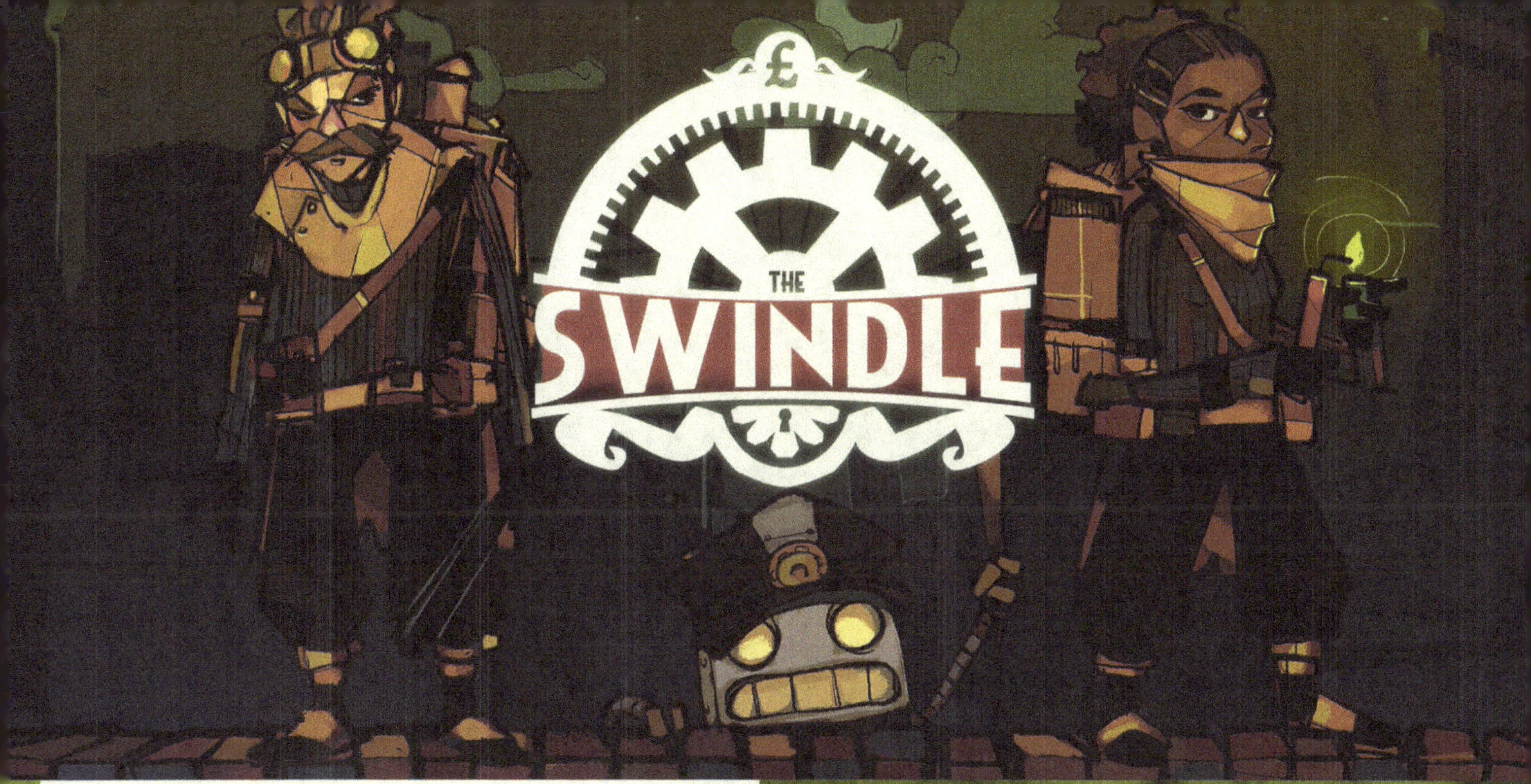

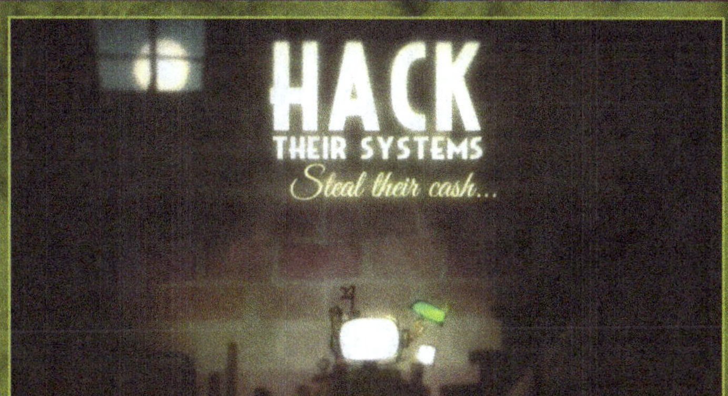

By Bella Blitz

"The Swindle is a steampunk cybercrime caper about breaking into buildings, hacking their systems, stealing all their cash, and quickly running away again before the police show up."

And, who doesn't like that, right? Right!

So, let me tell you what's more to enjoy: The Swindle isn't so much a stealth game - it doesn't care how loud or messy you are - as it is an RPG-like game. With clearly marked no-go zones and clearly defined level goals, it's easy to push yourself a bit too far and fall perilously to your permadeath.

What do you do with all that loot that you're looting? Why, you spend it on more upgrades, of course. As with any RPG-like game, you get to deck out your character skills, tools, and all manner technological atrocities. These upgrades will you help you take on bigger buildings - with tougher guard-bots - to reap the bigger benefit: more cash. Unlike most RPG-like games, you get to do all of this from the safety of your own outer space aircraft - albeit a rickety outer space aircraft.

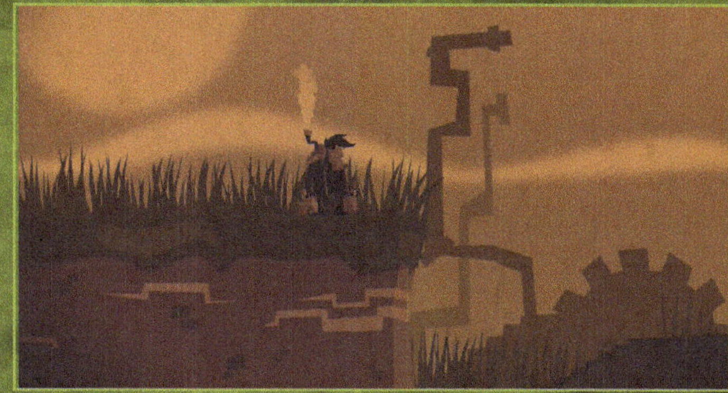

The icing on this heist cake is the wonderfully steampunk portrayal of London. Illustrator Michael Firman did a spectacular job of creating a landscape that is equal parts functional and collapsible. Paired with the adrenaline-inducing music of composer Tobey Evans, The Swindle may just have you capering on the edge of your seats.

The Swindle was developed by Size Five and is available on Steam, PS3, PS4, PSVita, XBoxOne, and WiiU.

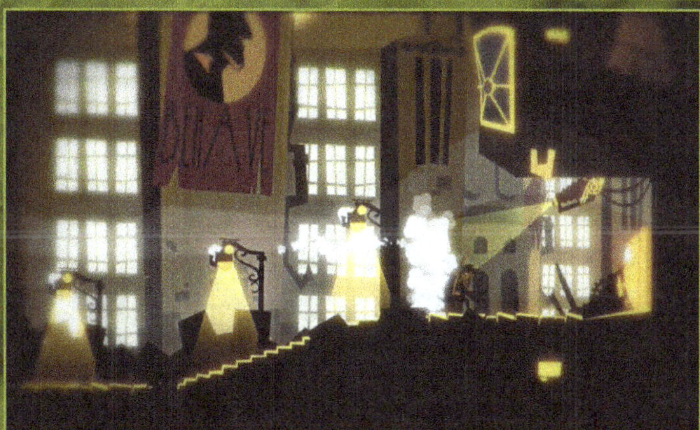

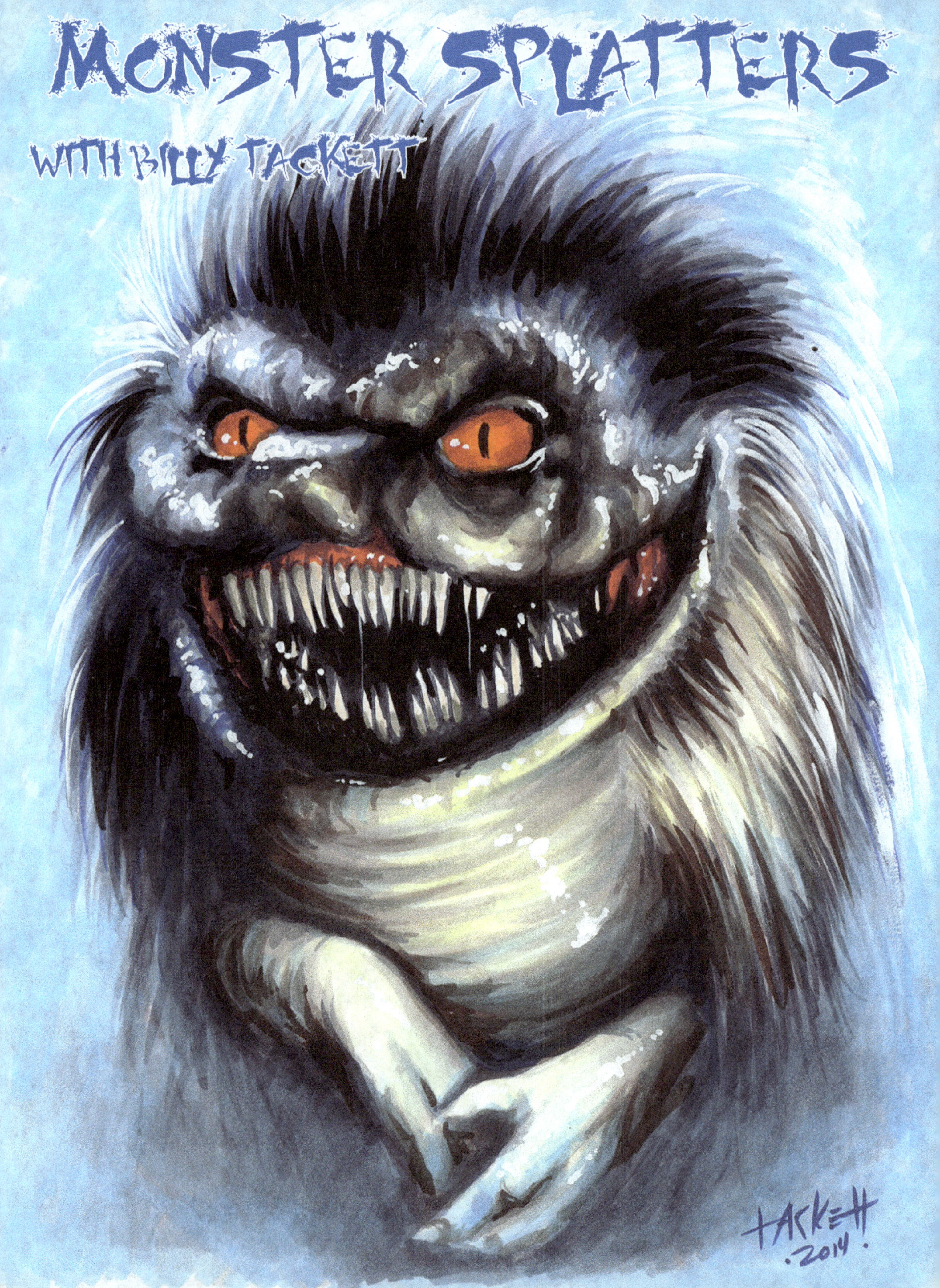

MONSTER SPLATTERS
WITH BILLY TACKETT
TACKETT 2014

By Zahara

Billy Tackett (Florence, Kentucky) has been creating pop culture mayhem and hellish images for over 25 years. He's best known for his zombie art, but this prolific artist has created a varied volume of work, including over 300 pieces for book/album covers, illustrations, and more. He and his wife renovated the former Florence Hotel into an art studio and gallery, where visitors can watch Billy's creations come to life.

[Zahara] *I always see your Daily Arting posts on Facebook. How do you keep coming up with ideas for sketching/painting every day?*

[Billy Tackett] The idea behind my Daily Arting was multi-purpose: For one, I didn't feel as though I was being as productive as I wanted to be; that my work habits could be tighter, so I came up with the idea to do one piece a day. The bonus was that I would focus on some things that I felt were weak points in my skills. Also, I had decided to use the sketch markers which were new to me, so I got some good practice there. Looking back over my body of work, I started out using heavy black lines, and then gradually moved into some gray-scale with blending. And then gradually, I began to add color and developed a really cool watercolor effect with them. It's pretty amazing to see the transition.

I never realized how hard it could be coming up with a new picture every day... REALLY hard. At some point, I started coming up with a comic book character and then trying to come up with another pop culture reference to mash it up with. That was pretty fun. Unfortunately, this year I had to scale back the Daily Artings to just Artings. I wanted to do fewer pieces, but higher quality pieces.

I've used almost every media, from oils to charcoal and markers. My favorite is whatever I'm currently focused on. Right now, that's my markers and latex splatter art.

[Z] *Can you describe the first time you did a Splatter Art picture? I'm fascinated with that technique. Your painting of Hellraiser's Pinhead is even more terrifying and gory as Splatter Art!*

[BT] For those who don't know, my splatter pieces are created by dipping my finger in paint and flicking it onto the canvas. It's very controlled and pretty precise.

About 10 years ago, I was doing a lot of graphic design work. If I ever needed a design element, I would try to make it myself. Like if I needed a brush stroke, I would grab a brush and paint and get to swiping until I had what I needed. At some point, I needed a splat and couldn't get what I wanted. I went through different paints and various methods of splattering them when I realized some of them looked like flowers. So I started with some really abstract looking flowers. I would create a few pieces a year, but I never really got into it. My wife encouraged me to do more, but I was focused on the zombie art at the time. I began to feel I wasn't growing artistically through the oil paint and finally took my wife's advice. Three years ago, I focused on the splatter stuff. I really began to push the medium and see what I could do with it. As I tell people all the time, I'm re-inspired! Moral of the story: Always be willing to try new stuff and listen to your wife!

[Z] *What's been your favorite commissioned piece or collaborative effort?*

[BT] Bicycle Playing Cards commissioned me to design a deck for them. Everything was created in oils, scanned and designed in the computer. It was a lot of work, but really fun. It was probably some of the last zombie pieces I created and definitely the most fun. (http://billytackett.com/index/bicycle-playing-card/)
And I've created nearly 300 book covers, illustrations, etc. I worked mostly in small press and independent publishers. I started doing the convention circuit years ago, trying to drum up more business, and kind of fell into doing the zombie stuff after that proved pretty popular. I still do a covers on occasion, but most of my commissions are for private collectors, corporate events, and galleries. Not much commercial stuff, and I'm OK with that. Although, I have a goal to get some of my splatter stuff on the cover of a "mainstream" comic book.

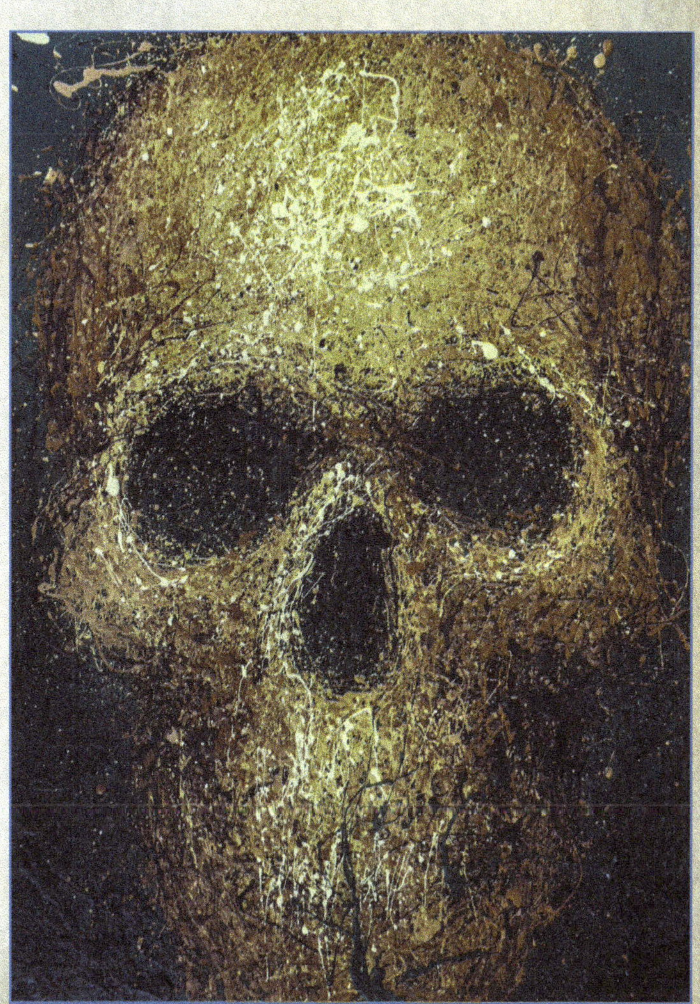

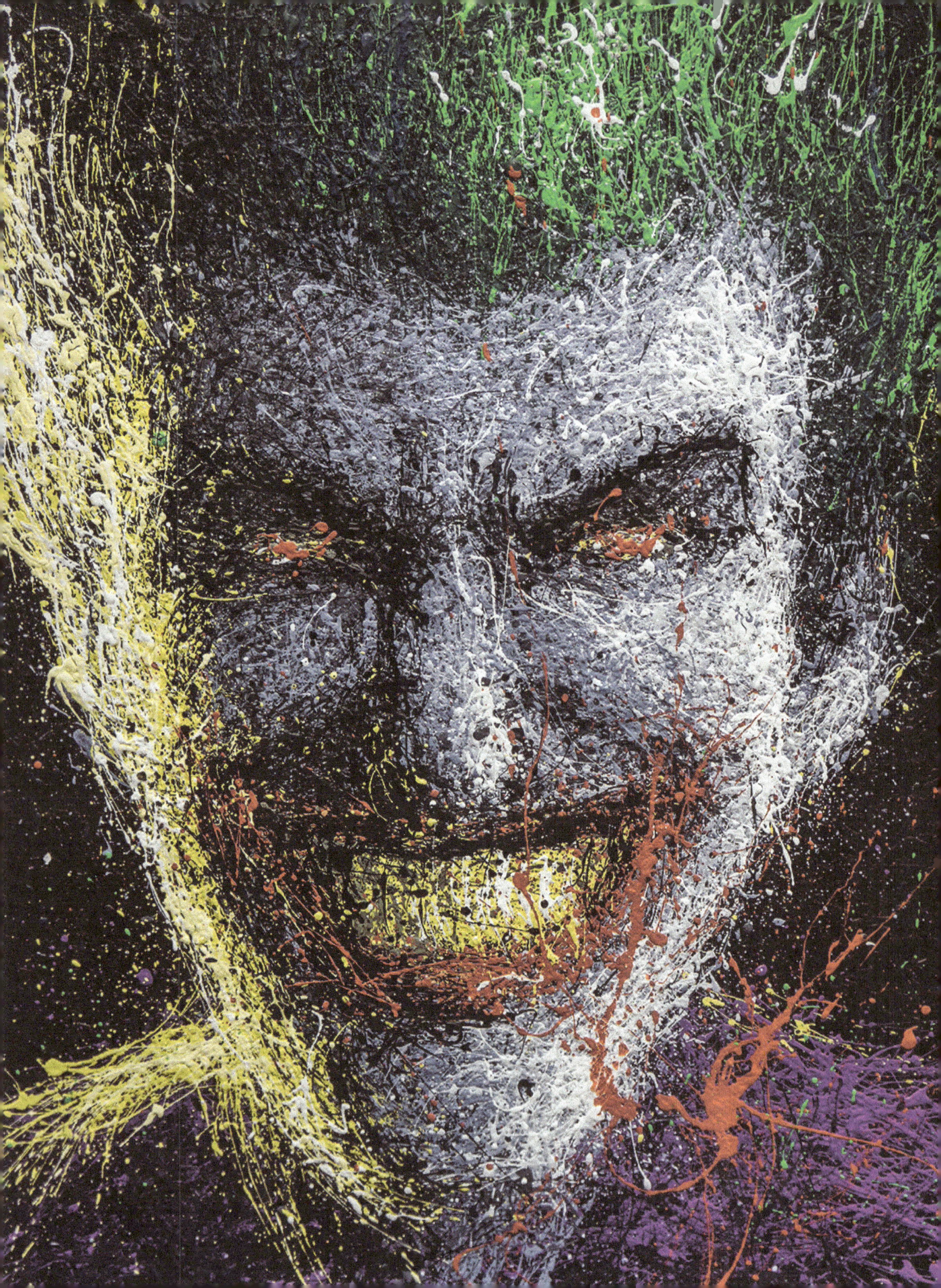

[Z] *That would be amazing! One thing I especially enjoy is the twist in many of your pieces, such as "Jailhouse Spock" and "Aqua-Jaws". What's been the most popular of your works?*

[BT] The zombie stuff was definitely hot for a while, and my Rosie the Riveter zombie was by far the most popular of those pieces. Now, I'm seeing something new start to sell… and that's my drawings of cars. All my life, I've loved cool cars and have wanted to get back into drawing them. My Daily Arting gave me that chance. I've been doing cars from pop culture. For instance, the truck from Sanford & Son, Ecto-1 from Ghostbusters and the Bluesmobile from the Blues Brothers. I've been working on the cars from the Mad Max movies, and by far, the best selling stuff has been the ones from the original movie.

[Z] *Any special upcoming projects you can share with us?*

[BT] I have a solo gallery exhibition this October here in Cincinnati, which will be monster-themed, so people can expect to see some cool horror-themed splatter art from that. Details will be posted on my website as they are confirmed. I'm also focused on publishing volume 2 of my Dead, White, & Blue comic. Other than that, it's pretty much business as usual. I pass along any new project info on my Facebook page (www.facebook.com/billytackettstudios).

And my fall/winter schedule is booking up pretty quickly! I've been booking more and more private and corporate events lately. I always keep my appearance schedule listed on my website (http://www.billytackett.com/), and I'm also here at my Florence, KY studio, which is open to the public.

Anyone interested in following my art as it is created is welcome to subscribe as a patron. For as little as $1 per month, patrons are able to see ALL new art I create a full 30 days before anyone else, giving them first dibs on their favorite pieces. My Patreon site is patreon.com/billytackett.

[Z] *Obviously, you're very passionate about your art. What's the most challenging aspect of being a full-time artist? What advice can you offer young artists who want to do this kind of work for a living?*

[BT] Making money is the biggest challenge! I'm very lucky in that I have a wife who not only is very supportive, but she has a head for business. She has been my manager since the beginning. Most artists don't have my wife and the art schools won't teach artists how to make money. For some reason, a stigma has been put on making money with ones art, and I don't get it. Art was a trade all the way up until the late 1800s, and then it became cool to be a starving artist. Screw that! I can't buy my comic books and beer if I'm not making money! Oh, and I also have a family to feed and a mortgage to pay…

If you're going to do this for a living, the first thing is to practice your craft. Don't be afraid to suck, because you can't improve without sucking first. Also, grow a thick skin because there are people who have no problem telling you that you suck. Learn to get over it. Then approach it as a business, like I mentioned earlier. The best way to be professional, is to act professional. Be prepared to start out doing things you may not enjoy. That's all part of it, and we all have to do it. Be prepared to work long hours for little money. And be prepared to be in it for the long haul, because it takes time, but the longer you do it, the greater your chances of being successful.

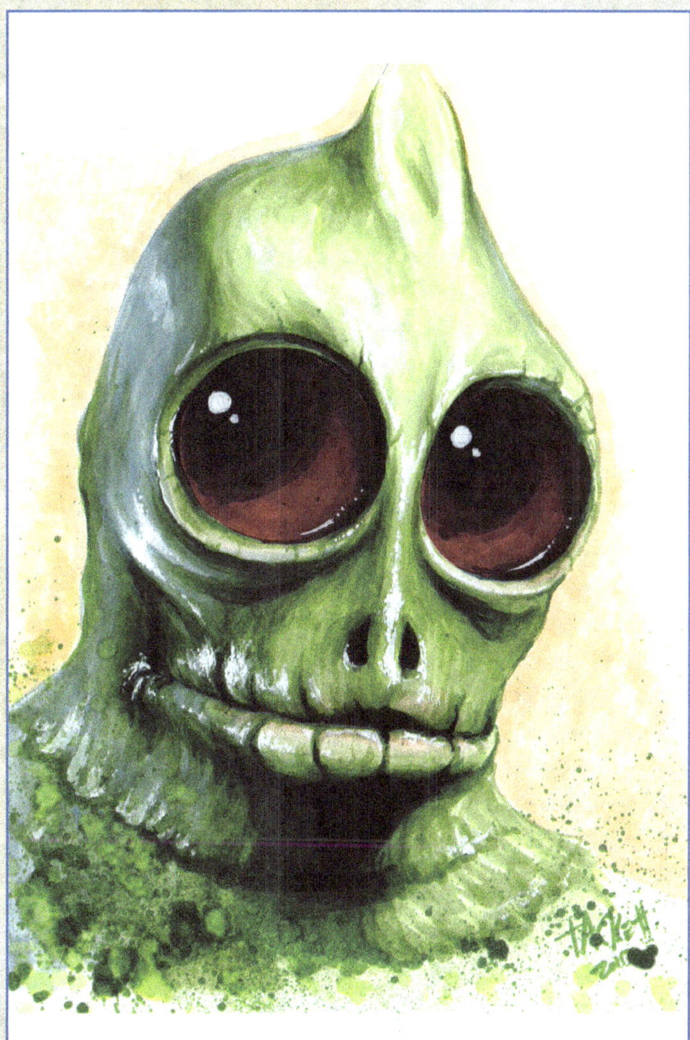

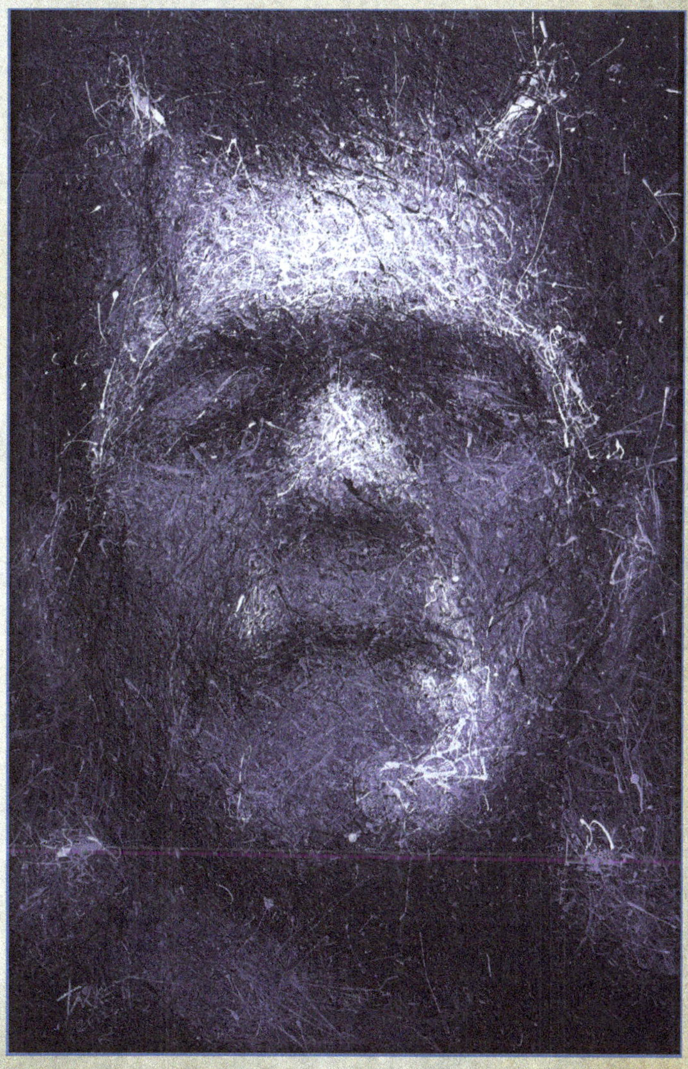

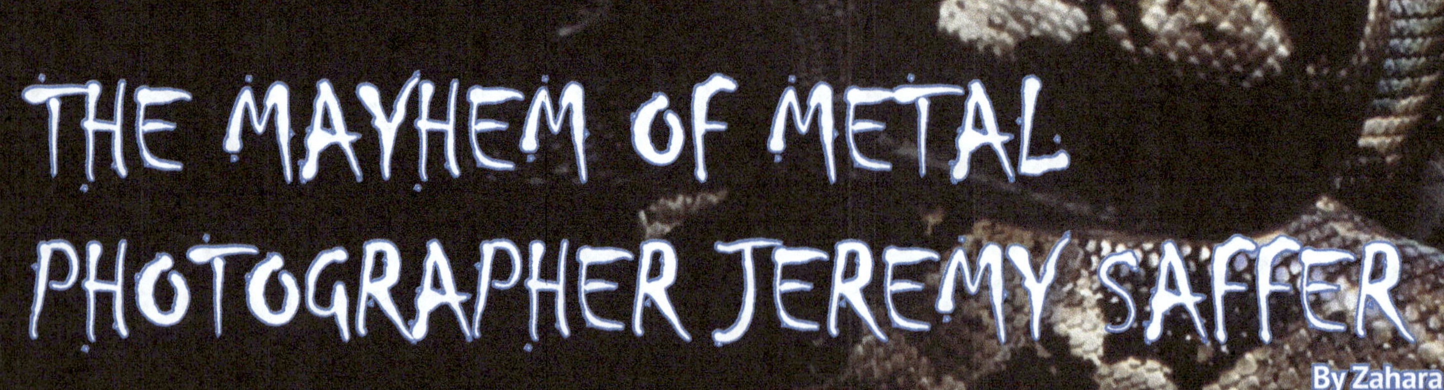
THE MAYHEM OF METAL
PHOTOGRAPHER JEREMY SAFFER
By Zahara

His photographs have graced the covers of Outburn, Inferno, and Xpressions. And his Corpse Paint project blends gorgeous nudes, featuring each model's own designs. Jeremy Saffer's website is filled with intense imagery, from the rock majesty of Alice Cooper to the haunting DVD cover for "Plague Town". Despite frequent travels and mingling with superstars, he remains down-to-earth, with a self-deprecating sense of humor. Not one to rest on his laurels, he focuses on his work, meeting new heroes every year, and working to bring his twisted visions to life.

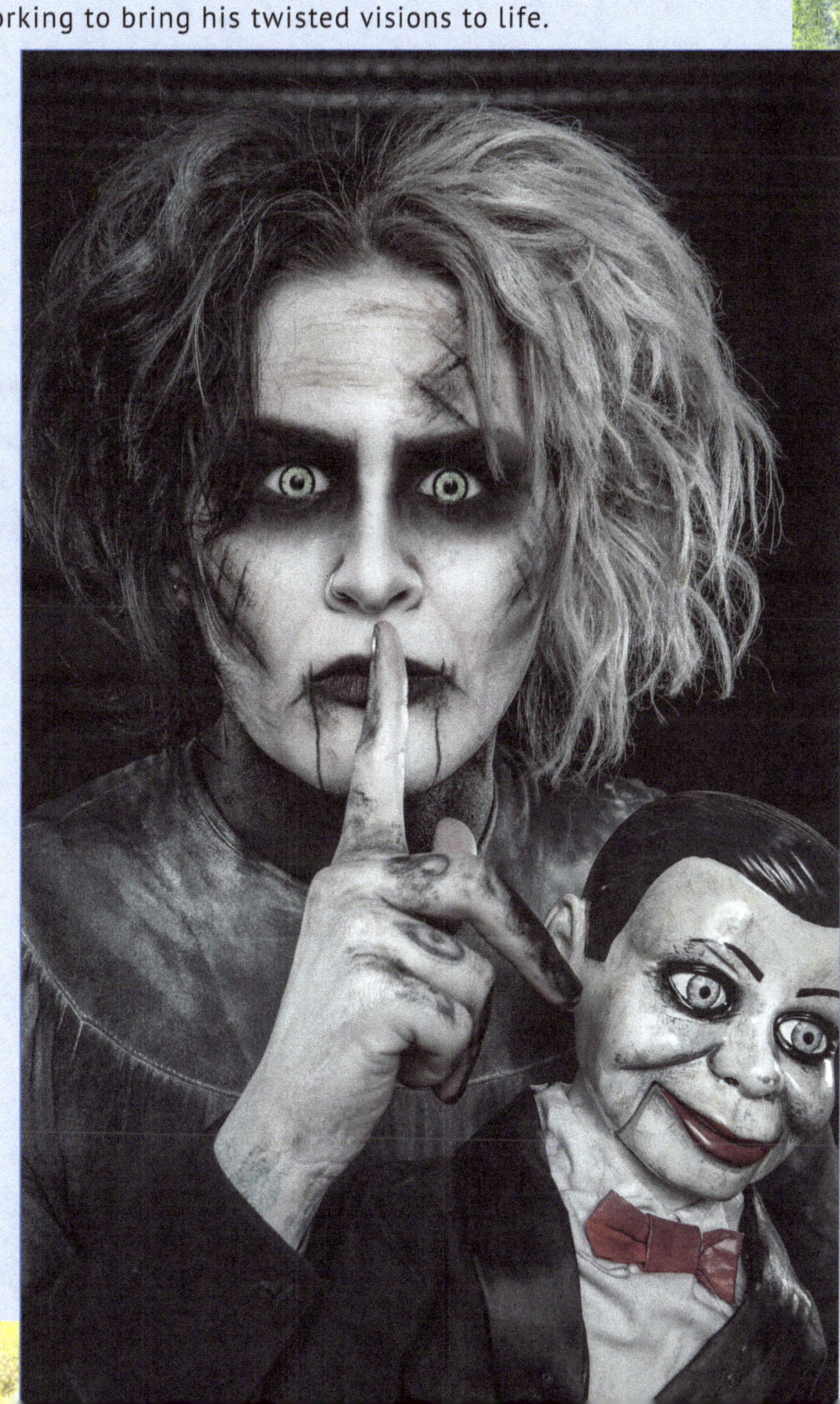

The concepts and characters in Saffer's photographs are surreal, intriguing and frightening. But Jeremy doesn't necessarily drive every shoot by himself. He often enjoys working with his subjects to co-create photographic works of art. "The majority of them are collaborative. I will come up with an idea and bounce it off the artist, who will put their spin on it. Other times, an artist will come to me with an idea. The best shoots are always the collaborative ones, because everyone worked to create it, and everyone is happy with the outcome (the whole point of working together)."

Jeremy has photographed some of the most recognizable faces in rock and metal. Yet he's very relaxed and not one to gloat about his accomplishments. When asked about any moments where he felt he "had arrived" as a photographer, his answer was completely in line with his work ethic. "I'm not there yet, and even if I was, I would never let myself get into that sort of mentality. I have a lot to learn and accomplish in my career. I never want to be content to the point where I stop trying to achieve my goals. That being said, I am very happy with my accomplishments thus far. Some are still so unreal to me, like the first magazine and album covers and getting to shoot people I've looked up to since I was young. Every time anything like that happens, I have my moment... then I get back to work."

Like most creative people, Saffer draws inspiration for his shots from everywhere, including movies, dreams, and life experiences. One of his covers looks like something right out of a black-and-white Victorian ghost story. It was the cover of the Halloween 2014 issue of X-pressions, featuring Ghost from Motionless in White. "Devin and I have an incredible working relationship and love for each other's art. Devin takes on a new character every tour (Charles Manson, Beetlejuice, Leatherface), and in 2014, he was doing the Dead Silence look with Billy the Puppet. We were doing a photo shoot with the band that day backstage at Tsongas Arena (Lowell, MA) and decided to do a cool Halloween-themed session for this cover at the same time. With Devin, all I have to do is know how to frame it up and light him properly, and he does the rest. There is no way to get a bad photo of him! He's a make up artist, model, and wardrobe stylist all in one." It's true that the majority of rock stars and actors already have a carefully cultivated visual presence. But it's the photographer's job to translate that physical presence to an image on a flat page, and Saffer excels in his efforts.

Typically, the biggest hurdles a photographer would need to clear would be related to continually creating new shots or staying busy enough to make a living from their photographs. He laughs that he's always catching up on editing. "I'm always behind!" But Jeremy faced a very personal challenge recently, which he has discussed on social media.

While in Los Angeles, Saffer woke up one day with blurry eyesight in his right eye. After a couple days of not being able to see very well, he went to a specialist. Although they didn't find any damage, he was still having problems, so he took a few days off from shoots and took a month off from editing. When he got home, additional tests were run, but they didn't turn up anything significant. Saffer was given glasses for editing, and sent on his way. While his right eye has not gotten worse, the damage is permanent, and he now wears glasses for editing tasks. "I kinda hit a depression, which made my work suffer. I've never felt anything like that before. One of the theories the LA doctor had was that it could be diabetes. So I told my eye doctor about the diabetes theory, and he quickly dismissed it." Eventually, Saffer was diagnosed with diabetes, which can rob the eyesight of those who have it. Jeremy knew he had to take immediate action. "I started dieting and working out, and now I walk five miles every day. Within a month, my diabetes was in complete remission, and I've lost almost 80 pounds since February. I am so stoked! I've never felt defeated and these daily walks really give me clarity. I'm back to working hard, and balancing my health with my work." Bouts of depression following a health crisis are very common, and it's encouraging to hear Jeremy say he's happy for the first time in a very long time.

There's an element of glamour surrounding band shoots, which makes it easy to overlook the immense amount of time and tasks it takes just to get one great shot published. There's no such thing as a typical day at work, and there are hours spent in preparation before a single picture is taken, not to mention the hours of editing afterwards. "An editorial feature/magazine (non-cover) shoot is usually set up where the band is playing, before they go onstage. I'll drive to the venue a couple of hours beforehand to scout locations. Then I plan out lighting, meet up with the tour manager, and usually do a 20-45 minute session with the band. Then they leave, and I stay to shoot the concert or head back to my studio. Some shoots can be as short as 30 seconds with bands like Behemoth, Slipknot, and Gwar, who have stage clothes/make-up on while they're heading to the stage."

Shoots for magazine covers can take even longer. "A bigger shoot sometimes happens over one or two days, shooting at the venue, studio, or both. I drive/fly to the location and scout a bit if necessary. Then we shoot for three to five hours a day (indoors, outdoors, etc.). But some cover shoots can get done in five minutes. Last year, I was flown to SDCC to do a cover shoot with Kirk Hammett (Metallica/ex-Exodus) and Gary Holt (Slayer/Exodus). I flew in to LA, drove to SD to set up, and waited around until about ten minutes before the doors opened to a secret show they were playing together. Then I did the shoot in three to five minutes... the doors opened as I was finishing! I stayed during the show, and then I flew home to Massachusetts." But there was no rest for Saffer after that particular shoot. He had Mayhem Fest the next morning and was busy snapping pictures of Korn, Ice-T, Asking Alexandria and 12 other bands!

Like many of our readers, I've also heard about Richard Prince and his unauthorized use of photographs ripped mostly from Instagram. Prince makes tiny modifications to the pictures and then sells them for a small fortune, without crediting the original photographer or getting a release from the model(s). It's shocking he's able to get away with this, considering it's very easy to track the original artists. Jeremy doesn't mince words on his opinion of all this. "Well, this is certainly a multifaceted (issue) with different

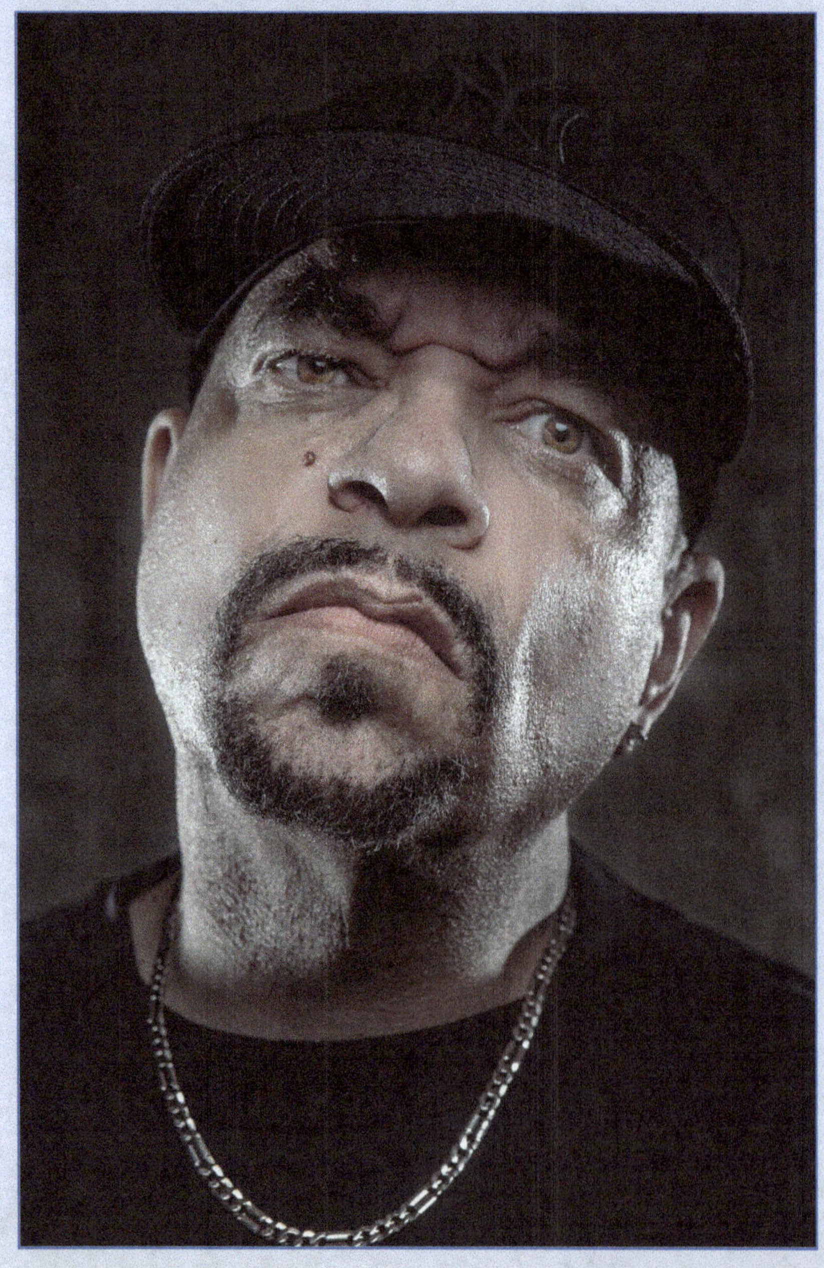

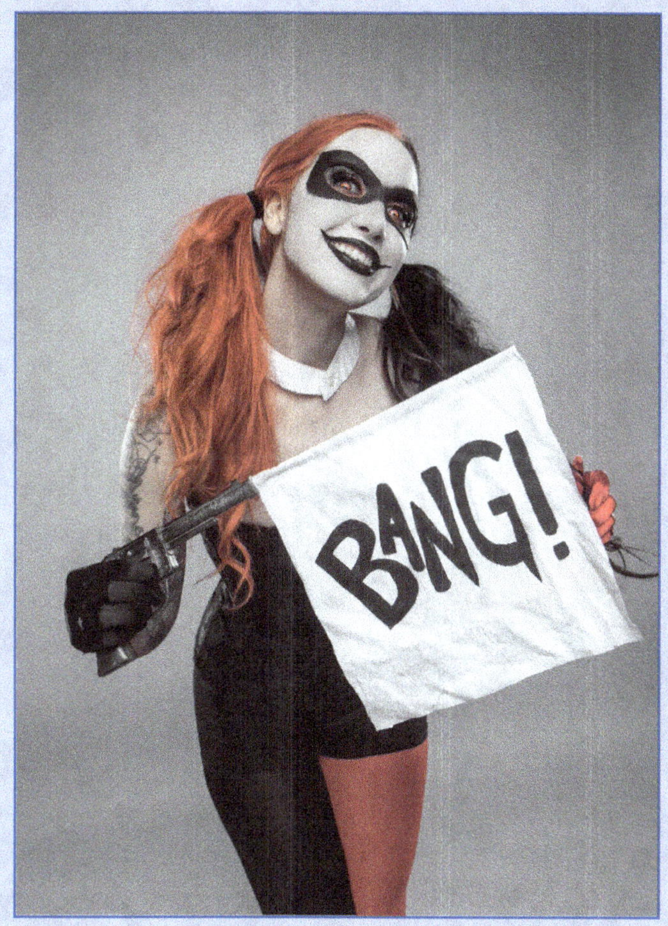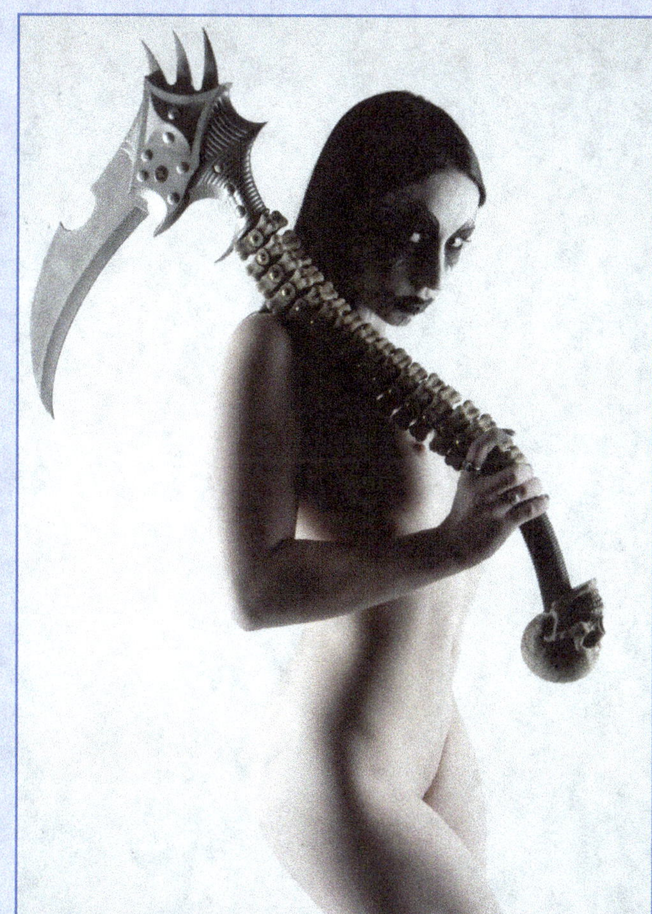

answers depending on the situation. Richard Prince is not an artist... only through legal loopholes can he exist in this capacity. And only through people who continue to buy his trash does he keep moving forward in his quest to offend every passionate, hard-working artist who knows of his misdeeds."

But the Prince episode (and many before it) has raised some serious problems for photographers who need to protect their work and income. "The DMCA (Digital Millennium Copyright Act) was a huge step forward. However, there are so many companies who give photographers a "work for hire/we own your copyright" contract, which strips it all away from us." And Jeremy, like most photographers, has experienced having his work used without his permission. "At first, I would freak out if someone posted an image of mine without my watermark on it, or if they cropped it out. I would get it deleted, and I would message that person. But I don't do that anymore. You'll see photographers go off the deep end over an artist posting a photo of themselves that the photographer shot (even WITH credit), saying something like, "You posted this on Instagram, so pay me or ELSE!" This is an amateur way to go about that. Being polite will get you much further."

Saffer says he's stopped freaking out about it, because it's going to happen and there's little anyone can do to stop it. It doesn't make any sense for photographers to stop posting images, as that's the most effective marketing tool they have. Much like musicians who find portions or all of their song being used without permission, there doesn't seem to be an easy answer or one that's completely fair to the creators, while still allowing for usage by fans.

Asking a photographer to choose their favorite assignment is like asking a parent to choose their favorite child. "I do love covers, no matter what or who they are. Some of my favorites have been those of artists I've looked up to since I was a kid. I call those "bucket-list photoshoots", and I'm fortunate to check a few off my list every year." And Jeremy hopes to keep adding to that list every year. When asked about people he'd love to photograph in the future, his choices are widespread. "Black Sabbath, Ozzy, Henry Rollins, Ron Perlman, James Hetfield, Die Antwoord, Elvira, Abbath, Madonna... the list could go on forever."

He'll be releasing his next book of band photography sometime in the next year, and he's just released his "Corpse Paint" book. But don't expect to see any paintings by Saffer in the future. "I have the artistic ability of Michael J. Fox and Ray Charles fighting over a paint brush on a roller coaster during an earthquake... at best. My handwriting alone has been compared to that of a second grader (and I believe that was a compliment at the time)." But he does have something in common with his rock star subjects. He was once a musician who played in metal bands (guitar, bass, drums, keyboards, etc.). After leaving Berkley School of Music to become a photographer, he left playing music behind. "I often say I put down my guitar and picked up a camera. I do play a few riffs here and there, but usually while on the couch watching TV."

Saffer has enjoyed many opportunities over the years and met many talented musicians and singers along the way. But as he said earlier, he still feels he has a lot to learn. And when it comes to wisdom already gained, he lists a few that may benefit future photographers.

1. Get the shot you need first (take the time to make sure your first shot is perfect).
2. Get it right "in camera" (to avoid extra editing).
3. Don't take business decisions personally.
4. If you ever get sick of what you love doing, take a break. Once you stop loving it, you'll stop doing your best work.

That last lesson is one we can all benefit from following.

Visit Jeremy at www.jeremysaffer.com or follow @jeremysaffer on Twitter and Instagram

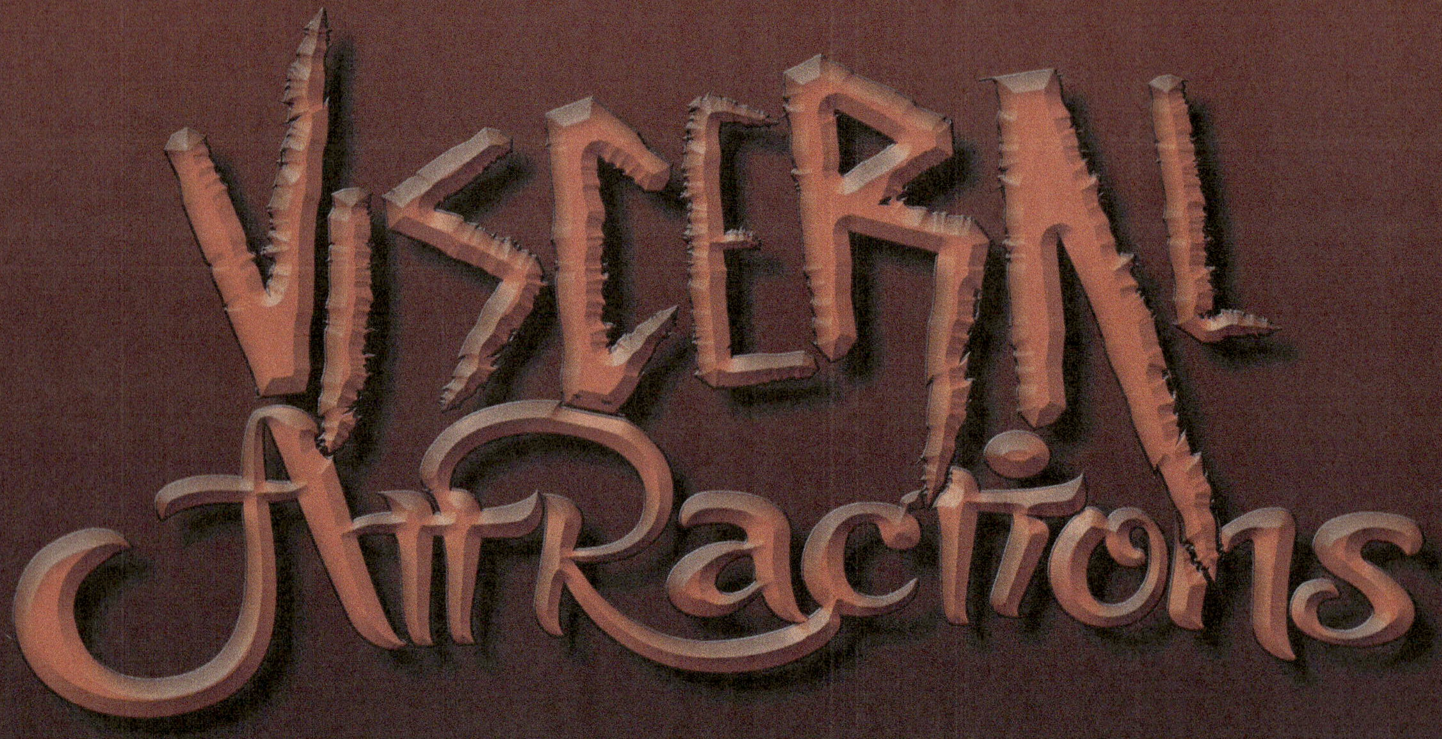

/VIS(ə)RəL/ -

coming from strong emotions; not pertaining to logic or reason

Visceral Attractions is Carpe Nocturne's official Fashion insert, spotlighting the most unique and decadent counter-culture fashion designs out there. Every quarterly issue features full page spreads of fashion, fetish and cosplay photographs to the theme of Goth, Fantasy, Sci-Fi and Steampunk.

THEMES:

Fall - Goth
Winter - Fantasy
Spring - Sci-Fi
Summer - Steampunk

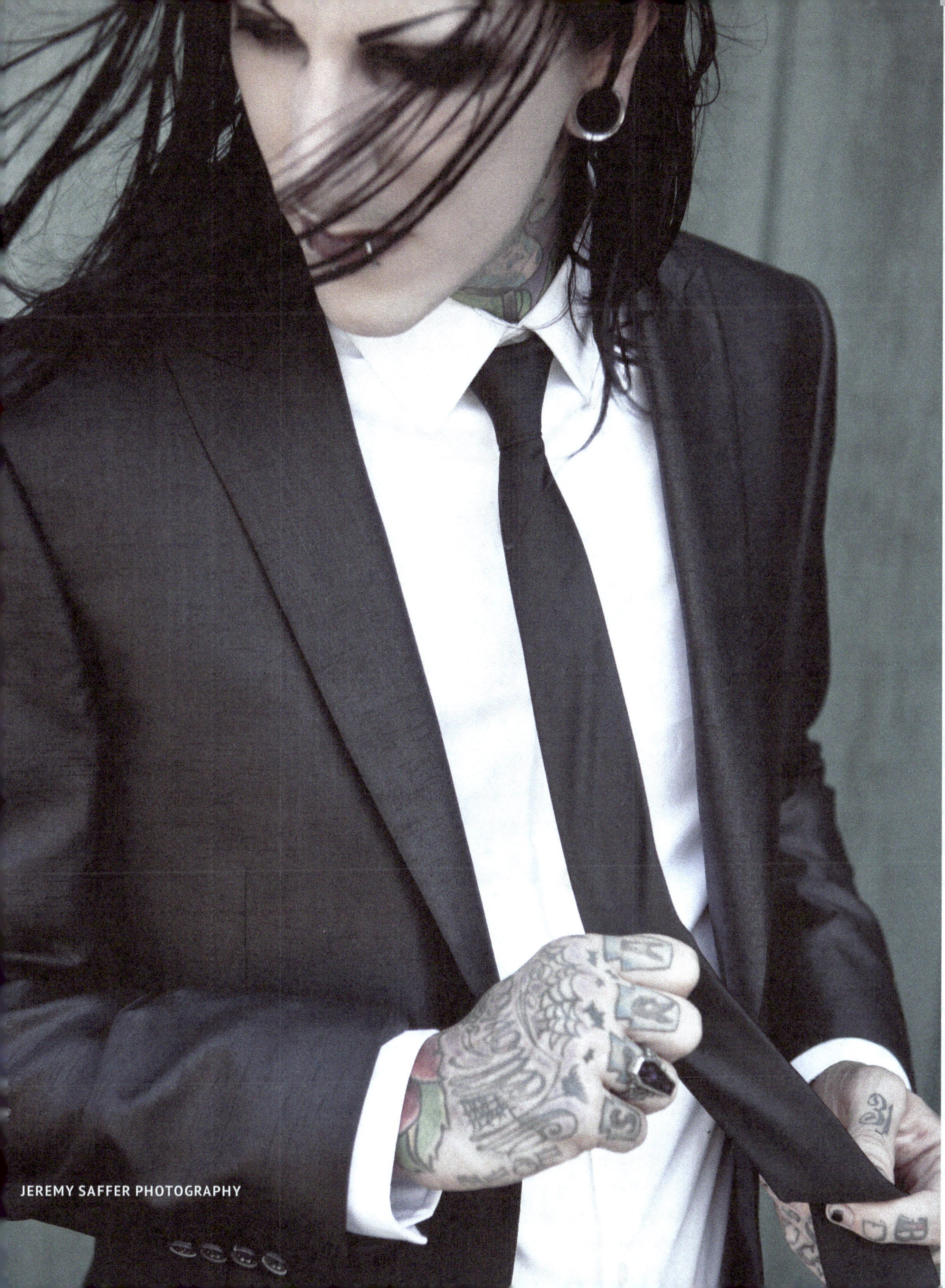

JEREMY SAFFER PHOTOGRAPHY

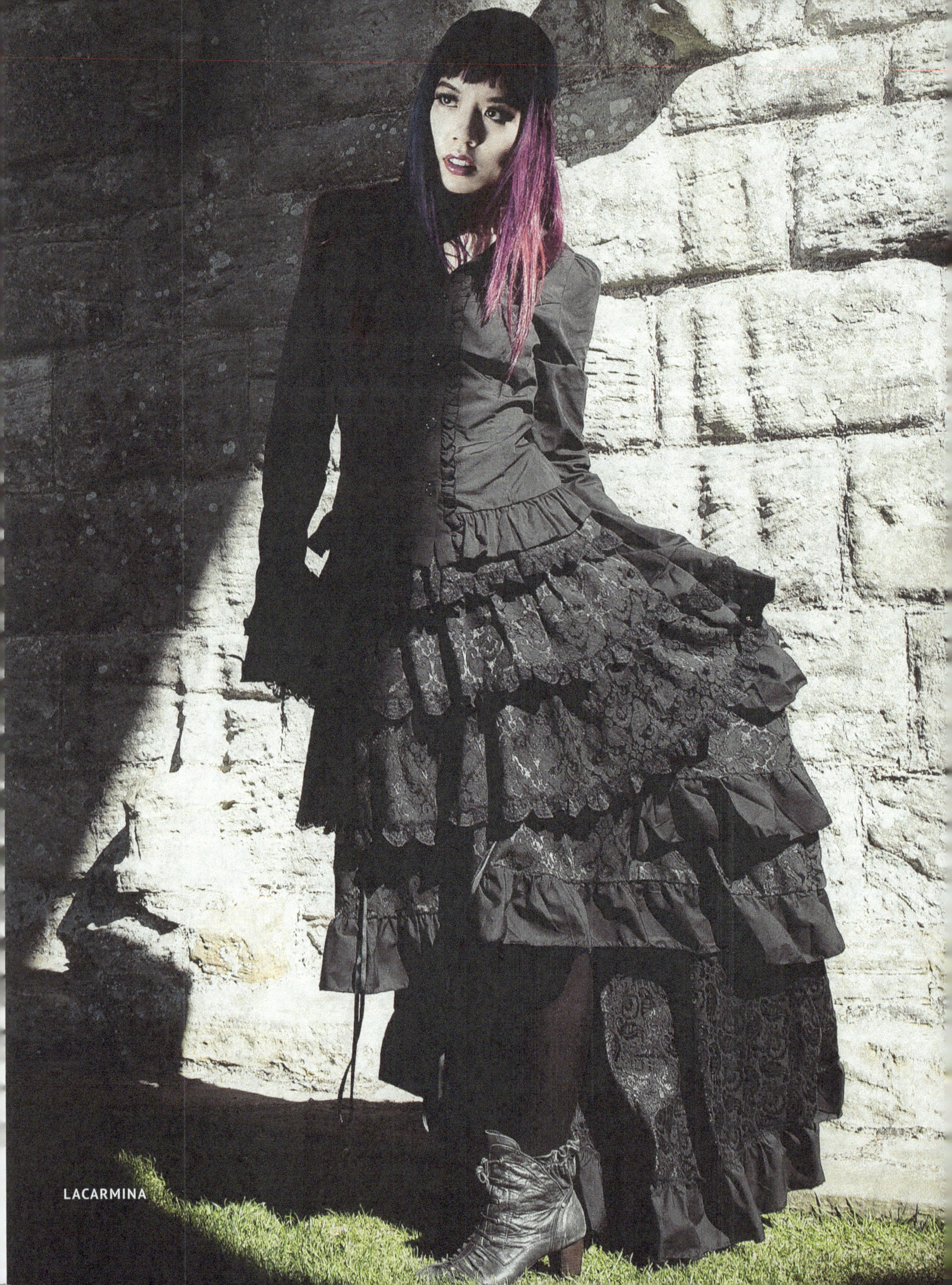
LACARMINA

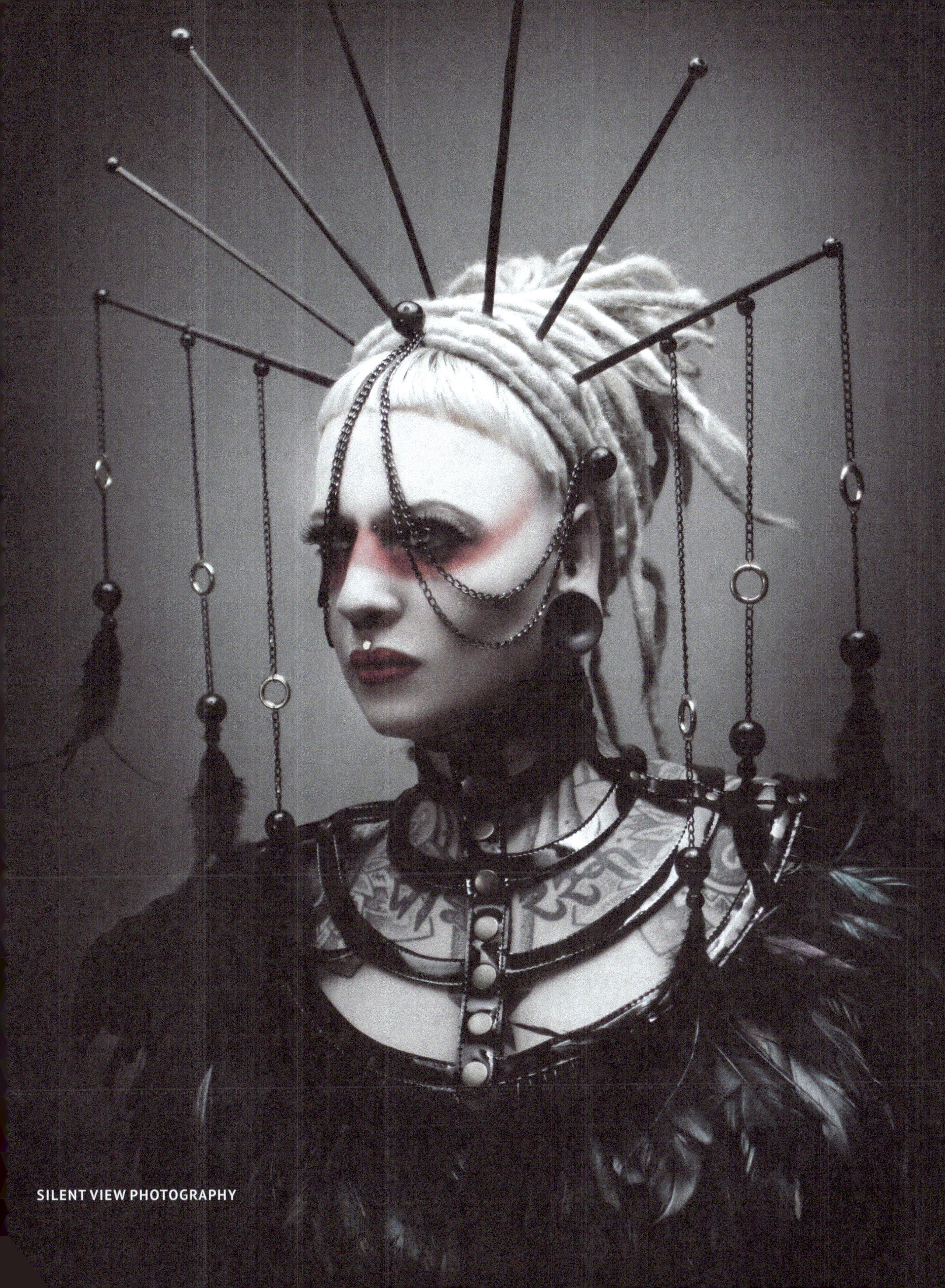

SILENT VIEW PHOTOGRAPHY

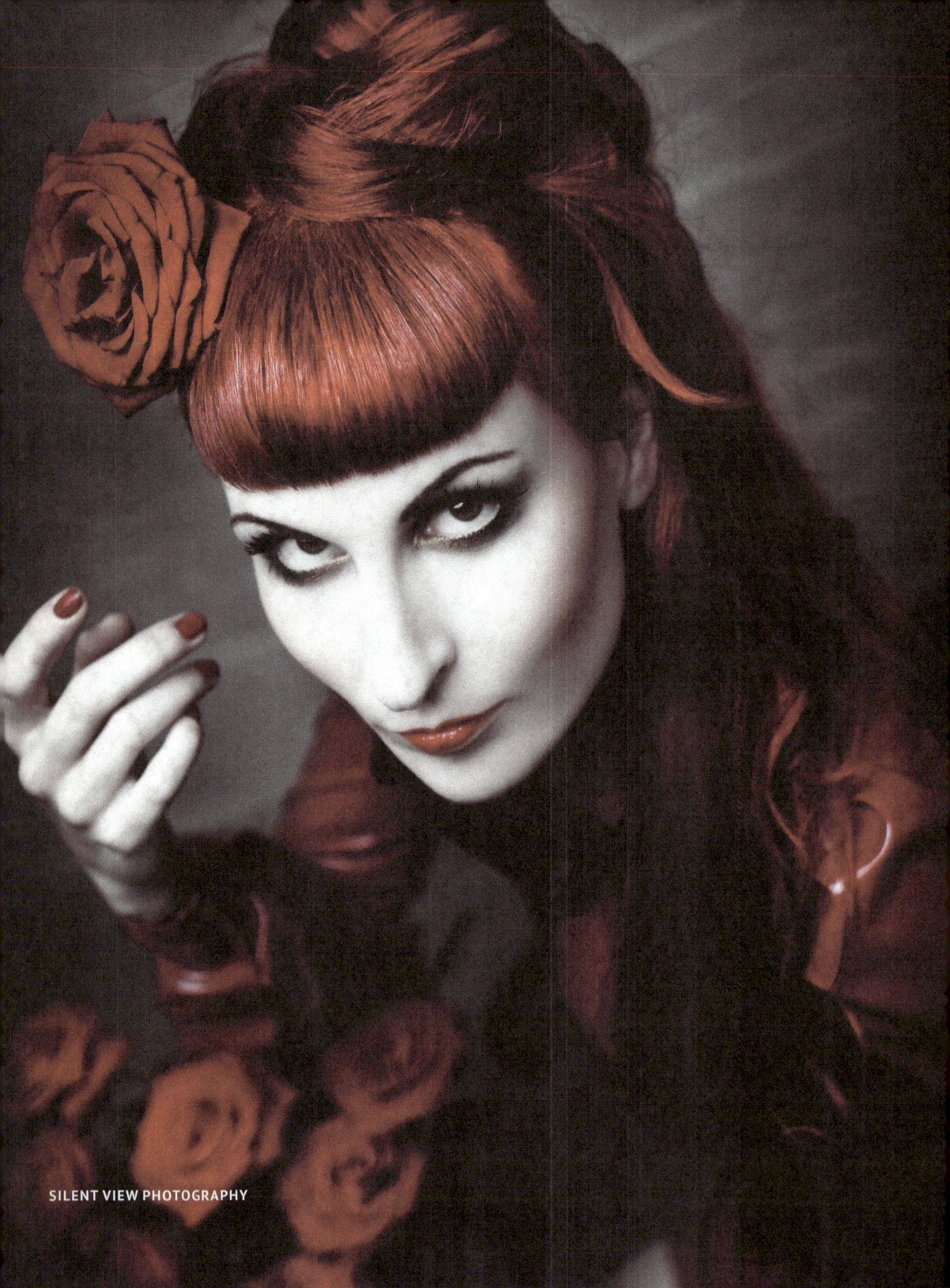
SILENT VIEW PHOTOGRAPHY

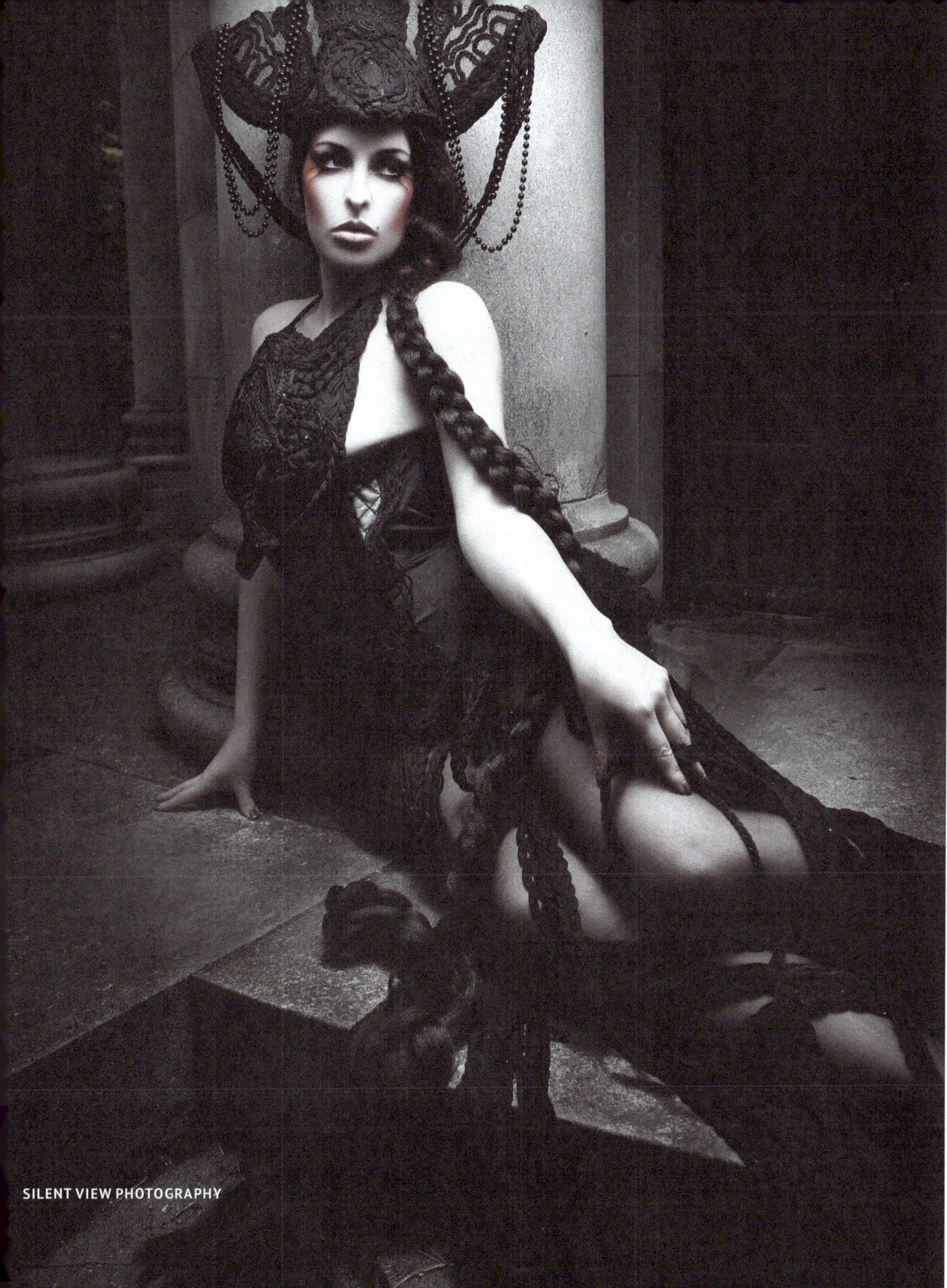

SILENT VIEW PHOTOGRAPHY

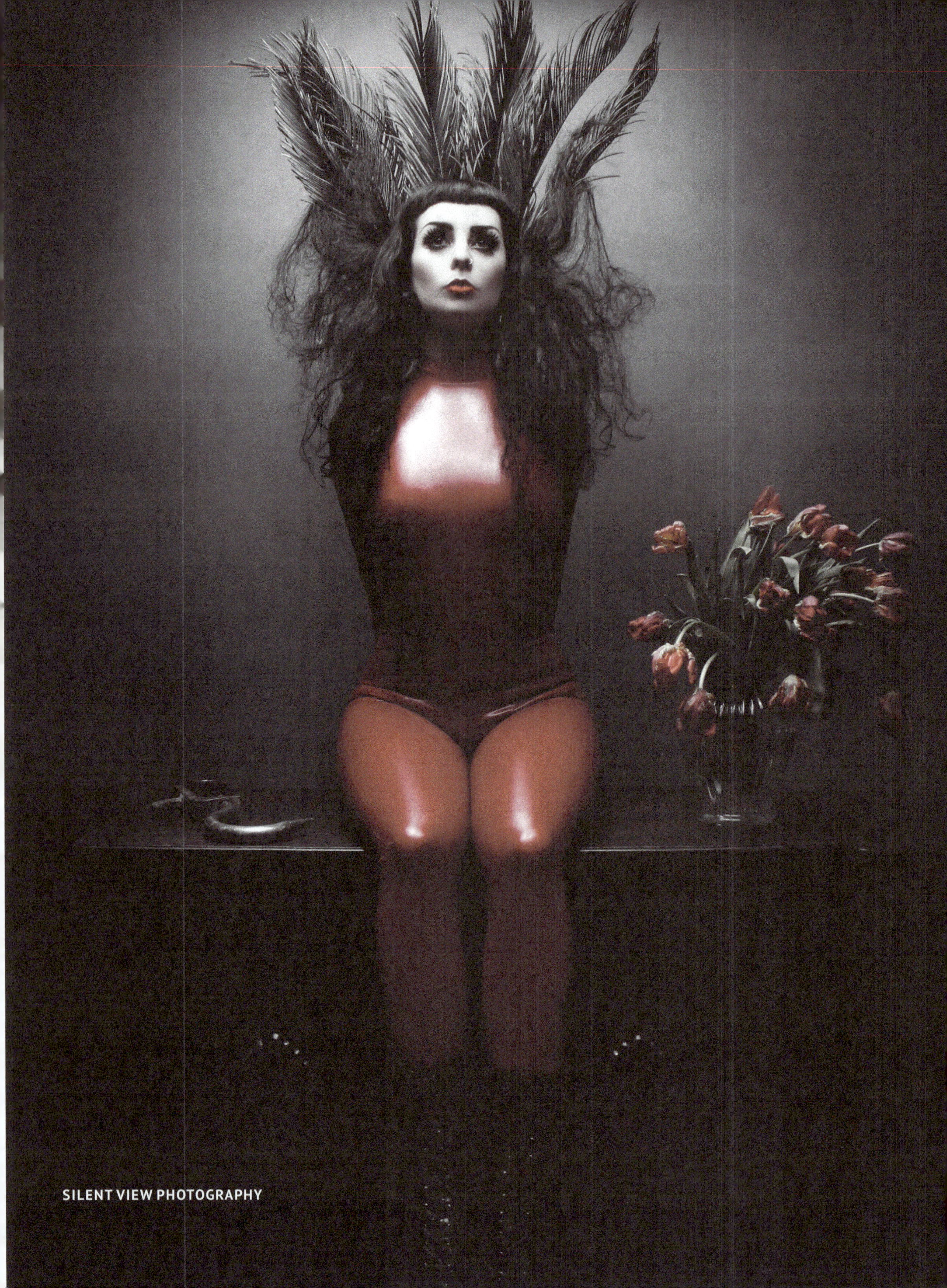

SILENT VIEW PHOTOGRAPHY

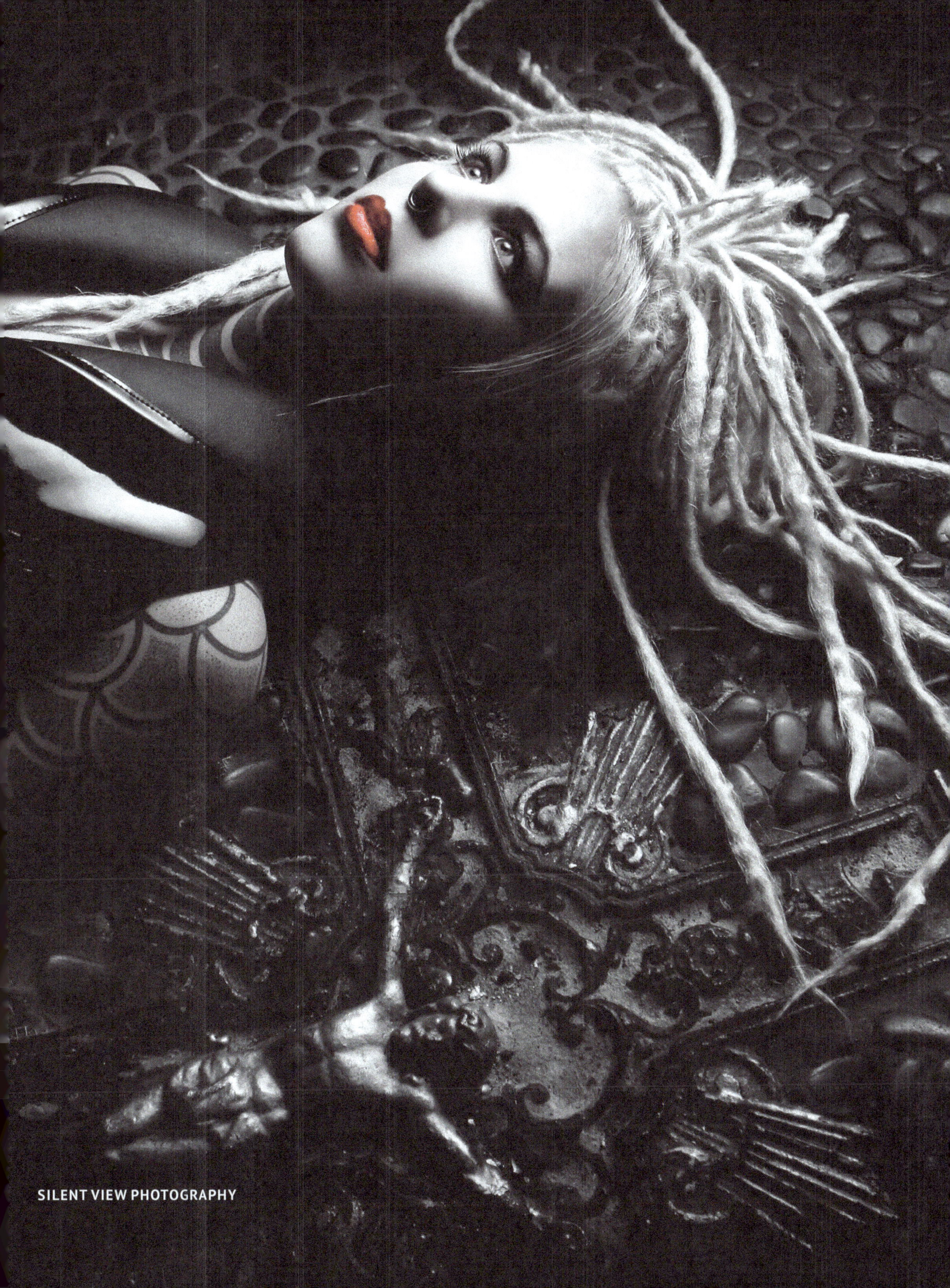
SILENT VIEW PHOTOGRAPHY

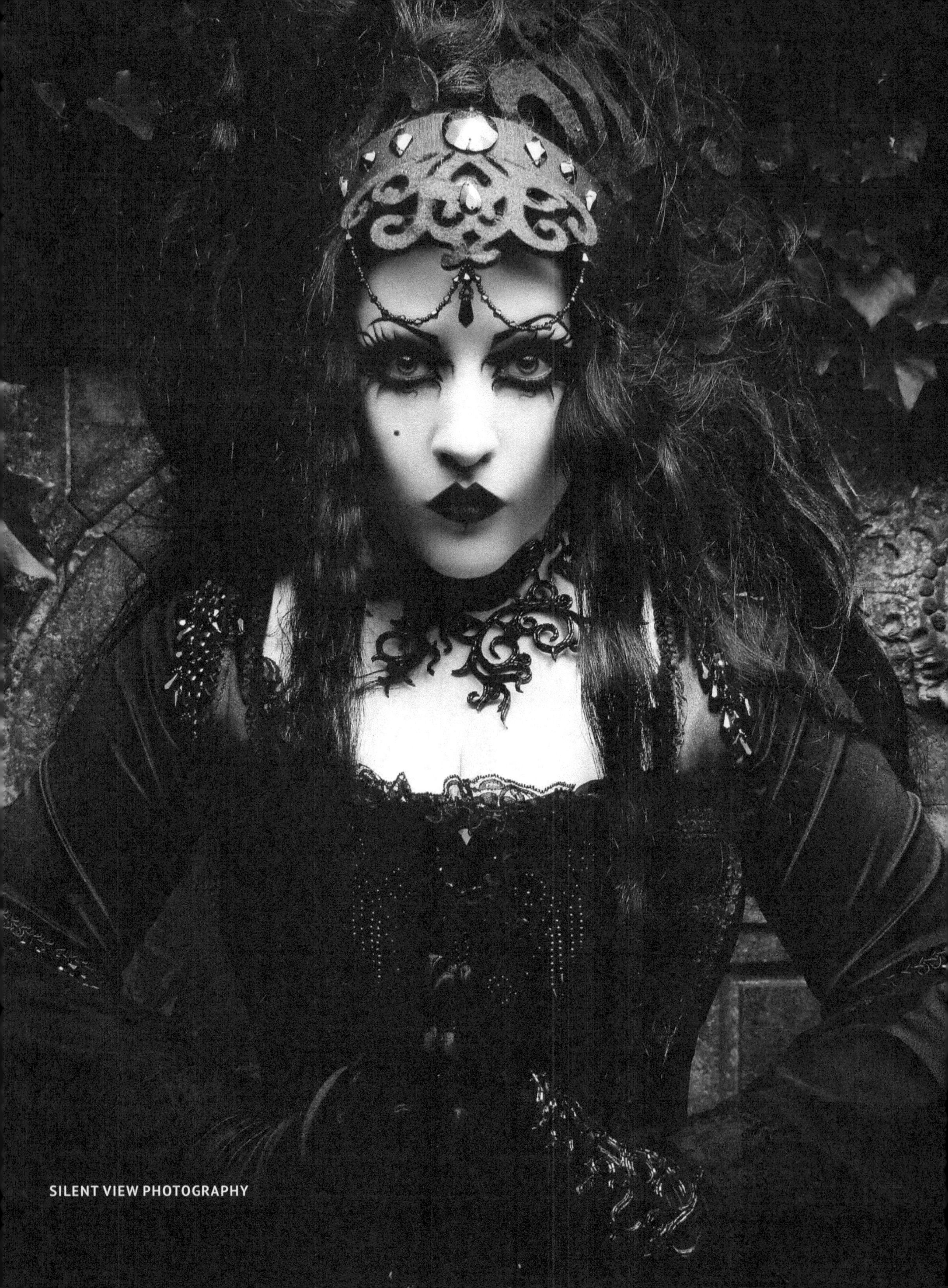
SILENT VIEW PHOTOGRAPHY

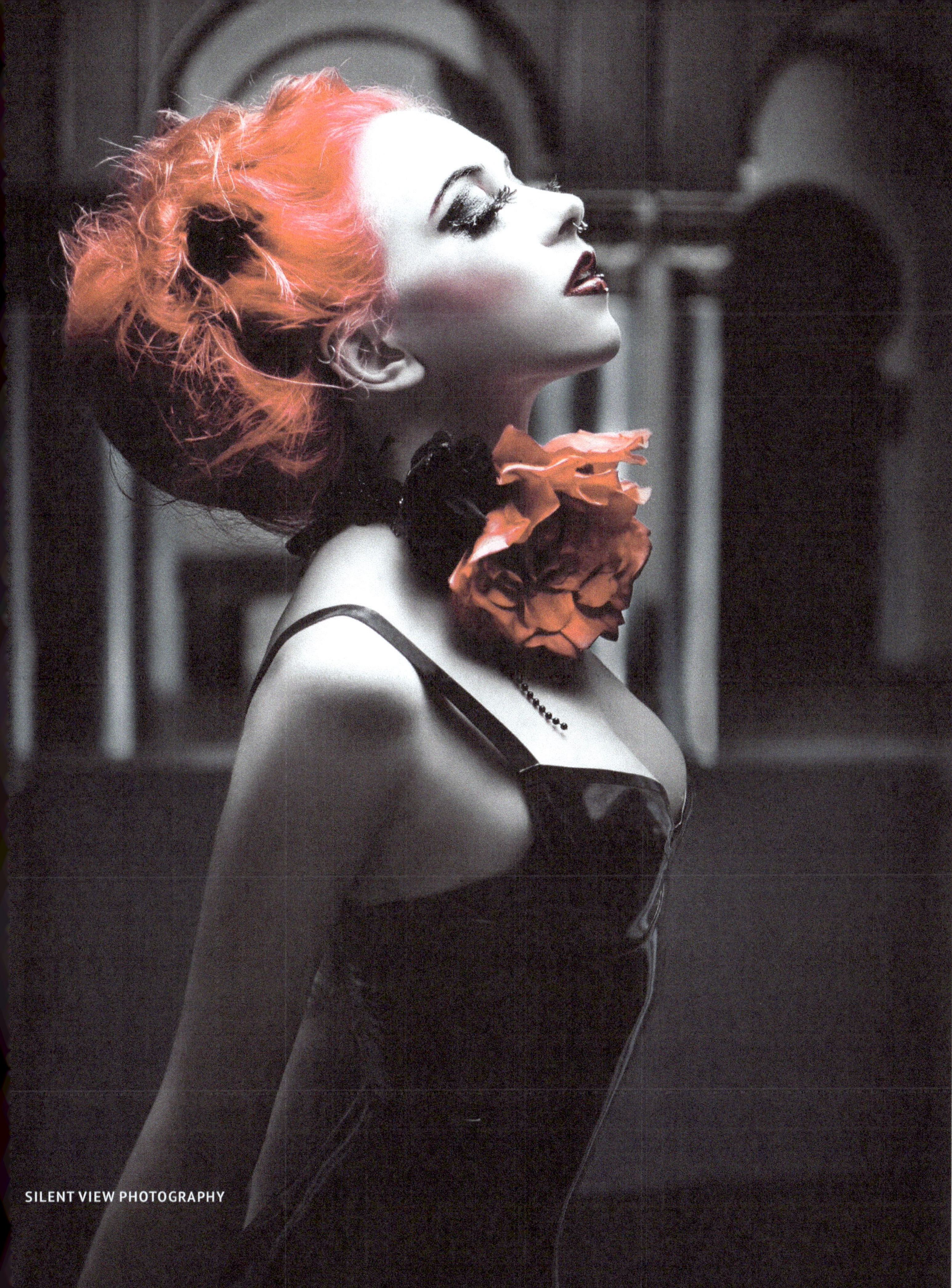

SILENT VIEW PHOTOGRAPHY

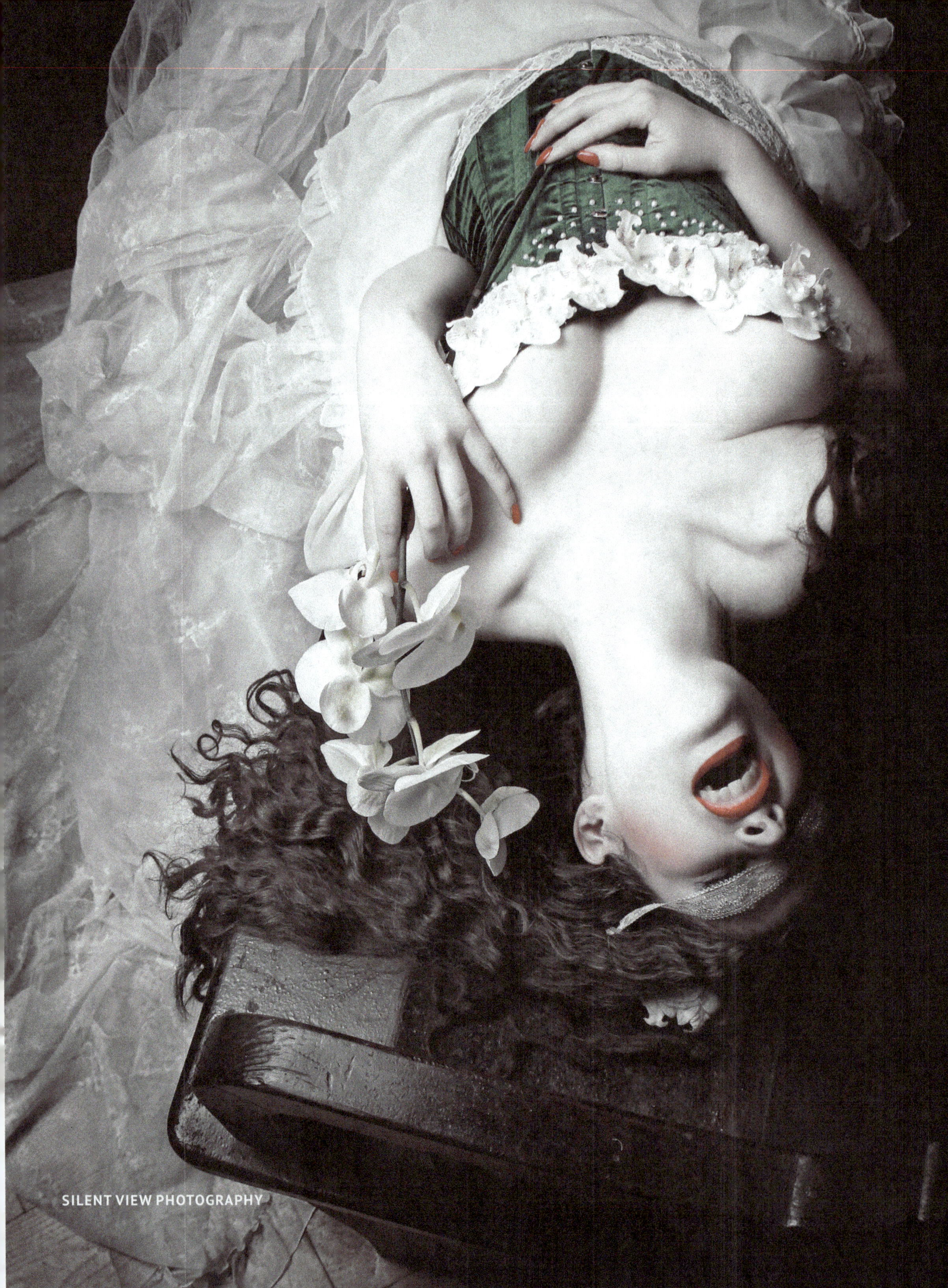

SILENT VIEW PHOTOGRAPHY

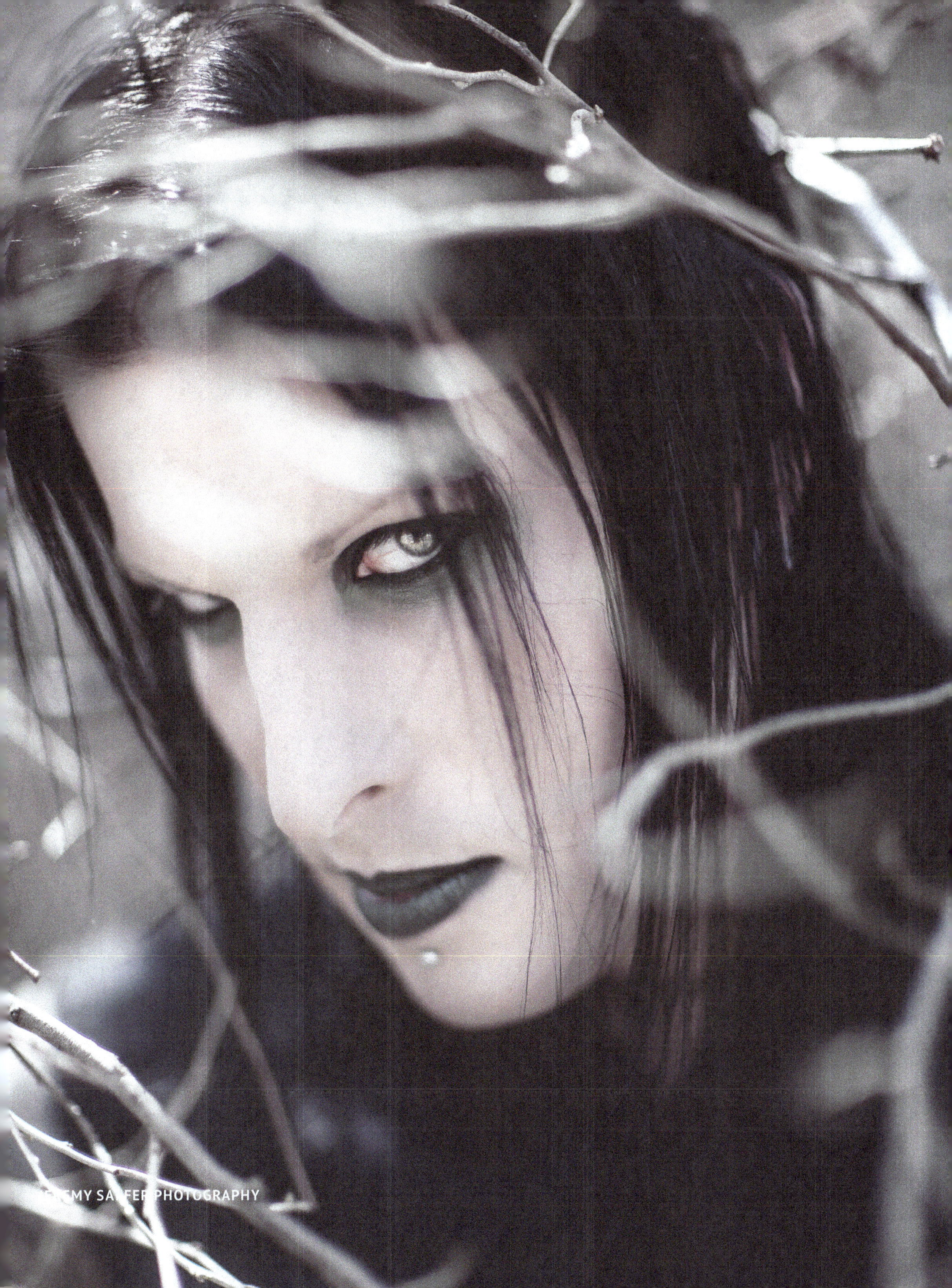

JEREMY SAFFER PHOTOGRAPHY

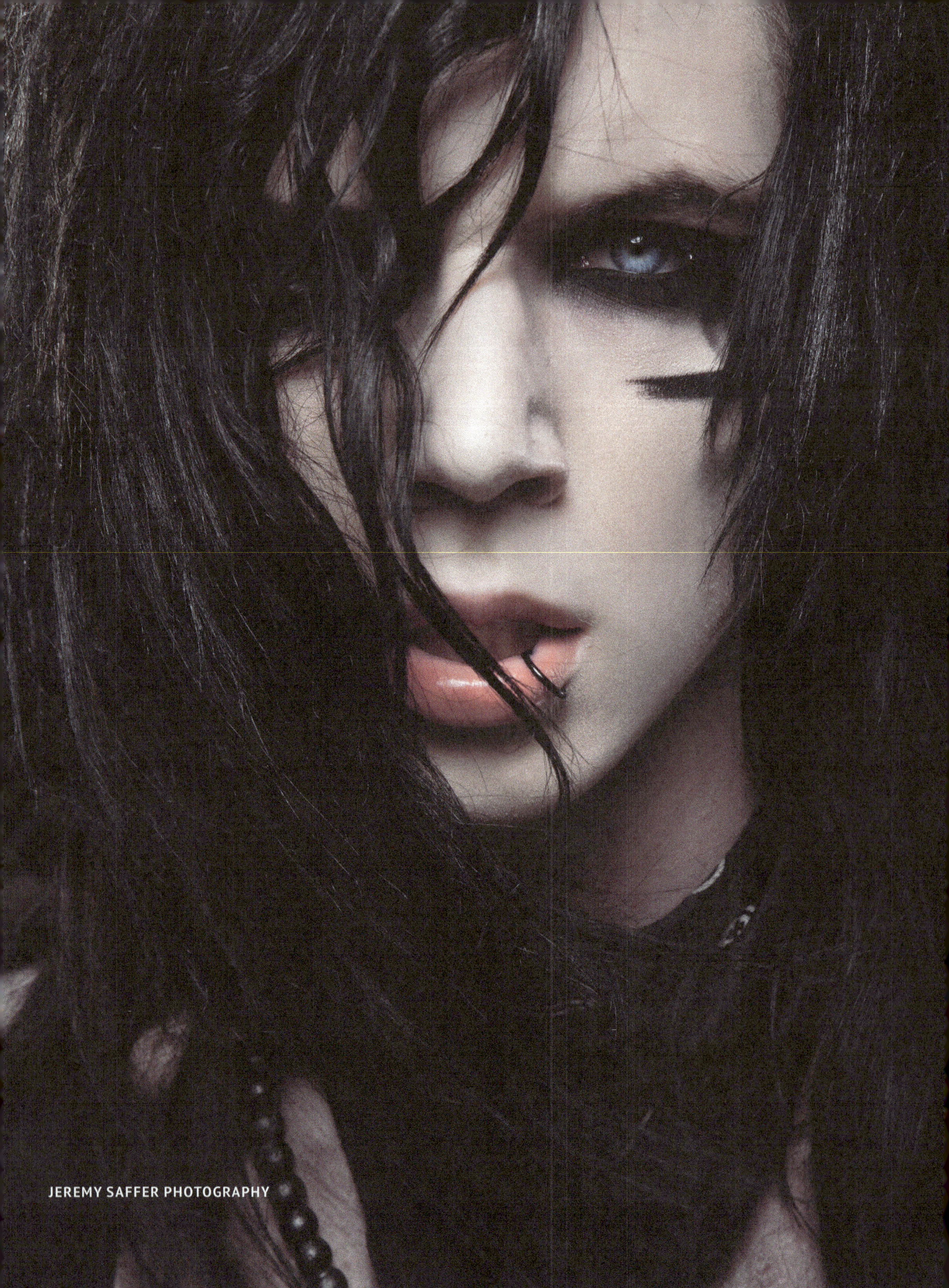
JEREMY SAFFER PHOTOGRAPHY

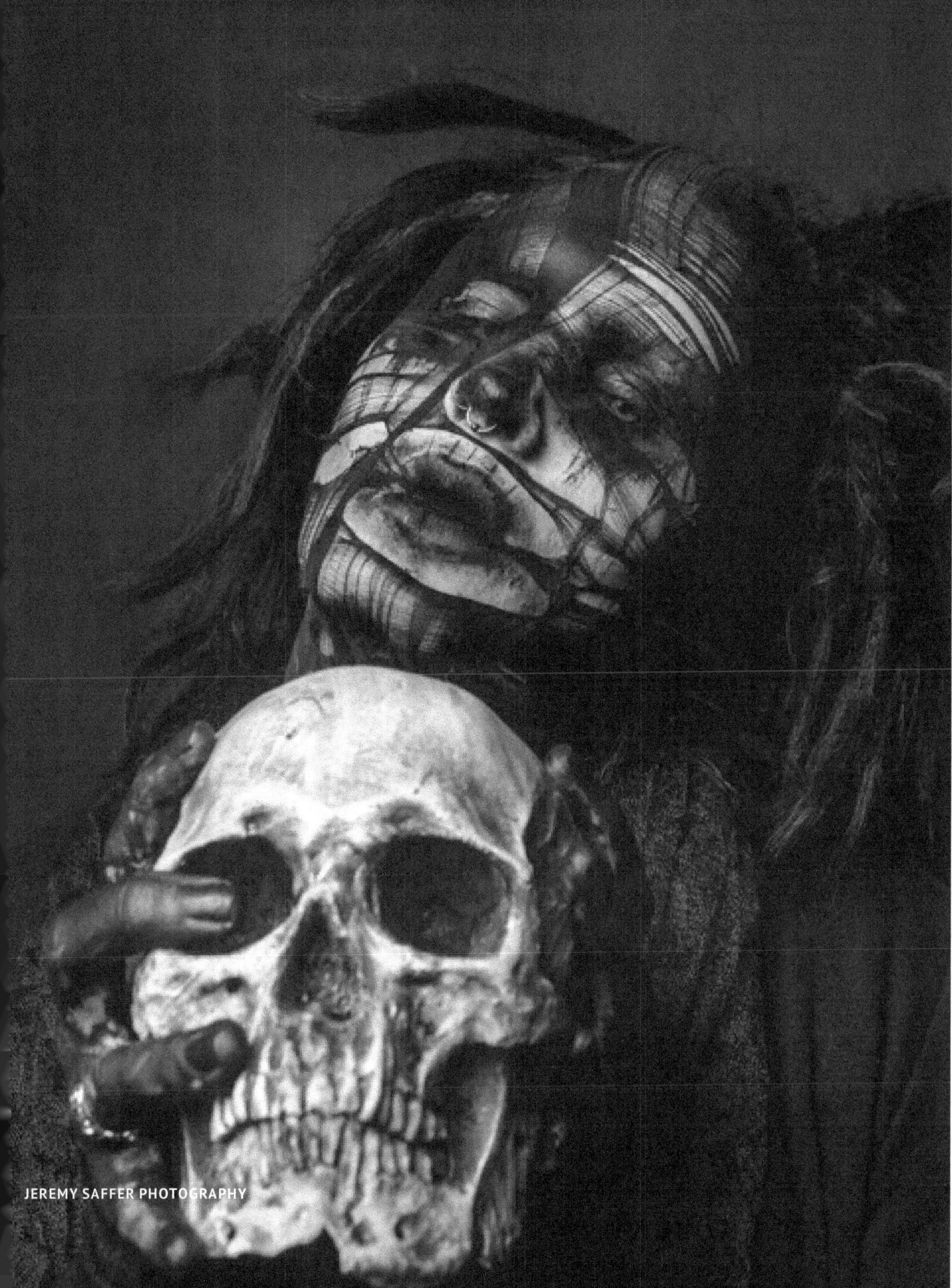

JEREMY SAFFER PHOTOGRAPHY

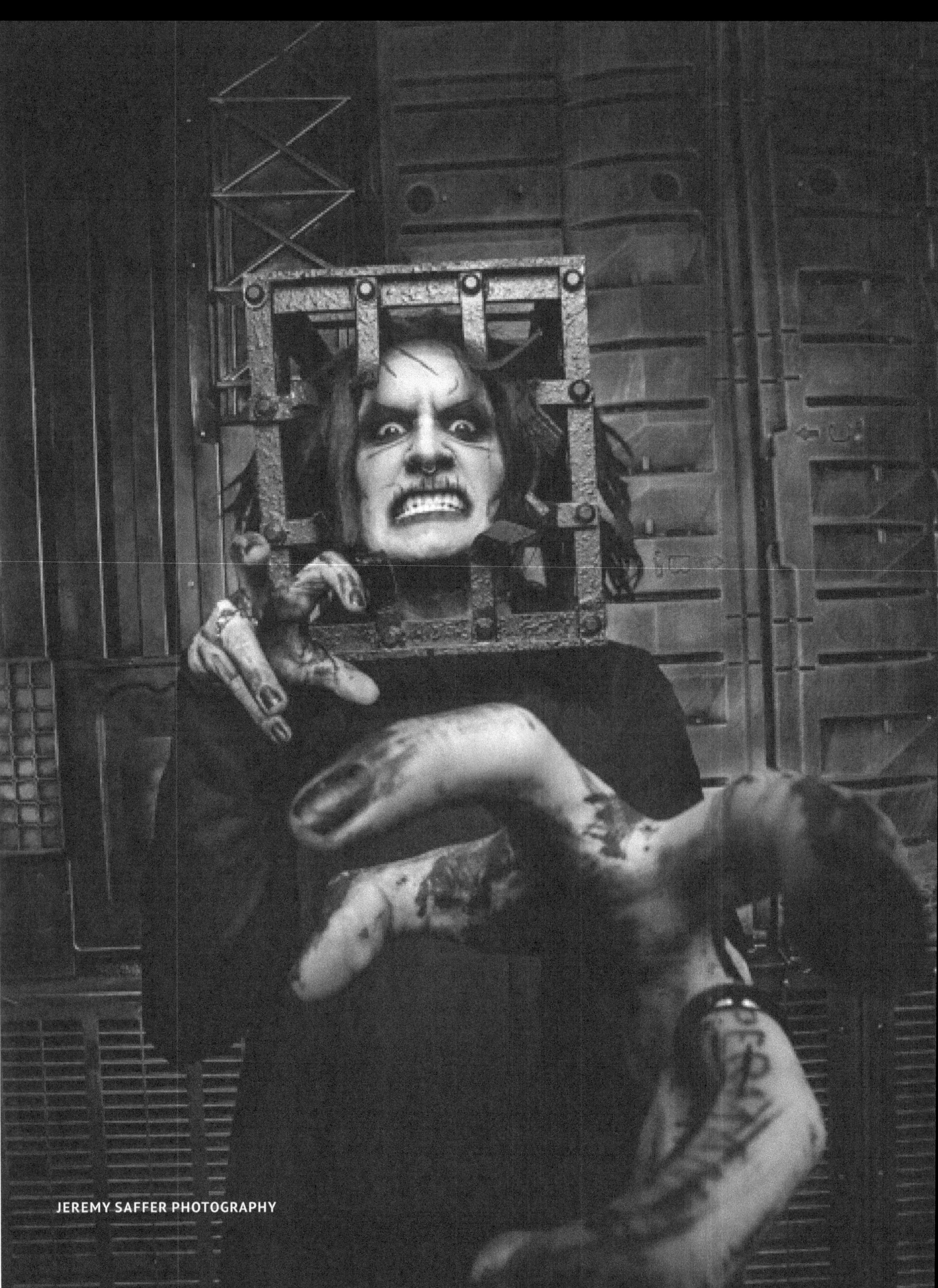
JEREMY SAFFER PHOTOGRAPHY

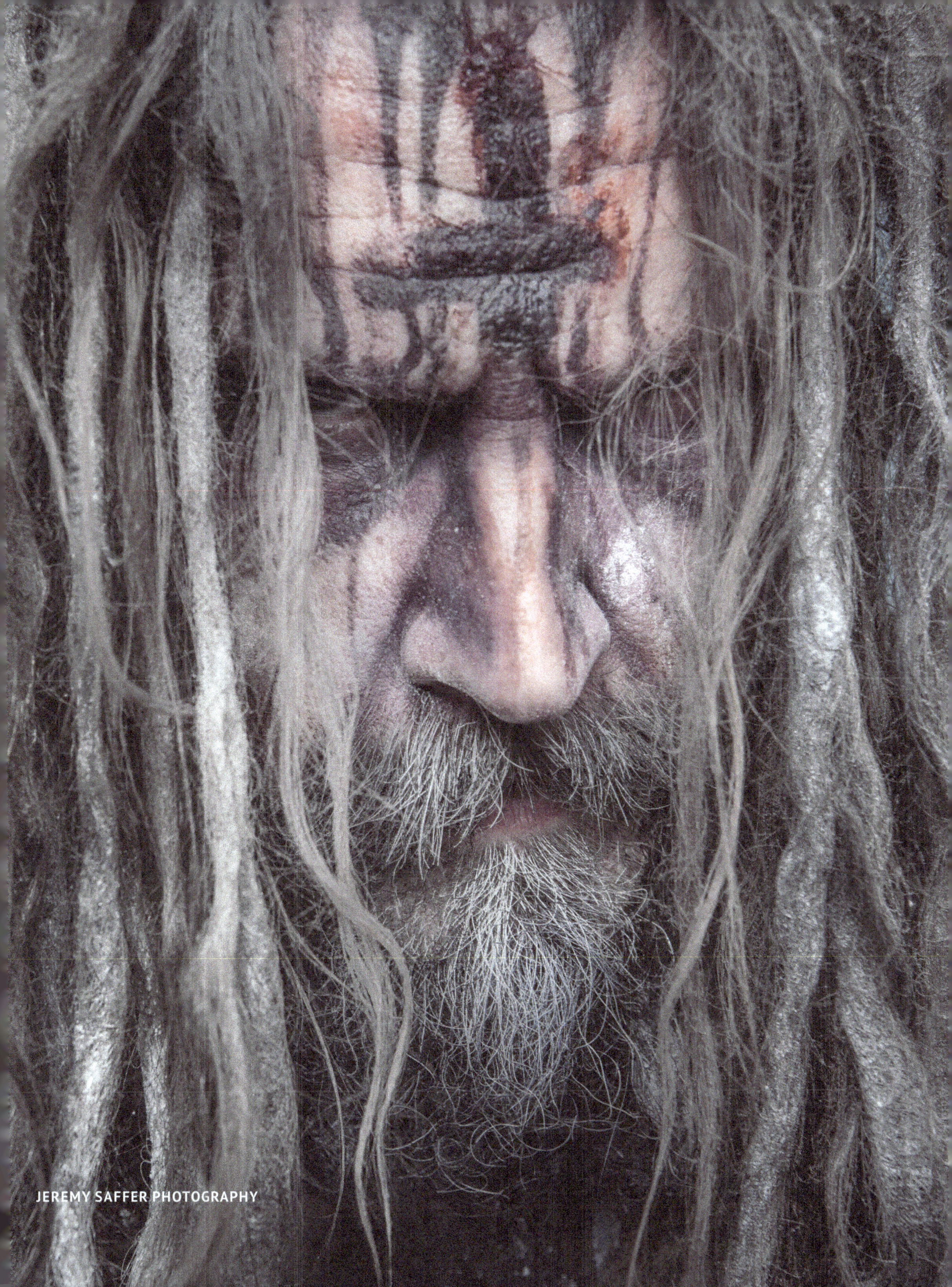
JEREMY SAFFER PHOTOGRAPHY

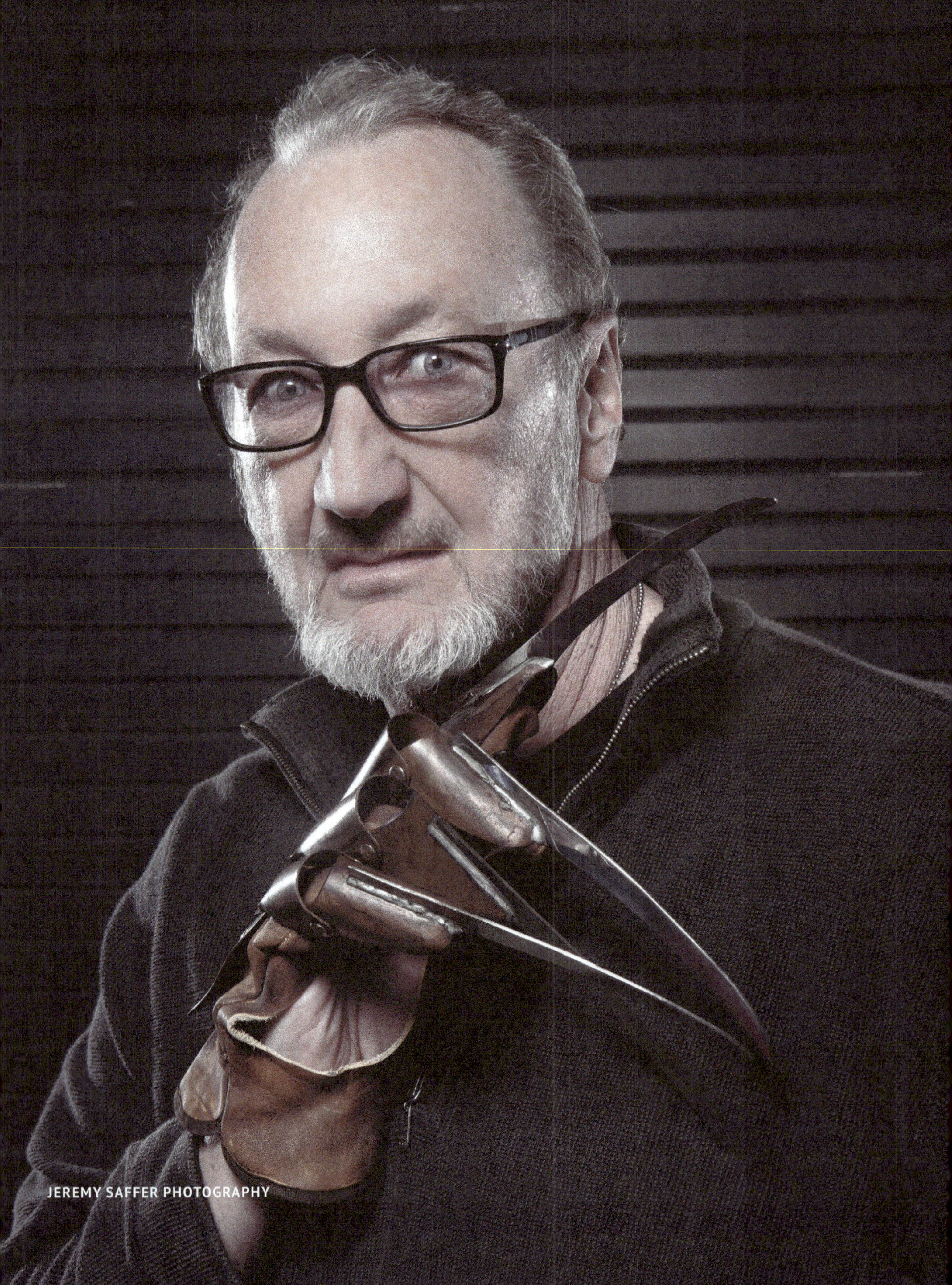
JEREMY SAFFER PHOTOGRAPHY

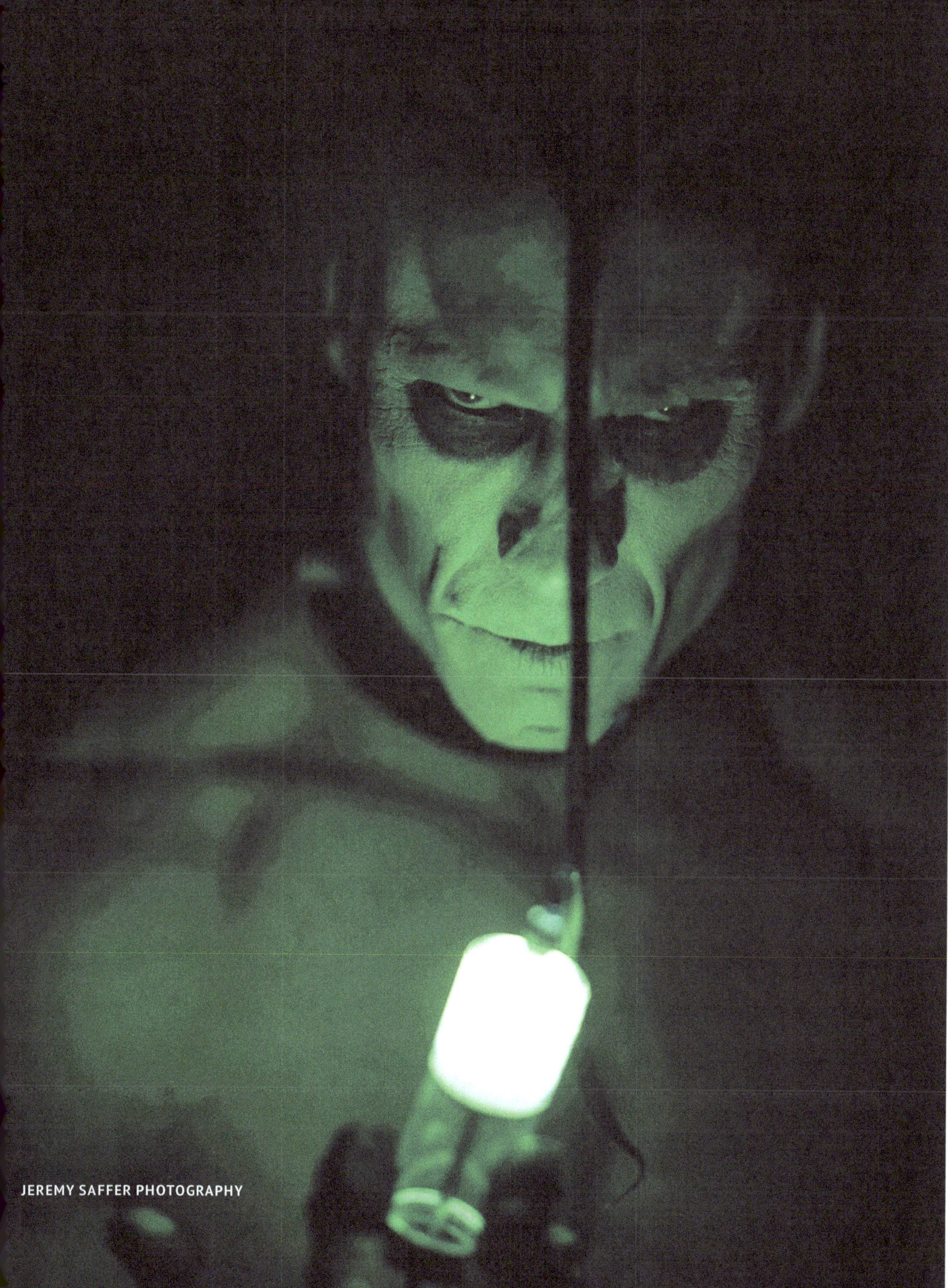
JEREMY SAFFER PHOTOGRAPHY

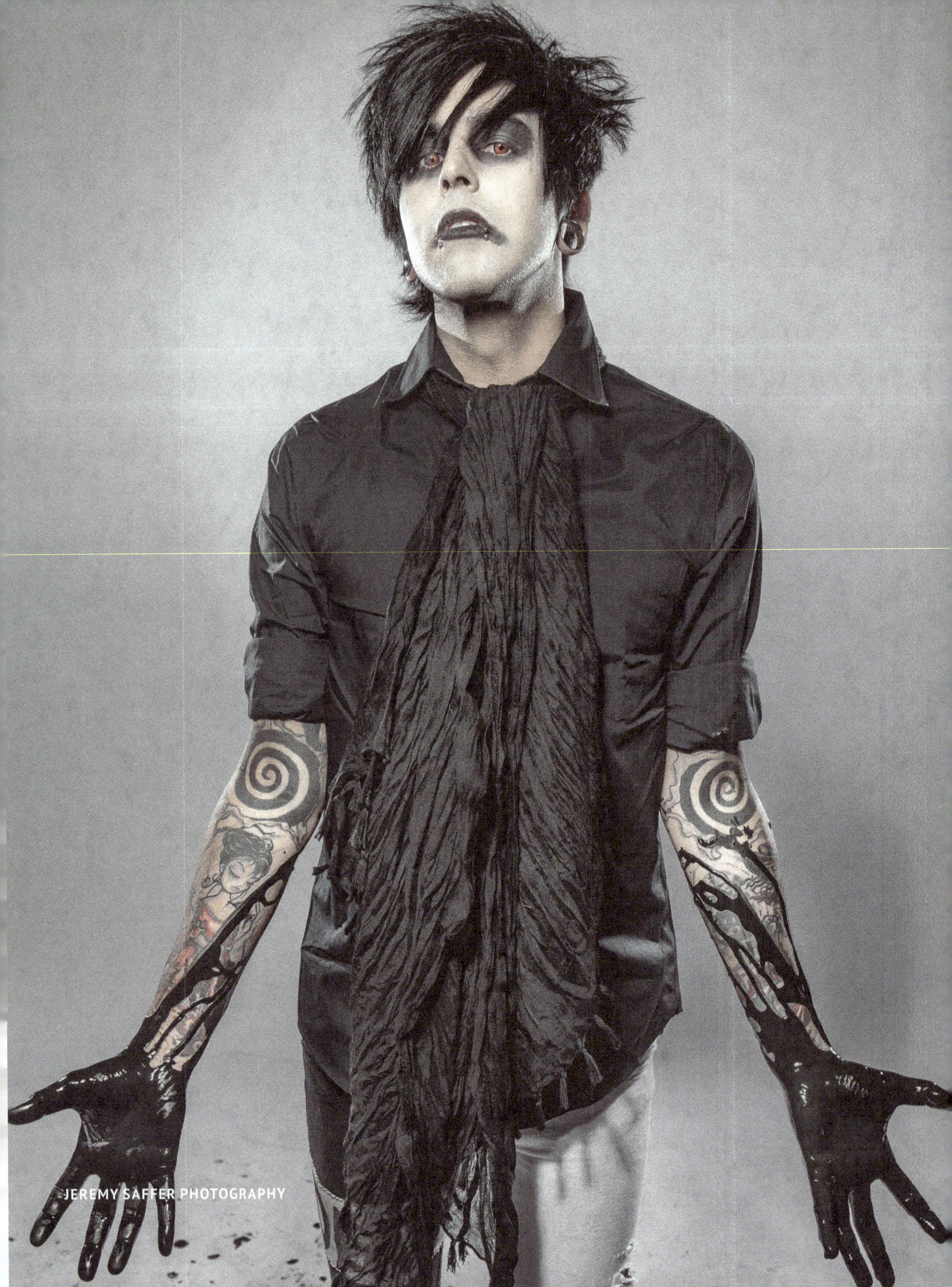
JEREMY SAFFER PHOTOGRAPHY

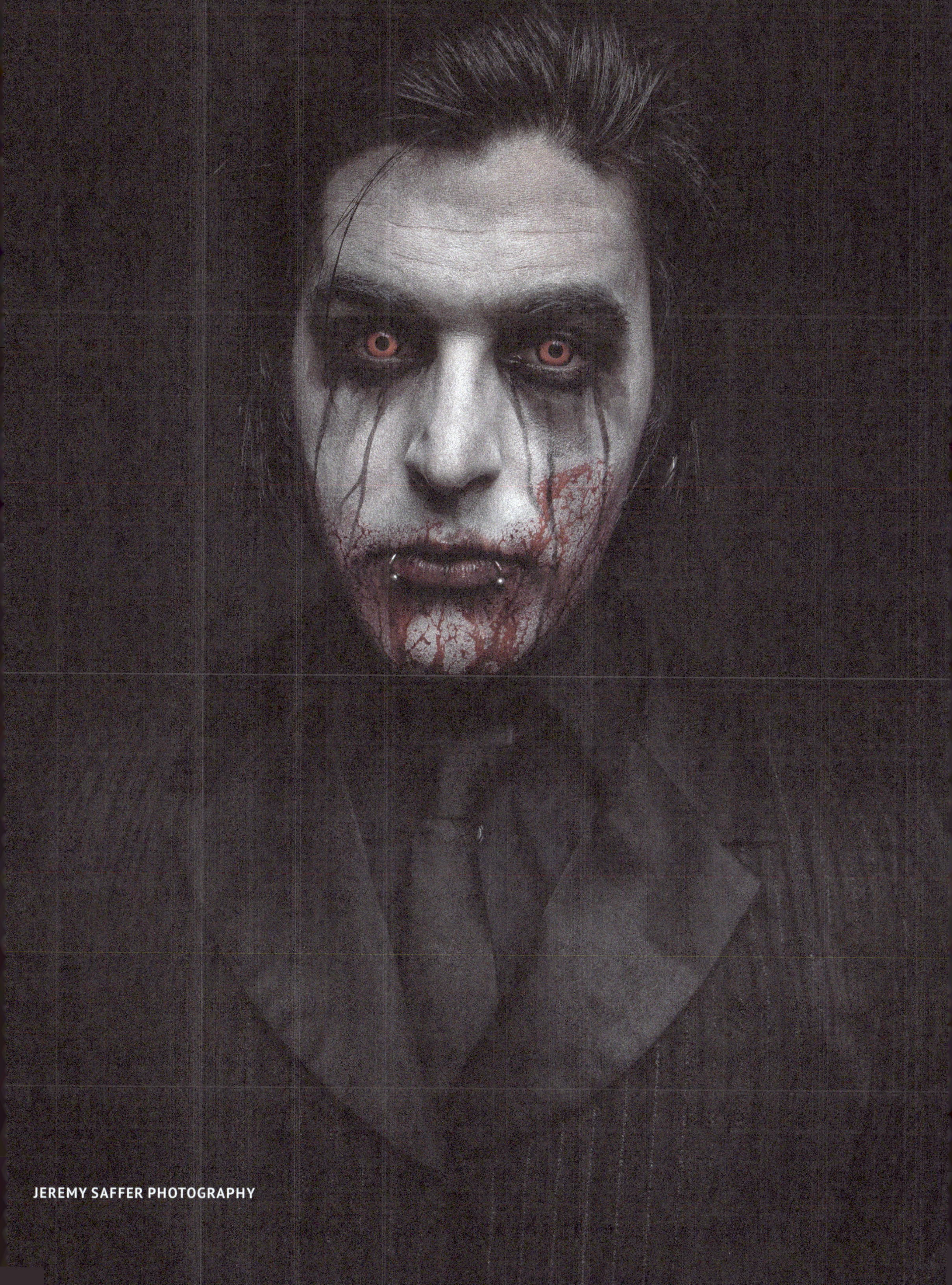

JEREMY SAFFER PHOTOGRAPHY

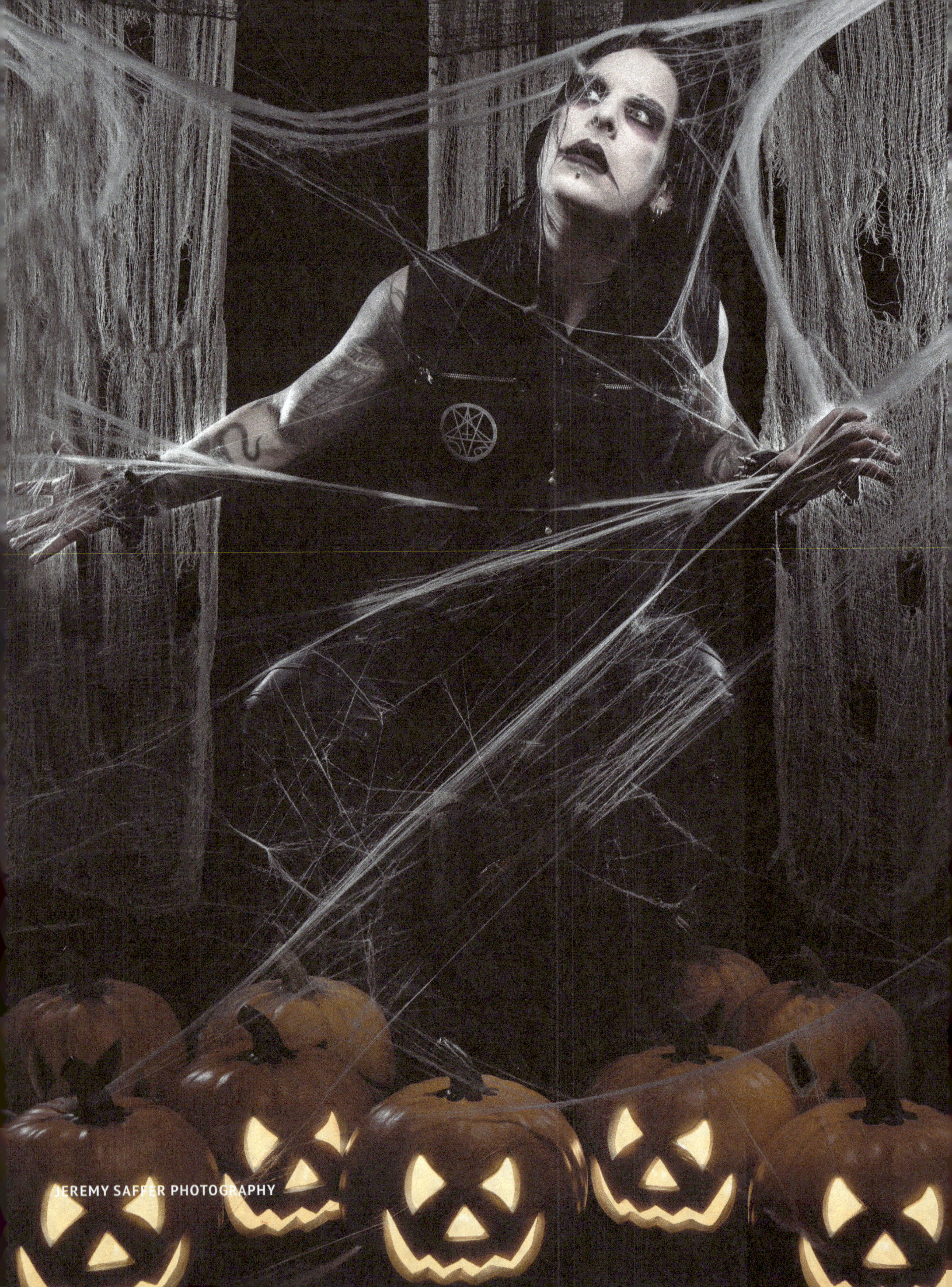

JEREMY SAFFER PHOTOGRAPHY

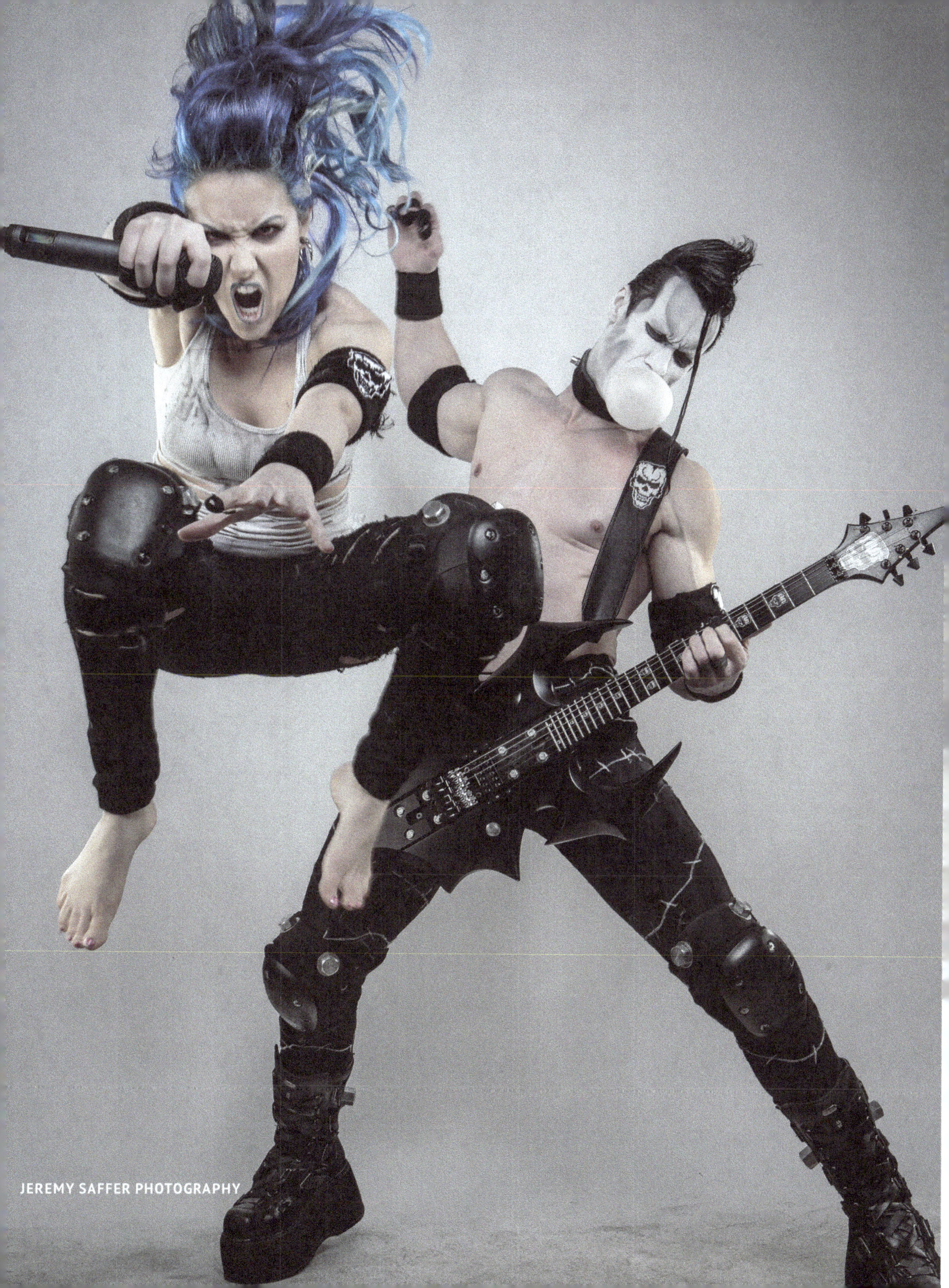
JEREMY SAFFER PHOTOGRAPHY

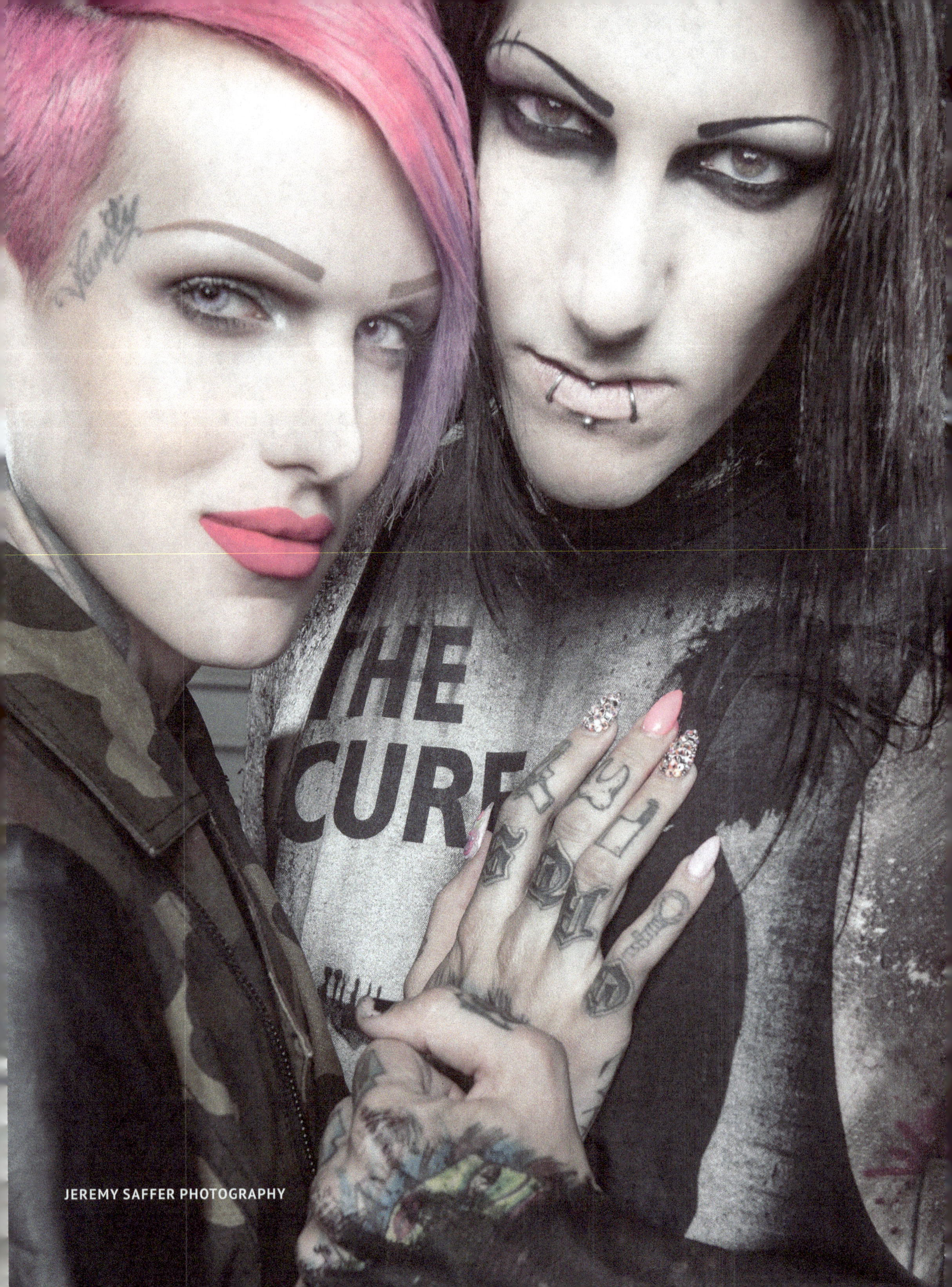

JEREMY SAFFER PHOTOGRAPHY

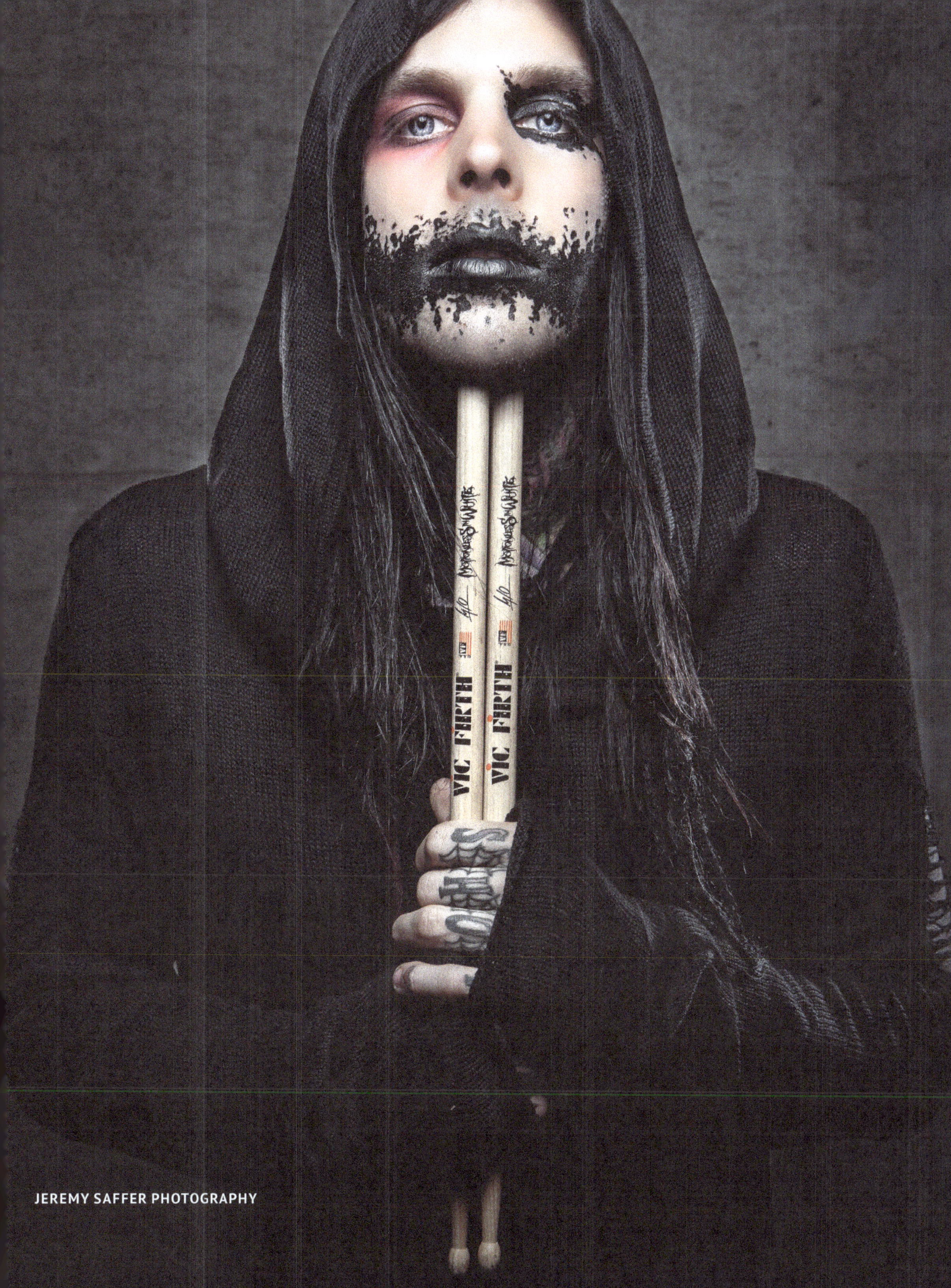

VIC FIRTH
VIC FIRTH

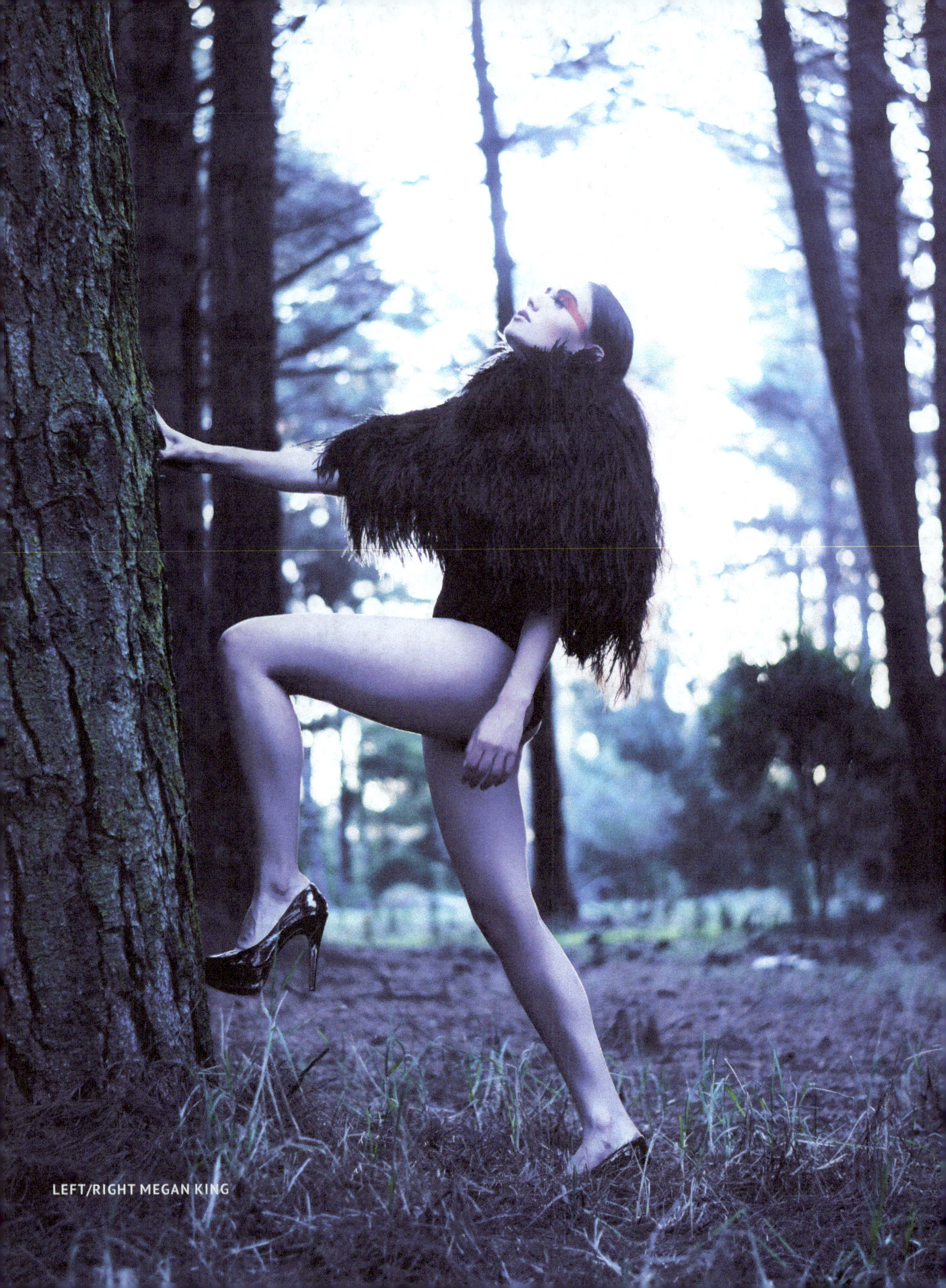
LEFT/RIGHT MEGAN KING

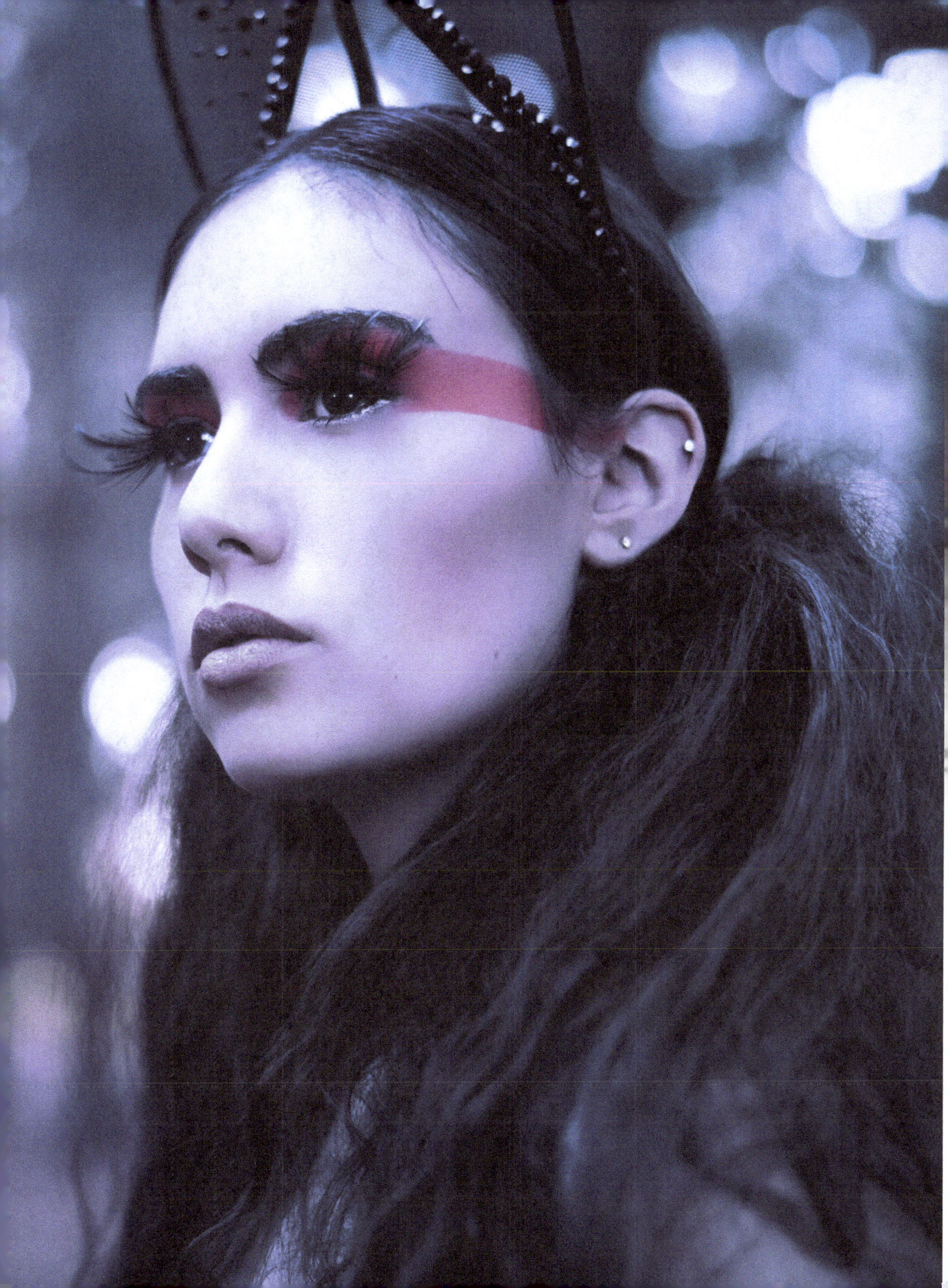

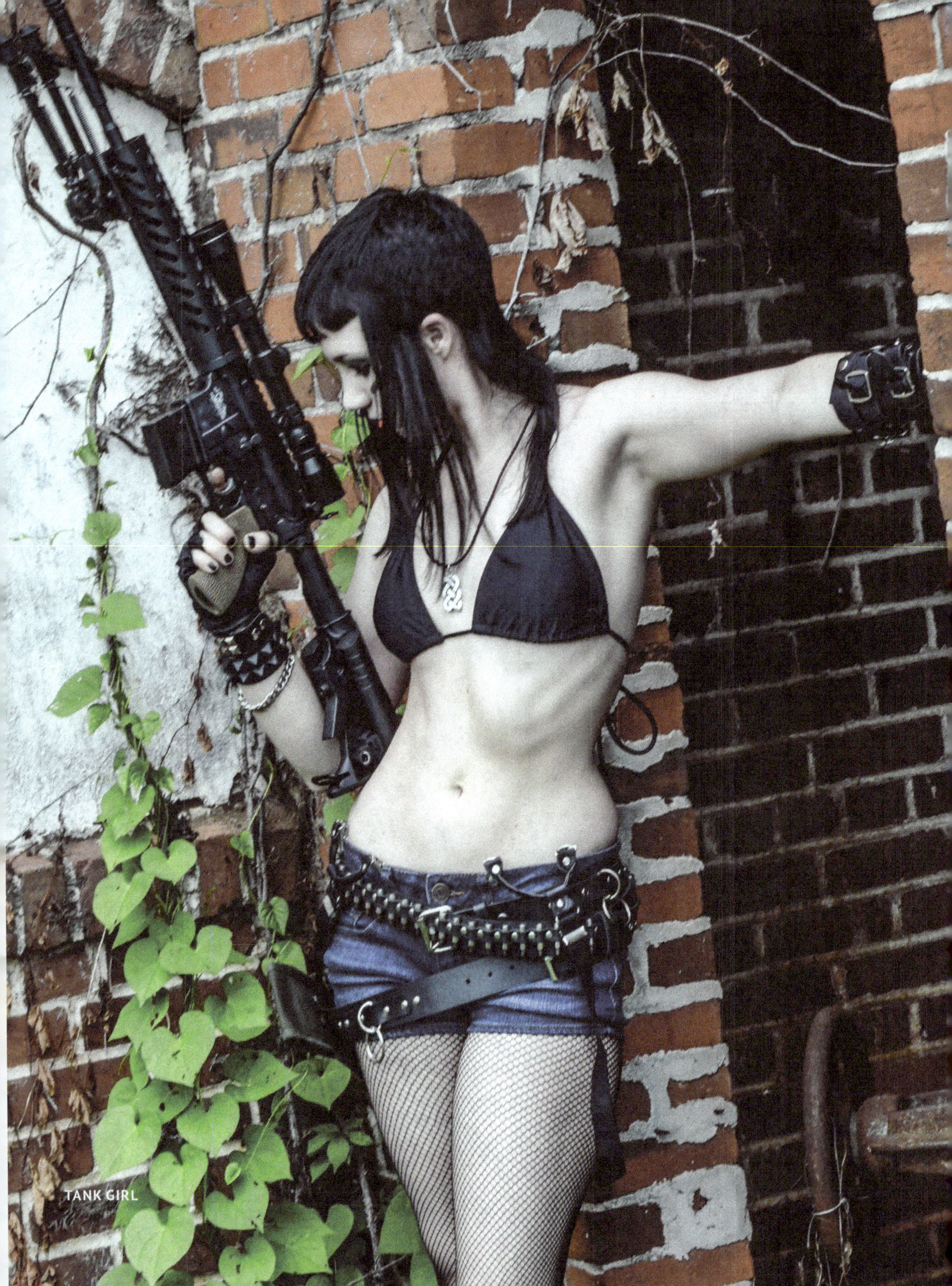

TANK GIRL

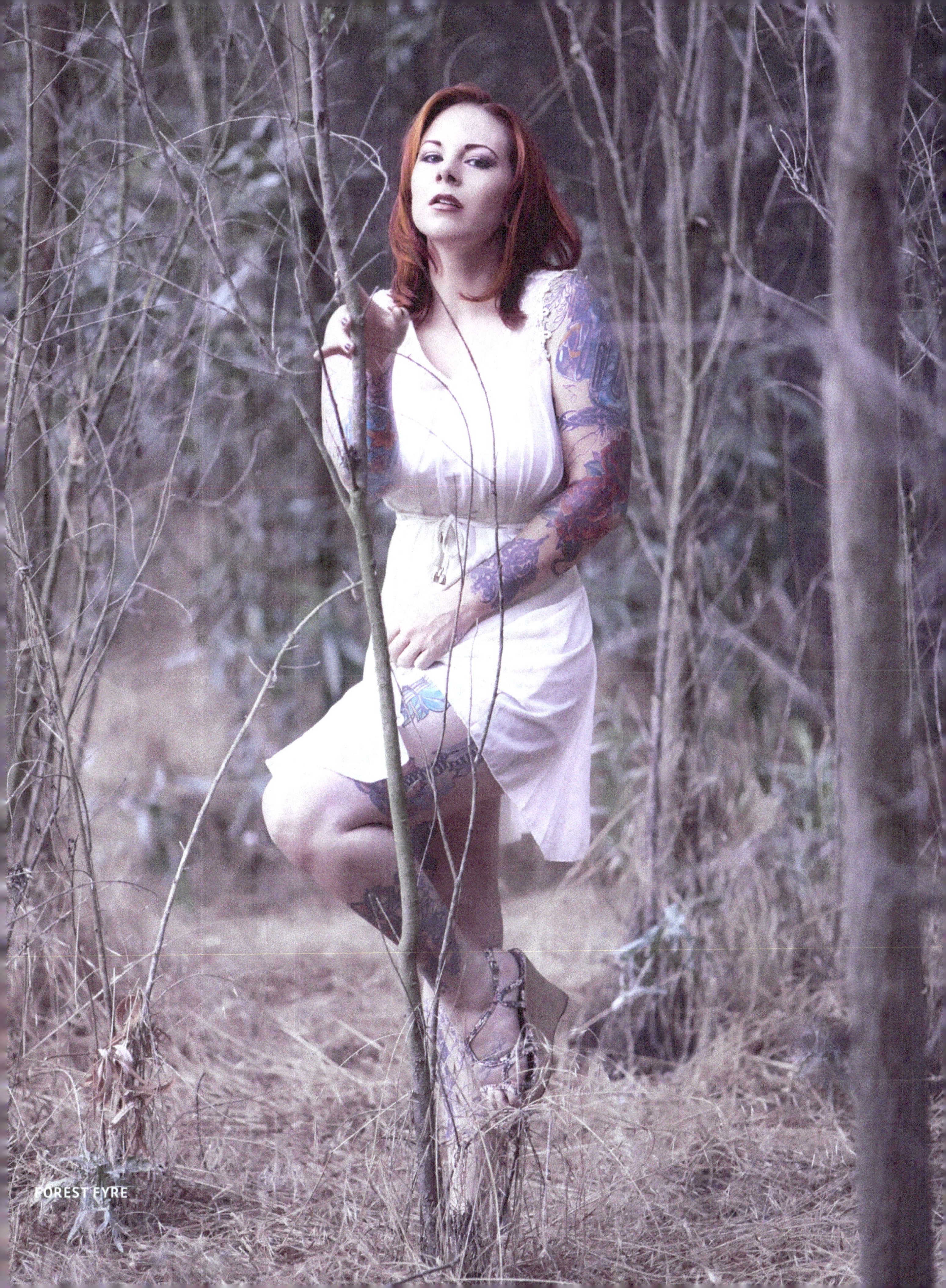
FOREST FYRE

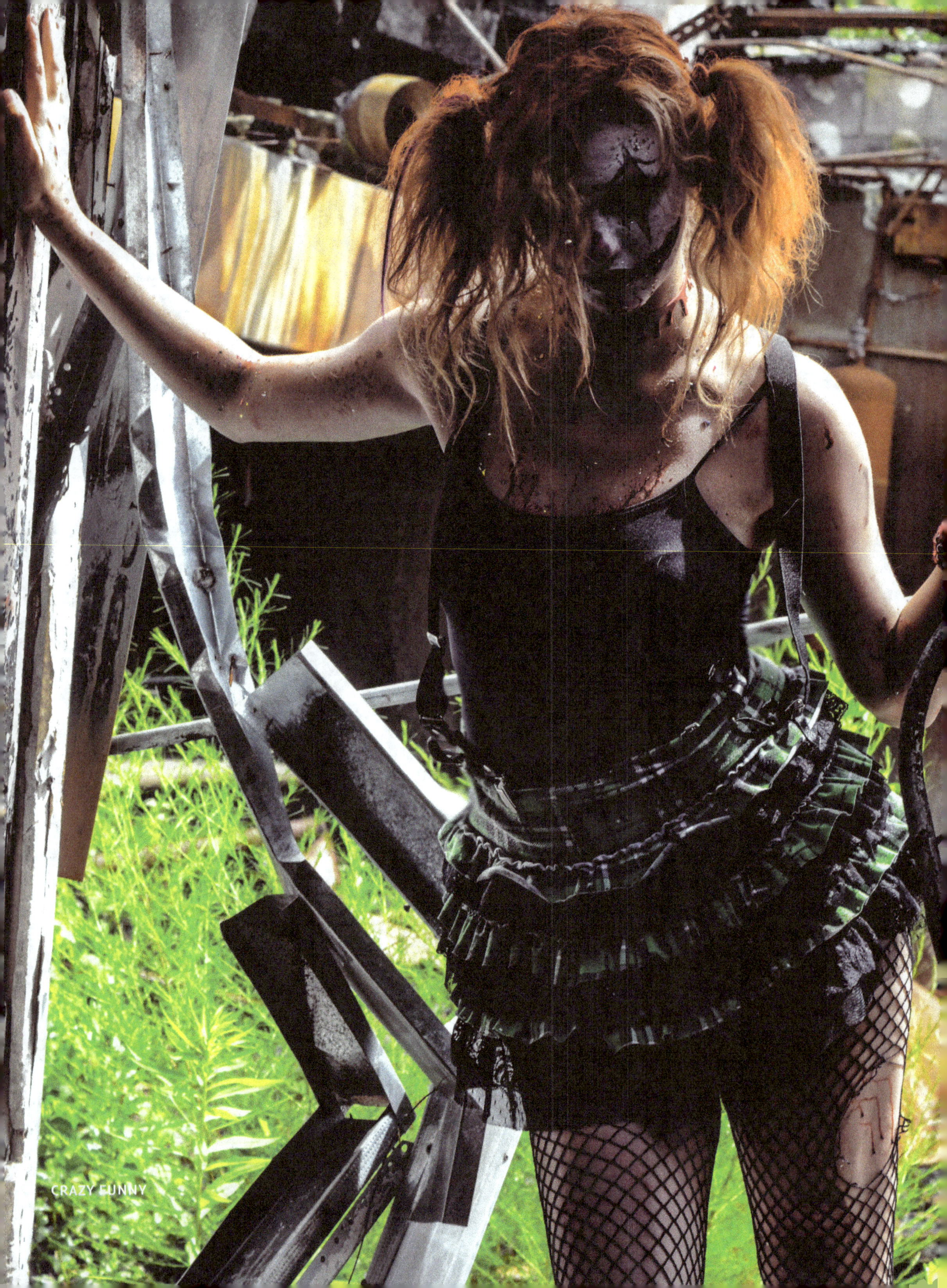

CRAZY FUNNY

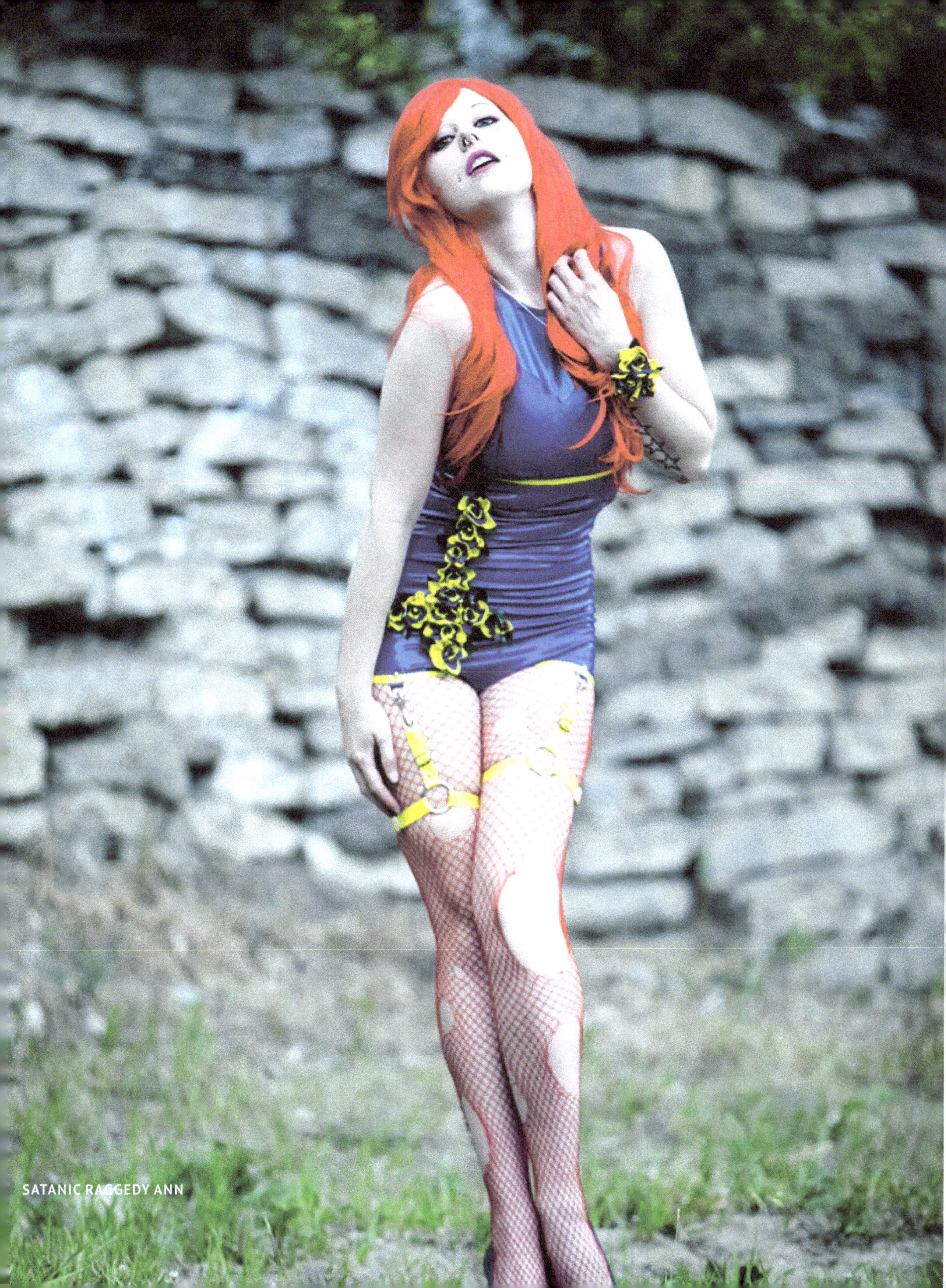

SATANIC RAGGEDY ANN

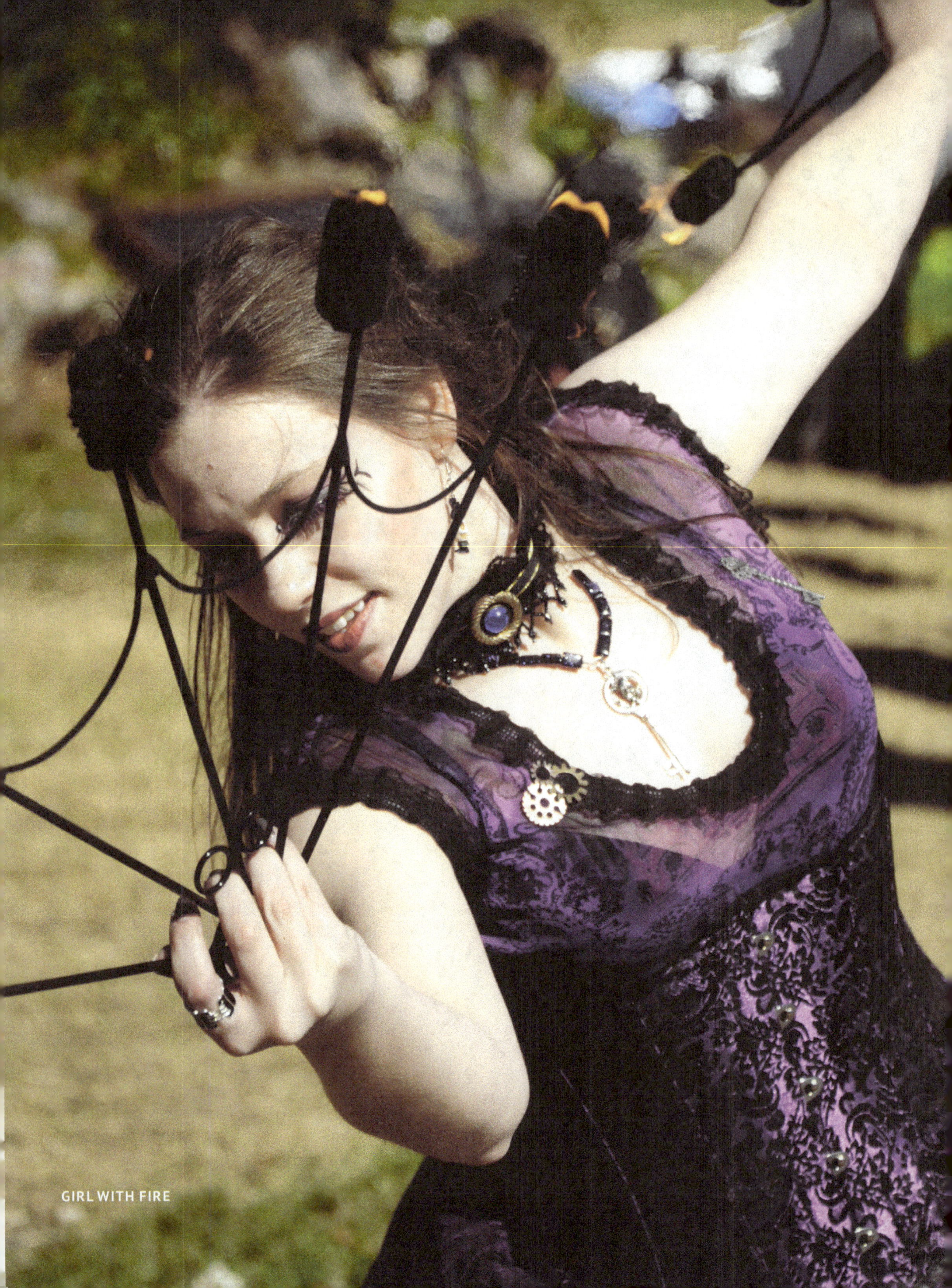

GIRL WITH FIRE

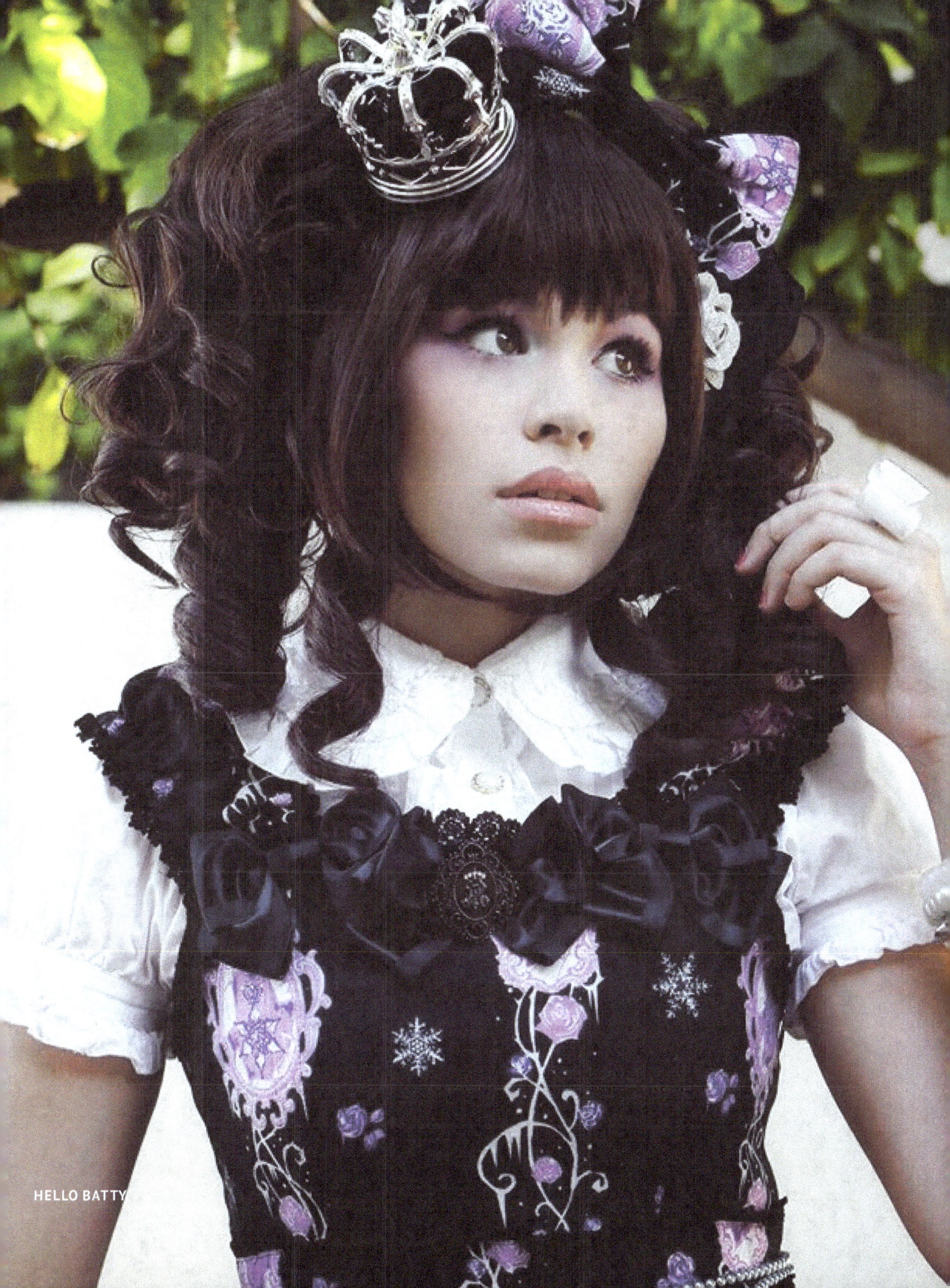
HELLO BATTY

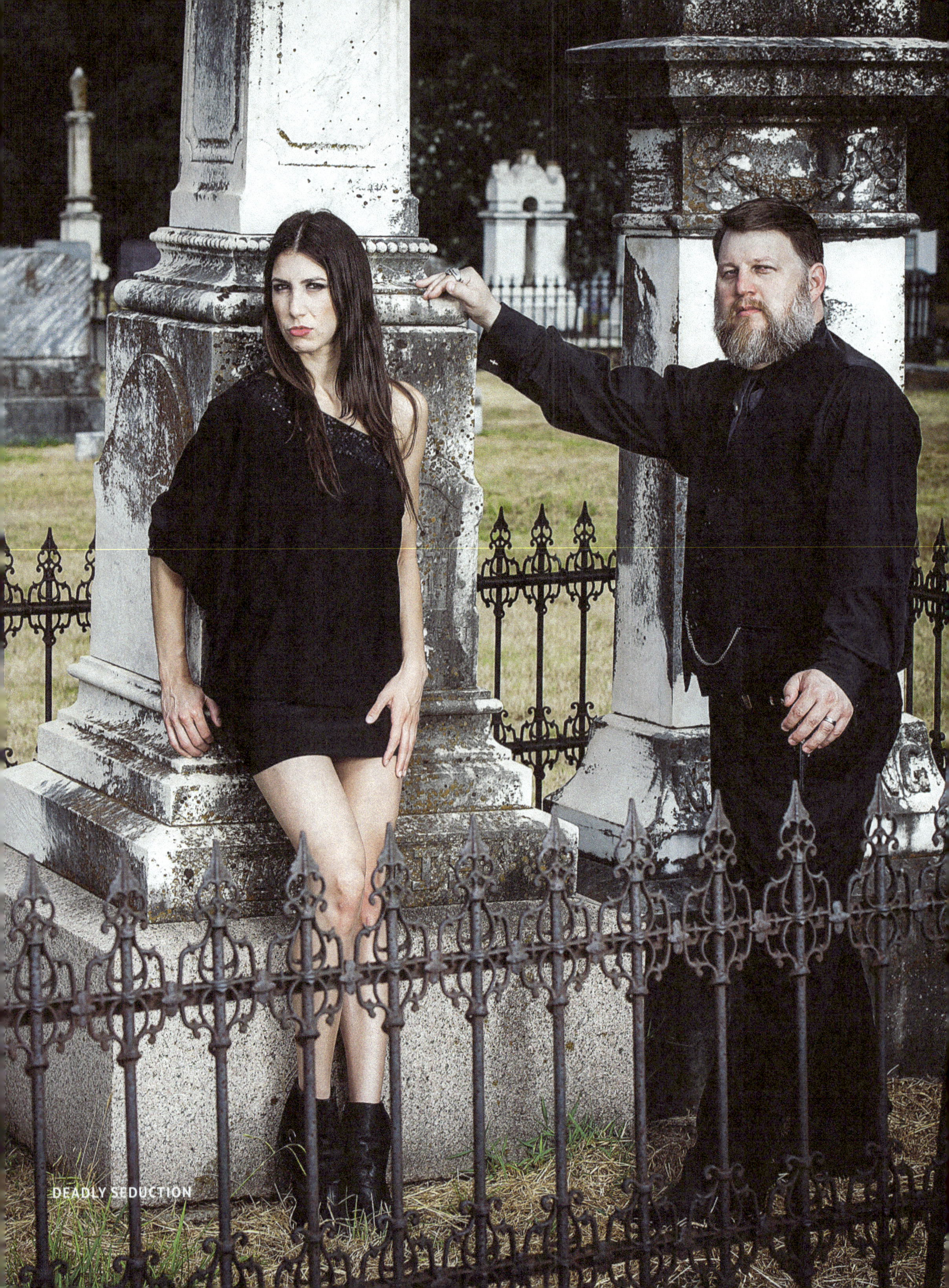

DEADLY SEDUCTION

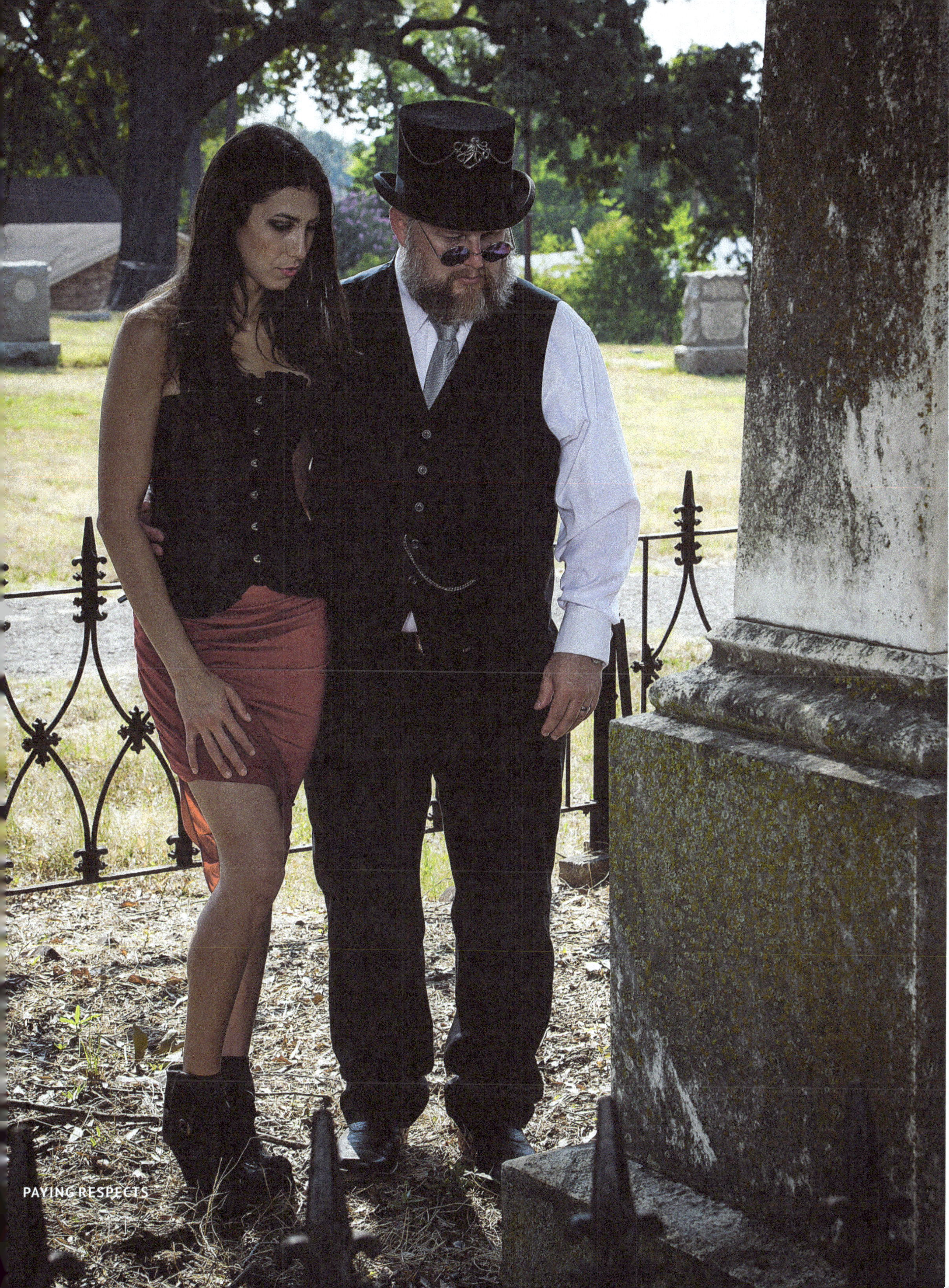
PAYING RESPECTS

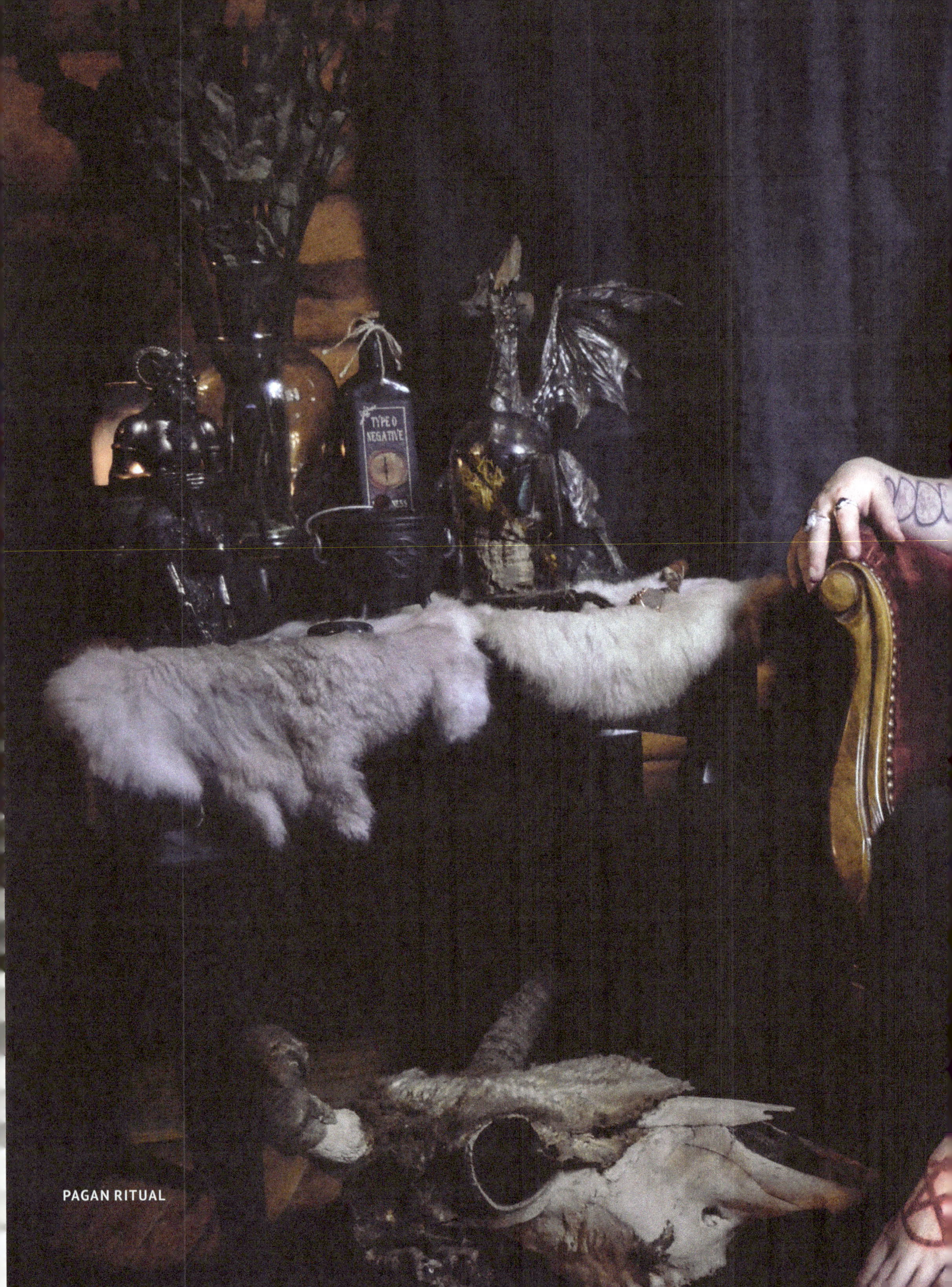
PAGAN RITUAL

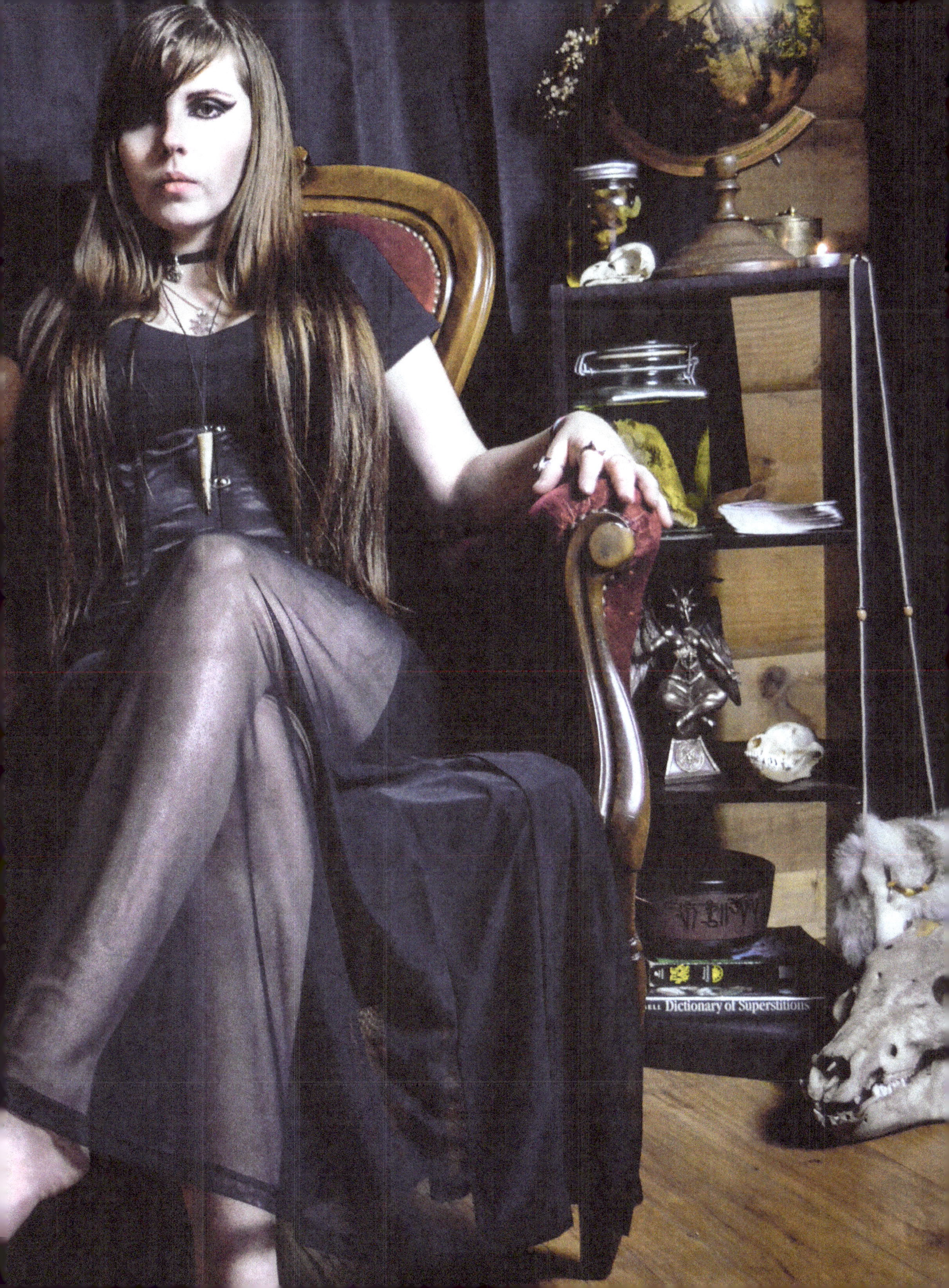
Dictionary of Superstitions

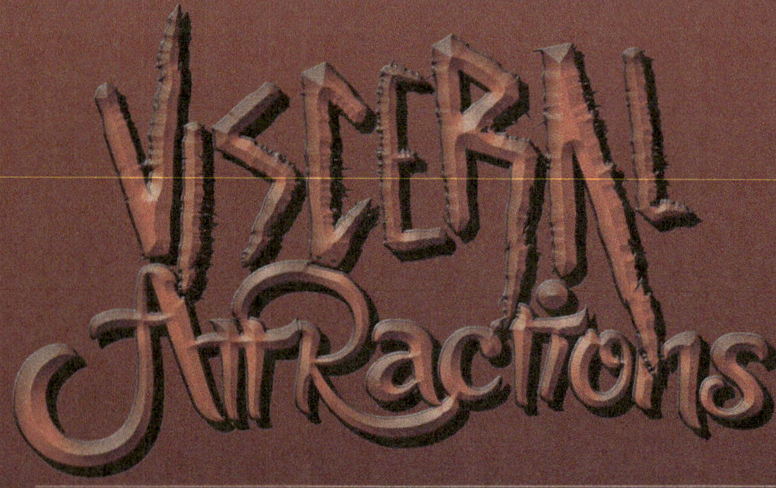

Credits:

If you would like to have your photographs featured in Visceral Attractions, please contact the editor at fashion@carpenocturne.net.

La Carmina
http://www.lacarmina.com
Instagram and Twitter - @lacarmina
Facebook - http://facebook.com/lacarminaofficial

Silent View Photography
www.silent-view.com

Jeremy Saffer Photography
www.jeremysaffer.com
www.facebook.com/jeremysaffer

Megan King
www.PhotographyMeganKing.com

Tank Girl, Model: Jessica Mispel
Photographer: Rewski Photography
Hair/MUA: Kayla King

Forest Fyre, Ms. Angi
www.facebook.com/modelmsangi
www.instagram.com/ms.angi
Photographer: David Noceti

Crazy Funny, Model: Krista Marie
MUAH: Shana Leigh Heagwood
Photographer: Rewski Photography

Satanic Raggedy Ann, Model – Chantele Smith
www.TwistedVisions.co.uk
www.facebook.com/www.twistedvisions.co.uk
Photography: Jen Hammer Photo, www.jenhammerphoto.ca
www.facebook.com/jenhammerart

Girl with Fire, Flower Island Photography
www.facebook.com/flowerislandphotography
flowerislandphotography@gmail.com

Hello Batty
www.youtube.com/thehellobatty
www.hellobatty.com
www.facebook.com/thehellobatty

Deadly Seduction
Paying Respects
Model: Erik Ethelwulf, Nina Larmeu
Photographer: H.M. Jelks Photography

Pagan Ritual
Model: Weslyn Rae
Photographer: Rewski Photography, David Noceti

NAIL SENSATION

Helpful tip for the fall season

Do you want to know how to keep your nails healthy and smooth during the fall season? Go out and purchase a good brand of vitamin E oil. At least 3 times a day rub the vitamin E oil into your cuticle area, this will help prevent dry cracking skin around your nail bed. According to Oregon State University vitamin E is a fat-soluble antioxidant that is essential for the maintenance of healthy skin.

With pumpkin spice everything and winter sweaters being dug out to keep warm, how quickly we forget something as simple as changing our nail color to match the transition into the Fall season. Take a look at some of our readers submissions.

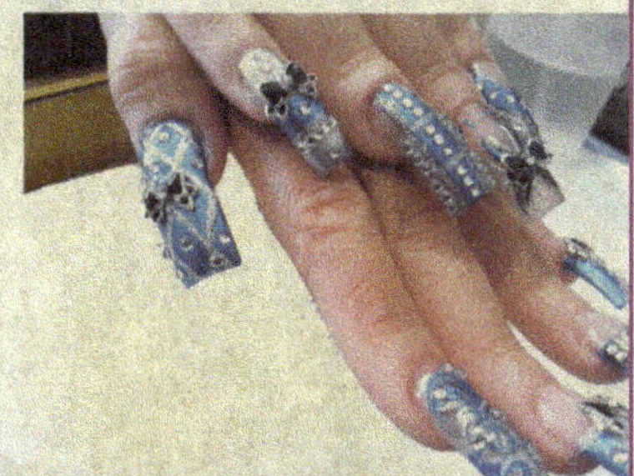

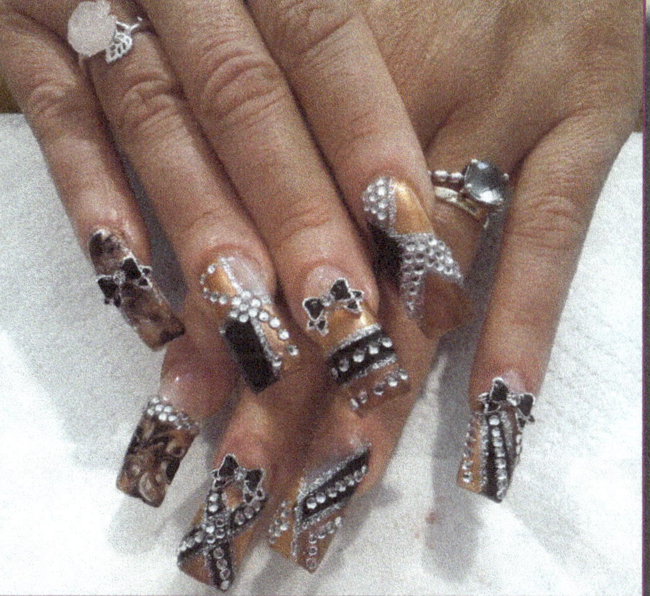

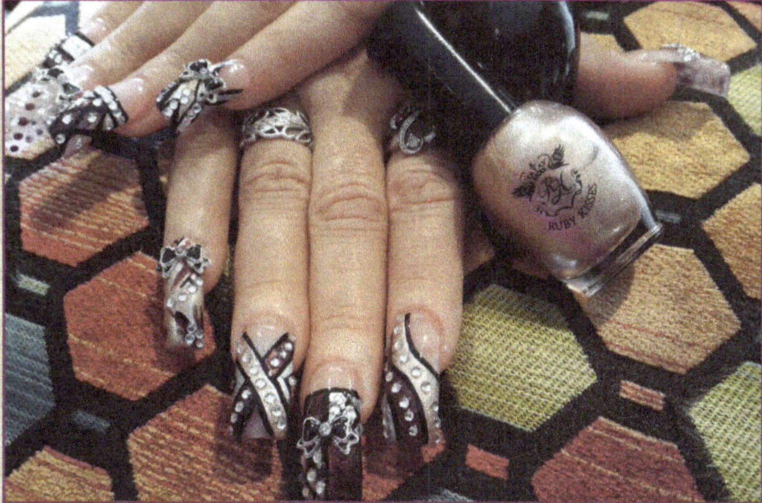

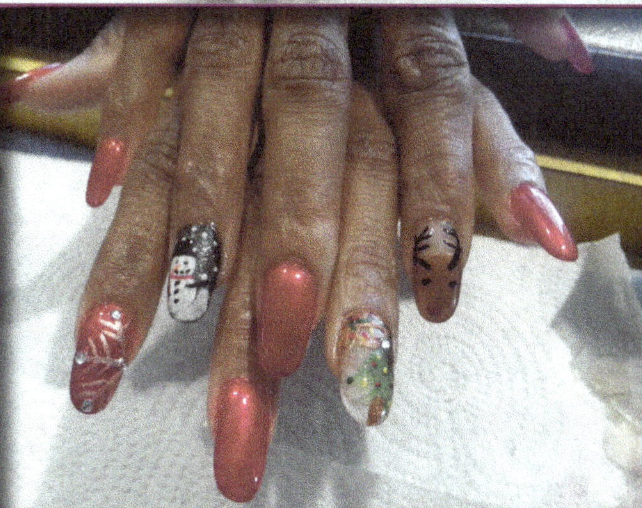

Delectable Darkness
A conversation with Miss T

By Sonnett57

On one of my journeys to the Bay Area of California, I encountered the lovely Michelle Tubby, founder of the New Zealand Gothic kitchen Miss T's. Our small community is full of people with a darkness to them, with an extreme appreciation for all things extravagant, eccentric, decadent and macabre. It is true we love the dark music, paintings, clothing styles, and culture, and now baked goods.

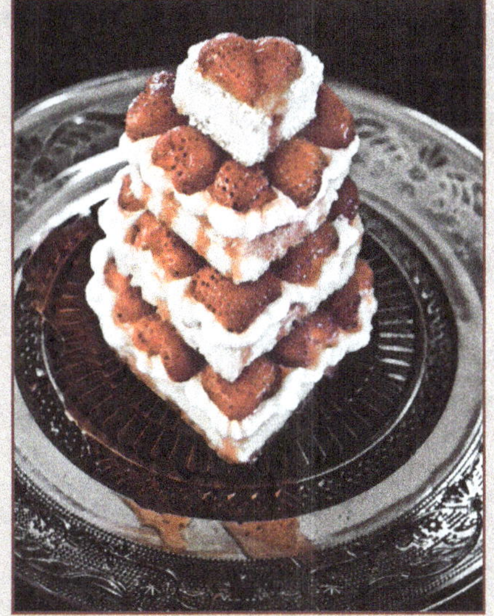

I am one who knows nothing about the kitchen, so any type of cooking fascinates me. I needed to know what inspired her to get into it. She said, "Isolation and necessity started me on the path to baking". She adds, "I spent a couple of years on my own after a long relationship ended and I needed to pour my emotions into something." An occasion arose that she needed a cake for her birthday and there was no one who could make what she wanted, so she decided to make it herself. She said, "I realized I had a talent for it, so I kept going." She realized there was a market for her craft when she started to look on the internet for gothic style baking and all she found were juvenile Halloween cupcakes. She said, "There were no mature or stylish recipes so I started creating my own and put them on Facebook and I had a great response." She added, "I had a bride ask me to make her a steampunk wedding cake for her Halloween wedding

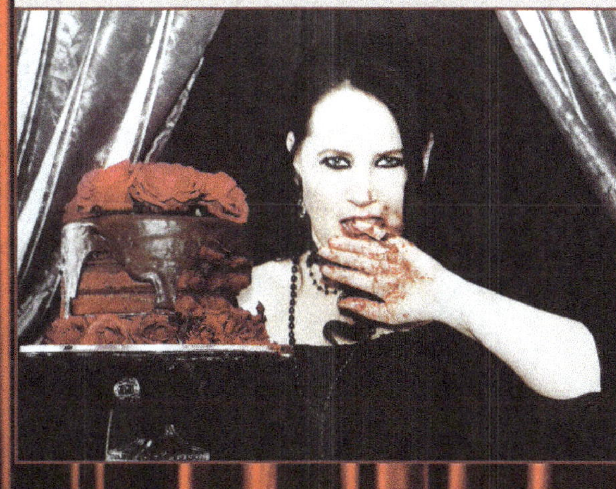

and it was very successful." She has also done commissioned cakes with themes like Day of The Dead and Monster High. So far her best seller is her Cameo cookies, and the most requested flavor is her rich and moist chocolate. Miss T's was started in 2011 and has been making dark confections since.

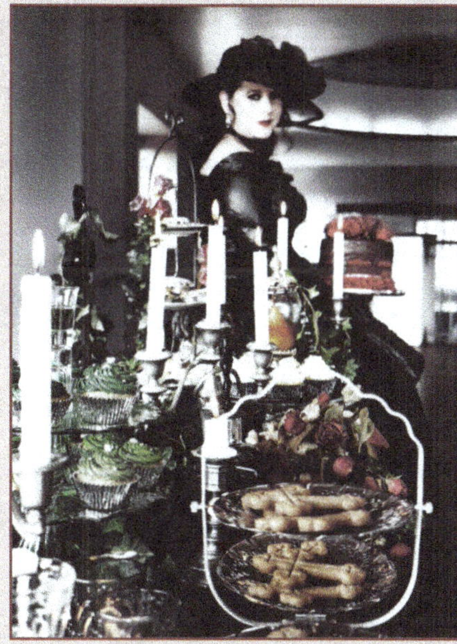

Miss T's creations are beautiful, and when asked about her inspiration she said, "I get inspiration from films, books, music and mood. I love the Victorian era and literature of the day. She added, "My absinthe cupcakes where inspired by a scene in Bram Stokers 'Dracula' where Mina was being seduced under the influence of absinthe by her dark prince. The crucifix cookies for example are also inspired by my vast vampire film collection." She is also in the process of creating a multi layered black crow cake dedicated to Edgar Allen Poe's 'The Raven' and the 'The Crow' movies.

The intricate detail she puts into her designs can only be described as amazing and innovative. She is so prideful in her creations and does not allow the most-minute design to be skipped. These are some very polished cookies, my darklings. When I asked how she did this she said," Solitude, patience, a steady hand and the right music." Music is what also pushes my creativity, so I was curious what the right music was. She said, "It all depends on the task at hand." She added, "I have found when covering my cakes in fondant, Godflesh is the best music for me. The droning guitar keeps me calm and focused". For the longer detailed work she said, "I will listen to The Cure, Echo and The Bunnymen, The Smashing Pumpkins, Portishead and Joy Division. Alice Cooper helps me cream my butter and sugar."

The flavors she come up with will truly take even the most cultured taste buds on and adventure, so I wondered about how she comes up with them. Miss T said, "Seasonal

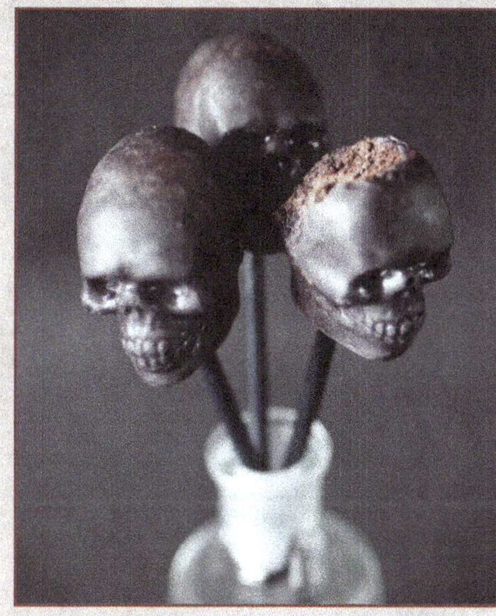

fruit is an inspiration." She will design a recipe around a berry if it's in season. A couple of examples of this would be her Strawberry Shortcake with bleeding coulis and Plum & Ginger Cheesecake. Alcohol also stimulates her creativity. Miss T has made St. Germain (which is an elderflower liqueur) poached pears in cupcakes and Cointreau Chocolate Fudge cake—with her favorite being the black forest cake soaked in Kirsch (cherry liqueur).

We have all seen television reality shows about bake offs, crazy kitchen chefs and contests about who can make the most interesting cake. Miss T's talent would intimidate any of the contestants on these programs. She lists her biggest challenge as an 8 layered, red velvet, 3D skull cake designed from the cover art off 'We Rise' by New Zealand rock band Devilskin. She said "I sculptured it by hand and covered it in fondant (sugar paste) and air brushed it gold and then watered painted it black for effect, complete with bullet shaped teeth."

When I asked what she envisioned for the future of her shop she said, "It's my ambition to publish a beautiful Gothic Baking Book and to open Miss T's Tearooms, a place where you can sit quietly in a dark corner and nibble on a Vampire Bite whilst sipping a brew."

If you are interested in ordering some of her devilish delights, she takes her orders through her Facebook page. She uses her special magic to ship all over the world so the Gothic goodies arrive fresh on your doorstep. I have my order in. You should get yours.

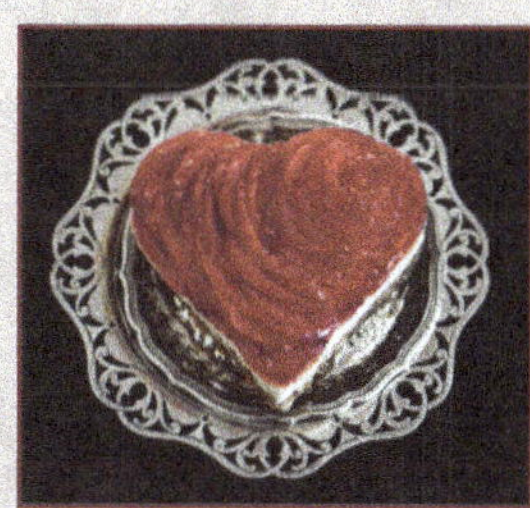

MEDUSA SEVAS TRA
OF
MOMENTO MORI

Rich, dark, raw, gothic, too beautiful to be terrifying but still dancing at the edge of macabre: everything that emerges from Medusa's studio Memento Mori, Inc., is as daring and distinctive as Medusa herself. While her style may defy description (hence, the pictures), Medusa herself likes to characterize it as "rogue taxidermy, wet specimens and macabre artwork dealing with bones and dead things."

Yes, my friends. Real dead things.

Whether bones or taxidermied animals, much if not all of Medusa's creations incorporate the remains of a once-living creature. It's a testament to her skill as an artist. Not to mention a poignant reminder that art can emerge even from life that has already passed.

The impetus for such creations comes largely from their scarcity in the marketplace. "If I see something is needed [in the art world], I want to make it," Medusa explains. "If it's never been made before, I want make it. Take my octopuses in jars, for example. People were selling 'specimens' like that that were just in jars. I took the octopus in a jar to a whole new level."

If you could have seen Medusa's table at RAW Natural Born Artists, you'd agree that it really is a whole new level. Her wares evince a distinctive mashup of gothic and steampunk (which I personally love) along with some medieval and Lovecraftian influences for good measure. The crowd at her table was three-deep every time I walked past. Probably because much of her work resembles the eclectic debris of a mad scientist's abandoned lair—and who doesn't love that? Especially when it's crafted from real bones and found animal carcasses?

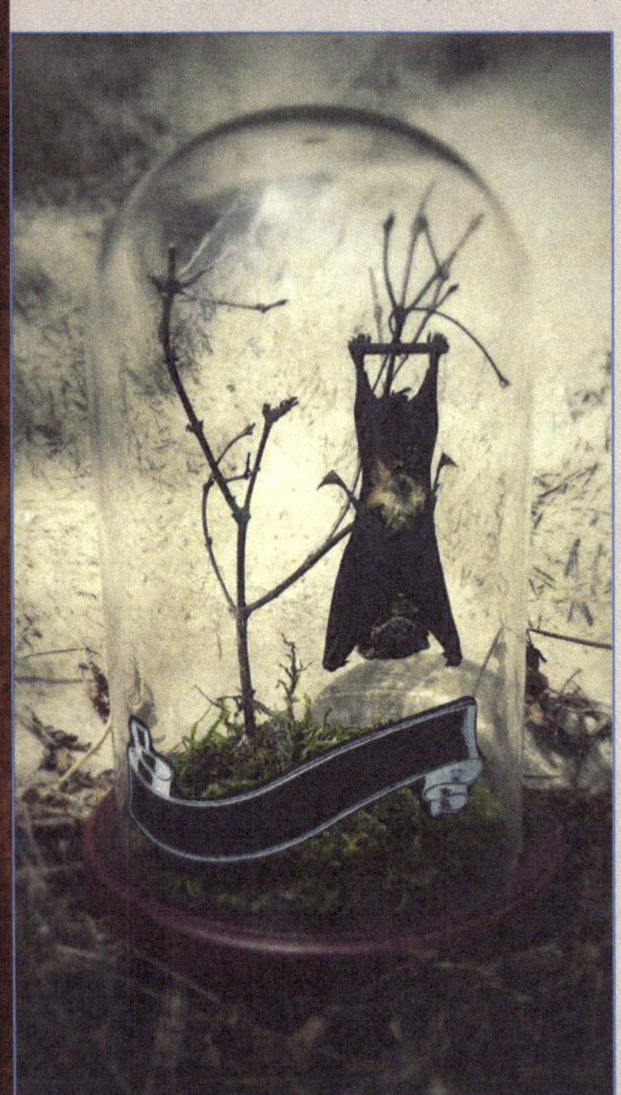

"I use all the health precautions," Medusa assures. "Plastic gloves, masks, respirators, goggles. I work with found specimens that expired in nature because I like everything to be as natural as possible. The octopuses are the only item I buy as prepared food. I defrost them and keep them in a special little jar."

Medusa's day job as a cake decorator plays well into her work. For one thing, it leverages the incredible hand skill she's developed in her work, which is often small or miniature in nature. On an average day she puts in her time crafting celebrations of life, then runs home to quite literally craft celebrations of the opposite.

It's an extreme Medusa takes with easy stride.

Luckily her roommates are able to do the same. They've even acquiesced to her using the small backyard for preparing the bodies of her future mammalian subjects. Medusa places each in a cat litter canister with holes drilled in the top and bottom. These she buries for months at a time, until the flesh "turns to mush" and drips into the earth. She can then remove the bones and take them through a mastication process to remove all the remaining debris.

Medusa's fan base has grown steadily over the last five years, but she's not sure all of them truly understand how much effort goes into each piece. Or that the specimens they buy are all real. Among her various offerings, her Vampire Heart installations are a perennial favorite. And while she did not start out doing jewelry, her first batch sold so well that she's continued to expand her line.

Sometimes the pieces are intensely personal, too. Customers send Medusa a baby tooth, for example, which she sets in resin and turns into a one-of-a-kind locket. Other times the piece may not involve so personal of a material, but the vision is just as original. For these Medusa will share sketches back and forth with the buyer until the right look is achieved. Then she must figure

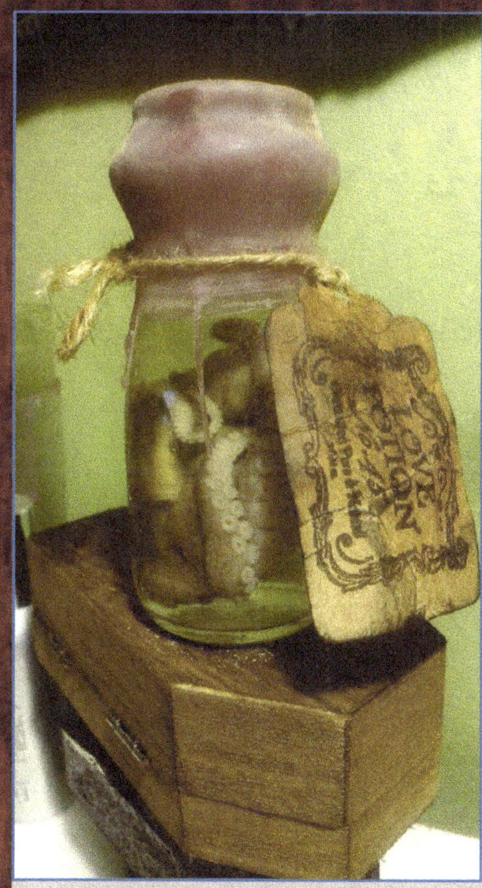

out how to execute it—often researching materials and techniques online to help her pioneer the production process.

So where did she get this amazing eye for art, using a set of materials most might overlook?

"It started about ten years ago, when I was doing haunts and horror makeup," she explains. "I began to realize that there wasn't a lot out there for the subcultures like the steampunk, horror and gothic communities. In steampunk, for example, everything is handmade. When it's churned out by a company, the fans leave. I wanted to answer the need for unique art."

But fandoms aren't the only markets that patronize her evolving line of limited-edition offerings. Medusa has also found an audience among roller derby players and fans, starting first with her own roller derby community at the BrewCity Bruisers, where she's been playing for several years.

Though Medusa's fan base and offerings have grown organically over the years, she's still a woman on a very serious mission. When asked about her creative influences, she referenced two women who may never have been mentioned in the same sentence

before: Otep—multi-hyphenate metal musician, slam poet, artist and painter—and the better-known magnate of lifestyle and decor, Martha Stewart.

Why these two specifically? "They're masterminds of their worlds," Medusa asserts. "Both of them have created a whole universe around themselves. Whenever you see their artistic output, you know it's them. It's unmistakable. That's my goal: to create my own unforgettable world."

From an outsider's perspective, Medusa is already well on her way to achieving her goal. Her courage and confidence exude in the form of easy grace. She knows her style. She knows that it matters, and though she already makes a tidy monthly income from her handmade creations, she forges ahead bravely with big plans for the future.

One of those plans in formal taxidermy school. Another is revamping her already-refined marketing strategies to afford her more visibility at high-profile fandom events for steampunks, goths and the horror community.

She smiles as she speaks of these plans, unfazed even by the constant uncertainties of being a working artist in today's world. When asked if she ever worries about what's to come, she reminded me of the many amazing performers and artists down through history whose vision carried them forward.

People like PT Barnum, for example. "When you start reading up on people like Barnum," Medusa says, "you discover that many of them went broke multiple times and then raised another empire almost overnight. They were forces of nature. Unstoppable."

It's this nimble maneuvering within singularity of purpose that makes Medusa herself as special as the art she creates. To all of us, her fellow artists and world-builders, she offers one piece of advice:

"Live in your bubble, and your bubble will come alive. Throw everything at it. Go all out . . . If you fail, tweak and go back at it. Never, ever give up."

With that, she hugged me and was off again. Maybe to frost some birthday cakes, or more possibly, to clean some dead animals. In the end, I don't suppose it really matters which.

For Medusa SeVesTra, it's all art anyway.

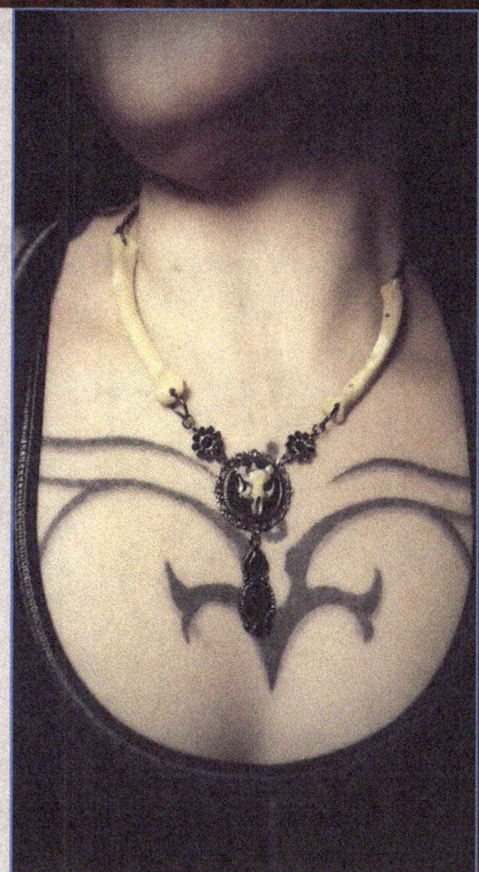

Discover Medusa's art for yourself at www.etsy.com/shop/MomentoMoriInc

Connect with Medusa www.facebook.com/medusahatesgerbils

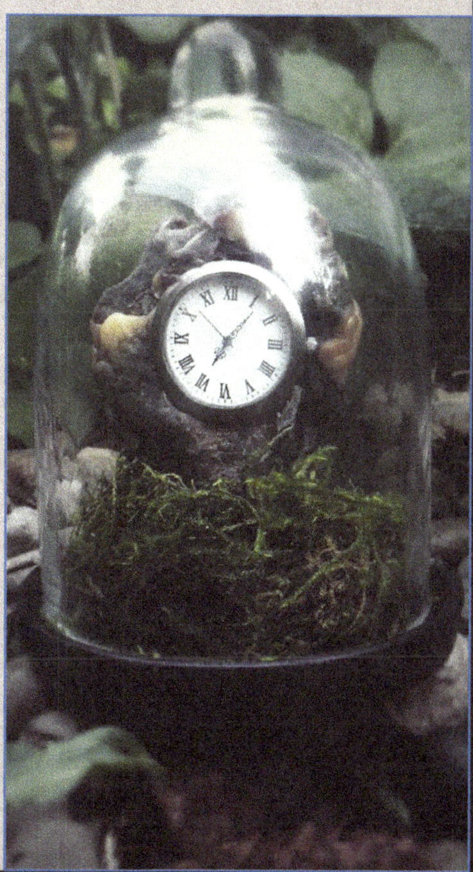

ONE EXPERIENCE WITH MEDUSA SEVAS TRA ART, AND YOU'LL ALWAYS BE ABLE TO FIND IT IN A CROWD.

STIMULANTS AND SEDITIVES: PART TWO

By Michael Jack and XXX ZOMBIEBOY XXX

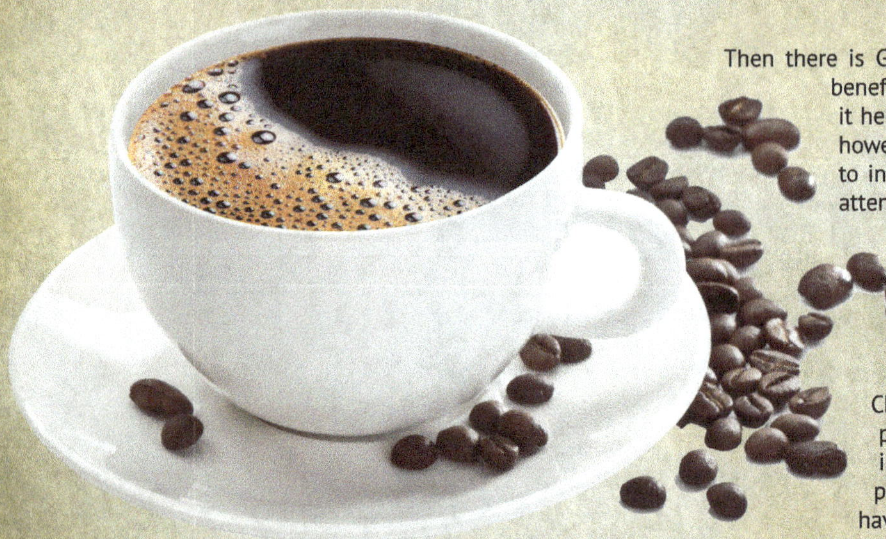

Then there is Ginseng. Korean Ginseng in particular has so many benefits (get your mind back in the gutter now because it helps that too). As we are on the subject of stimulants however I will focus on this benefit. Ginseng is proven to increase cognitive performance, as well as mood and attention span. Coupled with Gota Cola it increases blood flow to the brain, aids circulation, and reduces anxiety at the same time. As a side note, it also suppresses appetite and boosts the immune system.

I would like to take a moment to mention Chlorophyll. This is the green pigment you see in plants. What a lot of folks do not know is that it increases oxygen absorption to the cells. It also helps prevent cancer and I heard somewhere that if you have an arc reactor in your chest, it helps lower blood poisoning.

WAKE UP!! Mike got you does on some good stuff but I need you to wake back up again for some more advice. XXX ZOMBIEBOY XXX Here and I have some ups and downs for you as well. First, not to counter act Mike but don't ignore ALL Joe! Just Joe on the corner. If you need to get up from that night of seeing KMFDM and Motley Crue (like that would ever happen) then Joe is your friend! As in that blessed sweet nectar of the gods, COFFEE!!! Yeah, Mike mentioned this already. And I cannot agree more. Java is still the best thing in the world for that post ill-advised late night before your job at the call center, the bank or wherever your personal Hell is.

First of all, Coffee is loaded with antioxidants and actually fights a number of diseases! Once that caffeine... that GLORIOUS caffeine gets through your bloodstream and into your brain, it blocks an inhibitory neurotransmitter called Adenosine, which in turn fires up the neurotransmitters you want such as norepinephrine, which leads to the firing of more neurons. Drinking coffee and using caffeine also lead to weight loss, increased physical performance (get your mind out of the gutter, I am referring to normal physical activity), and can even lower your chances of type II Diabetes, Alzheimer's, Parkinson's and Dementia. Drinking coffee also helps fight cirrhosis; it is an antidepressant (unless the poetry slam is really bad), and even fights some forms of cancer. Not to mention IT WAKES YOU UP!! It is also one of the best excuses for a first date. I mean, lets face it. You don't exactly invite a love interest to meet you for a cup of orange juice.

Another excellent source of energy out there comes from the far away land of Brazil. This is the magnificent Guarana. Used in most of the South American sodas as a form of caffeine (but not actually caffeine), guarana improves cognitive ability, mood, focus and reaction time. It lasts longer than caffeine (8-10 hours) and it doesn't give you the jitters. When I was working as a tour bus driver in Portugal, I had a club owner hand me a two-liter bottle of Guarana soda. Twenty-four hours later we pulled into Germany. It is wonderful stuff!

Two of the most common ingredients in energy drinks are B-Vitamins and Taurine. The first aids in energy and focus but be sure that it is in the form of methylcobalamin or else it may just be genetically created trash. The later is an amino acid and has been known to improve athletic performance.

To get your Zef on try some Hoodia. This is a cactus like plant from South Africa and a proven powerful stimulant, which does not give you the jitters like caffeine does.

Then there is cocaine. Oh you took that? You are stupid. Moving on!

So now once more you are home from that waste of life office and jacked up on all the aminos and herbs that Zombie told you to put in your smoothies. Now you need sleep. HALP!

Though I am from the "I'll sleep enough when I am dead," philosophy of thinking, I do think that weeklong benders of no sleep are ill advised. You start to look like Jonah Hex with a hangover and inanimate objects start to talk to you. Shut up pencil.

There are a number of excellent alternatives to medication out there to help you get rested. One of them is now legal in Denver. That's all I need say on the subject. Michael already discussed one of these and that is Melatonin. The assassin that strikes after a big Thanksgiving meal. That's one of the reasons you always get sleepy from the beloved turkey leg. It is full of the stuff. Melatonin is gentle and it works. Sometimes it takes a while but it is good stuff.

Another excellent sleep aid is Valerian. This herbal extract has been proven to reduce anxiety as well as fight insomnia. It reduces the time it takes to get sleep and improves the quality of your rest. It also does not have the groggy morning effect that is so common in over the counter aids or antihistamines. It is not however a good idea to drive after taking it. Some studies show that it can impair mental capacity for a brief period much the same way as alcohol does.

One of the oldest and most popular sleep aids out there is Chamomile. As either a tea or a tincture, chamomile has a calming and relaxing effect that aids in getting to sleep. By itself however that is all it does. It helps yet there. Best to use in conjunction with something else.

Kava Kava has been growing in popularity and is in fact one of my personal favorites. It has seen such a growth in popularity that there have even been café's and bars opening up such as Kavasutra, which serve this in a drink form. It is excellent for fighting anxiety and relaxing the mind without effecting motor function. There is a mild danger of liver toxicity however so do not overdo it.

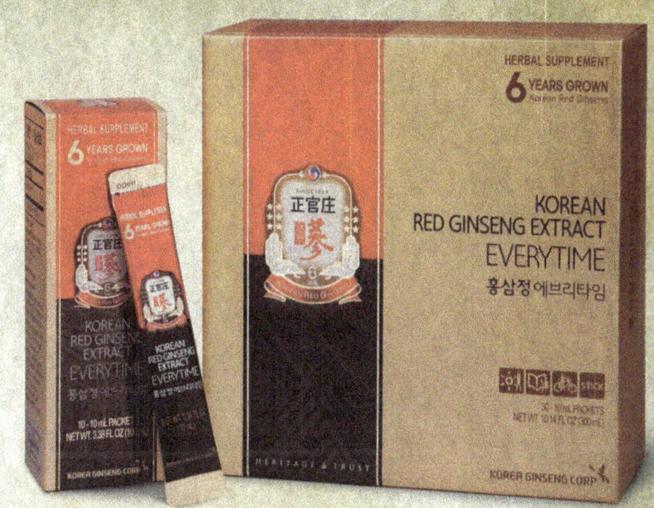

I will bring this to a close by mentioning Kratom. A relative of coffee, this herb is growing in popularity as well because it can work as a stimulant, a painkiller and a euphoria builder. Kratom has had very little research done on it and websites often conflict on how to use it. Some say to take one for stimulation and two for meditation. Myself I take one on the morning with my coffee and it really gets me going. It improves mood and does have a euphoric effect without affecting your mental capabilities. The over all opinion is that higher doses are sedative and lower doses are stimulating. Kratom is also effective as a mild painkiller and some studies see it as a potential way to get over addictive drug use. However, one should approach with caution and experiment to see how it affects you personally. A tolerance can be built, there is some evidence of dependency and addiction and if you take too much you may find it flying back out. It is great stuff. But you should not binge on it. Properly used however it can be stimulating and lead to feelings of warmth and contentment without grogginess or loss of mental capacity.

Toasts with my fourth cup of Café Du Monde Chicory Coffee
SLIANTE!

BLOODY Marvelous!

BLOODY MARY'S AND FOOD ODDITIES
By XXX ZOMBIEBOY XXX

Greetings and Salutations readers! As you may know I travel everywhere I can and when I do I try to find the best Bloody Mary in the land (though admittedly I prefer the Tequila version sometimes called a Bloody Maria). Having landed here in New Orleans I can certainly spend the next oh… millennia trying to sample all of the opportunities here, and possibly pickle myself in the process. I can tell you though that I have found some gems. For example Aunt Tiki's on Decatur has one of the best I have found ANYWHERE. Some other notables are The Brass Helmet, Frank's Italian, Mojos and the multi talented bartender that I am about to introduce you to. Modern Morticia is a dancer, a craftswoman, a model, an artist, a singer and a very talented bartender as I was to discover when I wondered into Little Tokyo. Her Murderous Geisha is a completely unique version of the Bloody Mary with a wonderful Asian twist. It has a flavor that is deep and delicious and has enough kick to keep up with the wasabi I put in my soy sauce. I will let her describe the recipe in her own words.

Modern Morticia: My Murderous Geisha is the ultimate Asian Bloody Mary! First, I rim the cup with Japanese rice seasoning and swirl Sriracha on the inside of the glass. Then in a shaker, I combine 1 oz of Absolut Peppar Vodka with another of Tito's Handmade Vodka (or Ketel One if Tito's is unavailable) a little bit of olive juice and low sodium soy sauce to taste, and about 3 oz of Zing Zang Bloody Mary Mix. I shake until it is mixed well, and then pour it over ice into your Bloody Mary glass. Then I garnish with a little bit of white pepper and green onion over the top, and some bokchoy, white onions, and green beans.

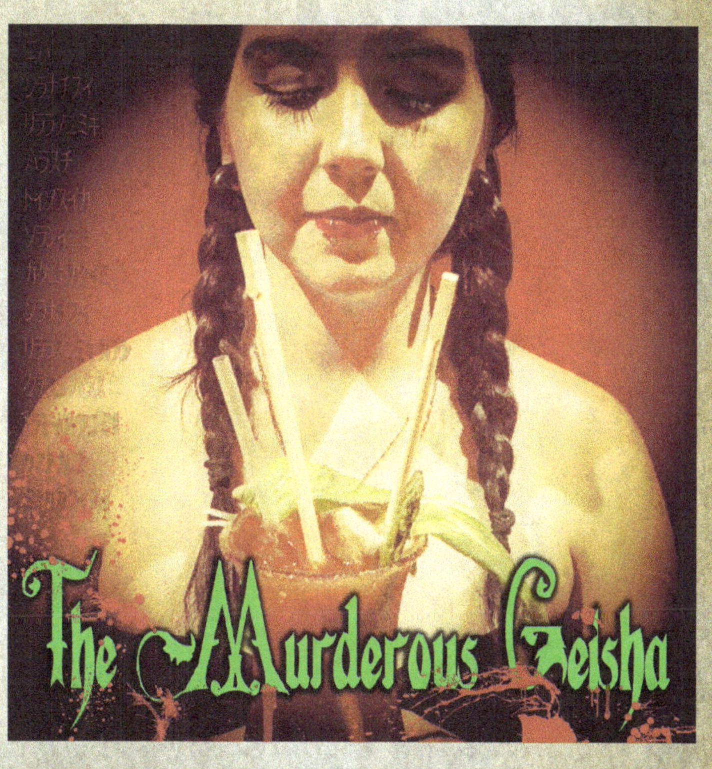

By Chirality

Most animals have only 72 hours from the time they are brought in to find a home. Black dogs are the hardest to house and we all know cats are always around. Only one out of ten dogs will find a permanent home. Every year 2.7 million dogs and cats are euthanized in shelters and homeless animals out number people 5 to 1. Animals need us, We domesticated them and they need our help. You can do something about it.

Karma Cat and Zen Dog Rescue Society is based in East Brunswick, NJ. Their mission is to provide a safe and peaceful haven for homeless pets and to provide a calm environment for those who have been neglected and abused. Their goal is to reduce the pets killed in shelters through spay and neuter programs, trap/neuter/returns and educational programs.

Adoptions are held every Saturday and Sunday at the Petsmart located in North Brunswick, NJ. They are there from 11am-3pm most days. You can also make an appointment to meet one of their lovely animals for adoption!

They do a lot of events to get people to adopt and to education people on pet adoption. On August 22, it was our scene who welcomed them to QXT's in Newark, NJ. Everyone came out to help with this cause and to help homeless pets. More then $1,000 was raised! It was all about dogs and cats galore on Saturday at QXT's. There was also a food donation for the Newark Animal Shelter and a silent auction where the proceeds went to the rescue.

If you wish to donate, volunteer or purchase a shirt you can go too http://karmacatzendog.org. You can also donate your time or funds to your local animal shelter or pound.

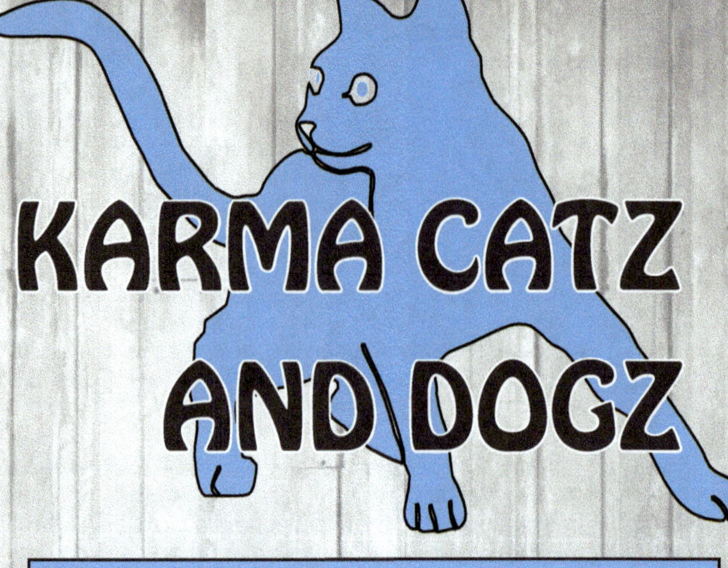

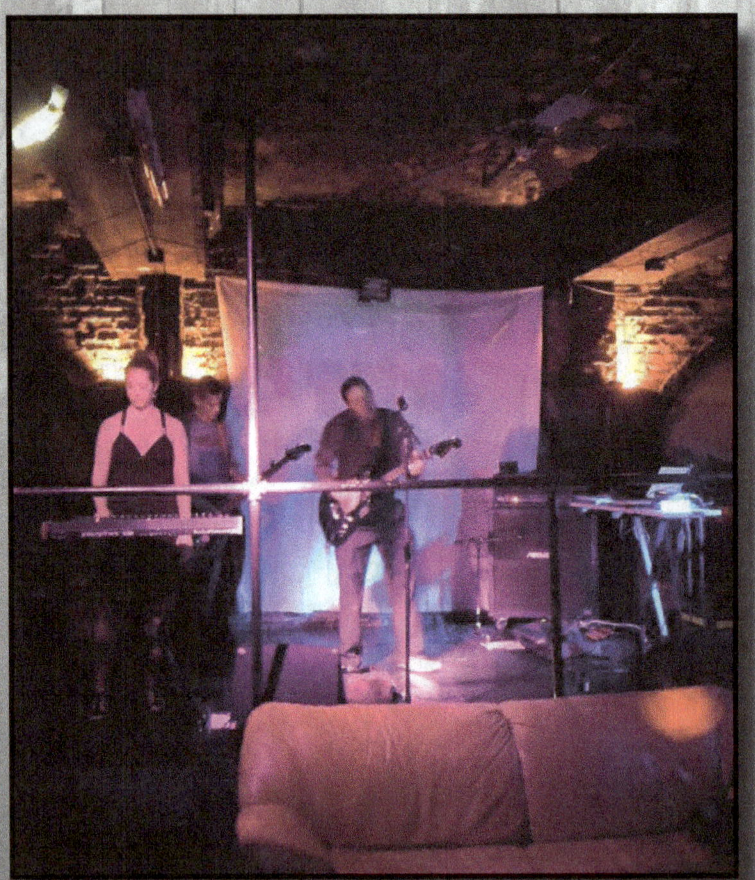

Auction Donors:

Theater of Terror
http://www.theatreofterror.net/

Suffer
https://www.facebook.com/pages/Suffer/

King of the witches
http://www.cauldron.club/

Zap Photography
https://www.facebook.com/ZapPhoto

Grindhouse Nights
https://www.facebook.com/
GrindhouseNightsAtCafeZ?fref=ts

Karnevil
https://www.facebook.com/Karnevil

Lillian Bustle
https://www.facebook.com/LillianBustle.

Dharmata101
https://www.facebook.com/dharmata101

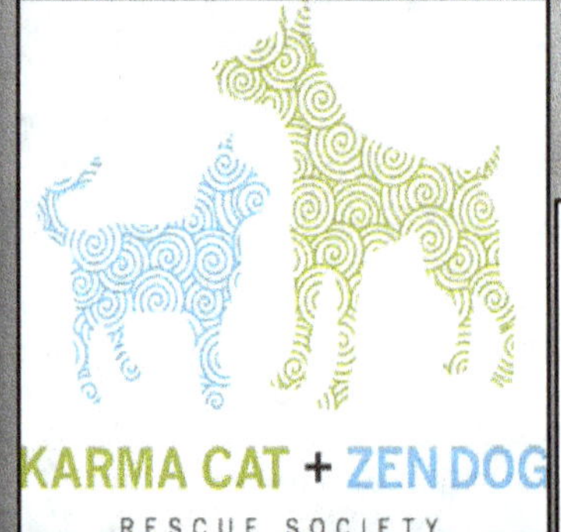

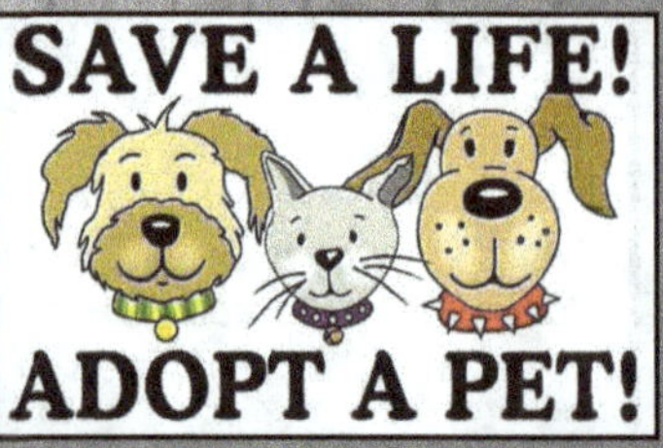

Marriage Equality for All

The time has come to celebrate, ghouls and gals. On June 26, 2015, the U.S. Supreme Court legalized same sex marriage in all 50 states. We finally did it! I live in Michigan, which still had a same sex marriage ban in place up until the Supreme Court ruling. All states must now recognize marriages between two people of any gender or sexual orientation. Society is evolving. Humans are embracing one another's differences. However, the fight is not over yet.

I heard the wonderful news and I was excited to share it with my family. I asked my dad what his opinion was on the ruling and he acted disinterested while my brother shouted out a homophobic slur. I wish I could say I wasn't used to this sort of behavior. Usually I would just blow it off. For some reason, it really affected me that day. When the world makes strides toward acceptance, but your family still doesn't accept you, it's hard to be happy. The whole country was celebrating and I was crying alone in my bedroom.

My mom saw how upset I was and had a talk with my dad and brother. They both apologized, which I appreciated. I think my relationship with my family will improve once I move out on my own very soon. We'll all have space and they'll have time to come to terms with who I am and how I want to live my life. I'll create my own supportive environment so that I can truly discover myself and have peace of mind.

My whole life, I never envisioned myself getting married. I thought marriage would take away my freedom and come with a lot of responsibility that I didn't want. I'm beginning to realize that what I didn't want to give myself was false hope. I knew it was against the law for me to get married and I couldn't imagine my friends and family happily celebrating my gay union. My mindset is changing now. I, too, have the opportunity and the privilege to marry whomever I want to. I can picture the ceremony and the support of my loved ones. I'll never say never again.

Beyond the legalization of same sex marriage, LGBTQ people still don't have equal rights. In Michigan alone, LGBTQ people face legal discrimination in public places, schools, when buying a house, when applying for health care, etc. Transgender people have to jump through hoops to change the gender listed on their driver's licenses and birth certificates. Michigan doesn't even recognize violence against LGBTQ people as a hate crime. We won a huge battle with same sex marriage, but we can't stop now.

That in mind, it's certainly okay to revel in the good news. Ah, I can see it now: A Halloween wedding in a sprawling Victorian garden with spooky candelabras and thrones for the grooms. I suppose I'm getting ahead of myself. I need to find a boyfriend first.

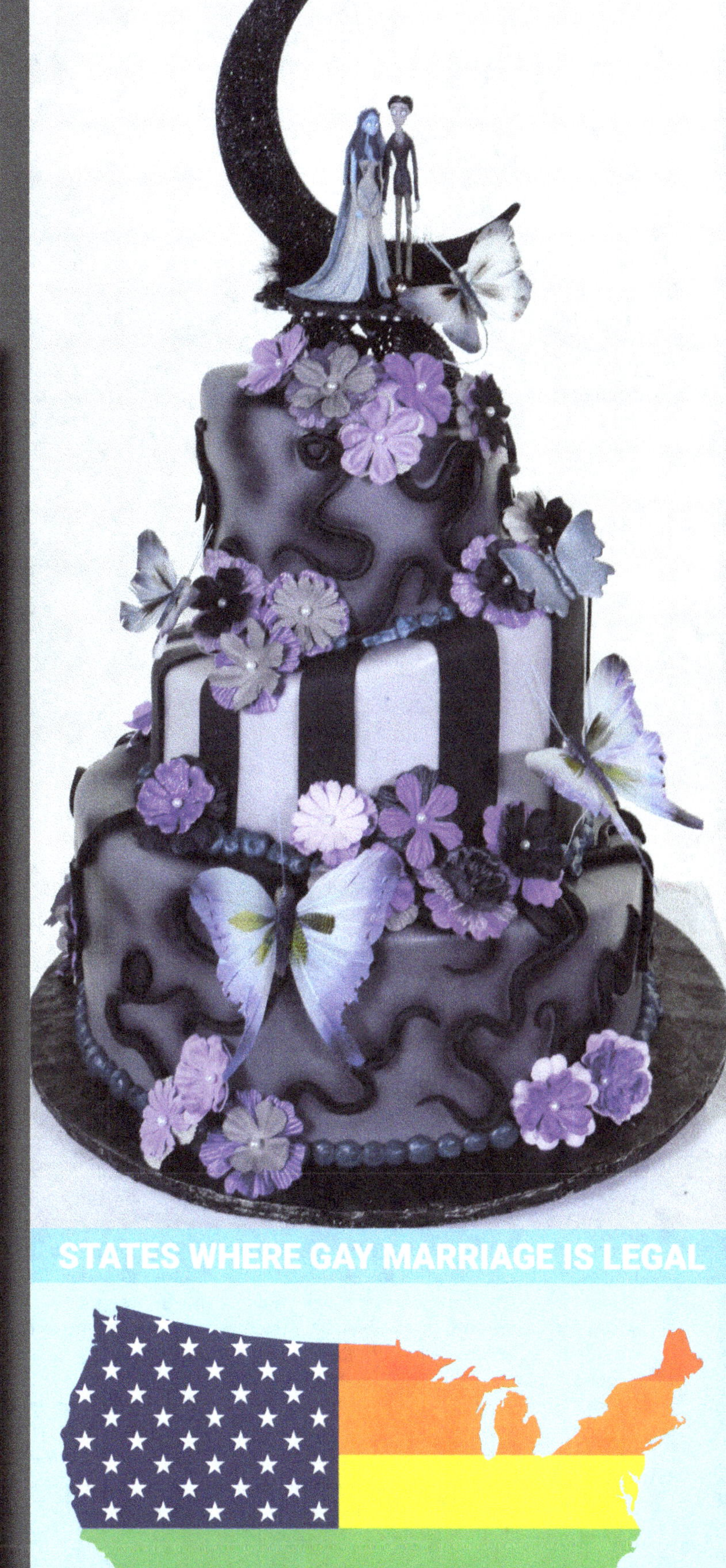

SURVIVING THE ZOMBIE APOCALYPSE

By XXX ZOMBIEBOY XXX

So I know some of you have been waiting on this one…

WEAPONS!

What to kill your friendly neighborhood zombies with! Before you go running for a white Katana or raiding the local Wal Mart, lets think about this. Because remember THINKING CLEARLY is the MOST IMPORTANT THING! It is why so many heroes in horror movies make horrible errors! There are pluses and minuses in every weapon. So what I will do is go through some of the old familiars. And then some.

Let us begin with the Katana. Oh the great and beautiful work of art from Feudal Japan that just makes you want to hold it to the sky and say, "There can be only ONE!" I hate to burst your bubble here but for many of you, this is NOT a good weapon to reach for. Before you lynch me or even worse, send one of our favorite Walking Dead characters out to take off my head let me explain. This weapon is not only awesome, but it deserves tremendous respect. It is a work of art that only a handful of people in the modern day know how to make and can take weeks or even months to make. It is as deadly as it is beautiful. Why shouldn't you reach for it? Because unless you have studied Kenjitsu, Iaido, or Kendo extensively, this weapon will be virtually useless to you. It requires a great skill to use it. It isn't like a machete that you can just pick up and start hacking away with. Chances are unless you are specifically trained with it, it will stick in the very first zombie you try to use it on. And it will take you a long time to get it out again. Also, there are very few real ones out there. A good Katana will run you hundreds of dollars. A great one in the thousands. Those ones you see for oh… $200 or so at the local market? The ones wrapped with cloth? Not real. They make great clubs and not much else. If you are interested in this weapon and serious about your interest I highly recommend you pursue that interest, go to a school teaching these amazing martial arts and learn the discipline and respect these works of art deserve. Everyone else? Don't pick it up. You will lose.

Moving on!

Machine Guns!! RatatatatatatTAT!!! No. Don't. It isn't like the movies kids. Trained soldiers, police and gun enthusiasts that DO KNOW how to use these, feel free to skip down to the paragraph below. Everyone else please listen. These are very complicated weapons (in general). You need to know how to load, clean, break down and put back together as well as maintain them. The idea of standing in front of a whole swarm of zombies and unloading in a heroic stance and a thunderstorm of glory is very romantic and a quick way to get eaten. Those that know how to use these can attest to how hard they can be to shoot and actually hit what you are shooting at. If you do grab one however, I recommend setting it to single fire. Ammo is going to be one hell of a precious commodity in the zombie apocalypse. Finding the right kind and the right amount to get you by is going to be a hard sell. I'm not saying don't grab one if you can. I am just stating the downfalls of making it your go to weapon. However if you do know how to use one and you have the ammo? Have fun.

While we are on guns, let us go through rifles and pistols. These are better options. The ammo is more common and easy to obtain. They are easier to control and last longer. Both make great clubs when they run out too. Just remember. You need the ammo, you need the gear to clean and maintain them, and you need to know how to shoot. If you have never been to a gun range, I highly recommend doing so. It is a tough world. I am neither pro nor con gun use in this column. I am however very pro

discipline and knowledge. Know what you have and how to use it well and you may just make it through.

Leaving guns behind for a moment let's go back to bladed weapons. In the Walking Dead we see our heroes use knives a whole lot. And the show has been pretty smart about where to stab to take down a zombie. As a side note, we are assuming that zombies are slow and that destroying the brain will stop them. I highly recommend having a good knife on you. Not a folding gas station $15 "Special Ops" knife painted in camo. Get yourself a good quality one. They are out there. Tanto knives will go through a car door. They also don't break easy. And a good knife is also an excellent tool for almost everything. Make sure you have a sharpener to go with it.

Axes are great as far as their strength and crushing ability. Just remember that it takes a lot of energy and strength to use one constantly. And they are also hazardous for getting stuck in that zombie's head. The same can truly be said for all bladed weapons. Be ready for this.

Machetes are decent as well. Cheap and easy to use. Just remember, you are trying to get through a skull. And forget about beheading that zombie. Ever try to take down even a small young tree with a machete? Forget it. They are however good tools and they can pack a wallop.

A word on bats. This is and always will be my favorite weapon against zombies. Solid, strong and crushing. No ammo needed, no cleaning, no upkeep. Just good old-fashioned skull crushing fun! An aluminum bat will last longer. I am however a traditionalist. I love me a good old Louisville Slugger. Even if not your

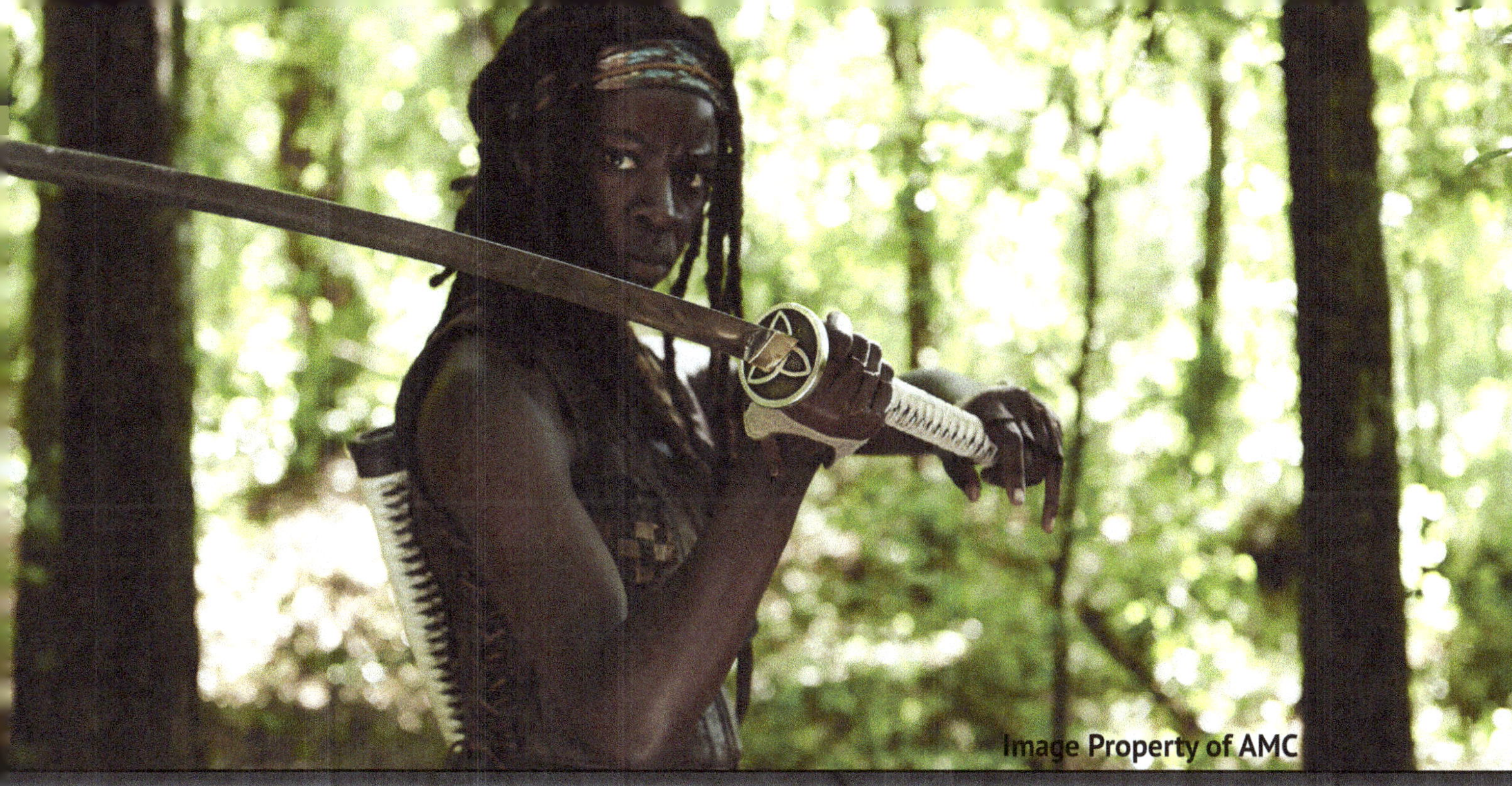

favorite weapon, have one with you. They are a great back up if nothing else.

Explosives! You have fun with those. Very... very far from anywhere I am. Enough said.

Now just for a moment and perhaps throwing out all I just told you, let me introduce you to two zombie-destroying friends. The AA12 assault shotgun and the minigun. The AA12 is a fully automatic assault shotgun that can be loaded with a drum clip and pretty much evaporate a whole crowd of zombies right in front of you. They can even be loaded with mini-grenades firing at the same rate. And the minigun is a chain fed weapon usually used on combat helicopters. See Predator and look for "old painless". These two weapons are devastating and awesome. They are however quite rare and again, you need to know how to use them, how to maintain them and have the ammo for them.

Shotguns are easy to come by and so is the ammo. Just remember that depending on the type of ammo you are using, they are designed to spread out (generally). Close range these are wonderful. At long range you are far better off using a good rifle with a good scope. This scenario is honestly the best case!

I will make a quick shout out to the cats at Zombie Tools. They make some pretty great anti Zed stuff!
Check them out at: http://www.zombietools.net/

Where does that leave us? Surrounded by zombies!! So, barring all I have said, use anything you can get your hands on! I myself keep a decent zombie killing tool within reach everywhere in my home. When it all comes down, anything can be used as a weapon of some sort. Guitars, kitchen knives, shovels, boards, crowbars, framed paintings, shopping carts, rubber chickens, it doesn't matter. This is the zombie apocalypse! Grab whatever you can and use it to the best of your abilities. There are a whole lot of the dead out there.

al blood drops
Artist Sarah Segovia
Boutique
DU
Vampyre

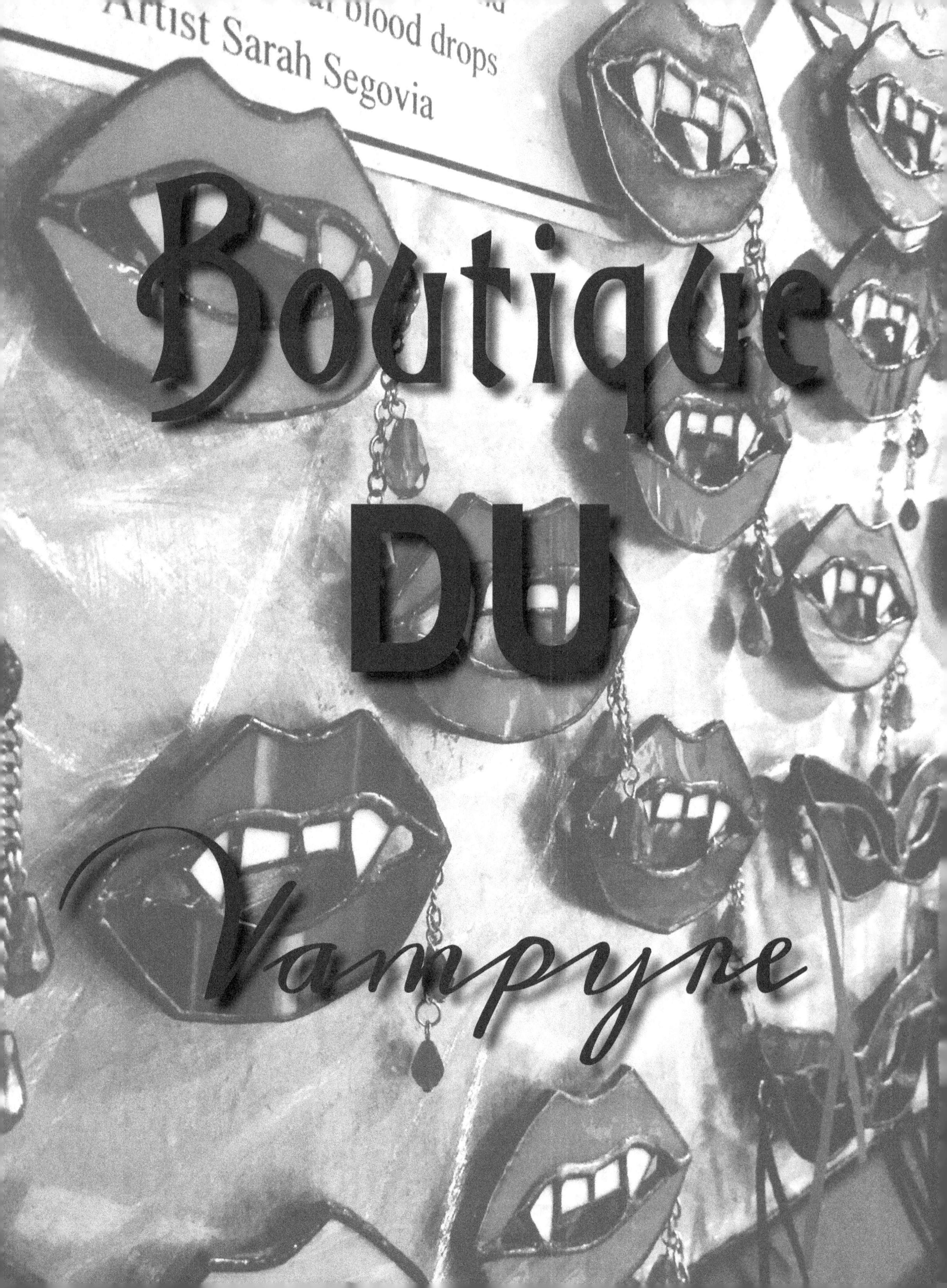

"Upon entering the little boutique I knew I had re-discovered a treasure."

By XXX ZOMBIEBOY XXX

Once upon a long time ago I found myself in the Veux Carre once more. I could not say with any degree of accuracy what year it was or my purpose for being there other than to indulge in history, beauty and vice; all of which this lovely part of the world has in enormous measure. On my way to the Pirates Alley Café to sit beneath an oil painting of La Fee Verte and indulge in her spirit, I came upon a small window with paintings and a dark interior. I was intrigued and within discovered a small boutique dedicated to Vampires. Thrilled, I walked out with a painting of a Witch called "Trick or Treat" from a local artist named Melody (no last name) and a small vial of deeply intoxicating rose created from the oldest perfume maker in New Orleans. I would return years later to find my little treasure gone. Unbeknownst to me however, the boutique had only moved in the wake of Katrina. Moving to the area I re-discovered the boutique and delighted at the chance discovery, I immediately sought out the owner Marita Jaeger to hear the story of the **Boutique du Vampyre**.

Upon entering the little boutique I knew I had re-discovered a treasure. Their motto was Carpe Noctem and I couldn't help but mention our magazine Carpe Nocturne which Marita immediately loved. And as she said to me, "My personal motto since college had always been Carpe Diem. I've always woken up with a good attitude and ready to hit the ground running, so why not translate that into the vampire world as well!" I asked Marita if she would mind my doing a little write up on the shop for our upcoming autumn issue and if she would tell me a little of her story.

She first set foot in New Orleans in the late 90s. Originally from Germany, she was immediately charmed by the historical aspect and feel of the city just as I had been long ago. In fact, we both agreed that we felt immediately at home. That the city has a way of pulling you in. It is so very true.

Marita had come on business and found herself creating more and more short business trips to the Quarter. Finally on one such trip Marita decided to rent a small apartment on Royal, right across from Pirate's Alley which runs along side the St. Louis Cathedral. Her thinking was that she wouldn't feel as sad leaving every time, if she had an apartment here. She came to stay in the apartment Halloween weekend 2001, and like so many others before her, never left. She sold her house in California over the phone, flew home and picked up her dogs. And anyone with pets will pretty much agree that once they are moved, it is official!

I glanced around at the shop again. So unique. Not a horror shop but a vampire shop specifically. And if there were

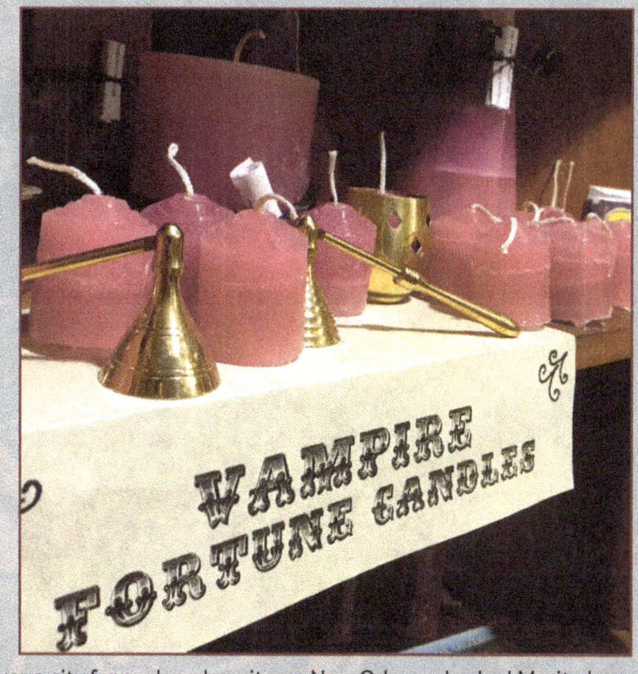

ever a city for such a place it was New Orleans. I asked Marita how she came to such an idea, to cater specifically to fans of vampire myth and legend. She remembered drinking Vampire Wine in California, and had never seen it in New Orleans. She actually contacted the owner of the company and he agreed to meet with her to review a marketing plan. So it turns out that Marita introduced the wine to New Orleans. On this score I had to thank her as it is one of my own personal autumn treats. She even worked with him to create Fangria. And from this exchange came the idea of a Vampire themed boutique.

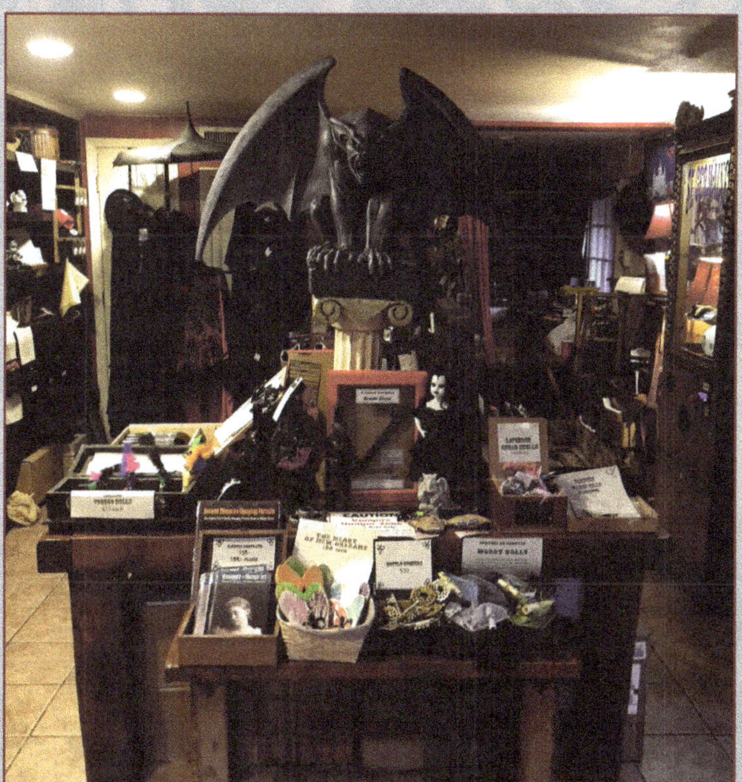

"I really wanted to create a magical place, that when people entered our shop, they would be temporarily transported into, if just for a moment, a fantasy. Could vampires really exist?" She asked. I explained that on all supernatural creatures I was very open minded. That I myself was looking to do ghost tours. She went on to tell me, "Our Mission Statement is: To create a unique shopping experience for vampires and mortals alike, by featuring handcrafted items with a New Orleans flare, as well as enriching each customer's visit to New Orleans through personal attention, building strong bonds and customers for eternity. We started with just six products: Our fortune candles that have little charms inside, and we select the correct candle for each customer, my artwork, greeting cards by a local artist, boutique T-shirts, Vampire Wine's energy drink VAMP, wine gift boxes, and a game I created called Duel to Dawn. It was a struggle at first, but we added local artists and moved the shop to Cabildo Alley, where the shop thrived until Katrina."

Katrina. I realized while talking with her that it was almost the ten year anniversary of that terrible storm. I had a feeling that this was the reason for the change in location. Katrina caused a tremendous amount of economic damage to the French Quarter, and vampires were certainly not excluded.

"We ended up having to temporarily close the shop six months after the storm. We kept our website going however, until we were able to reopen about 8 months later, once again on Orleans behind the Cathedral. For various reasons we moved twice more until we found our current location at 709 ½ St. Ann Street at Royal. This has been a wonderful spot for the Boutique. Just off the beaten path, there is plenty of foot traffic, but the location has a "secret" feel to it, by being on a side street."

Yes, Katrina was a tragedy on a horrific scale. I told Marita how I remembered going to find the boutique to re-supply on Bouquet du Vampyre and being saddened to find it was gone. Then being delighted again when I just happened to (possibly literally) stumble across the boutique again at its current location. I took a moment to wander the store as customers came in. And marveled at how much I could have dropped in one visit had I been "in funds" at the time. First there were the books. A huge bookshelf of vampire novels. To my delight I discovered that most

if not all of them were signed. Then there were candles, scents, marvelous hand made jewelry and even bottled vampires. What struck me was a lack of "Made In China" stamps on the wares. I asked Marita when she was free, if everything was local.

"Over the years we have attracted an amazing group of talented artists, mostly local, but also several across the country that make exclusive items for the Boutique. Almost everything in the shop is handcrafted just for us. We are so fortunate in New Orleans to have a vast pool of talent to

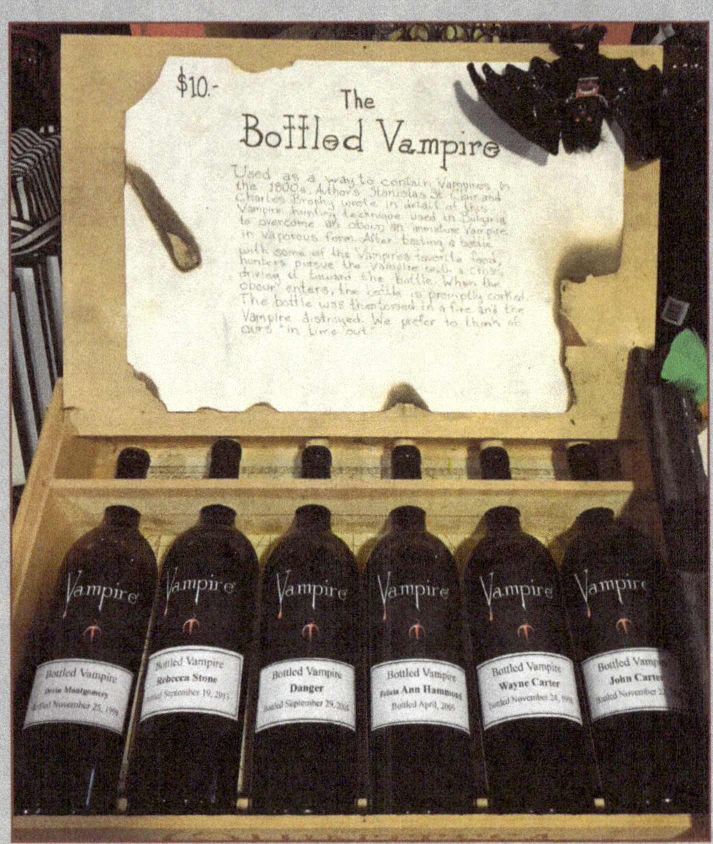

> **"It was nice to see such interpersonal exchange in a world swarming with corporate moguls who could care less."**

pull from. Our magical city attracts magical people. I feel that when tourists come to visit the city, they certainly don't want to find things made overseas, and given the talent we have here, it would be crazy not to put that to use. It's what New Orleans is all about." When I asked her about all the signed books she stated, "As far as books, in addition to attracting artists, New Orleans feeds peoples souls, giving them so much to write about. It makes zero sense to me to carry books that are not signed. We have such limited space, so introducing our customers to books where the authors care enough to come to the shop for book signings and meet their readers is certainly a wonderful addition to the shop."

I myself came picked up a copy of the Casquette Girls by Alys Arden. It was lovely to see that she had signed it. Something I geek out about. The Casquette Girls is Alys' first book. She was apparently very nervous to approach the boutique to sell the book. Marita is very careful what she chooses to put on the shelf, because the boutique has a very loyal following of readers who have come to trust their library.

"I told Alys, who lives just around the corner, that I would read the book, and let her know.

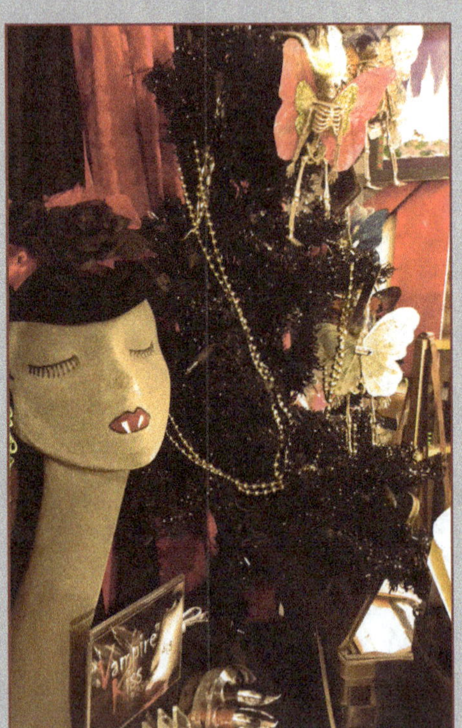

Well, I was blown away, and not only began to carry her book, but also introduced her to Anne Rice, who is also now promoting the book. It is so much fun to be in a position to be able to help artists and authors," she told me with enthusiasm.

It is a wonderful symbiotic relationship and greatly appreciated by the community. As to the other artists, many of them have approached with unusual items. And many of the artists they carry started as boutique customers.

"It is amazing the number of regular customers we have that are very talented artists. Like Sarah Segovia, who makes our stained glass items, such as our awesome signature Fangnets, refrigerator magnets that are lips with fangs and Swarovski crystal blood drops. Or Stephanie Knight, who makes our one of kind Creepy Dolls. Each one is a masterpiece. There are too many artists to mention, but each one is special to me, and they know it."

It was nice to see such interpersonal exchange in a world swarming with corporate moguls who could care less. And the artists they carry are both eclectic and talented. I asked Marita how she generated interest in the shop given its almost hidden feel. She started a blog called VBITE, Vampire Business and International Topics of Entertainment and she does it almost nightly. It is meant to be a vampire news spot.

"I try to cover vampire world news, and then throw in something about the shop. It's all in good fun, and gives vampire enthusiasts something to tune into." The boutique have been a long supporters of the Endless Night Vampire Ball, hosted by Father Sebastian and held at the House of Blues the Saturday of Halloween weekend.

"We also help promote the Anne Rice fan club ball every Halloween weekend on Friday night, and we are a major supporter of the New Orleans Witches Ball, held at the Elms Mansion on St. Charles, also the Saturday of Halloween weekend," she continued. "We also have a nightclub that pops up occasionally called Vampyre Cabaret. It's a private club, but members can bring the same guest twice, before they must become a member. It's also a lot of fun, but a lot of work, so it has been open less frequently than I like." This is an event I hope to do a write up on myself soon.

To focus on the subject matter, Vampires have gone through many portrayals and evolutions, sometimes revolutions it seems, in our popular culture. When I asked Marita her opinion on what is it about the vampire that continues to fascinate through the years and the many portrayals.

"It is a crazy phenomenon. People in the dark ages were terrified of various interpretations of vampires, and today modern culture has morphed the vampire into something very sexual and desired. I believe it really stems to the fact that they offer eternal life, and they drink the life force. Those two things give people a mystery to ponder that is alluring." We then geeked out about vampires in cinema and their many incarnations. Films ranging in style and format from After Dark to Lair of the White Worm and Lost Boys.

" I personally like them all – the terrifying and the beautiful. I really enjoyed the recent film Only Lovers Left Alive. I think it is the most realistic of what being a modern day vampire would be like. Let the

Right One In is wonderful, Lost Boys, of course "Interview with a Vampire", "Dracula" both new and old, gosh, the list is truly too long. I actually really miss the old black and white vampire films they would put on in the middle of the night; my brother and I would sneak out of our rooms to watch. Like I said, I love them all."

At this point more customers found their way into the store. After purchasing a bracelet for my girl Viola, I wandered back outside to meander the streets a while longer. Yet, something was itching in my brain. The one question I wanted to ask but felt a little cheesy asking. And as you know, it is always that one thing that stays and stays. So in the end, I made my way back into the shop. Marita smiled and welcomed me back. Asking perhaps was there another book I wanted to add to my collection. To this my response was typical. That I was a greedy bibliophile and would take the whole lot if I could. It was one last question however I wanted to know.

"Ask me then," she invited warmly.

"Would you dear Lady Marita, bare your own neck to a true vampire if ever given the chance to meet such?"

My question was not as cheesy as I had thought for she considered for a long moment.

"I've often wondered that too – what would I do? It sounds so romantic, to be a chosen one by someone who can give you the gift of eternal life. However, I had a very realistic dream once in which a very ferocious vampire was about to bite me, and I knew it would change my life forever. I was terrified, and when I woke up and realized it was just a dream, I had wished I went for it to see what would happen - however, in my dream, I fought him off. There are so many consequences that would surely be devastating."

With my final answer, I bid her farewell for the time being. I have since revisited the Boutique du Vampyre a number of times. Spending time in the quiet and peaceful dark shop pondering my own question and also checking my budget to see what I could get my hands on next.

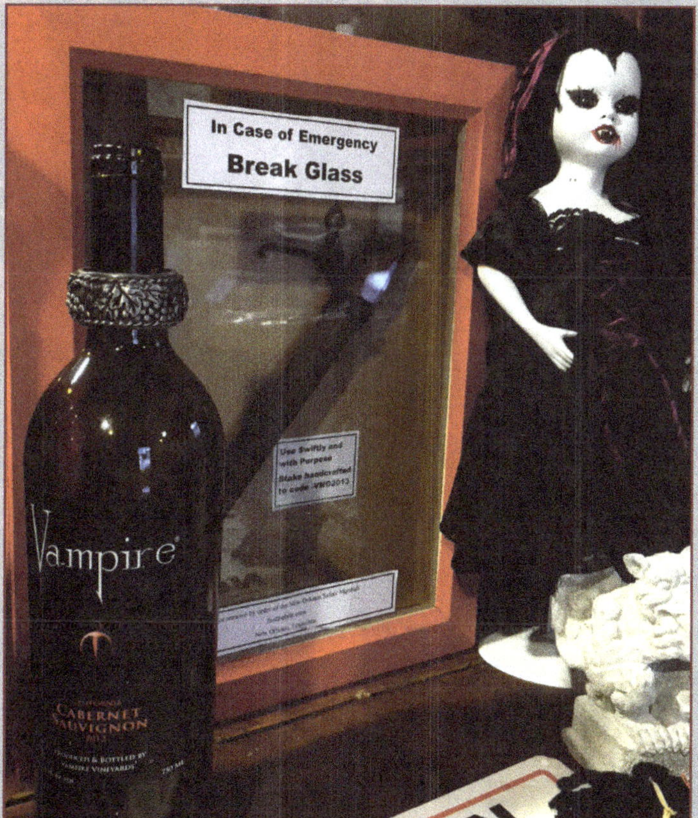

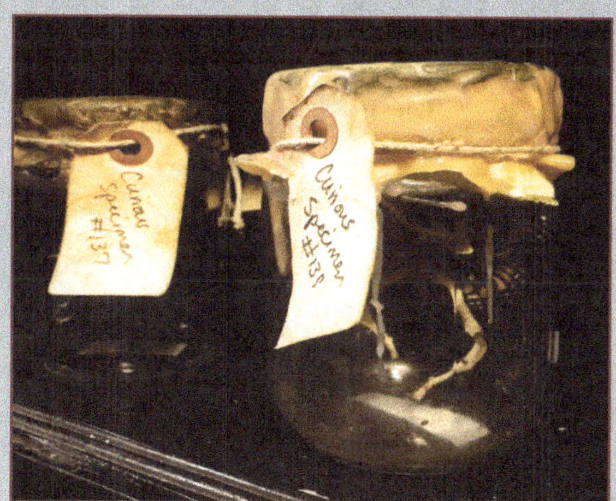

You can find the Boutique du Vampyre as of this writing at the following address and links:

709 1/2 St. Ann Street
New Orleans, LA 70116
(504) 561 - 8267
http://www.feelthebite.com
https://www.facebook.com/BoutiqueduVampyre

Misrepresentation in the Alternative Community:
Life as a Goth of Color

By Hyde Falkenstein

This is a topic that everyone has always seemed to look over and never really pay attention to. When you see pictures of alternative people in magazines, on the internet, or on T.V., you all see that they are white people most of the time. There is rarely enough representation of goths of color. Something that has always been a big unofficial characteristic of being a Goth is pale skin. All over blogging sites such as Tumblr, many of these people are praised for their pale skin. It is normal for many people to ask them how they got their skin as white as all these people fawn over them. Tutorials about skin whitening are all over Youtube. The rising of "pale/glow" blogs has not helped this either. When confronted with these issues, many Goths are quick to say that "it's all about contrast! It's all about looking dead!" Well, where does that leave the Goth people that

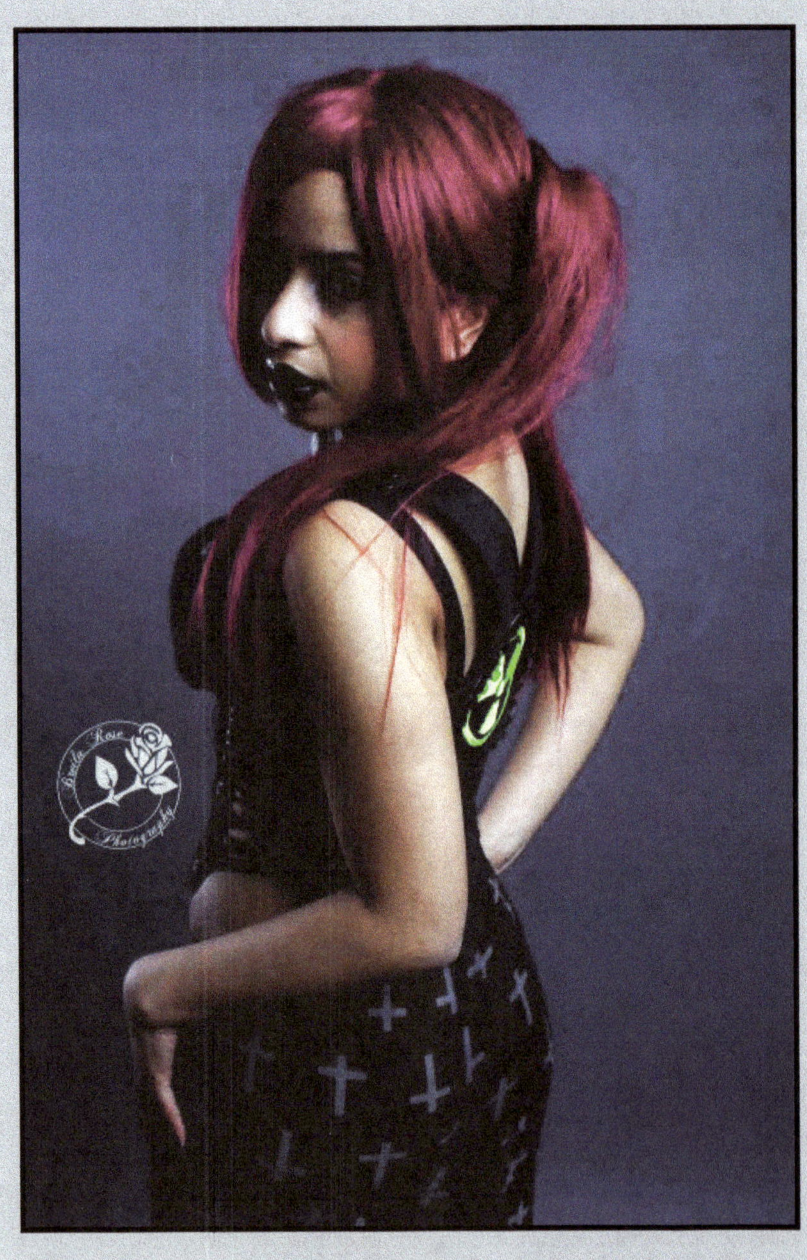

are not white? As a biracial person that is heavily into the alternative community, I want to see more people like me. Where are the Black goths, the Asian goths, or the Latinx goths? People should to realize that the Goth subculture was never only for white people. I asked a few Goths of color about their personal accounts in the alternative world.

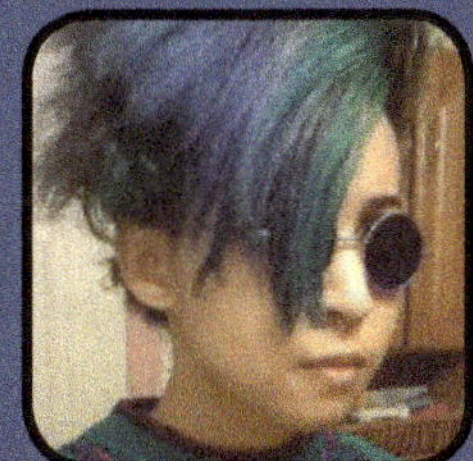

Hyde Falkenstein

What has been your experience as a Goth POC?
Have you ever felt excluded or were told you did not belong?

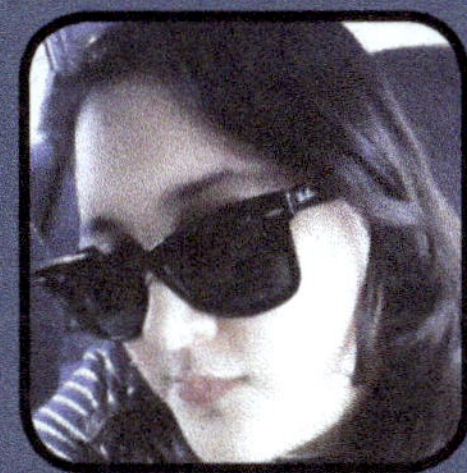

Lelia Age 28

"My other Goth friends and I would talk about how much we hated being so dark-skinned because all of the Goth related things we had ever seen featured white people and we questioned whether we would be allowed to identify as Goth or Punk. That deathly pale skin aesthetic that's so revered in the Goth community is tough on brown people and those of us who, when pale, look a sicklier yellow-green and a lot less like porcelain."

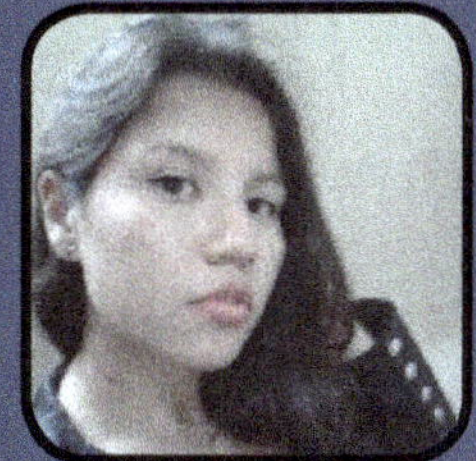

Irene Age 21

"I've always had a love for religion and the occult, goth aesthetic, metal music and punk ideology. Now don't get me wrong, I am a Latina and I say it proudly. But back then it was kind of hard to feel pretty when all the Goth guys liked a thin, frail-looking fairy with snow-white skin or some succubus with a face so white she made bond paper look tan. And since I never saw any other gothic Latina women in media or in my city, I felt like I didn't fit in. Yeah, the predominant beauty aesthetic in the Goth community is pale skin, long black hair and no flaws, but that doesn't mean that I am not beautiful. That doesn't mean that I am anything less."

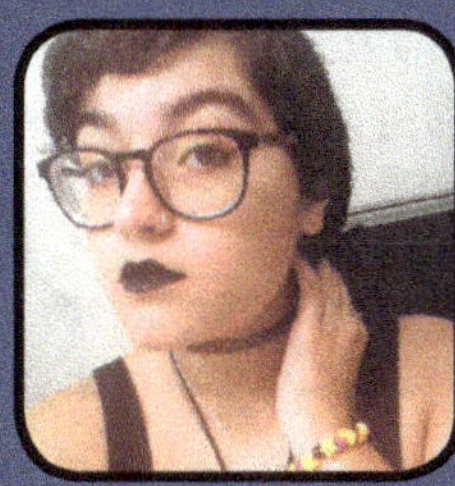

Alex 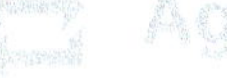 Age 20

"I spent years trying to lighten my skin with makeup and straightening my hair and wearing contacts because glasses weren't "goth" enough. I'm 20 now and love myself and how I look in the dark colors. But I often get fetishized by men for being a color and fulfilling their Goth fetish."

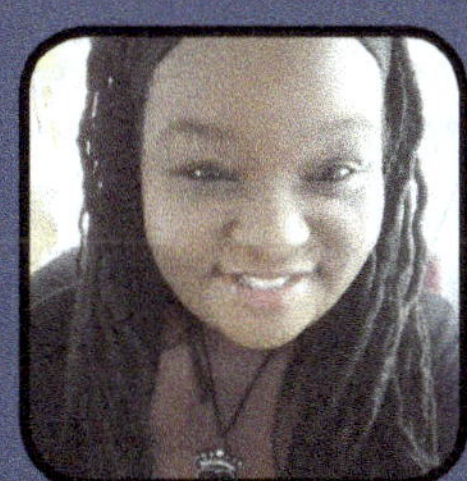

Nocturne 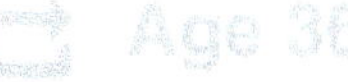 Age 36

"When I first got fully involved, I immediately got questions as to what I "was" & was told that I couldn't be Goth because I am black. The discrimination came from the Goth community, the non-goth community and the black community as well."

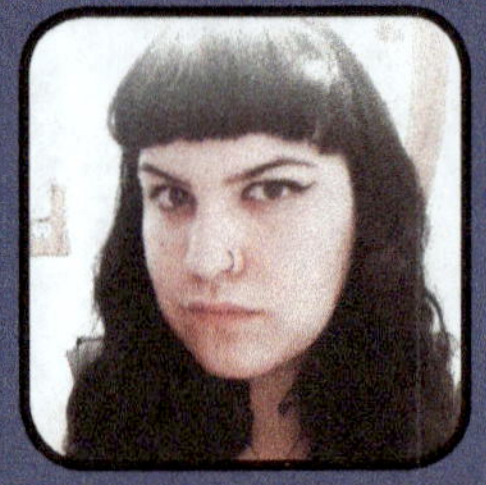

Gabi 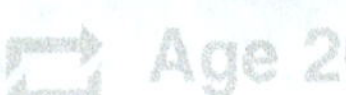 Age 20

"The key to me being happy was just realizing that I will never be the stereotypical goth girl with flawless pale skin and perfect make-up, that can wear the expensive brands and just have everything. Am I still ridiculed for being a Hispanic Goth, yes, especially by other Hispanics who are very traditional or even just don't like the style because its disrespectful to them. The only one that I've seen on T.V is Flaca from Orange is the new black and she is just perfect as a character because she still speaks Spanish and isn't white washed. Being Goth is always pegged as a white girls rebellion, but it's not. It's a sub culture that has its own music and fashion. It should be open to all races and genders without stereotypical ridicule."

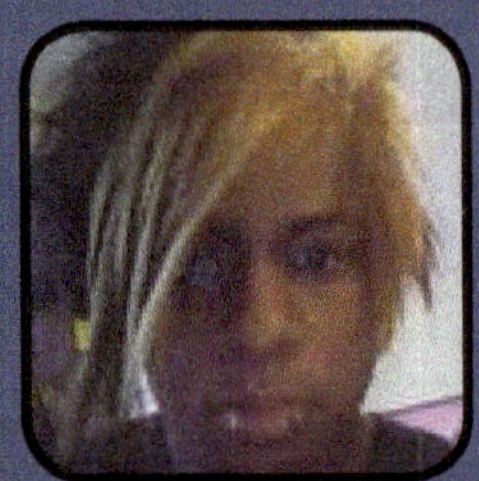

Syverenn 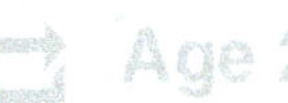 Age 26

"I've had many exclusionary and racist experiences mostly centered on the never "looking pale" sort of thing. I've just learned to associate with those against it and point out when people are harassing me or others. It's not a new part of my reality, just one when I was younger thought wouldn't exist in the subculture, but it's everywhere not just in being Goth. Confidence is everything even if you don't feel it."

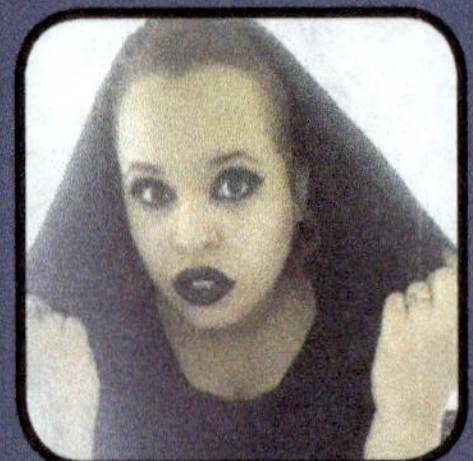

Victoria  Age 22

"I embraced the witchy Goth fashion heavily, and I've been told I wear it well. There's still the 20% of asshole people/"friends" I deal with daily, like "no don't shave your eyebrows that only works for pale women, don't wear that, it look only works if you're skinny and pale (shorts, short skirts, garter socks and thigh highs)", and because I'm not pale, my black makeup doesn't contrast as much even if I wear the same amount so therefor, somehow, I'm not goth."

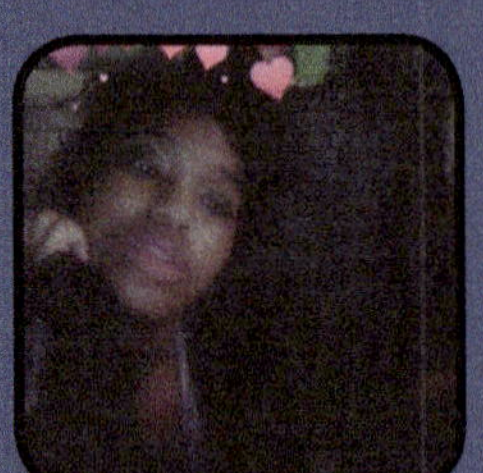

Salem  Age 19

"There is some kind of sense of not belonging because I'm black and especially with the basic stuff (pale skin bullshit, European obsession, appropriation, etc.) which kind of led me to make my own kind of Goth. [On Goths making skin whitening tutorials and being praised for their pale skin and claiming it's all about contrast and looking dead] I really think it's bullshit and unfair. People with dark skin don't turn white when they're dead. And sometimes I think I'm just being bitter but it kind also goes with white people (especially in the Goth subculture) almost literally drawing on features that POC are considered ugly for (cheekbones, lips, dark eyebrows)."

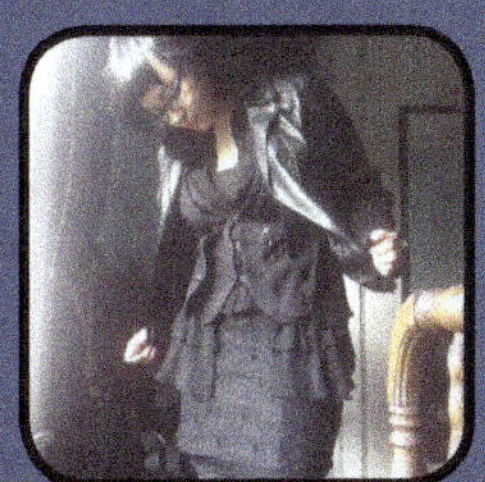

Obsidian   Age 28

"I feel like beauty is unattainable for me from here, from non-whiteness. At least not in the mainstream/conventional sense, you know? It's like getting dressed and trying to feel good about it, but at the back of my head, there it is- this would look better if you were paler like a white person, if you were lankier like a white person, if your eyes were bigger or brighter or fingers more slender. It goes on and it's awful. There's so much particular value placed on the paleness in it. It's inescapable. Days when I see other POC out with any level of a Gothy look and it's so validating. Sometimes I try to be that person for others too. Sometimes I feel good enough and have enough energy to want to just go all out and show people that not all goths are pale. It feels empowering those days. Like, here is an aesthetic that was developed with a huge racist element, and I love it, and I'm pulling it off, and I'm killin' it."

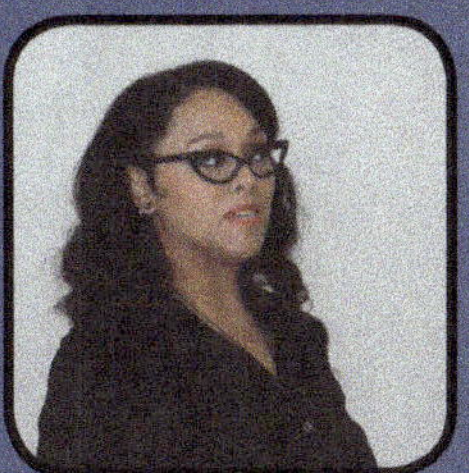

Murphy   Age 31

"The couple of posts that I have seen on Goth folks "favoring white skin," they normally say that's just part of the "goth aesthetic" or something along the lines of "I just think being pale is more beautiful, there's nothing racist about it!" This is kind of tough for me. I just want more people to realize that a cornerstone of Goth should NOT be skin color."

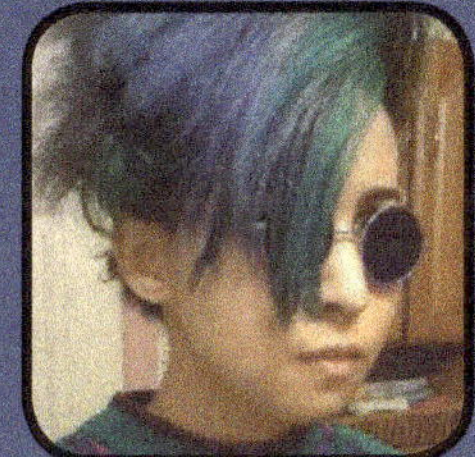

Hyde Falkenstein   Carpe Nocturne Magazine

If you are a POC Goth and need inspiration, here are some blogs that cover goths of different races.

fuckyeahblackgoths.tumblr.com
alt-and-black.tumblr.com
tokyo-fashion.tumblr.com
iamsogothiwasbornblack.tumblr.com
prettyblackpastel.tumblr.com
altgirlsofcolour.tumblr.com
diningwithdana.net

Support POC Goths, disabled Goths, LGTBQ Goths, religious Goths and everyone else in the community.

Nightfeverking is a blog started in July 2014 by Hyde, a sophomore in college and an aspiring artist, writer, and film maker. He focuses on Japanese/Alternative culture, art and cinema. From D.I.Y tutorials, Japanese fashion, art work, film reviews, and weird things in general, his blog has something for everybody interested in the darker and stranger side of life.

By Chirality

I don't think I need to go into who Alice in Chains was and who Layne was. Alice in Chains apparently is still even around just minus Layne. Metal, Goth, or not, you cannot deny their impact and his impact on music. When Seattle was howling and growling, Layne seemed a bit more sinister. I remember watching Man in a Box and being genuinely freaked out. He seemed tormented, but in a different way than Kurt. Between him and Jerry Cantrell they were a powerhouse with Alice in Chains, Mad Season and then Class of 99. Not much was heard from Layne after 1996.

From 1999-2002 Layne became very reclusive. Hiding out in his apartment. He gave one final interview in December of 2001 where he said, "I know I am near death, I did crack and heroin for years. I never wanted to end my life this way." He also spoke of the damage the heroine caused his body. It was apparent in his appearance with missing teeth, pale yellowing skin and looking emaciated. He claimed to be "dope sick" and said it was a horrible way to go.

His friends left him alone stating if they had not heard from him they didn't think anything of it and moved on. On April 19, 2002 Layne Staley was found dead. It is believed he had been there two weeks. It was his mother who dialed 911 and when he was found, he was surrounded by drug paraphernalia and needles. His former band mates expressed their remorse for not checking any sooner. The singer was 86 pounds at the time of his passing.

The band Cold released a song called "The Day Seattle died" in 2003 marking the deaths of Layne and Kurt and essentially the death of grunge. They took it with them. Some count this as a victory, but I do lump them in with this life. They all struggled, they were all lost. I think Layne would have been a kick ass person to hang out with. I remember the interviews on Headbangers Ball wishing I could chill with these guys.

Hit Parader Magazine named Layne 27 in the top 100 metal vocalists. His influence cannot be denied and if you were a kid or teenager in the 90's you know what I mean.

RIP Layne. I hope you have found your peace hanging out on your Angry Chair.

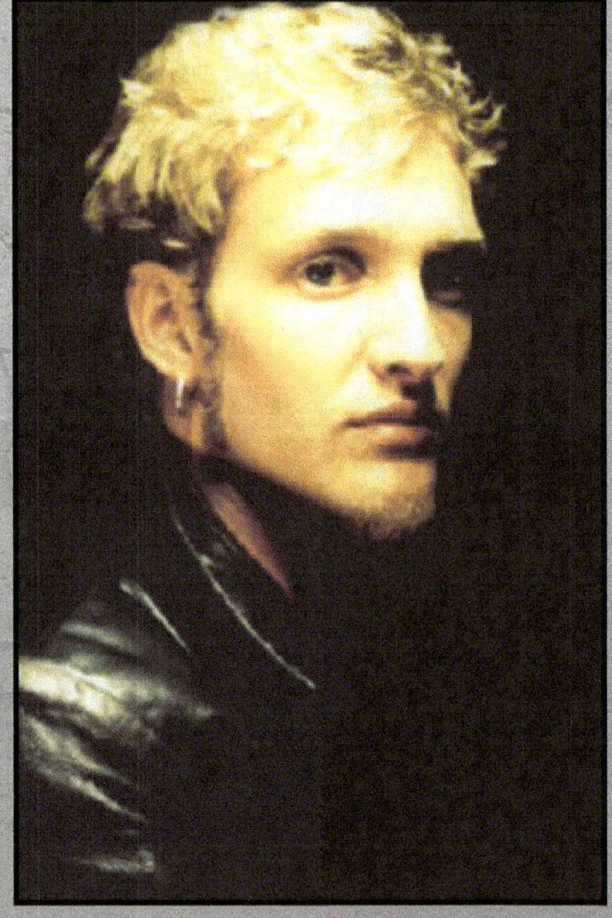

Layne Staley
August 22, 1967 - April 5, 2002

FAREWELL TO THE MASTER OF NIGHTMARES

August 2, 1939 - August 30, 2015

Legendary film director Wes Craven passed from brain cancer this past August at his home in Los Angeles. He was best known for the creation of classic horror franchises such as A Nightmare on Elm Street and Scream, but a few of his other great works include The Hills Have Eyes, The Last House on the Left, and The Serpent and the Rainbow. If you haven't had a chance to pay tribute to Mr. Craven's memory yet, take a look at his filmography and set aside a night to bingewatch the old classics. You won't regret it!

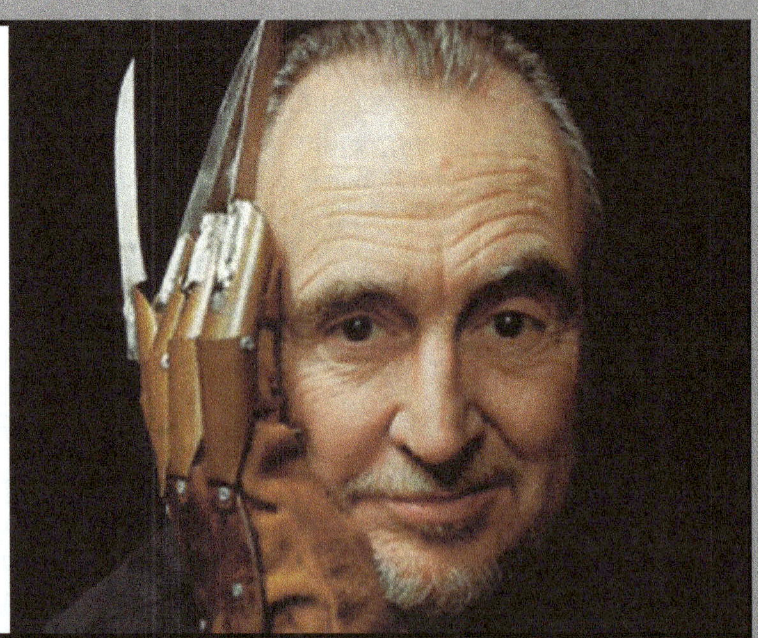

Historically HENNA

By Isolde de Mortimer

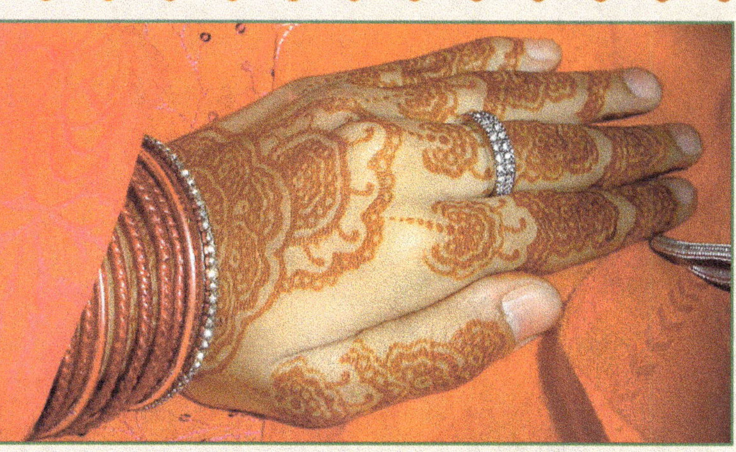

Camphire in Latin; mehndi in Hindi; kina in Turkish; kafer in Hebrew... truly, henna, by any other name, would be as beautifully versatile. With its name spoken in many ancient tongues, it shows henna has claimed a wide-reaching influence and suggests that, like belly dance, henna use had more than one point of origin. Used for dye, cosmetics, medicinal purposes, and protection from evil, henna's history transcends religion and has played a role in the traditions of ceremonial occasions and celebrations for over 5,000 years in many parts of the world by Muslims, Hindus, and Jews alike.

The leaves of the small flowering shrub Lawsonia inermis are gathered, dried, and finely ground. Though the power produced from these sub-tropical plants is green, it contains hennotannic acids which cause the resulting red-orange color. The powder is then used in any number of secret family recipes to stain the skin and nails a deep orange, color the hair, and soothe and cool the skin.

Henna will add highlights to dark hair and darken lighter hair. Reportedly, it will condition hair and improve dry or splitting nails. Due to its antiseptic and antifungal properties, henna can help suppress infections of the skin, so it is used to seal wounds, soothe mild burns and stings, as well as calm inflamed cuticles. Because it is cooling and astringent, it is said to lower body temperature which can soothe headaches and fevers, and of course, temporarily stain the skin for those gorgeous henna tattoos!

Henna Powder

Marriage is the transition from single spirit to coupled life and many cultures believe it to be a vulnerable time for the couple. As a safeguard, a henna ceremony to apply a protective patterned stain to the twosome prior to the wedding is customary in Islamic and Hindu countries.

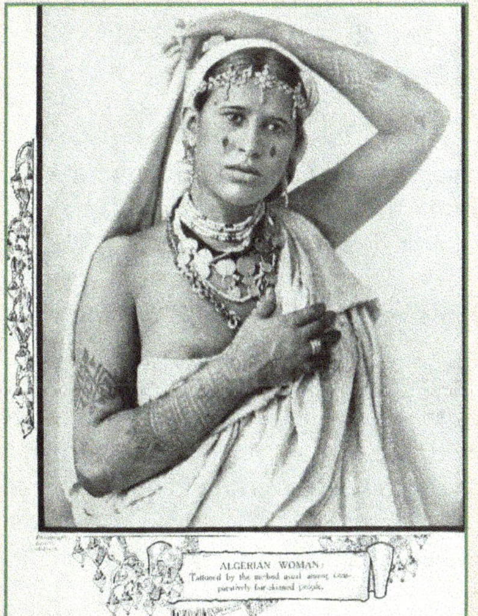

In the Jewish Yemenite tradition, henna is a symbol of protection and happiness. Prior to the wedding, the hands and feet of the groom are colored simply. The bride's henna is more detailed and completed in phases over the final days before the wedding. Her fingertips, nails, hands, feet, and face are colored, while accompanied by dancing and singing.

In North Africa, the practice of the Night of Henna strengthens and protects. Dancing, music, and feasting follow a ritual bath and henna painting for the bride.

Afghanistani custom includes a Night of Henna for the bride. Female relatives of the groom paint her right hand with henna. Her left hand and those of the guests are also painted.

Indian tradition has the henna artist include the groom's name within the bride's intricate henna patterns, and the groom looks for his name on the wedding night. Red is considered a color of great promise, so the deeper the color of the stain on a bride's palms, it is believed the more her husband will love her.

An Egyptian bride will celebrate a Night of Henna with close friends. She takes a lump of henna paste in her hands and each guest adds a coin. Once she has collected many coins, she scrapes the henna from her hand, and then more henna is painted onto her hands and feet.

Armenian Christian practice includes a henna party the night before the wedding. The guests dance around the bride and dip their pinkies into the henna paste. The henna is visible the following day at the church symbolizing the family's support of the marriage.

Just as the word for henna varies by country, so do henna body art designs. Patterns and techniques tend to be specific to a particular area and conform to the cultural standards of beauty and tradition for that region. North African designs are bold and geometric, while the Indian method uses stylized floral patterns and Arabian style favors vines and scrolls. Contemporary designs combine a collage of styles and images and are not restricted to regional customs or beliefs.

You can have henna designs professionally applied at fairs, festivals and specialty salons. Traditionally, clients didn't make requests; the pattern was left to the discretion of the professional. But today, you can request placement and can choose a design from which the artist will take inspiration and create a similar custom design for you. Commonly applied to hands and feet, henna stain on the palms and soles will reach a deeper color and last longer, due to the thicker skin on these parts of the body. However, you can now also have henna applied to arms, wrists, shoulders, belly buttons, chest, and neck. Once henna is applied, keep it on at least 8-12 hours to dry, and don't get it wet during this time. For best results, henna should be applied in the evening, so it can rest overnight. The intensity of the stain will depend on how long you allow the henna to set and your skin tone; the same paste can give different results on different skin types. Avoid harsh soaps, and your design can last two to three weeks and will slowly fade.

This is the first in a series about henna.

Becoming Entranced

By Jezibell Anat

The reason this dance has so much to say and so much to offer is that it is both a physical and emotional experience. - Ibrahim "Bobby" Farrah

The zar, or zaar, is not a just a dance, but a community ritual that uses drumming and dancing to heal illnesses believed to be caused by spirits. The word zar may derive from the Arabic word for visitation (ziara). It is most often found among lower class married women in East Africa and the Middle East, and is one of the few indigenous traditions in which females play the prominent role. Thus, it has become part of the belly dance mystique.

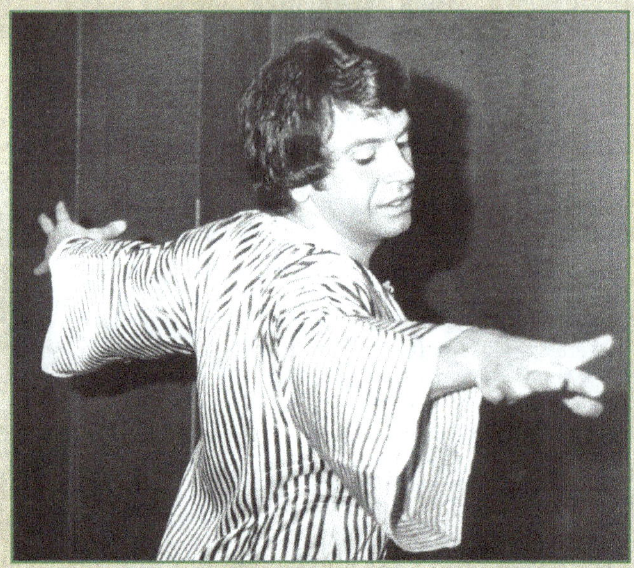

We are not sure of its exact origins. Some claim that this ceremony goes back to Pharaonic Egypt, and concepts of spirit possession appear in ancient Middle Eastern religions. Another theory is that the zar originated in Ethiopia or sub-Saharan Africa because of its similarities to ritual trance in other African-based traditions.

Some believe that the zar became more prevalent during the eighteenth century as a response to colonial oppression. The zar ceremony was first documented by Europeans in the Sudan in the 1820's and in Egypt in the 1870's. Today, it is practiced in various forms throughout northern Sudan, as well as in Egypt, Ethiopia, Somalia, Arabia, and southern Iran.

Considered un-Islamic, the zar is forbidden during Ramadan. At times, it has been banned outright by conservative Islamic authorities, but ceremonies have continued in secret. Still, most women who go to a zar are devout Muslims, and they praise The Prophet after each dance. Occasionally, Christian women attend. An upper class woman will rarely go to a zar; to her, it's something her servants do.

The zar has fascinated and repelled Westerners. The concept of spirit possession reinforced nineteenth-century stereotypes about the backwards and benighted people who were not Christian. Even today, beliefs in spirit possession still freak out many people. The zar, with its raw energy and unrestrained movements, has gained a reputation of being a dark, mysterious rite of exorcism, but this reputation lures artists and mystics.

The actual zar is a ritual of catharsis, and the spirits who trouble these women are considered red djinn. The djinn, translated into English as genie, are supernatural creatures of Islamic mythology. White djinn are benevolent, black djinn are malicious, and red djinn are somewhere in between. Also known as zayran, these red djinn are egotistical and wanton.

The djinn have their own multifarious cosmos, and most of the djinn that afflict women are male. They may be perceived as ancient forces of nature, ancestral spirits, Muslim saints, Turkish pashas, or even European colonials. Through the zar, a woman can contact her djinn to find out what he wants, and she will only be healed when he is placated. To do this, she may drink, smoke, or dress up - activities that would usually be forbidden.

Generally, the women who attend a zar are poor, socially subordinate, and they are expected to conform to a strict code of conduct. For them, the zar serves as a technique of healing that helps them balance their interior lives. The zar is a culturally sanctioned outlet for them to let off their frustrations and justify behavior that would be otherwise inappropriate.

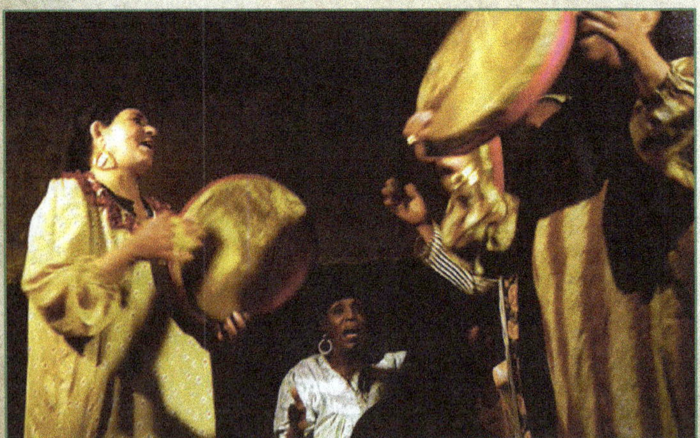

Usually the zar is a private ceremony which involves considerable expense for food, musicians, perfume, and whatever gifts the djinn demand. In a way, being diagnosed as possessed and in need of a zar forces a woman's husband to spend money on her. A less expensive alternative in some urban areas are public zars, often held near the shrines of local saints.

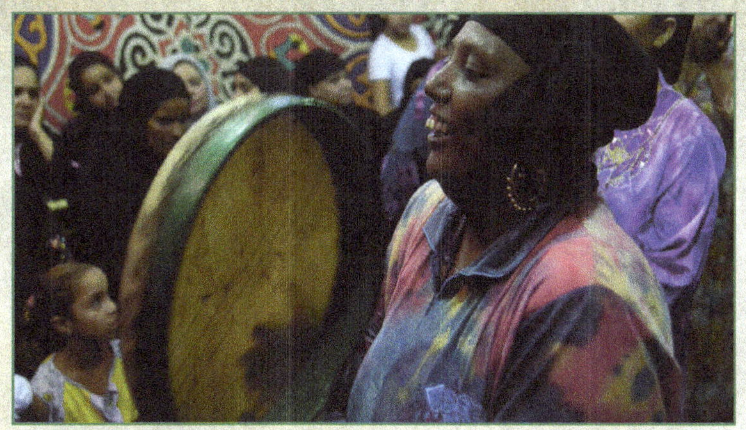

Like many religious services, the zar begins with incense, usually frankincense, which is lit and passed around to all the participants. These scents are believed to cleanse the souls of the guests as they breathe in. The specifics of the ceremony vary between regions; in some villages, the afflicted may wear white, in other areas she may wear red. Often an animal, usually a chicken, is sacrificed, and its blood is sprinkled on the afflicted. The animal is cooked and eaten in a shared meal after the ritual, and, in places near the Nile River, the leftovers may be taken and dumped into the water.

The zar is led by a woman who has inherited the role of ritual leader from her mother. In Egypt, she is called Kodia and in Sudan, she's known as the Sheikha. Usually, she has been possessed herself. She has learned to handle her djinn and is thus able to guide others. She knows the rhythms of her region's particular djinn, and she directs the music. She may have a collection of colored scarves, costumes, and props to help the woman express her djinn. Chants accompany the ceremony, as the singers use their voices to enhance the trance experience. The ritual may last for several hours, or for as long as seven days.

The afflicted woman relaxes into the rhythm and allows her body to follow spontaneously. The other women may join in to offer encouragement, sometimes becoming possessed themselves. Movements associated with the zar included wild tossing of the hair, flinging hands, swaying motions, a descent to the floor, pounding the ground, and a collapse. However, the nature of the dance varies greatly depending on the region, as well as the requirements of her djinn.

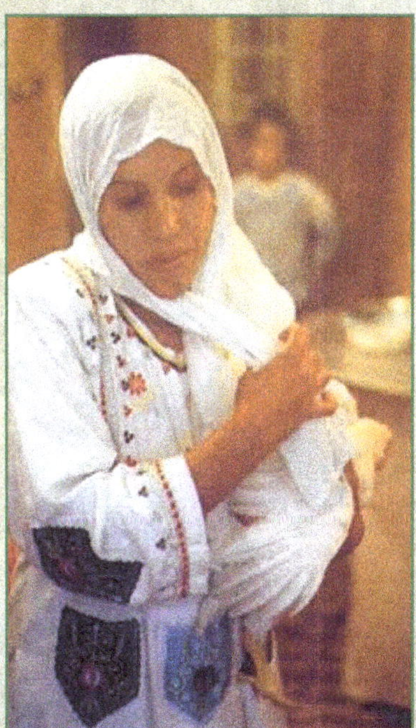

Within the context of the zar, the bonds of the djinn are released, and the woman feels a deep sense of calm. The djinn is not actually exorcised, but the woman learns to work symbiotically with him. After the zar, she is advised to attend to her spirit and to avoid dirt and negative emotions. In many cases, the zar must be repeated every year.

The Western skeptic may dismiss all this as superstition, but from a practical perspective, let's look at the benefits of this ceremony. A woman with few options in her life receives much-needed attention and support, and the physical activity provides relief by raising her serotonin levels and generating endorphins. The zar brings a sense of community, a refuge where she can express whatever she needs to. An Arabic word for a possessed person is ma'zura (excused).

Psychologically, these djinn can represent other parts of the woman's personality that have been repressed, the aspect that in Jungian terms would be the "shadow self." This is the primal side, dark and creative and powerful. The shadow contains all the traits that are socially unacceptable. Even those of us who don't live in a culture that expects women to be satisfied with a subordinate status still struggle with our inner demons. The zar acknowledges these aspects, which is why it is both appealing and frightening.

The zar was never intended to be a performance art, but in the twentieth century, many ethnic dances of the Middle East became theatricalized for Western audiences. The legendary Egyptian belly dancer Nadia Gamal (1937-1990) was the first to occasionally include a zar-inspired piece in her cabaret show.

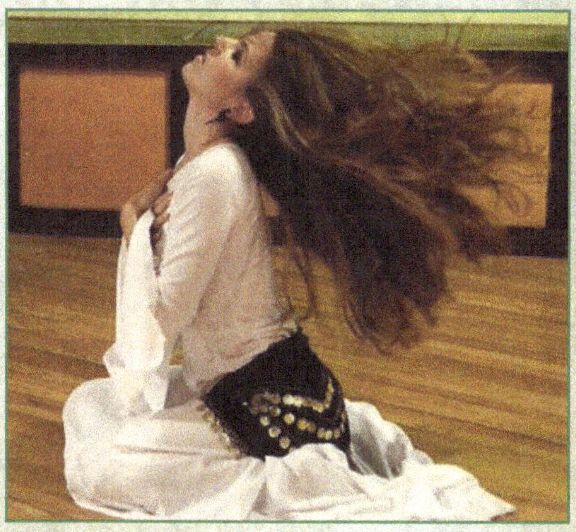

Ibrahim "Bobby" Farrah (1939-1998), an American-born dancer of Lebanese descent, was a major influence in belly dance in the United States from the 1960's through the 1990's as a choreographer and teacher. After seeing Nadia's show, he researched the zar and created a dramatic version called Bait el Zar (House of the Zar) which introduced the zar to America. Performed by his Near East Dance Ensemble, Bait el Zar is 15 minutes long and begins with a chanting high priestess. Then the high priestess reaches out to the woman who is possessed, and they begin to move as the drummers and other dancers enter, including Bobby himself. The piece intensifies into a beautiful and expressive stage performance.

The Bait el Zar performance featured the ayub rhythm, which is the pattern most commonly associated with the zar in the West. The ayub is a strong two beat, similar to a heartbeat. This rhythm itself is sometimes called the zar, and percussionist Hossan Ramzy describes it as "very spooky." It is often played by Middle Eastern drummers, whether they know the zar or not, and dancers will often incorporate some dramatic hair tosses when they hear it. However, the traditional zar does not always use this rhythm, instead incorporating many complex patterns which are specific to particular djinn.

Since Bobby's heyday, many dancers have since been inspired to perform the zar. Many have done further research, which is much easier to do now than in previous eras, and they strive for a more accurate presentation. Some dancers feel that, because of the personal nature of the zar, it should only be done privately among friends. Others choose to wear a belly dance costume, focusing more

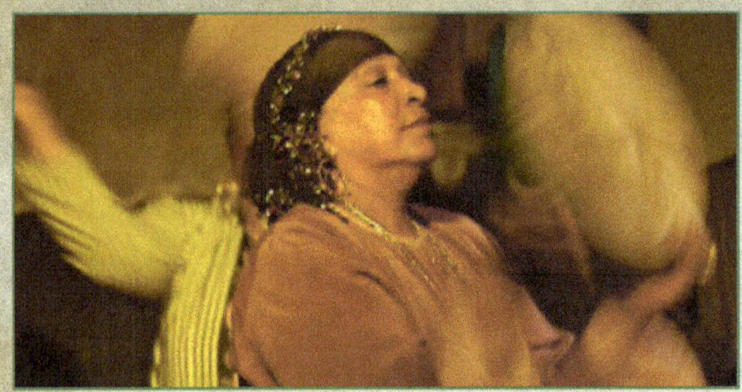 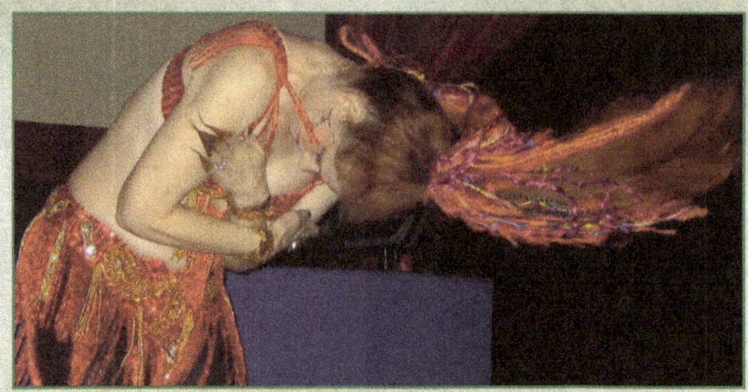

on the emotion and spirit of the zar than anthropological correctness. Some audiences may understand and appreciate its context; others can simply enjoy the show, even if they don't know all the nuances.

I do include some zar aspects in my performances. The big head spins with flying hair are the move usually associated with the zar. Bobby says that is because the hair is the last place the spirit clings to before its release. Personally, I love these head spins because I have long red hair that looks very impressive when flung about. However, these movements may not work for everyone, and they can be dangerous if done incorrectly. If you want to do them, the important thing to remember is that they originate from the torso, not the neck. The chest makes the big circle, and the neck simply extends the motion through the hair.

After one dance, an audience member complimented me on what she called my "headbanging!" I was surprised at first, but then I realized that to many people, the zar hair toss does look like the head banging motion of punk and heavy metal music. So perhaps this is a cross-cultural motion to release socially imposed restriction and an organic response to intense emotion.

I have been particularly drawn to the spiritual healing aspect of the zar. The week after my Mom passed, some friends took me to a community drum and dance event where we gathered outdoors around a bonfire. Late in the night, the drummers began to play the ayub, and I started moving. At that time, I was at a point of emotional devastation, and I simply moved into the sound, feeling the vibrations pull me across the earth and swirl through my body.

Extending my energy from the inside out, I danced to the point of exhaustion, and without even trying to do any particular moves, I was stomping, spinning, swaying, flailing my limbs and torso, until I finally collapsed upon the earth. I realized that this prostration was not a position of servility, but of regeneration, a connecting with the solid energy of the earth. After a few moments, my friends gently helped me up and brought me myrrh, frankincense, and pomegranate wine.

They told me that my dance had a dynamic power they'd never seen before, but it is not something I could ever recreate on a stage for an audience, even if I wanted to. To me, it was proof that this ancient ceremony of healing still holds power.

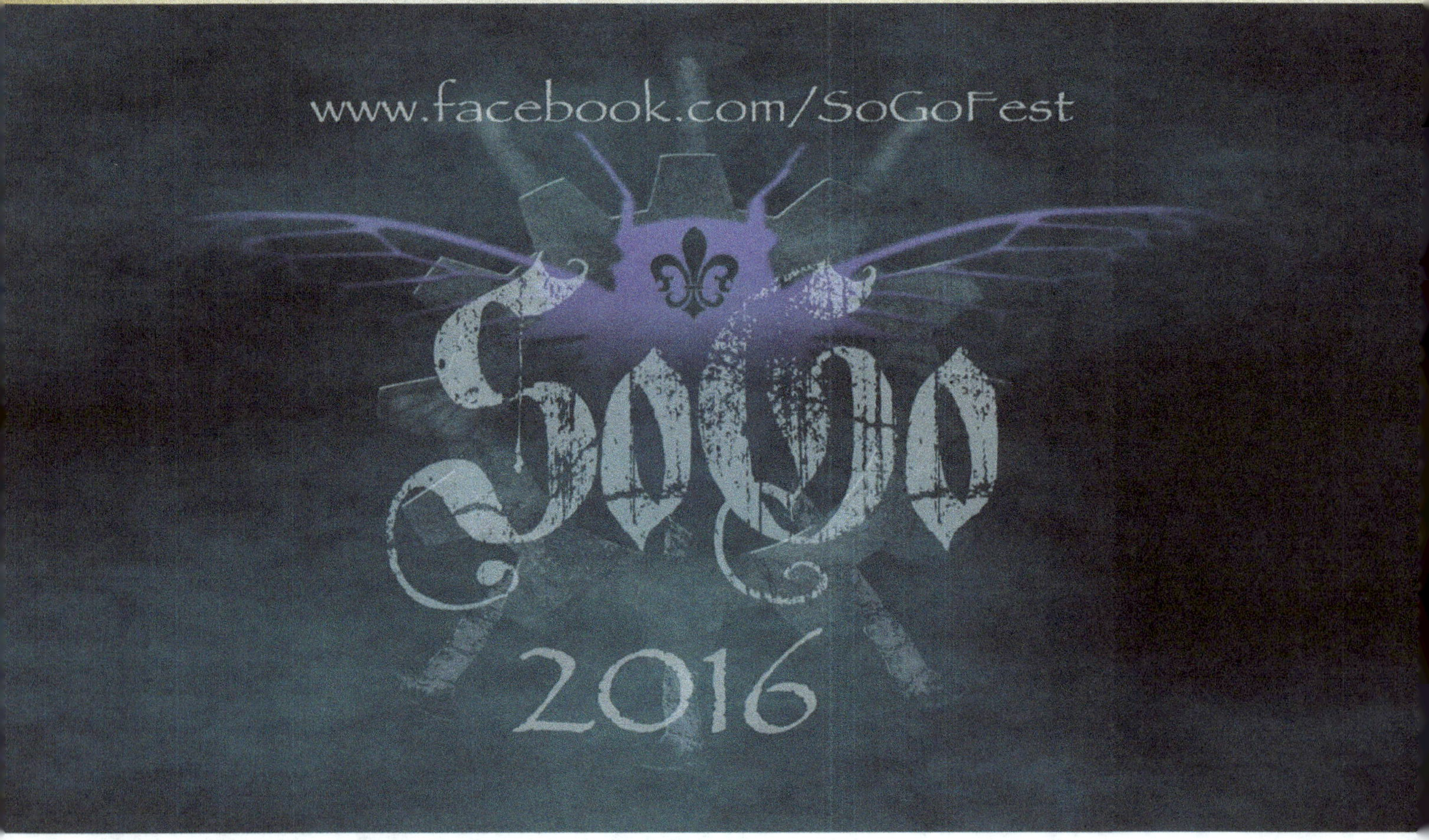

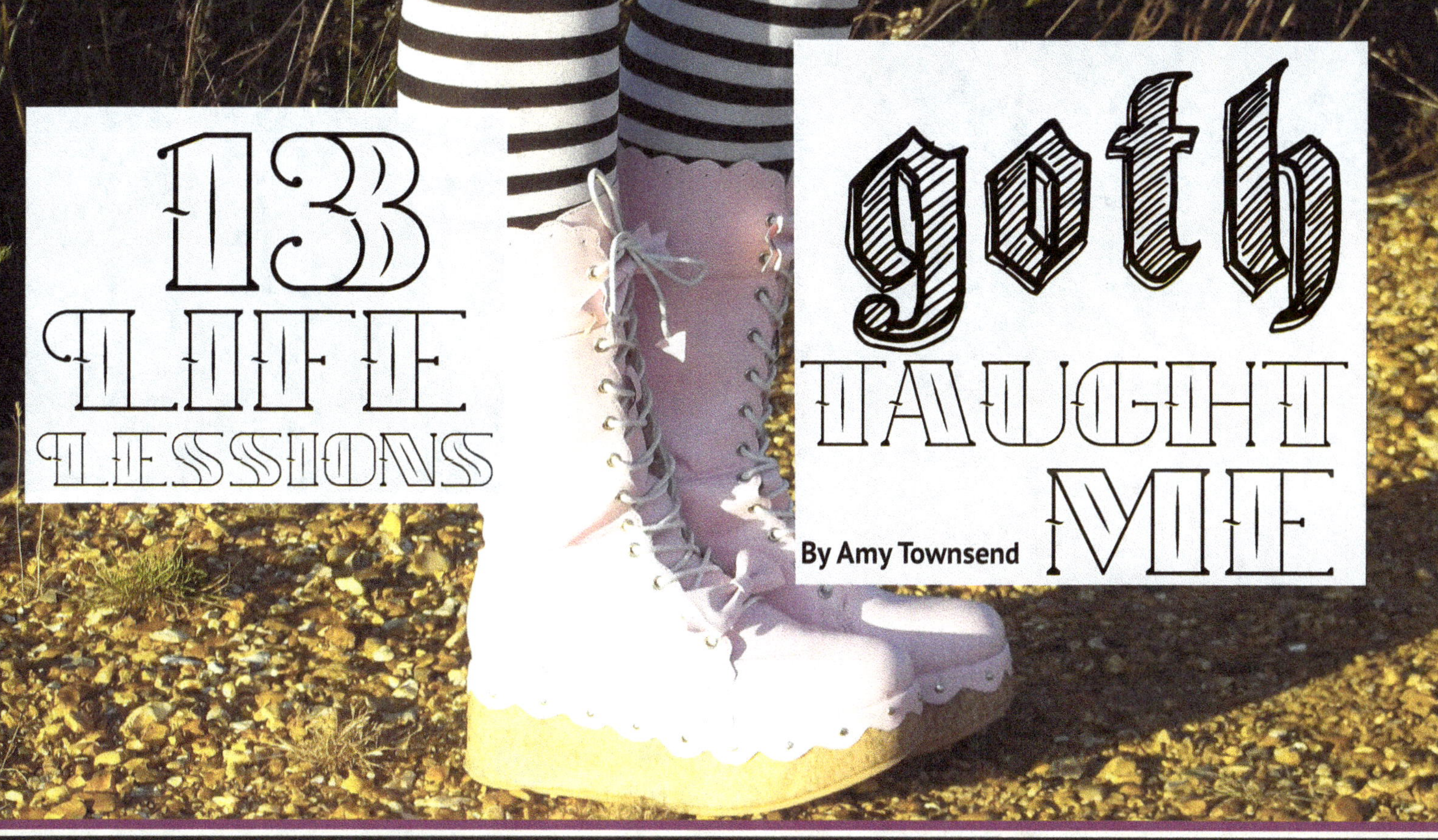

1. *Being yourself is more important than any label. Don't get so caught up in crafting your 'image' that you don't leave yourself room to grow.*

2. *Colour is overrated. I'm not saying I don't have a special place in my heart for a flash of blue hair or a shimmer of pink glitter, but the basics, the backbone, of a wardrobe is generally a neutral. Nowadays I often give stormy greys and navys precedence, but the current trend for minimalism always reminds me of the years I spent creating a wardrobe consisting of one colour and one colour only - black.*

3. *There's no school like the old school. Old-school post-punk and deathrock music AND style never fail to fill me with a vaguely reverential sense of awe, and mainstream fashion shows us that the best 'new' ideas are often nothing more than cleverly-recycled old ones. When looking for inspiration, it never hurts to look backwards.*

4. *The best of friends are found in the strangest of places. The greatest friends I have found in life don't like me despite my eccentricities, but because of them. Do what makes your black little heart happy, explore your interests, and make friends who won't roll your eyes if you ask them to come with you to Goth night or the Renaissance Faire.*

5. *Screw the 'male gaze'. If I want to wear thirty layers of impenetrable velvet and an improbable hat, I will. Similarly, 'You looked so much prettier before you had that mohawk/piercing/tattoo/hair colour never seen in nature' is a ridiculous statement implying that what you see in the mirror should be tailored to suit other people. Nuts to that.*

6. *Pretending to be bored in an effort to look cool doesn't actually make you cool. If you don't want to do the thing, don't do the thing. If you DO want to do the thing, why get all pretend-morose about it? Being 'alternative' gave me the freedom to geek out over the things I'm interested in, and dispense with the faux ennui of trying to be cool, popular, or impressive to strangers on Instagram.*

7. *You know when you're a teenager and well-meaning people pat you* on the head and tell you you'll be embarrassed in ten years' time? They're right, but not for the reasons you think. Young'uns, think twice before you post your poetry/vampire fanfic/outfit photos online (or use a pseudonym).

8. *Hair grows back.*

9. *Eyebrows don't.*

10. *Being creative and expressive is the most awesome thing ever. Even if your poetry is dire and your eyeliner is wonky, you tried. And one day your poems won't be dire and your eyeliner hand will be rock-steady and you'll be able to look back and see how far you've come.*

11. *Don't worry about what everyone else is doing. And especially not about whether people are doing things 'differently' or 'better'. Ignore those who lecture about how to be 'real' this, 'real' that and 'real' the other. They're insecure.*

12. *Question everything. Perhaps this comes from Goth's more political cousin punk rock, but I found that being involved in the Goth scene led me to question many of society's standards. Why must we look/dress/ act this or that way? Why is this body shape 'acceptable' and this one not? Questioning standard models of dress and behaviour (right down to 'I don't like this radio station... where is the decent music?', a query which can start a person on a journey all on its own) taught me a very different lesson than that which a lot of teenage girls learn; that my body is fine, that I am fine, that it's OK to take up space in the world and that I can dye my hair whatever colour I want.*

13. *OK, so you may never get your Hogwarts letter (sorry), but the world doesn't have to be bland and boring if you choose to make it otherwise. Look for the extraordinary in the everyday. Be the extraordinary. Don't lose the sense of whimsy and wonder you had when you were a child; the love of the unusual that made you dye your hair green (or whatever) in the first place. There is magic in the world, if you make it so.*

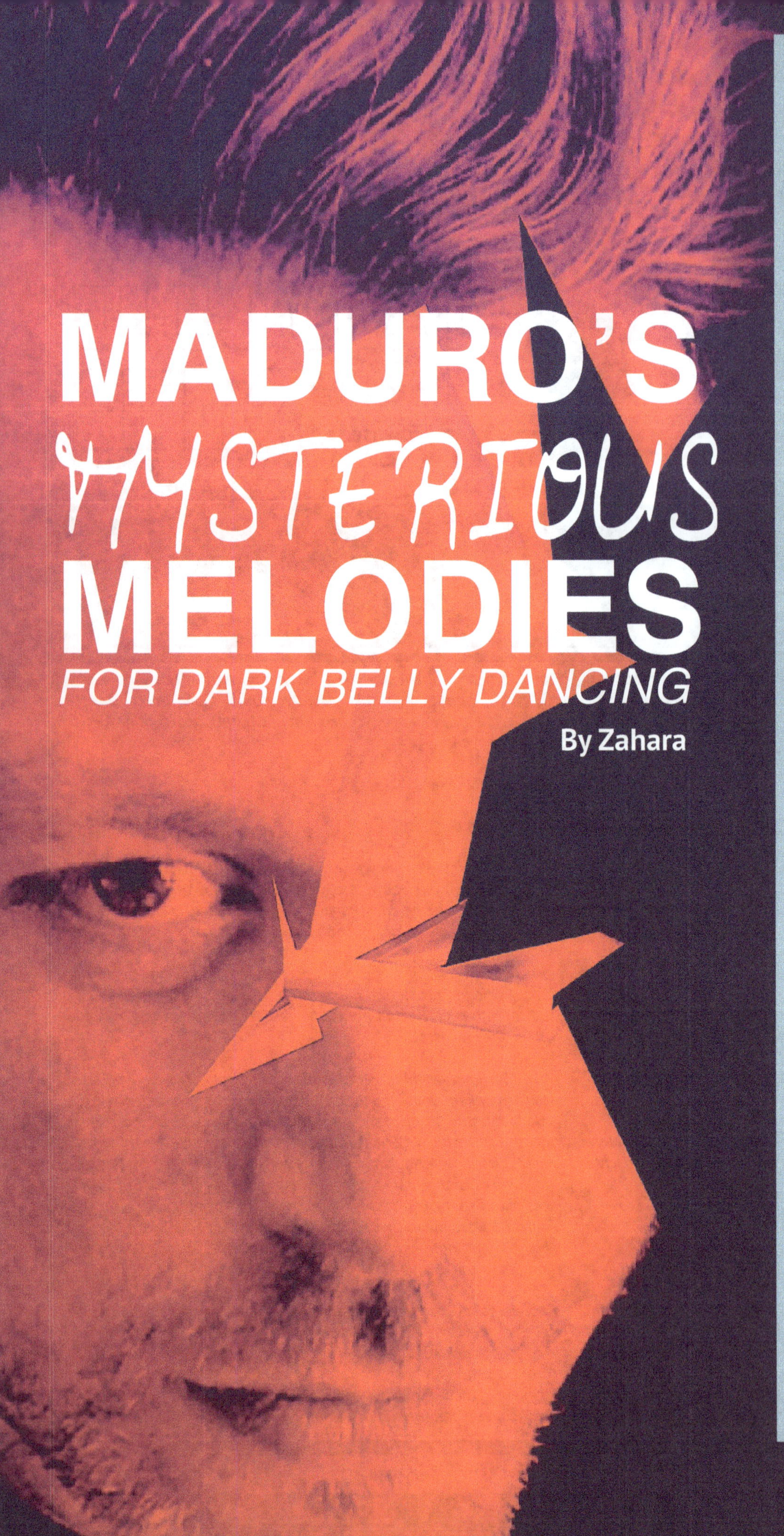

MADURO'S *MYSTERIOUS* MELODIES

FOR DARK BELLY DANCING

By Zahara

I remember very clearly the first time I heard "Akkadian", from Maduro's Shimmer Sustain CD. I was at a local belly dance show, and a tribal belly dancer did a routine as The Devil to this futuristic song. It was intense and textured, with extraterrestrial accents and a surreal melody creeping over a thumping Middle Eastern percussion. I had never heard anything like it, and since that time, I've regularly turned to Maduro's songs for inspiration. His early offerings were definitely World Fusion Electronica, with strong percussion rhythms acting as a foundation for other-worldly tunes. But even with his more subtle Middle Eastern vibe, his latest creations offer fusion belly dancers an opportunity to move in unique ways.

Maduro has been making electronic music for over a decade. He started with recording all dark electro on hardware only, but gradually moved to software as his sound diversified. At first, he gave away recordings to local DJs in the Washington DC goth/industrial scene, but it was difficult to get his music heard if he didn't play live (which he didn't enjoy doing). He got into the world/tribal scene when his tribal dance friends ran out of new music to use, so he started incorporating Middle Eastern progressions. He says Shimmer Sustain was hastily put together, yet it continues to be a favorite among belly dancers. "But I made dark electronic music long before I met dancers, so I did not start out as a belly dance musician. I just made albums that went that way for awhile. I really hope to see dancers try to use my newer stuff. It's vastly different than Shimmer Sustain."

Each album has a unique, quirky theme. Some songs are really ambient and delicate, while others are moody. As you listen to each release, you begin to notice the subtle influences (jazz, world music, etc.). "I get quickly bored with ideas and techniques and try to change things from one album to the next. While I still have many friends in the dance scene, I really stepped away from it all in 2009, although the 2012 EP Cover Your Eyes is a pretty tribal release. So while I don't make belly dance music anymore, I hope that creative dancers will continue to use my music as inspiration to push their art - as I push mine. It has always been the greatest honor to see dancers interpret my music. There is a beautiful symbiotic relationship there." Fortunately for us, there are 20 Maduro albums that have been released since Shimmer Sustain!

Some of my personal favorites are listed at the end of this article.

Maduro retains the rights to all his work, and this gave me the opportunity to ask him how and when dancers should ask permission to use his music. "If you are going to perform to a piece of my work and/or video tape your performance with my track, that is totally fine and free. However, if you are going to make money on a product, like sell a performance or instructional video using my song, then we get into a license fee." All musicians/bands operate differently, so it's best to contact them directly and ask if there is a license fee to use their work.

I was pleasantly surprised to find out he's released music as Teleoptyk, which I like to use in class for drills. "I've released music under numerous names, because I record a lot of music that takes on its own persona and really falls all over the genre spectrum. I release about three to five albums a year. I've recorded four albums as Maduro already in 2015. Genres are lame, though. I make dark electronic music - the end. I even put out an industrial techno EP Fisticuffs on a British techno label as Maduro a couple years ago. While I record most of my work as Maduro, I have recorded two albums as Darkened, about five industrial/ebm type releases as Teleoptyk, and other projects under Obelism, Luminous Dials, Baphometrics, etc. I identify with the industrial/goth scene the most, so Teleoptyk was a logical output, and I was happy that it made some rounds on compilations and at clubs. I'd like to continue making heavier industrial tracks in the future, ideally collaborating with a band or starting one."

The volume and variety of Maduro's work is impressive! He's mostly inspired by artists and music, going through phases of listening to particular genres that eventually bleed into whatever he's making at the moment. "Right now, I'm listening to a lot of old acid house techno, and old 90s rave and big beat music. This influenced Nights on Neptune, which was just released as well. I have musical ADD."

Some of his work would make a great soundtrack. And although none of his pieces have been used in commercials or movies yet, I feel it's only a matter of time before his work gains the attention of sci-fi producers. For fusion belly dancers, who often pride themselves on dancing to unique pieces of music, there's a lot of interesting, layered work to absorb for inspiration. He recently signed with Component Records, and will be releasing works with them and on his own. "Last year, I released two albums that I thought would be great for film, as they were this chaotic, cinematic dubstep set of releases: Black Ice Ballet (an homage to William Gibson's cyberpunk vision, which I'm proud of) and Blood Turns Black. I was dabbling in the sound and making it my own." Both releases got great reviews internationally, and I would encourage dancers to listen to these. "I've had friends tell me I put out too much music, that I over-saturate. If I think something is worth sharing, I release it."

His work is available on iTunes, Amazon, Spotify and eMusic. And if you're looking for obscure recordings and limited-time offerings, be sure to visit http://maduro.bandcamp.com. "I will often release an album that I only keep in circulation for a year or two, so don't wait to explore the catalog! I stopped putting out physical CDs as Maduro in 2008. Everything is digital, and I can release more work this way."

Like many artists, Maduro does more than produce amazing music. "I'm pretty busy writing poetry (I have a collection I'm putting together for a small press in LA), and I also get caught up in making the digital art I release on my instagram account (@maduromusic)."

Maduro's music has been a great fit for modern and alternative styles of belly dance, including dark fusion, sci-fi and steampunk. His wide range of offerings make it easy to find a song that speaks to me, no matter where I find myself in my dance journey. And because he's always releasing new work, I'm constantly finding another CD to use. Listed below are some of my favorite Maduro works for belly dance.

Black Magic Kingdom - Intense vocals and crushing beats ("Fatima") with a subtle jazzy feel.

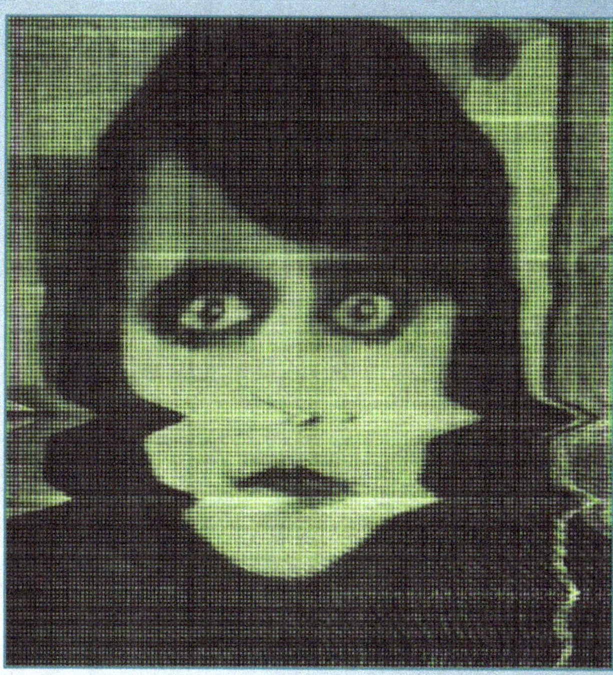

Nights on Neptune - His latest release is upbeat and bouncy, especially "Punch It" and "Patrons of Pluto". The title track is reminiscent of Fin de Siècle.

Black Ice Ballet - I especially enjoy the brassy sass of "Monochrome" and the 80s vibe of "Hidden Hologram".

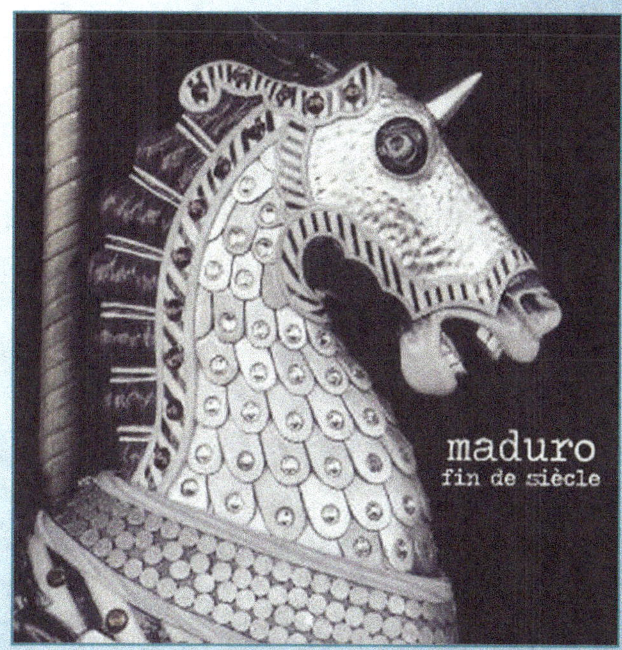

Fin de Siècle - If there was such a thing as an "Other-World's Fair", this would be the music piped through the carnival. There are some great songs to use for steampunk and sci-fi belly dance.

http://maduro.bandcamp.com
@maduromusic on Instagram

SHATTERING BOUNDARIES

By Asylum Attendant

Lindsey Stirling

I grew up appreciating and performing classical music, but I also developed a love of electronic music. I never would have thought to combine the two. That's just what the tremendously talented dancing violinist Lindsey Stirling did. Lindsey has carved out her very own spot in the music industry using the raw energy of EDM and her dedication to classical training. With millions of YouTube views, album sales and adoring fans, Lindsey still remains grounded. Her worldwide Music Box Tour in support of her new album Shatter Me has been wildly successful, even bringing her to South America for the first time. The new choreography, bubbly energy and diverse audience make Lindsey's live shows a sight to behold. The trailblazing superstar's thoughtful responses to my interview questions reveal the wonderful role model that she is.

[**Asylum Attendant**] *Thank you so much for taking time out while on tour across North America to answer some questions. What's been the most enjoyable part of The Music Box Tour?*

[**Lindsey Stirling**] Well, this is probably the biggest production I've ever done. It has been so fun to see all of my ideas for the stage come to reality. It's also the first tour I've had female backup dancers (girl power!) and that has been amazing! So much fun being able to perform with these amazing women!

[**AA**] *You have a massive following on Youtube. How do you come up with the magnificent visuals/concepts for your music videos?*

[**Lindsey**] It depends on the song, but sometimes I create a vision in my head of what I want to convey or a story I want to tell, and then I create music to tell that story. I've always been a very visual person; I love symbolism, and I love the triumph of light over darkness/good over evil. Ultimately that is the basis of my work as a musician and the message I want to convey...that light will always prevail over darkness. And I believe that my faith in God and reliance on him is what fuels the inspiration behind my work.

[**AA**] *Why did you decide to release your music independent of a major label?*

[**Lindsey**] Honestly, in the beginning no one would take me haha; now that I've made it without a label I love having the creative control and I'm very hesitant to give that up. At this point I really don't see much that they can offer me that I don't already have.

[**AA**] *When composing your songs, how do you tell a story and evoke emotions using only instrumental soundscapes?*

[**Lindsey**] I believe that the energy and emotions we feel when we create something actually becomes a part of the creation itself. And that those same emotions and energies and visual images that I put into my music can be felt, seen, and heard by anyone actively listening to it. Music is a mode of communication; an unspoken language. It has the power to penetrate the heart and mind on a level I don't think mankind has had the ability to fully understand or tap into yet.

[**AA**] *What would you say to music snobs who believe that classical music has no business mixing with other genres such as trance and dubstep?*

[**Lindsey**] I'd say they're sticking their heads in the sand and are being closed-minded. People can try to argue and litigate and fund-raise, but the fact is, orchestras are failing all over the country because people aren't willing to pay to hear the same classical music as much anymore. The world we live in is a world of progression and change, and music is no different. I have a great appreciation for classical music, and I think that it should be honored and performed regularly, and I owe my profession to the study of it. But ultimately when I was conforming and only learning and performing the classics...things that had already been written and performed for years...and having to play them "just so", without any creative liberty...I wasn't happy. Once I combined the music I enjoyed with the classical base I was given, I thrived. I think that's the case with anything. Take your base/what others have done before, learn from it, and build on it. We are creatures of creation, not regurgitating machines. It's been shown time and time again that professions that foster and encourage creativity typically have a higher satisfaction rate, while the latter produces a lot of not-so-happy employees. So I think that it's important, in any profession really, to take what you've learned in school or whatever, and adjust it or re-define it and make it your own. Validate the ideas and thoughts that inspire you. Make consistent goals and follow-through. I know it keeps me going.

[**AA**] *Your second album, Shatter Me, recently won Top Dance/Electronic Album at the Billboard Music Awards. What was it like to receive such an honor and perform in front of the biggest names in entertainment?*

[**Lindsey**] I was honestly blown away...it was very surreal. It was very humbling; taking it all in...felt overwhelming that all the work and all the support from my family, friends, fans, and God has gotten me to this point...and it's just crazy to me. It was funny; after the awards I was getting ready to take pictures at the photo booth and Taylor Swift called out, "Hey Lindsey, get over here!" We got some pretty fun photos haha. My jaw about fell to the floor haha; never thought I'd see the day when celebrities I've looked up to for years would actually know me by name.

[**AA**] *You're a very dynamic performer. How difficult is it to dance and play violin at the same time? Ever had any accidents?*

[**Lindsey**] Haha; oh yes! There was one time I totally biffed it on stage at one of my concerts; tripped on myself and fell backwards on my behind. I had to just get up and keep playing as if nothing had happened XD. Years ago I was performing at a business convention and I went to do a backbend (had done it many a time) and realized at the bottom of it that I couldn't get up. So I fell back on my head, rolled over, got up, and took my bow. I tried to pretend like it was part of the act but it was so embarrassing! As far as difficulty is concerned, learning to dance and play is like learning anything really; you take it one step at a time and eventually habit/muscle-memory kicks in, like learning to ride a bike.

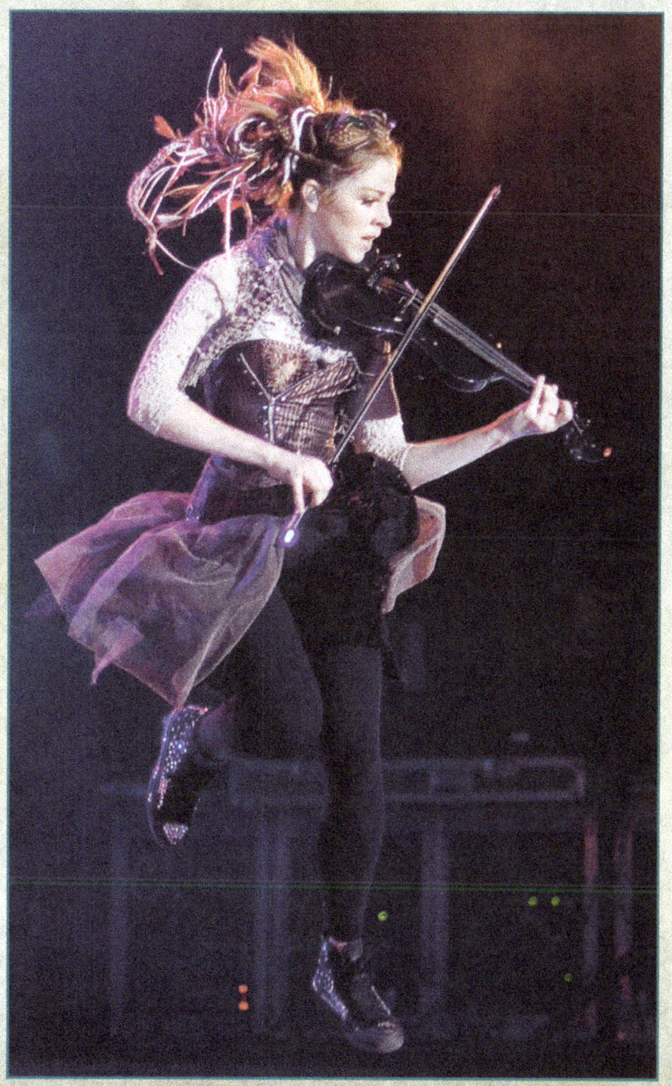

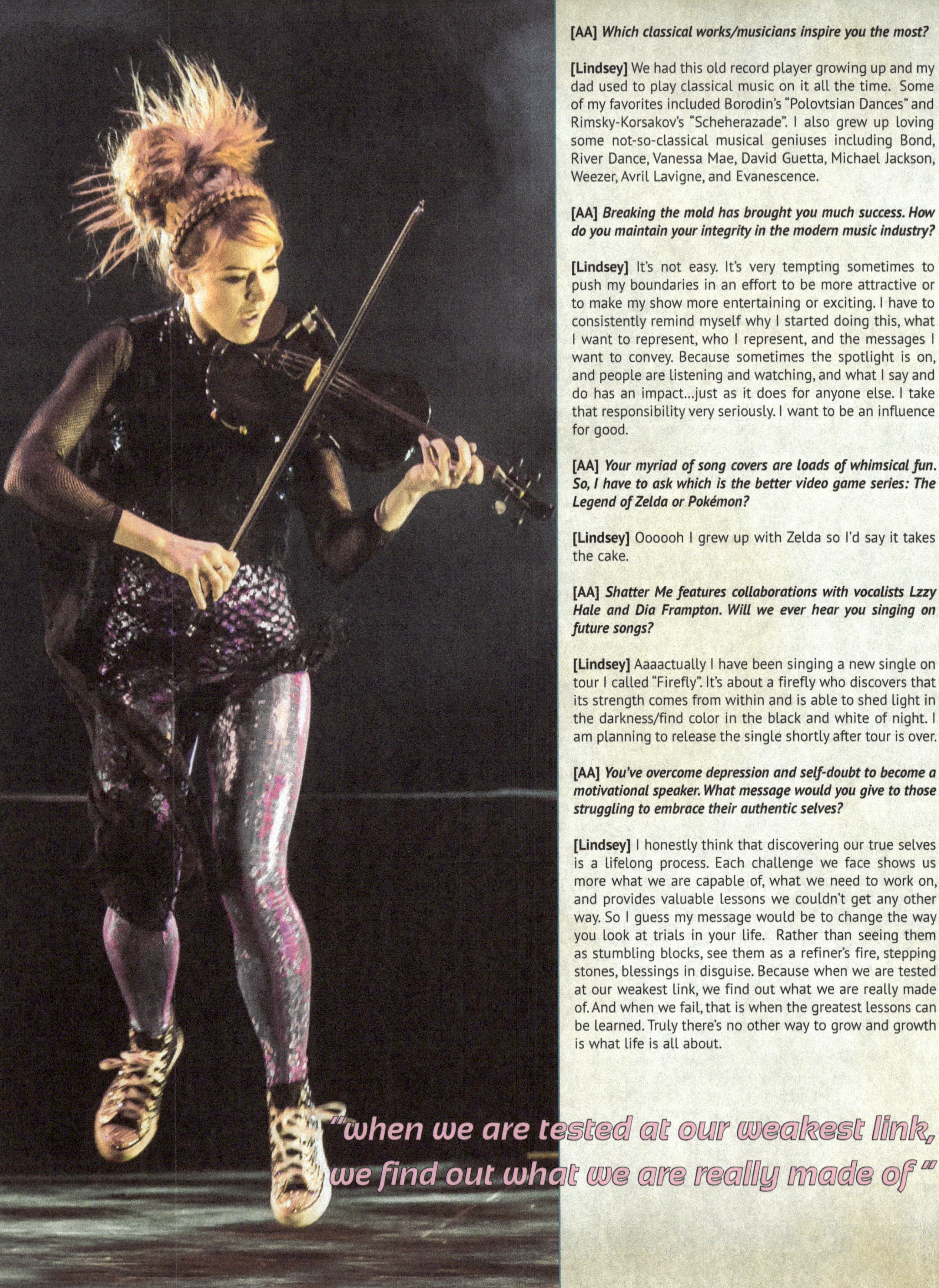

[AA] *Which classical works/musicians inspire you the most?*

[Lindsey] We had this old record player growing up and my dad used to play classical music on it all the time. Some of my favorites included Borodin's "Polovtsian Dances" and Rimsky-Korsakov's "Scheherazade". I also grew up loving some not-so-classical musical geniuses including Bond, River Dance, Vanessa Mae, David Guetta, Michael Jackson, Weezer, Avril Lavigne, and Evanescence.

[AA] *Breaking the mold has brought you much success. How do you maintain your integrity in the modern music industry?*

[Lindsey] It's not easy. It's very tempting sometimes to push my boundaries in an effort to be more attractive or to make my show more entertaining or exciting. I have to consistently remind myself why I started doing this, what I want to represent, who I represent, and the messages I want to convey. Because sometimes the spotlight is on, and people are listening and watching, and what I say and do has an impact...just as it does for anyone else. I take that responsibility very seriously. I want to be an influence for good.

[AA] *Your myriad of song covers are loads of whimsical fun. So, I have to ask which is the better video game series: The Legend of Zelda or Pokémon?*

[Lindsey] Oooooh I grew up with Zelda so I'd say it takes the cake.

[AA] *Shatter Me features collaborations with vocalists Lzzy Hale and Dia Frampton. Will we ever hear you singing on future songs?*

[Lindsey] Aaaactually I have been singing a new single on tour I called "Firefly". It's about a firefly who discovers that its strength comes from within and is able to shed light in the darkness/find color in the black and white of night. I am planning to release the single shortly after tour is over.

[AA] *You've overcome depression and self-doubt to become a motivational speaker. What message would you give to those struggling to embrace their authentic selves?*

[Lindsey] I honestly think that discovering our true selves is a lifelong process. Each challenge we face shows us more what we are capable of, what we need to work on, and provides valuable lessons we couldn't get any other way. So I guess my message would be to change the way you look at trials in your life. Rather than seeing them as stumbling blocks, see them as a refiner's fire, stepping stones, blessings in disguise. Because when we are tested at our weakest link, we find out what we are really made of. And when we fail, that is when the greatest lessons can be learned. Truly there's no other way to grow and growth is what life is all about.

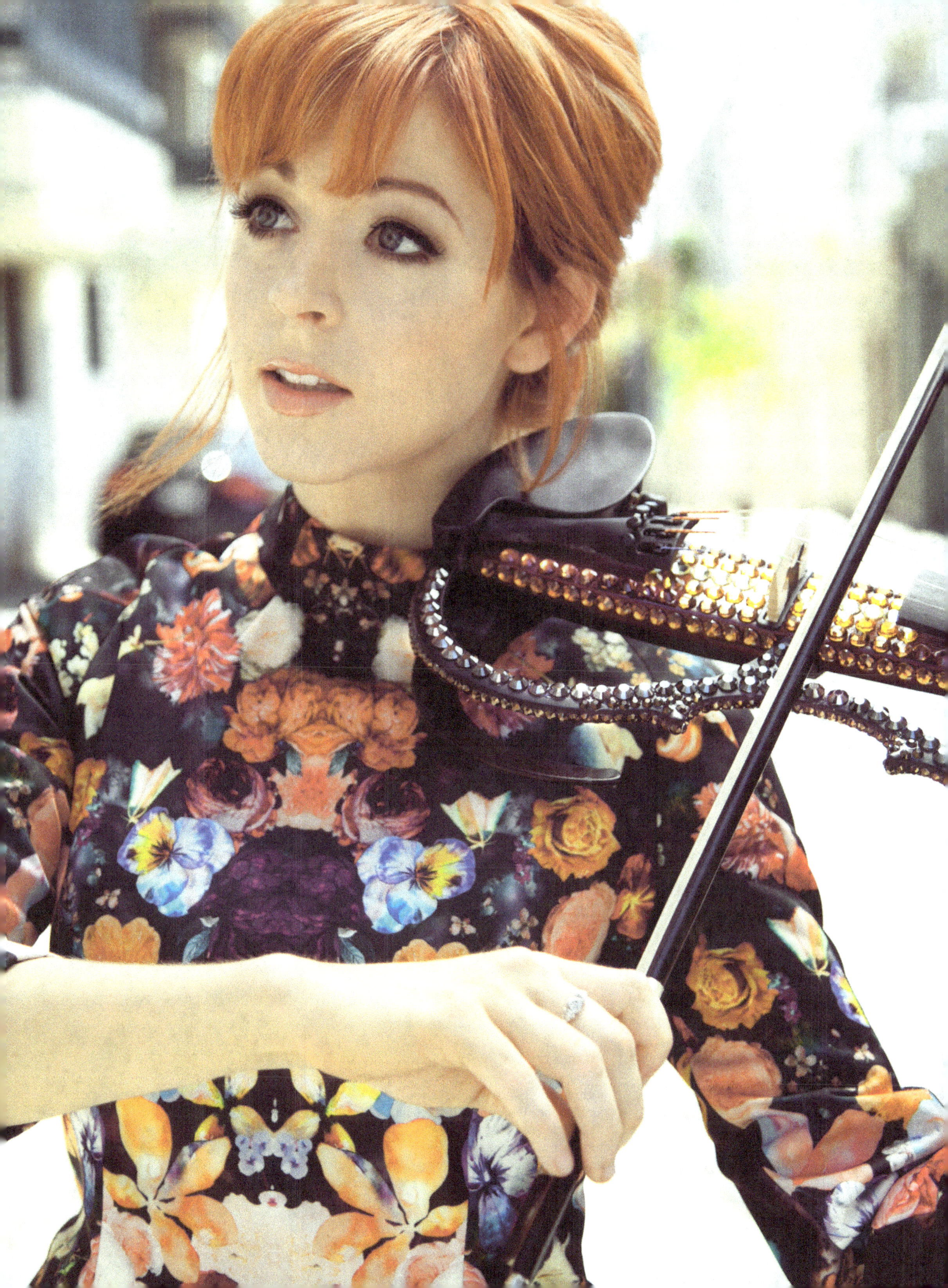

Caligo Bastet

By Asylum Attendant

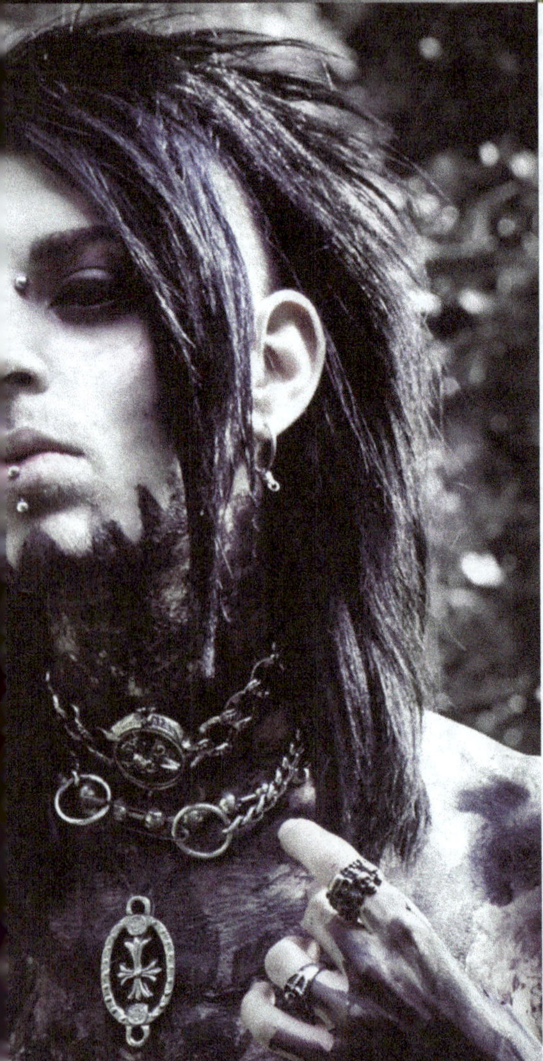

Photography by Lucy Ekel and Zhenya Gore

I think a lot of alternative people take for granted the freedom to express themselves through their appearance. Sadly, not every place in the world values non-conformity and diversity. Even still, brave souls disregard their oppressive societies and display their individuality proudly. One of these people is Caligo Bastet and his signature dark and edgy wardrobe, informative YouTube videos and liquid latex fascination all set him apart from the crowd.

Caligo is an alternative model and musician from Israel and often vents his frustrations regarding the traditional values of his home country and how judgmental a lot of the people there can be. He's very talented with makeup and clothing alterations, posting tutorials and advice videos on his YouTube channel. A lot of Caligo's tutorials are geared toward Goth guys, which is great because it promotes acceptance and inspires guys to experiment with their looks and rock who they are. From eyeshadow to contouring to hair, Caligo is a knowledgeable guy to learn from. His fashion is pretty particular, with all black pieces, platform boots, spikes/studs and vests/shirts worn open. Caligo even paints liquid latex on himself similar to the band members of Black Veil Brides and Motionless in White.

Caligo studies music at a university and is a singer/songwriter. His song covers include the bands Evanescence, Solar Fake, Emilie Autumn and more. Caligo has a deep, powerful voice that will aid him in his future musical endeavors. He is also vegan and a strong activist against animal cruelty. Caligo lives a drug-free life and wants to be a positive influence on the world. His thoughtfulness and sweet demeanor have gained him thousands of followers on social media.

What's to come from Caligo? He plans on moving to Germany to launch his music career and realize his many dreams. You can keep up with all of Caligo's beauty tips and adventures on You Tube at xCaligoBastetx. He's one Goth guru you'll want to get to know.

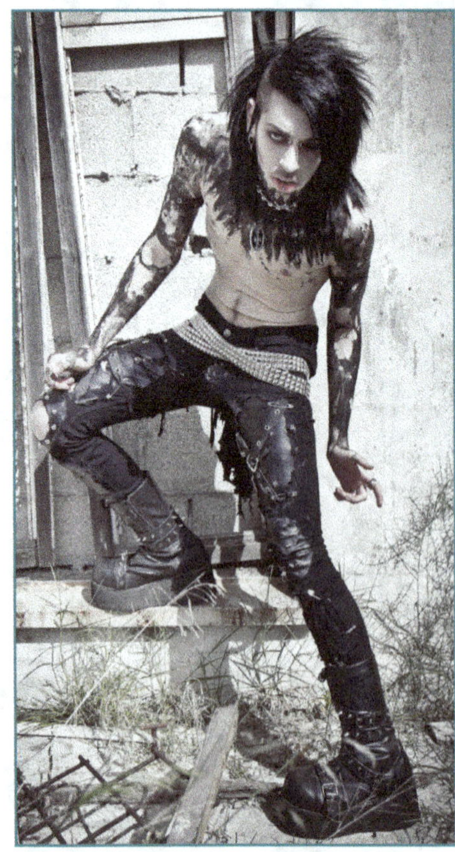

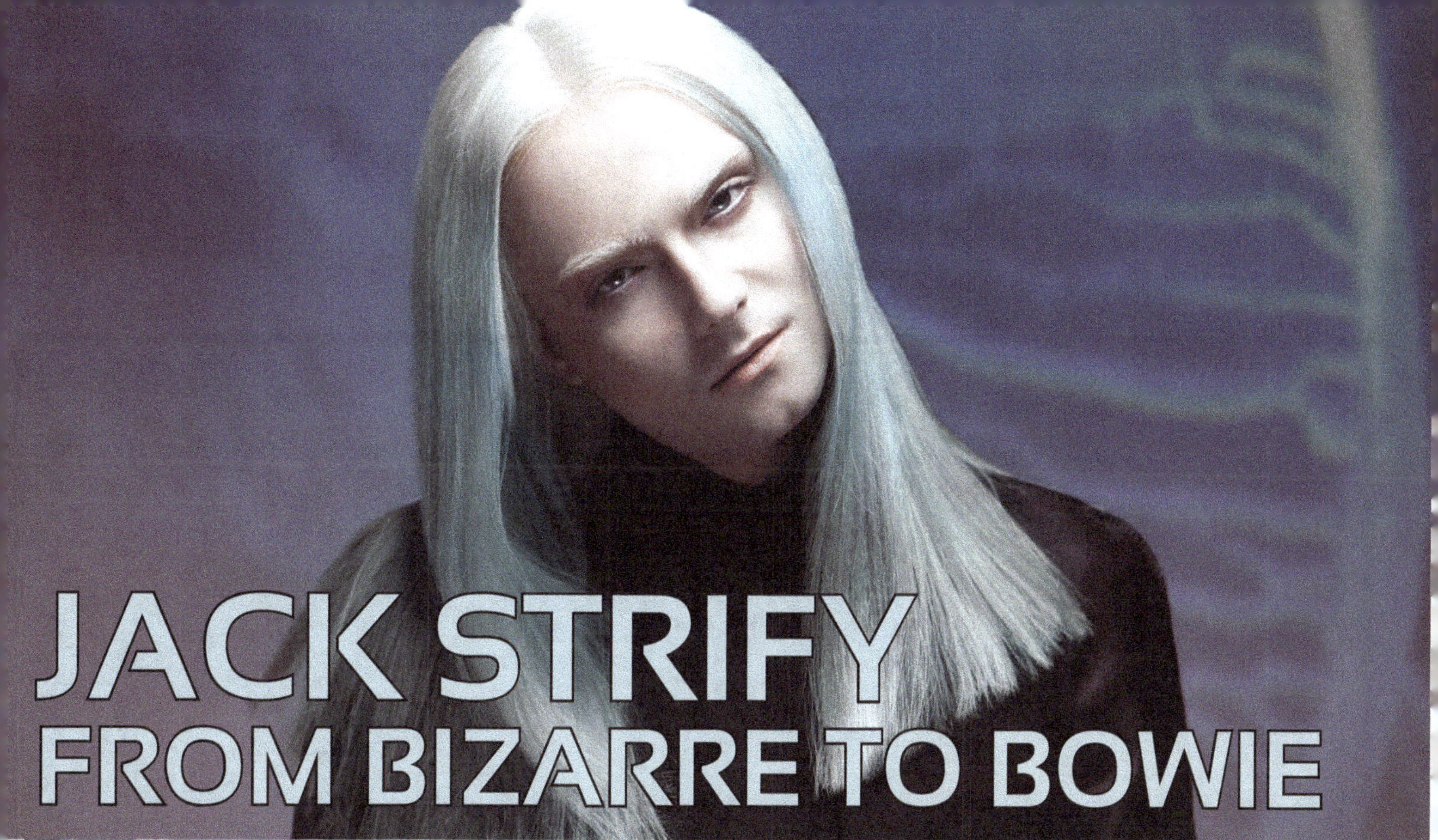

JACK STRIFY
FROM BIZARRE TO BOWIE

By Asylum Attendant

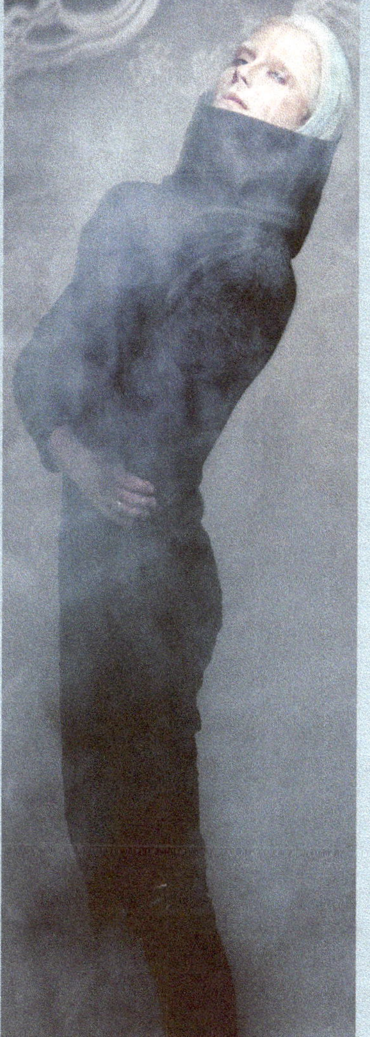

Musically, I am most inspired by synthpop and new wave artists from the 80's. These musicians include Depeche Mode, Yazoo, Soft Cell, Visage, etc. Well, when I came across a contemporary artist with the exact same influences as me, I knew it was fate. That artist is Jack Strify and his androgynous appearance and so-called synthwave music will have you reminiscing over MTV's early years.

Anyone remember glam pop band Cinema Bizarre? Jack Strify was their lead singer and that's where his music career began in 2005. The members of Cinema Bizarre met at an anime convention and were all very interested in the visual kei movement originating from Japan. Visual kei musicians wear elaborate outfits, lots of makeup and have a gender-bending look about them. Cinema Bizarre adopted the edgy fashion trend and released their debut rock single "Lovesongs (They Kill Me)" in 2007. Their first album Final Attraction quickly followed and was quite successful in their home country of Germany.

Cinema Bizarre reminds me a lot of another German pop rock act, Tokio Hotel. Both groups had flamboyant lead singers and droves of teenage fans. Cinema Bizarre released their one and only U.S. album BANG! in 2009 and toured North America as the opening act for Lady Gaga. By early 2010, the band decided to call it quits and Jack Strify became a solo artist.

In 2012, Jack released a stunning music video trilogy displaying his solo work. His music was clearly moving in a more electronic direction and his visuals were in no way lacking from his time with Cinema Bizarre. Jack's love of science fiction novels is evident on the song "Brave New World", which lyrically describes a dystopia. These darker themes marked Jack's maturity and artistic growth. He released his first EP, Glitter + Dirt, in 2013, much to the joy of his loyal fans.

Next came work on Jack's solo album Illusion. In order to fund the production of the album, Jack set up a project on the website PledgeMusic where fans could donate money in exchange for prizes and exclusive updates. Illusion was released in 2015 and is a deep new wave odyssey through the future where love is hard to find. The industrial first single "Burn/Fear" and accompanying video are captivating. Jack has morphed into a fierce creature with long ice blond hair and all-black attire. "Metropolis" is a creepy song about a loss of freedom and individuality with a Depeche Mode vibe. Jack gets a bit sweeter on "Lovers When It's Cold", a sleek synthpop love song with a campy music video straight from the 80's.

I really value diversity and authenticity. Jack Strify embodies both of those qualities. He is not afraid to make the music he likes or to look however he wants to. Jack has meaningful thoughts to share with the world through his current new wave persona. He has found a home amongst my music playlist of artists La Roux, Orchestral Manoeuvres in the Dark, and Purity Ring. I'm sure he'd make a great addition to your playlists, too.

Music Review:
Zeitgeist Zero
Ghosts of Victory

By Omen

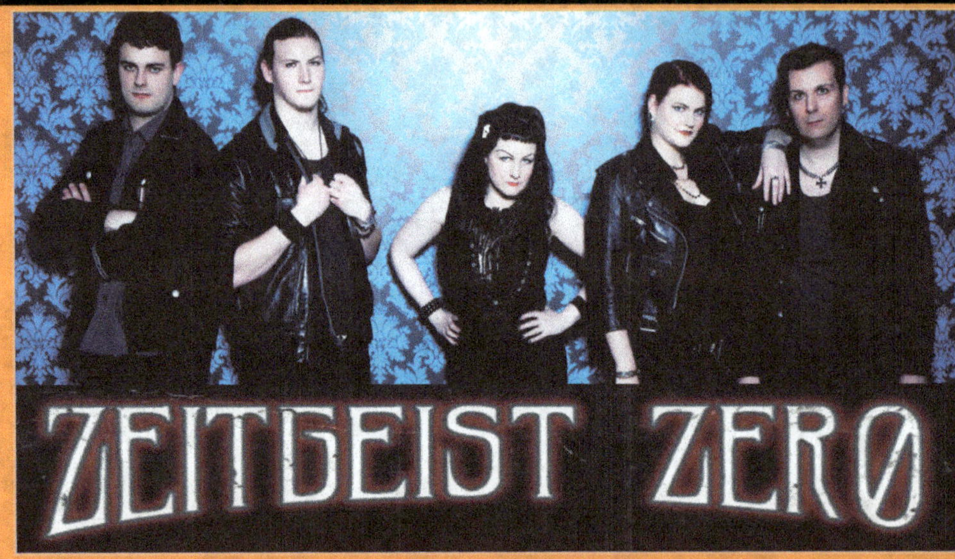

Review Focuses
Production: rates how everything is assembled and directed to support the title or focus of the song. It includes sounds and breaks designed to enhance the purpose of the music and storytelling together while controlling the attention of the listener
Storytelling: rates the writing (lyrics) and vocals of a song, cohesively.
Music: measures the structural environment of a song created by instruments. It dictates the feel of the track using rhythm, tempo, harmony and melody.
Presentation: measures the level of visual immersion surrounding a product and/or brand (CD graphics, art, imagery, etc.)
Note - Review scores are based on a scale of 1 to 5 with a score of 3 as average and 5 being the best.

Zeitgeist Zero – Ghosts of Victory
Overall Score: 3.5
(Really good, Above Average)

Individual Tracks Reviewed:
Domestic Blitz
Production: 3
Storytelling: 2
Music: 2.5
Summary: The chaos of destruction is clearly felt through the heavy guitars and trilling sounds, great Production. The cuts created by the brief lyrics and vocals enhance the urgency. I definitely wanted another verse of this experience.

The Jekyll in Me
Production: 3
Storytelling: 4
Music: 3
Summary: Smooth beat-runs with a strong focus on storytelling; this is a piece of art in which the vocals support the strength of the writing. The mix-up in the production fully stands out and impresses. Interest is held by the variety of sounds and high tempo. This is one of the stronger tracks on the CD... very enjoyable.

Dust and Bone
Production: 4.5
Storytelling: 4
Music: 3.5
Summary: A late 1930s to 1940s noir feel with an industrial, bebop tone. The 'up-bop' is extremely fun and immersive. Dust & Bones delivers a welcomed contrast to the lyrics of some of the other tracks on this CD by taking us a quick journey through time. The voice and synth are seamless. This is an EXCELLENT production; one of the most stylish tracks of the entire CD.

Don't Pop My Bubble
Production: 2
Storytelling: 2
Music: 2.5
Summary: Starts with a smooth and busy tempo which escalates into a drum rhythm colliding with the bass to create a trance of emotions. The background vocals acted as a needed echo to make this track solid.

Pushed to the Edge
Production: 2.5
Storytelling: 2.5
Music: 2
Summary: This track was standard until the break in the final quarter of the song. The break pulls the attention back to the song and forces one to listen to the lyrics more intently. This is a 'headbounce' song with complex storytelling asking for multiple playthroughs to absorb. The vocals were at the edge of being swallowed by the music.

Loose Lips Sink Ships
Production: 3
Storytelling: 3.5
Music: 2.5
Summary: A welcomed regret letter written with a voice that stands above the ovation of music meant to support it. These vocals drag the listener to a dark place beneath the surface of this tale's emotions; the written lyrics were the weights to aid this occurrence. The ending was an elegant composition.

When the Lights Go Down
Production: 3
Storytelling: 4.5
Music: 3.5
Summary: A war chant of sultriness and 'down-to-earth' sexuality. The guitar rips the innocence from any lies that want to be digested as truth. This rhythm echoes attitude and is the 'neck-twist' to the vocals. The listener is reminded that this is a mature and confident woman speaking... she will not be ignored.

A Last Farewell
Production: 4
Storytelling: 4
Music: 3.5
Summary: This is a masterful piece of art which spotlights the entire production aspect of its tale. The backup vocals offer an ethereal undertone that provides a level of wonderment and empathy; it is the glue in this song. The piano is without comparison, the fingers pressing those keys should be commended. So dark.... so deep... so beautiful... very well done.

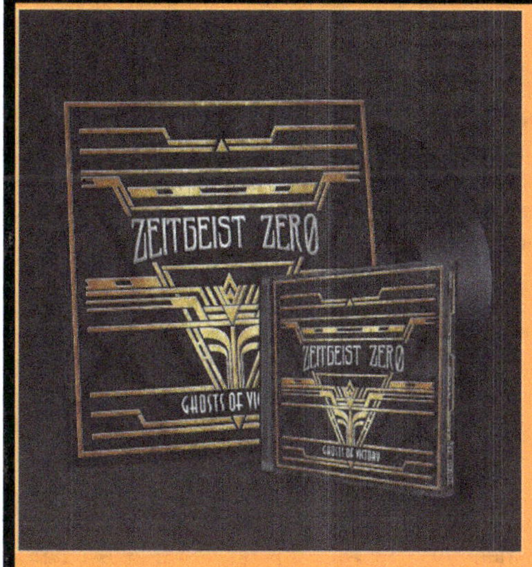

United in Black
Production: 2.5
Storytelling: 2.5
Music: 3.5
Summary: This is a dank and fun, dance floor song. A safe thumping reverie and escape from being normal, is celebrated in this track. This is a 'head-bouncer' to be enjoyed in the car when waiting at a light and ignoring those around you.

From Stun to Kill
Production: 3
Storytelling: 2.5
Music: 4
Summary: This 'stance-of-rebellion' song, recruits the listener with its hypnotic beat. The writing is complex and yet, simple to understand. This is a musical song in every sense. It strives to prove a point and successfully achieves it. Set the volume from stun to kill – stand back, aim, and fire at will!

Overall CD Visual Presentation: 4
Summary: There was a lot of attention to detail taken with this CD case, as well as the booklet. The art and photography reflects an understanding, the listener is staring at every pixel and picture associated with this product while escaping into the music. The very splashes on the inside case photo became relevant when listening to the impact of the first song. The old-world color palette combined with the textured wash, did not distract from impeccable clothing and the essence of the musical artists gathered. The slick dark pages in the booklet and unique golden borders complemented the single photos displayed on each page opposite of the lyrics. It allowed the listener time to get to know the artist spotlighted. It left us wanting more (which is good).

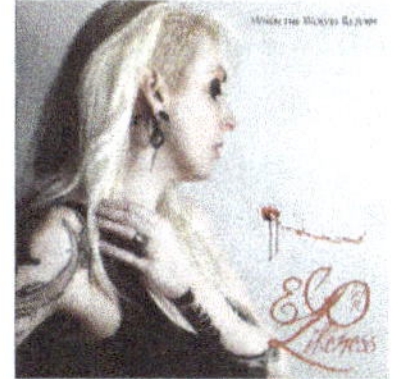

Ego Likeness
When the Wolves Return

- Lyrics by Donna Lynch

I confess
My crimes of hopelessness
And excess

You should know
That out there in the dark
This terrible girl
was torn apart

I don't want pity
That would make it all about me

There's nothing to forgive
It's the price you pay to live...

Take these lessons
Make them count
Make it worth the pain you felt
Before your time runs out

Take these lessons
Make them count
Make it worth the pain you dealt
Before your time runs out

When the lights go out
All you'll have is what you felt
When the sky goes dark
They're gonna leave a mark

When the wolves return
All you'll have is what you learned
When the wolves return...

Then the wolves returned
And all I had was what I learned
Then the wolves returned.

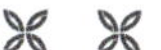

It seems like forever ago when Ego Likeness released the video for "Treacherous Thing." It was 2012, in fact. This was a taste of their upcoming album. Three years in the making, "When the Wolves Return," was finally unleashed onto the world this past July. The expectations were high, and Steven Archer and Donna Lynch did not disappoint. They never disappoint. As much as I completely love "Breedless" and "Order of the Reptile," "Wolves" may very well be the best thing this duo has ever done.

Like everything else they do, this CD is undeniably Ego Likeness. However, I find a lot more diversity among the tracks than any of their previous works. Donna showcases her amazing range more in "Wolves" than any of their earlier releases. This album definitely has a more electronic feel, but there are plenty tracks with those crunching guitars we are used to from Steven. I feel the Stoneburner influence, but it's subtle. There is no one better at setting that haunting atmosphere than Ego Likeness, and "When the Wolves Return" is built for the darkness. It is a sweet nightmare you will want to relive over and over again.

Normally, I would break down individual tracks for the reader, but I have something better in store. First, I must say the biggest surprise for me on "Wolves" was the inclusion of the song "Persona Non Grata." This incredible song was originally released on the very limited edition "East" EP. I've had the pleasure of hearing Ego Likeness perform this song live, and was blown away. I have been disheartened ever since that I couldn't buy it on iTunes or through their website. Now, I finally have it. Thank you Donna and Steven!

Now the bigger thing...check out our Winter Issue when I will be interviewing Ego Likeness, and giving you a more in-depth and insightful look into the duo I consider to be the best Industrial Rock band out there today. In the meantime, do yourself a favor, and buy "When the Wolves Return." You can thank me later for the recommendation.
- MICHAEL JACK

SOUNDS OF THE LIVING DEAD

ALBUM REVIEWS

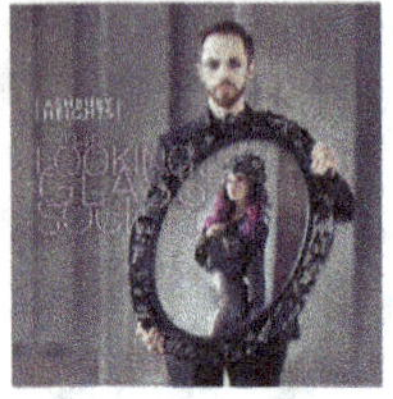

The Looking Glass Society
Ashbury Heights

Swedish synthpop band Ashbury Heights is finally back after a five year hiatus with their new album The Looking Glass Society and it's packed full of just as much imagination as anything Lewis Carroll could come up with. This album is decidedly more pop than anything else Ashbury Heights has ever released, but this is refined pop music for intellectuals and elegant aristocrats. One can sing and dance to the prominent synths and irresistible hooks on The Looking Glass Society, yet still encounter the Gothy themes that give Ashbury Heights their edge. New female singer/songwriter and model Tea F. Thimé joins founder Anders Hagström to create futuristic Victorian soundscapes with mass appeal. I think Anders may have uncovered the perfect formula for world domination together with Tea.

"Phantasmagoria" is a great example of the band's dark electro pop that could sneak onto Top 40 radio. The ghostly bells and spooky lyrics are certainly a nod to Carroll's poem of the same name. Anders' and Tea's beautiful vocals really mesh on "The Number 22", complete with a delicate carousel-esque break from the driving electronic beats. The harpsichord and strings at the beginning of "Hollow" unexpectedly lead into Tea's sultry vocal stylings and danceable instrumentation.

Ashbury Heights' implementation of strings into their music adds another dash of class to their multidimensional dance songs.

The anthemic "Ghost Spirit Mother" is certainly my favorite song from The Looking Glass Society. The song is about losing someone close to you, but continuing on in their legacy. "Ghost Spirit Mother" is uplifting and hopeful, turning a dark experience into something positive. The whole album is like a high society theatre show with plenty of dramatics and shadowy undercurrents. I can't wait to hear the companion album to The Looking Glass Society, entitled The Victorian Wallflowers, which is soon to be released. The modern maturity and fairy tale charm of Ashbury Heights will definitely guide listeners into Wonderland.
- **ASYLUM ATTENDANT**

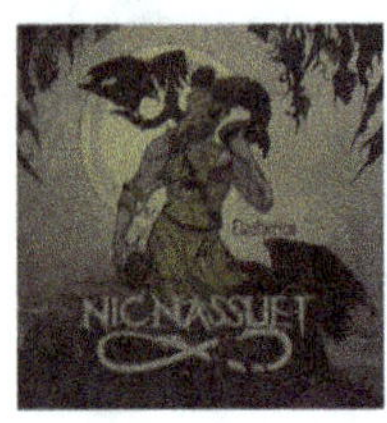

Nic Nassuet
Eleutherios

Gothic folk rock is not an easy genre to pull off. Singer/songwriter Nic Nassuet excels as an unclassifiable artist on his first album Eleutherios, a work that can be appreciated by fans of acoustic music with depth and those who dwell in the shadows.

The ancient legend inspired "Immured" tells the tragic story of a bride entombed alive. The evocative lyrics and sorrowful strings make the legend real to the listener. The vocal stylings of Nic Nassuet and Catrina Grimm emote the desperation of taking one's last breath. Nic has a way of adding power to his voice without ever losing control. Soft or gritty, Nic is comfortable showing many dimensions of himself through his music.

"When It Falls", an up-tempo break-up song, marks Nic's descent into introspection and "The Nothing" is him baring his soul. Nic pulls from dark experiences, but there is beauty in the complete honesty he shares. "Goodnight, Goodbye" is an acoustic lullaby with just Nic and his guitar. His tremendous talent cannot be denied when stripped down to the basics. "Black Dress" conjures up an image of a female grim reaper, with a vibrant string solo to bring her to life.

Eleutherios is a refined debut with intrigue and heaps of feeling. I can see the audience to Nic's music being very diverse. Rock fans will dig his booming voice and guitar skills. Goths will enjoy his theatricality and gloom. Pop aficionados will appreciate his lush melodies and hooks. I think Nic is just beginning to show us what he can really do.
- **ASYLUM ATTENDANT**

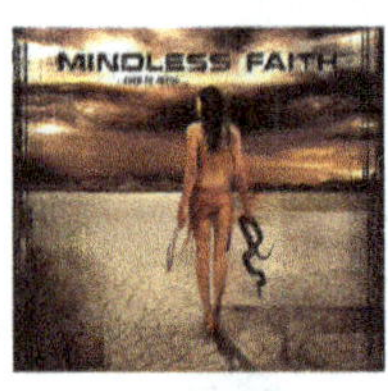

Mindless Faith
Eden to Abyss

Mindless Faith is back with their sixth full length CD, "Eden to Abyss." There are reasons this band has longevity and a devoted fan base...consistency and quality. "Eden to Abyss" might not be the epic earth shattering release that completely changes up what they do and leaves you with your jaw hanging open. Instead, Mindless Faith builds on what they already do great...intelligent and complex arrangements, political outcries, guttural vocals, and hard electro-rock. If you are a fan of Mindless Faith, you will love this album. If you are not, you may want to give this CD a listen because it just may change your mind.

From the opening song, "Devil May Care," Mindless Faith hooks you in with driving dance-able beats and nightmarish ambiance. The song explodes with the chorus, and instantly you are bobbing your head and pumping your fist. The second song on the album, "Shit Show," infuses funk, and features guest vocals by Monica Durant. This gritty song delivers that experimental style that has helped to define Mindless Faith. By the time you hit the third track, "Red Halos," you begin to realize how much this band is truly pushing the limits of what they do. This song contains a 40's jazz style blended perfectly into heavy guitars and rhythmic beats.

From beginning to end of this CD I found myself amazed with the not so-subtle, and sometimes subtle, use of varied music styles within the songs. I also laughed at bawdy themes like "The Fluffer." As a complete work, I rate this album as one of the best things they have done so far. Its arrangements are brilliant and flawless, but then again, they always are. I said it in the opening paragraph, and I'll say it again, there is a reason for Mindless Faith's longevity. To date, they have never released anything that has not been of top quality, and "Eden to Abyss" is no different. This album is a must-own.
- **MICHAEL JACK**

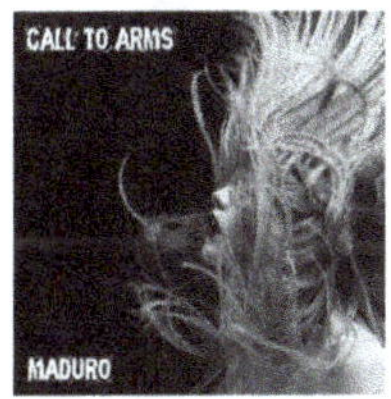

Maduro
Call to Arms

Prolific electronic music artist Maduro takes the listener on a spacey trip, featuring distorted melodies and intense beats. "This Is Where It Begins" and "Arcane Lore" are reminiscent of the rainy cityscapes in Bladerunner, and the title track offers an endless climb and heaviness not found in the other tracks. The songs range from delicate and deliberate to frenzied and overwhelming.

Each song contains layer upon layer of beats and accents, starting with opening tracks "Vapor Guns" and "Detect Magic". The distortion and echoing signals your arrival in Maduro-land, and there are surprises at every turn. While "Orchid Crush" and "Sine Pollution" are very danceable, the rest of this release has a sinister and cavernous feel. The piano melodies in "Orchid Crush" are soft and soothing, overlying a brooding percussion that makes the listener want to move.

"Beguiled" offers a more relaxing vibe, acting as a calm point during this alluring synthesizer storm. Call to Arms ends with the eerie "Moments Before the Light". It's as though one had a dream where the details are difficult to recall... but the feeling remains upon awakening. With over 20 releases to his name, Maduro consistently delivers dark electronica that's futuristic and compelling, yet enticing. And Call to Arms is no exception.
- ZAHARA

The Sweetest Condition
Truth and Light

Like other bands of their generation, The Sweetest Condition have grown up in the worship of a certain British New Wave, founding in Depeche Mode a peculiar source of inspiration. But Leslie Irene Benson and Jason Reed Miller, live not merely in this comfortable amniotic fluid. These two guys raised in Indianapolis and now based in Nashville, have in their hands many other cards to play.

The five songs on this EP ranging from synth-rock to a not-so-harsh industrial style, sometimes also dance-floor oriented., however always dark-tinged. It Is always recognizable an extreme accuracy and capacity to draw melodic plots, each containing inside a distinctive spark. Even if it is evident the debt with Mr.Gahan and his group - "Give Me The World" - for example, they possess a strong personality.susceptible to further future developments There's imagination, fluidity and lyricism inside this work, above all in the dramatic shape of a piece like "The Ghost and the Girl", enriched by the high quality lyrics written by Benson. She's also a very talented singer and uses her voice in the most expressive manner. There's some promising material here and their first album is coming soon.
- SERGIO MANGHINA

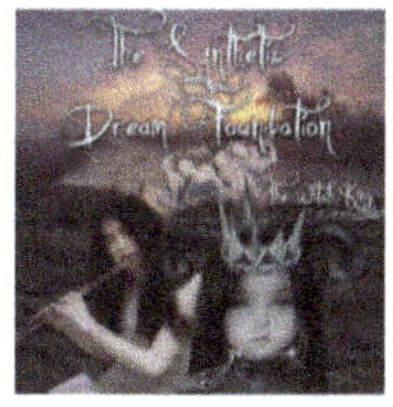

The Synthetic Dream Foundation
The Witch King

Eclectic and ambitious, Brett Branning, the man behind the name The Synthetic Dream Foundation, ably handles several styles of music such as Industrial, Dark-Ambient, Goth, Classical, EBM. The Witch King, his new work, represents a very complex project which these three songs, are only a part, the first movement of a pocket symphony.

Solemn and epic, with a masterful use of choirs, "In The Realms Of The Unreal" starts with powerful telluric energy, combining rhythmic subtleties as well as sophisticated timbres, unusual in not academic music. The classical element is not stuck as a mere ornament but instead is a completing part of the structure of this and the other pieces.

Human Harvest elicits a drastic change of perspective to a robust electro-beat with some reminiscence of the Tangerine Dream '90s edition, while the final track, "Letters of Black Night", increases, if possible, the overall rate of dramatization between classical tradition and dark electronic. This EP is the first segment of a soaring trilogy and also an elegantly designed, impressive demonstration of musical quality.
- SERGIO MANGHINA

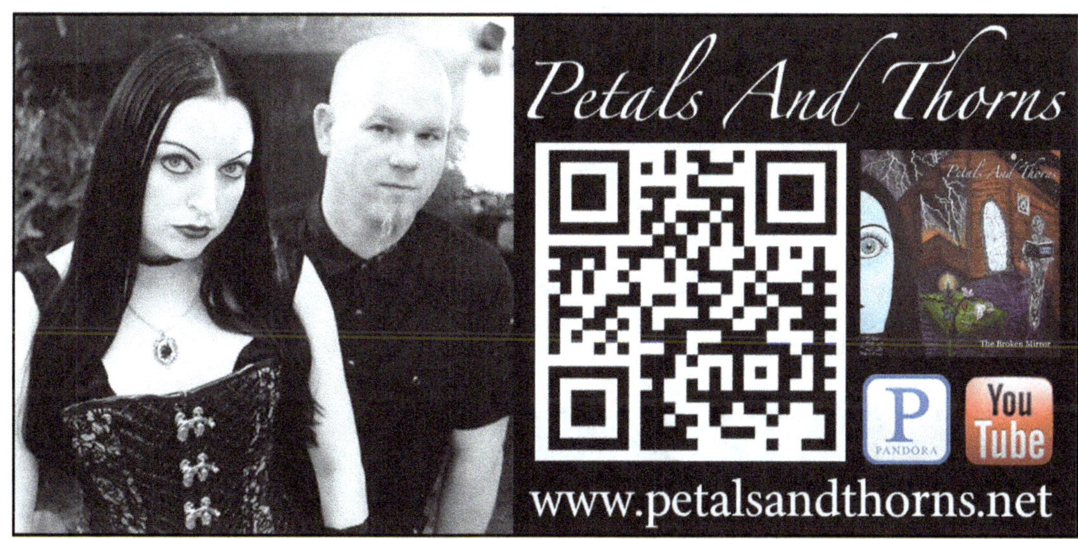

CHAINED SHADOWS

A GATHERING OF THINGS IN NOIR STYLE

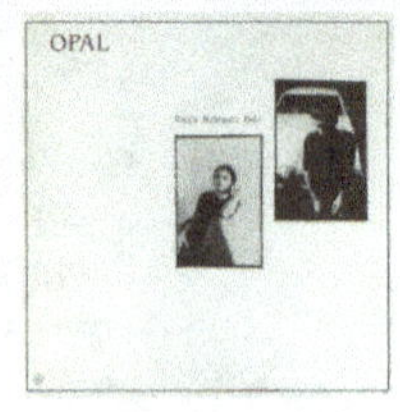

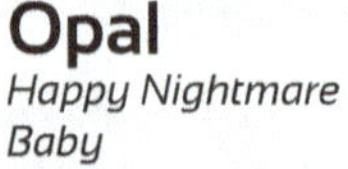

Opal
Happy Nightmare Baby

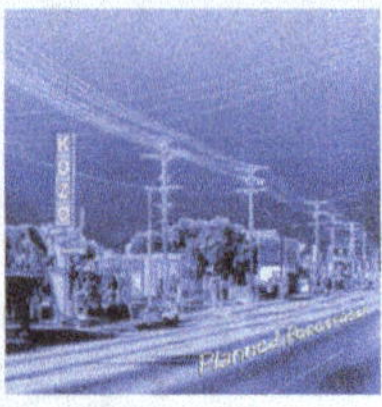

Kozo
Planned Penetration

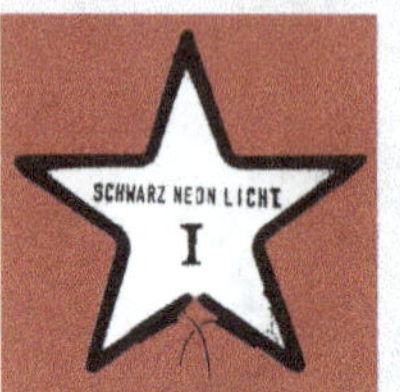

The Chill Marks Bending
Schwarz Neon Licht

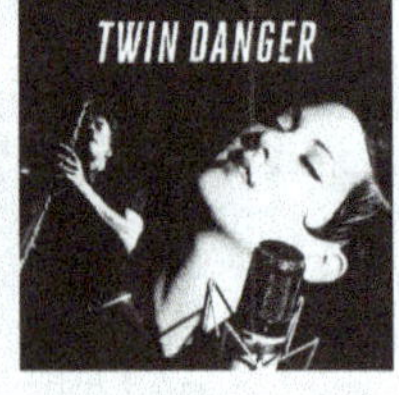

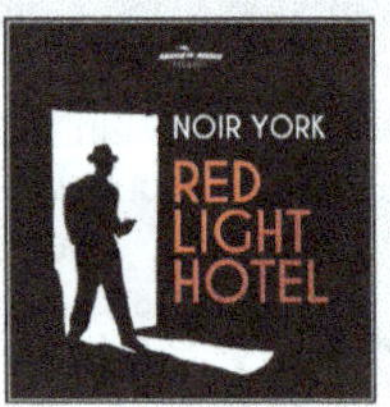

Twin Dangers
Decca

Stewart Matthewson, saxophonist and composer, was one of the key players behind the success of Sade, the coolest British chanteuse.of the '80s. Vanessa Bley, is the talented daughter of a master of jazz such as Paul Bley.

Some time ago, the couple gave birth to a creature called Twin Danger whose debut album is an amazing collection of sparkling songs, a happy combination of seductive melodies wrapped into a noir mood. However, the cherry on the top of the cake is the ultra-sophisticated "I love Loving You", four minutes of pure pleasure, ideal for certain smoky nightclubs illuminated only by table lamps.

Noir York
Red Light Hotel

Aron Erdmann is a prolific Hungarian musician, above all he's an ace in the art of sampling and hits in full the right noir mood, thanks to a deep knowledge of the subject. "Entrance" is the revolving door for a mad foray, split into twelve episodes inside the rooms of this "Red Light Hotel". The fragrant mixture of electro-swing, voices and sounds - stolen from old radio broadcasts and movies and then cut and sewn in surgical samples - is an exciting sonic adventure. No cheap lounge-exotica here, but solid nu-jazz, shaken by classic swing and frantic bebop breakbeats. Fun for everyone.

flew away from the short-lived '80s Paisley Underground mosaic. Among those neo-psychedelic guys, David Roback had been the Byrdsian guitar of Rain Parade and Kendra Smith the disturbing muse of the first Dream Syndicate. Roback spreads gasoline and corrosive acid on his Rickembacker, that is now more sharp and hard, while a noir shade is the dowry that Kendra brings to her new band.

Opal is precious, with iridescent and perhaps even magical colors. But the dream is actually a nightmare and the street in the night does not lead anywhere. Similar to the oniric video clip of the title track - filmed by Kevin Kerslake - the convertible runs on the edge of the solid white line into the night and toward the sea. The Doors appear in the mirrors like wandering ghosts and a bit of their "When The Summer Is Gone" lives again in this Happy Nightmare Baby.

Kozo is little known outside his native Japan, and yet he's a fine multi-instrumentalist. His style is a neurotic ambient jazz, absolutely noir in imagining scenarios of contemporary urban desolation, in some ways not so far away from an industrial-cybernoir aesthetic.

The twelve tracks of this album have in common a compact sound space shared between solo trumpet and an unceasing electronic breakbeat. The first track, Room Service, is a game of distorting mirrors, in which the same trumpet - played with and without wah wah - feeds an opposite sense of lyricism and grinding. Miles Davis is obviously the greatest inspiration for Kozo, apart from the digression of "Voodoo", a tribute (unstated but evident) to another great trumpeter, the esoteric Jon Hassell.

They seem directly come out from Bristol, England, and its somptuous factory of electronic sounds around the mid-nineties. Instead, The Chill Marks, are a current project of the lively Israeli scene, even if they have released so far only a handfull of songs. "Behinding" is one of those, included in this sampler by a small label called Schwarz Neon Licht.

It is a nocturnal piece characterized by a spectral singing - in evident debt with Beth Gibbons - and a piercing saxophone, desolate like a scream in the night.

Some years ago, Portishead and (sometimes) Goldfrapp disseminated traps and pitfalls here and there and even today, fortunately for us, someone falls into them.

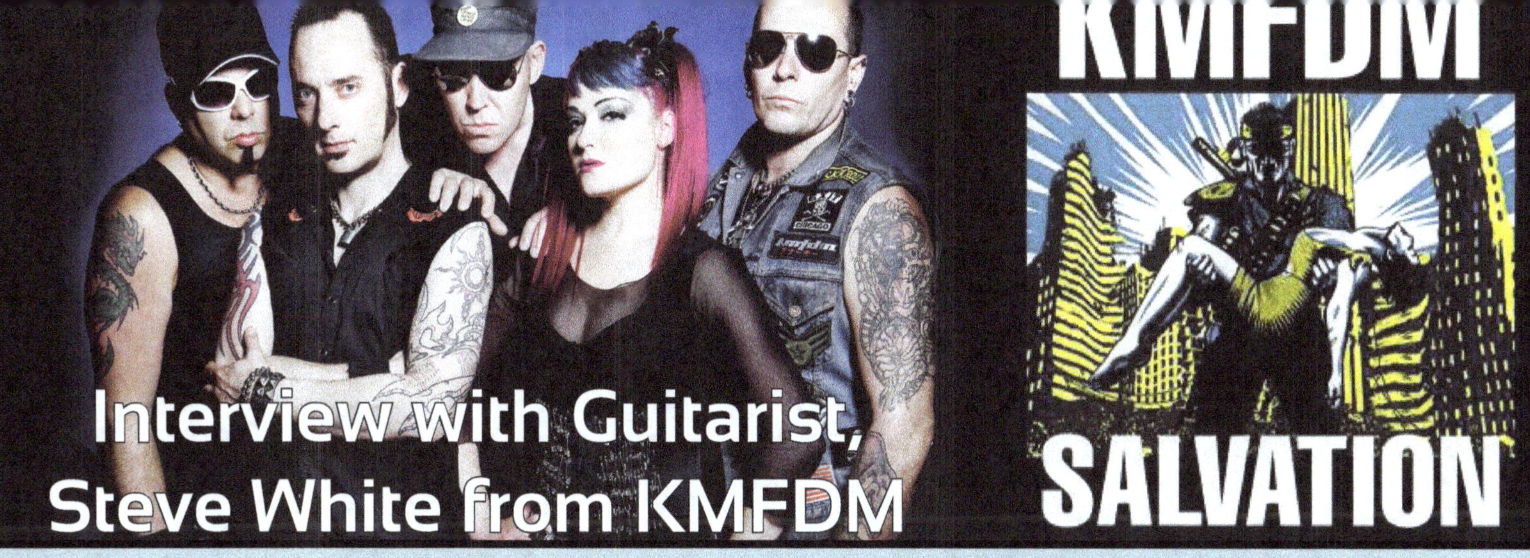

Interview with Guitarist, Steve White from KMFDM

KMFDM is still today, one of the front running Industrial-Metal acts, formed in 1984 by Sascha Konietzko in Hamburg, Germany. Since then, KMFDM has performed in North America, Europe, Asia, and Australia. KMFDM's earliest performances were as a local act in Hamburg. Their first major tour was in support of Ministry in 1990. Since then, KMFDM has headlined all of their tours, and has been a major influence to many Industrial bands. They are recognized in the Urban Dictionary under "Industrial Music" as forefathers of the genre. I had the pleasure of talking to the (always witty) KMFDM Guitarist, Steve White, who resides in Seattle.

[Carpe Nocturne] *Steve, you are getting ready to go on tour with KMFDM. How long is this tour going to last, and are you touring the US or the US and abroad?*

[Steve] Funny enough I am, as it happens. We are spoiling the Yanks for a month or so, teasing the Canucks, and just ignoring Europe right now.

[Carpe Nocturne] *What/whom would you say inspires you as a guitarist?*

[Steve] I have to say, the good life...and a certain cake maker from Tacoma. Once you've seen a fetus on "You Tube "playing your shit at twice the speed, it's all pretty irrelevant, really. Oh, what was the question again? Erm, I love Geordie's guitar playing in Killing Joke, but I met him recently and it turns out that he's a bit of a wanker. That is strangely inspiring, to not be him.

[Carpe Nocturne] *Haha! How many bands/projects are you in presently?*

[Steve] Single figures, these days. I only have 2 tits to suckle on.

[Carpe Nocturne] *You are also quite the talented soundman. How long have you been running sound on the side for other bands?*

[Steve] Too f###ing long. It started as a mission to improve the player/listener experience. I would recommend that all bands become familiar with the sound projection process, as it can only benefit all parties concerned. However, most people in this business could not find their asshole to scratch, let alone tune that plank of wood round

their neck. Being a Sound Person has morphed from: getting your gal into a show for free, to a charity with uninsured therapy classes beckoning.

[Carpe Nocturne] *What is your favorite thing to do, besides touring, of course?*

[Steve] See, I got into this business, like teachers for the holidays. Where do I start? Hmmm.... I largely like eating and thus cooking. It's all downhill from there, really Sailing and eating.....erm.... drinking and eating (particular favourite). I suppose, professionally speaking, I like collecting free plug-ins and making gentile, harmonious ditties for my (which I am too scared to form indie band that all my

By Dawn Wood

SEATTLE SOUNDS

band members would hate. You know how it goes. Haberdashery comes in at a close second.

[Carpe Nocturne] *What is Steve's biggest pet peeve?*

[Steve] If only I could confine it to 'pet' ..Oi , Don't don't get me started. It's been a nice day, so far, as I have not had to deal with any other being. Let's keep it that way. If forced, I would say the present trend amongst people to advertise their limited vocabulary and futile observations. Particularly the abuse of the verb, preposition, conjunction, adverb , noun etc...'LIKE'...I will have to leave this country when the valley kids eventually dispense with all vocabulary in favour of 'Like' and 'Awesome', delivered with question inflection or ...'You know wot I'm saying ??' or 'Do you feel me ??' Hurumph ...

[Carpe Nocturne] *Who are some of your favorite artists/bands to see/ listen to?*

[Steve] That's an easy question for young people." Me? Ha! Whatever one randomly finds on the web /radio or heaven forbid, somebody's recommendation. I am a guitar player, so tick all the usual boxes of course. See previous comment about You Tube, begs the Spinal Tap line, 'I could play Stairway to Heaven on my guitar when I was just 21 and Jimmy Page did not write until he was 27?' I think that says a lot.

[Carpe Nocturne] *What would be your advice to an aspiring guitarist?*

[Steve] Don't go Raga.

[Carpe Nocturne] *Where are some of your favorite places to tour with KMFDM?*

[Steve] Well, I consider myself very fortunate to go anywhere. However, the good ol' US of A has been particularly kind to us and the fine people who support us are second to none. There is nothing finer than being on a posh tour bus with your oldest mates and being paid to be delinquents. Particular highlights of foreign travel would have to include our 3 shows over 2 weeks in Australia and our legendary 24hr ferry ride from Stockholm to Helsinki (in which too many rock and roll clichés happened to so many). Eventually culminating with the incarceration of our roadie who took the rap for the tour manager (whom can no longer visit Finland legally). If such a thing was possible on a boat, it all started innocently enough with 20 Swedish birds doing Karaoke.

[Carpe Nocturne] *Anything you would like to promote?*

[Steve] This is where I say something profound, particularly to make up for the last paragraph? I hear Nano Technology is doing fine without my endorsement, so I will have to give a shout out to the band: Murder Weapons and...world peace, naturally. Oh, and I whole heartedly endorse a cheddar cheese toasty with Marmite, Heinz baked beans, bit of tuna and mayo while watching a British period, costume drama...All dressed in black of course.

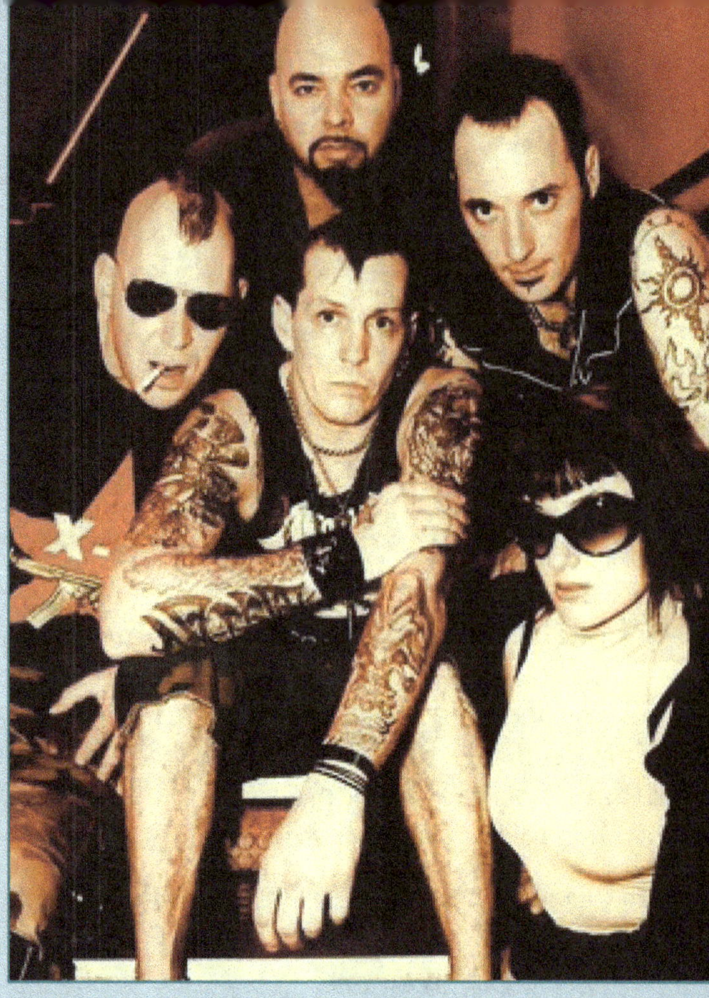

In the event that you haven't heard KMFDM's "awesome" ;) music, I encourage you to check them out at:

Web: http://www.kmfdm.net
Lastfm: http://www.last.fm/music/KMFDM

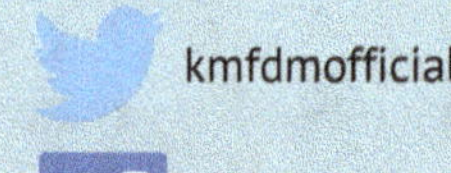 kmfdmofficial

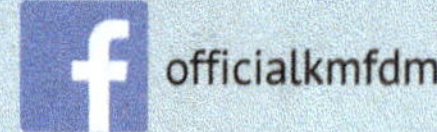 officialkmfdm

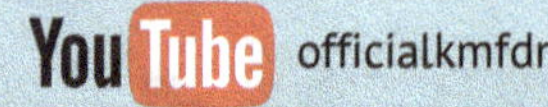 officialkmfdm

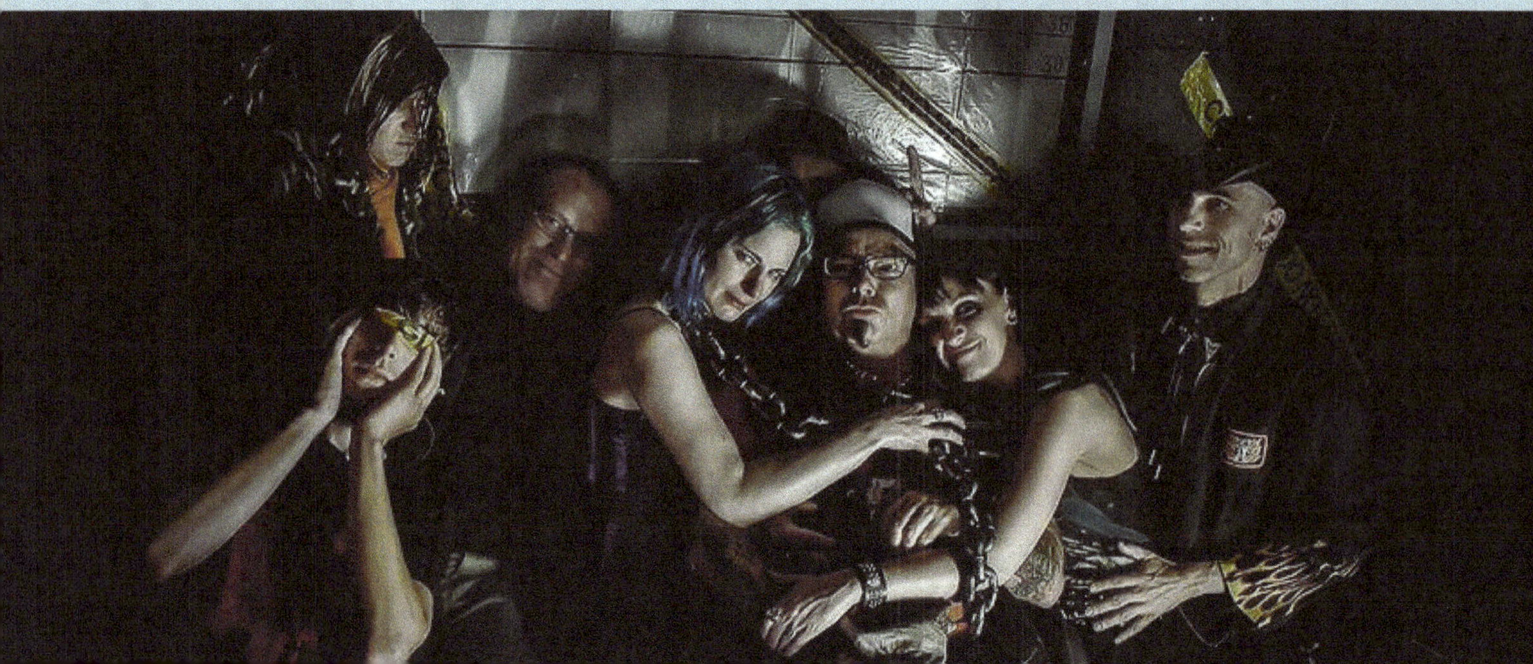

Pamela Moore is best known as Seattle Heavy Metal Goddess "Sister Mary" for Queensryche's <u>Operation Mindcrime</u> concept albums. She is the cousin of Teri Nunn of the 80's New Wave iconic group, Berlin. Pamela is also an extremely kind-hearted mentor and vocal coach to students both in the Seattle-area and abroad. I have to say, she is honestly one of the kindest people I have ever had the privilege of knowing. I have interviewed Pamela previously and sat down with her in June to catch up with what has been going on in her world. We discussed her successful career, upcoming projects and other musings.

PAMELA MOORE INTERVIEW

[Carpe Nocturne] *Pamela, have you always known you would be a singer? Did you have other career aspirations growing up?*

[Pamela Moore] "When I was a young girl, around the aged of 7, I wanted to be an actress. My Mother always said if I was going to be an actress, I had to learn to sing and dance. We didn't have the money to take all of those classes. I taught myself how to sing, play the guitar and the piano. I did some acting in High School. My Mom was an inspiration because she acted in small local theater productions."

[Carpe Nocturne] *When did you begin your career in music?*

[Pamela Moore] "I began at the age of 14. I was with a band in high school. I was mortified because my Mom was involved in making sure she knew what we were doing and making sure everything was OK. It was good because I wasn't old enough to make those decisions for myself. I am glad that she had that concern for me."

[Carpe Nocturne] *Were you inspired by any singers?*

[Pamela Moore] "I have always been inspired by many different kinds of singers. I have a tough time answering questions like this because I don't want to pigeon hole myself into a specific type of singer. Back in the day, I loved listening to Paul Rogers and Anne Wilson. They were on the radio at the time. Most of the time, I was more inspired by songs, as opposed to specific singers. Really well written songs in Country, Metal, R&B can really sing to your heart."

[Carpe Nocturne] *How did you become first involved with Queensryche and take on the role of Sister Mary?*

[Pamela Moore] "1989. I had already released two albums with First American Records (1981-1982) and was in Boy Toy at the time. It all started because I had gone over budget on my 2nd album and worked out a trade with the studio to record a commercial for Guitars Etc... The ad wound up being played all the time on the radio and television. I then started working by day at Guitars Etc... and at night with Boy Toy. I met Chris DeGarmo (one of the founding members of Queensryche). He introduced me to Geoff Tate. They actually came out to a Boy Toy show when we played at Pier 70 on the Seattle waterfront. Some time later, I got a phone call from Chris. He explained that Queensryche was in Montreal recording. They wanted me to 'come up and sing a part' for them. It was a duet for Geoff. I couldn't hear it before hand. He explained it was a conceptual album and they were holding it very close. They flew me to Montreal and told me about the concept of the album. We went into the studio, recorded the song and some voice over stuff for the Sister Mary part. I was pretty lucky. I was in the right place at the right time and did the right thing."

By Dawn Wood

SEATTLE SOUNDS

[Carpe Nocturne] *I understand you are involved with a horror project now. Tell me about it.*

[Pamela Moore] "I submitted my song Paranoia for Draghellpictures.com: The Zombie Meat Lovers. It was fun and quite hilarious.

[Carpe Nocturne] *Tell us about your teaching of vocal lessons and performance coaching?*

[Pamela Moore] "I started teaching part-time in the 90s. My notoriety has put me in a situation where I can show people my vocal techniques. I have really been doing this full time since 2009. I now have a recording program for my first time students so they have a chance to record a song for the first time in a professional studio. It is great to give back something that I have learned."

[Carpe Nocturne] *What are your current projects?*

[Pamela Moore] "I recently returned from a rock cruise doing an acoustic set and have plans to do another rock cruise in 2016 with my band. I have been continuing to build by business as a vocal coach and working on new material for the Pamela Moore Band.

Pamela can be found on the web and on Facebook. Check out her page and give her a like. Her voice is amazing.

www.ratpakrecordsamerica.com/pamela-moore
wwe.pamelamoore.net
www.pamelamoore.net/pmdream/lessons.html
www.facebook.com/pages/Pamela-Moore/45621380661
www.draghellpictures.com

Video trailer for The Zombie Meat Lovers:
https://www.youtube.com/watch?v=9q-prbNSs9Q

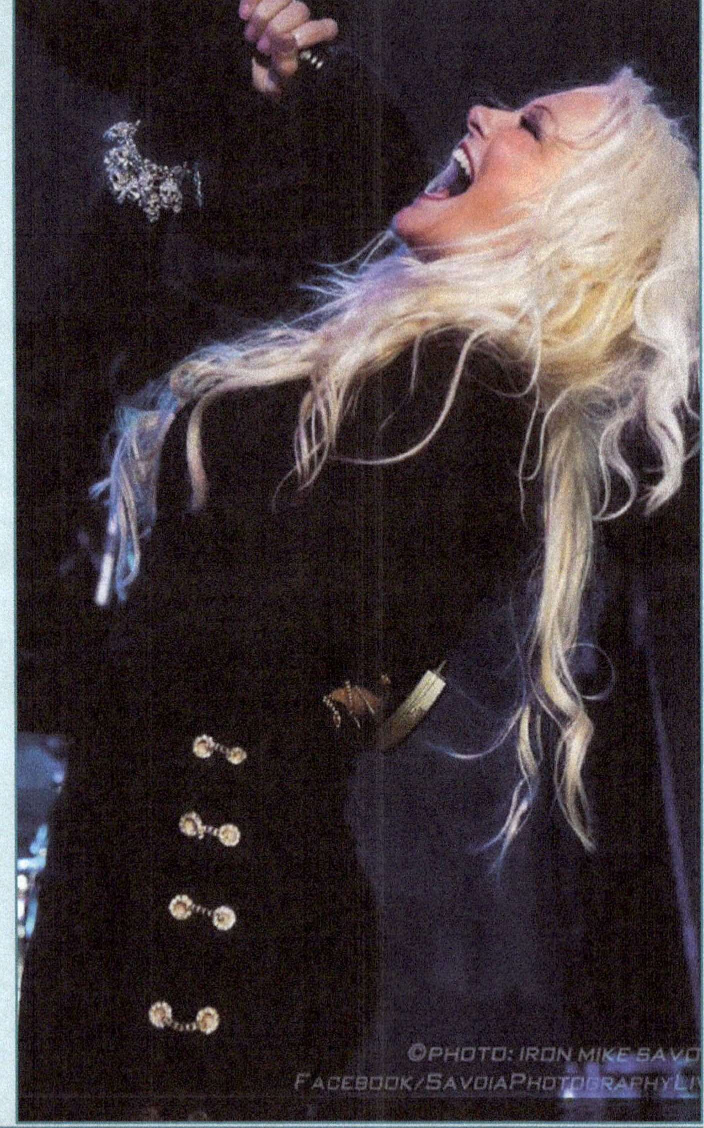

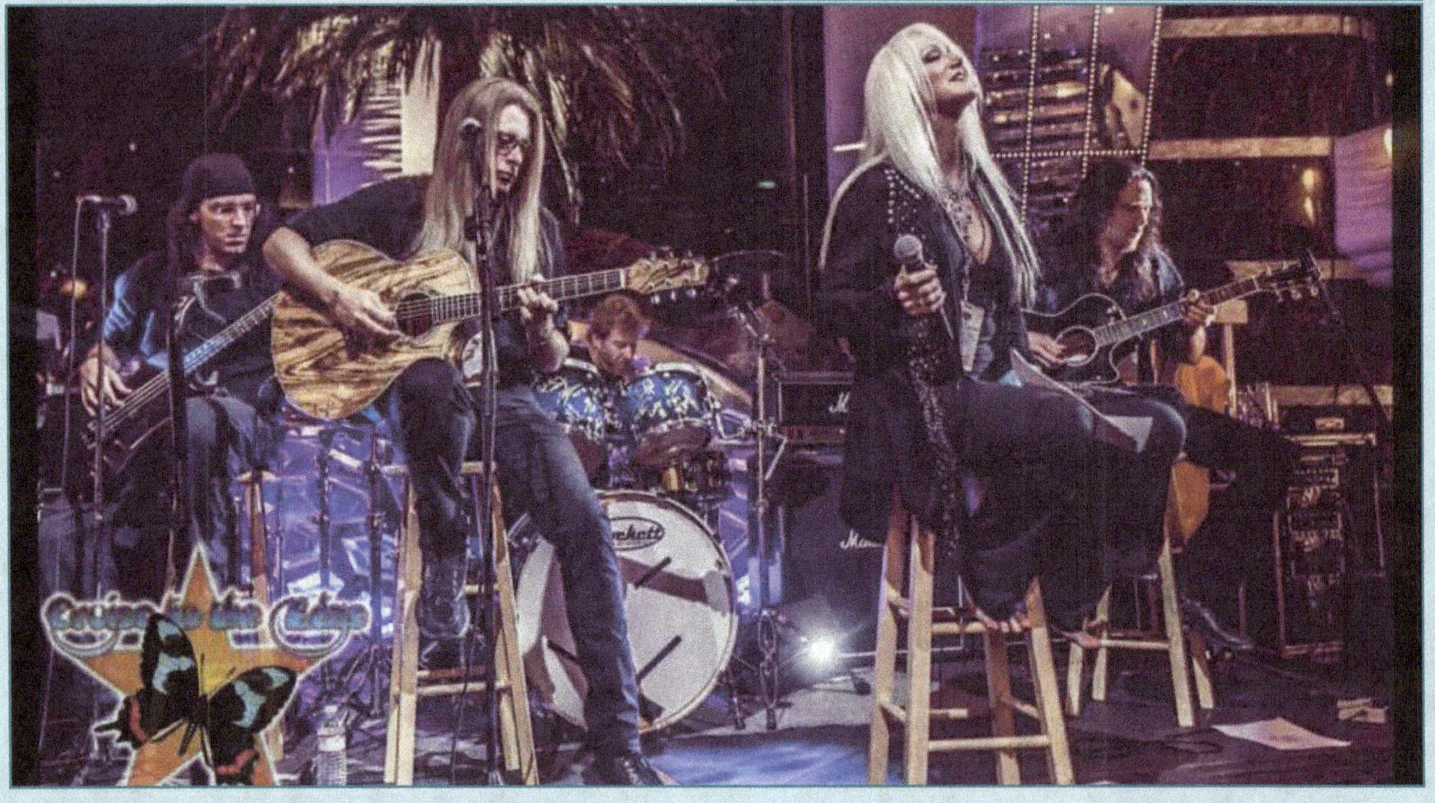

SPOTLIGHT FEATURE

There are a lot of truly talented people out there, especially in our culture. Some use this talent simply for passing the time and personal growth, while others develop their talent to create services, works and objects for others to enjoy. Some post their creations on their website and never try to sell their works, while others use their talents to supplement or create their income. Carpe Nocturne Magazine admires, respects, and supports YOUR TALENT!

Whether you are creating to sell or only for personal enjoyment,
LET THE WORLD SEE WHAT YOU'VE GOT!
There is NEVER A CHARGE to be Spotlighted or Featured!

The feature within Carpe Nocturne Magazine spotlights artists, designers, photographers, crafters and others with a creative side.

Does your work relate to the subject matter of this publication. Whether you do what you do for self-enjoyment or to sell your craft, we support you.

Contact: art@CarpeNocturne.net
Subject Line: Spotlight Feature

ARTISTS • COSPLAYERS • CRAFTERS • DESIGNERS • MODELS • MUSICIAN • PHOTOGRAPHER

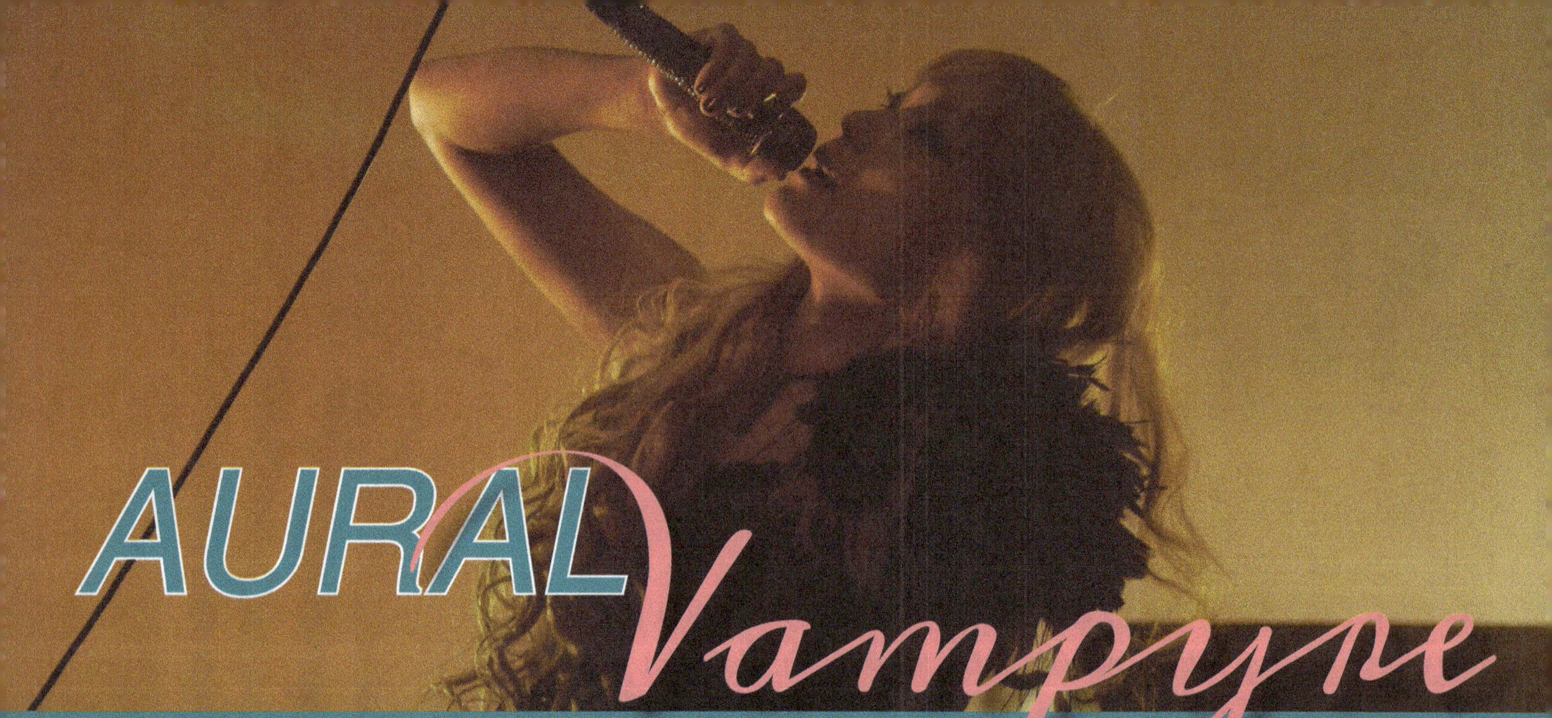

AURAL *Vampyre*

By Michael Jack

What happens when a vampire vocalist meets a mysterious serial killer sound producer? Although this may seem like a hypothetical question, it has already been answered. Enter the energetic dark sounds of the extremely charismatic band Aural Vampire. Although known to the world mostly for their chic, Anime and Lolita inspired Gothic fashion, Japan has a vibrant underground music scene. Active for over a decade, Aural Vampire have established themselves as the premier Japanese Gothic band. They are very J-Pop heavy, but combine strong elements of Industrial, rock, and Darkwave to their music. I would say this former duo has created the perfect blend of East meets West music for the discerning Gothic ear. If you have not heard them before, I suggest you give a listen.

Aural Vampire began simply as two kids in high school who shared a love for 70's and 80's horror movies. Exo-Chika was a natural performer who loved to sing and dance. Raveman avoided social situations, and preferred to spend his time collecting and playing with sounds. The almost natural result was a collaboration. For their stage presence, Exo-Chika embraced her love for vampires, although her style goes way beyond her pointed fangs. Raveman donned a sadistic mask, and became the image of the horrific slasher. Together they would create a world of Gothic horror, although they didn't fully realize what culture they were about to appeal to, or what culture would embrace them.

Exo-Chika and Raveman began primarily as a live band. In 2004, they released their first full-length album, "Vampire Ecstasy," on an independent label. The CD was very Pop oriented, but embraced the darker side of the duo within the lyrics, voice sampling, and heavy electronic beats. In 2005, Aural Vampire released an online single, "Death Folder." The next three years would see the duo remain very active as a live band, but not active in the recording studio. In 2007, the band saw their first overseas trip, and toured Germany. Their popularity was growing.

In 2008, Aural Vampire was signed to the major label Avex Trax. Later that year, they released three self-titled EP's, and were invited to perform at Anime Matsuri in Houston, Texas. This was only the beginning of their convention appearances. Aural Vampire was welcomed back to Anime Matsuri in 2010, and performed at various events throughout Germany, including AnimagiC. Their name was becoming known among Anime fans and Goths worldwide. In 2010, Aural Vampire released their first full-length album under Avex Trax titled, "Zoltank." This CD was still heavily J-Pop oriented, but contained stronger elements of Rock and German-Industrial influences than their previous works. Following their release, the duo embarked on their first North American tour. In 2011, the duo released the EP "Kerguelen Vortex," and it would be their last through Avex Trax.

2012 saw a lot of changes for Aural Vampire. First, the duo signed with Yottabyte Records. Next came the additions of new band members Wu-CHY (Bass), Higuchuuhei (Guitar), ZEN (Keyboards), and IZU (Drums). They were now a six piece act. With the new

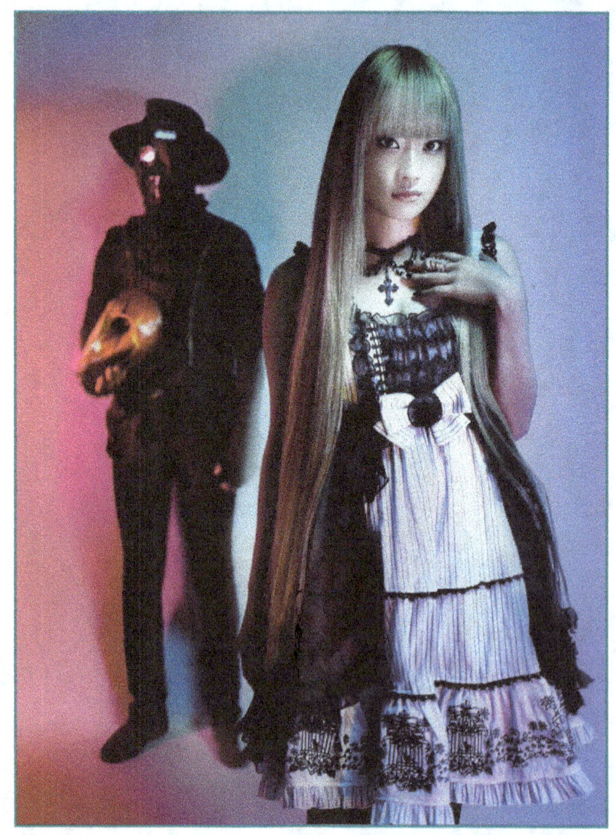

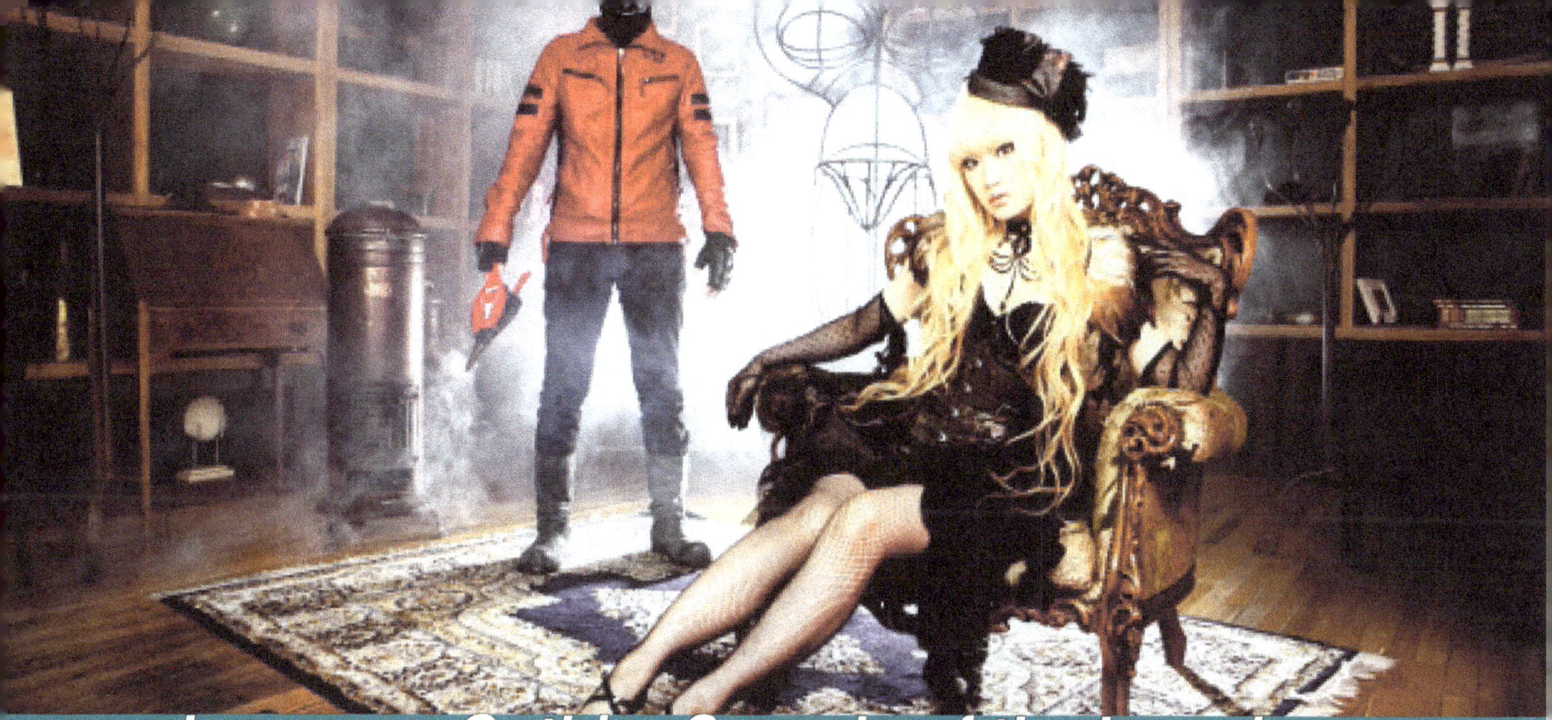

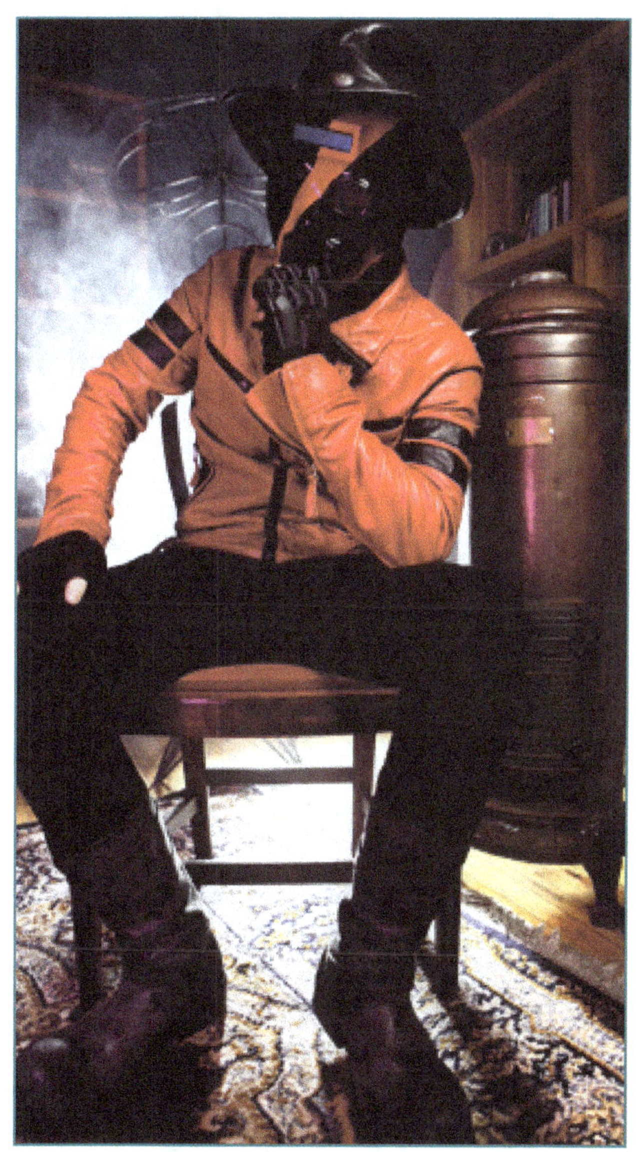

Japanese Gothic: Sounds of the Invasion

lineup, Aural Vampire released their third full-length CD titled "Razors on Backstreet." It was the first to not feature front-woman Exo-Chika on the cover. Instead, they opted for total soundmaster Raveman, depicting a play on the 80's horror hit, Nightmare on Elm Street. The new album swayed heavier towards the rock side of music, bringing an even darker feel to their already macabre sound.

Aural Vampire has the distinguishing honor of being the most popular Gothic band from a country rich in the dark underground. Their sense of horror style blended with Japanese Anime has brought them international attention. People are captivated by Exo-Chika's fangs, which are, in fact, permanent. Raveman is never seen without a mask. He even has one to eat with, which further adds to the band's mystique. Then there is the music. It's catchy, fun, and sadistically twisted. Although Aural Vampire has been active for over a decade, I feel this is only the beginning of what is going to be an international underground love affair with the former duo. Aural Vampire's sound is growing, widening it's appeal, and the world is taking notice.

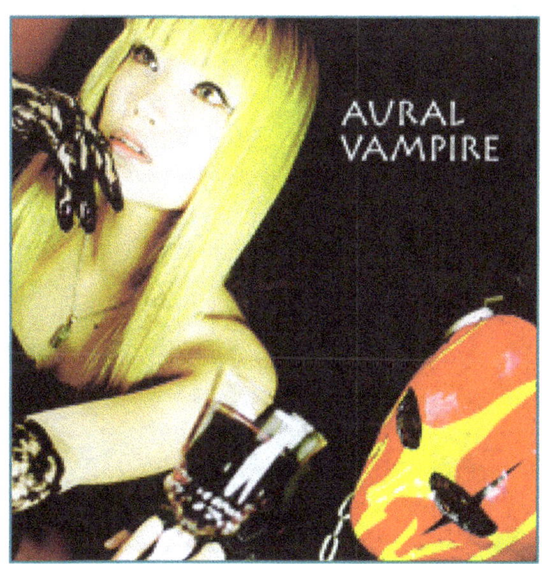

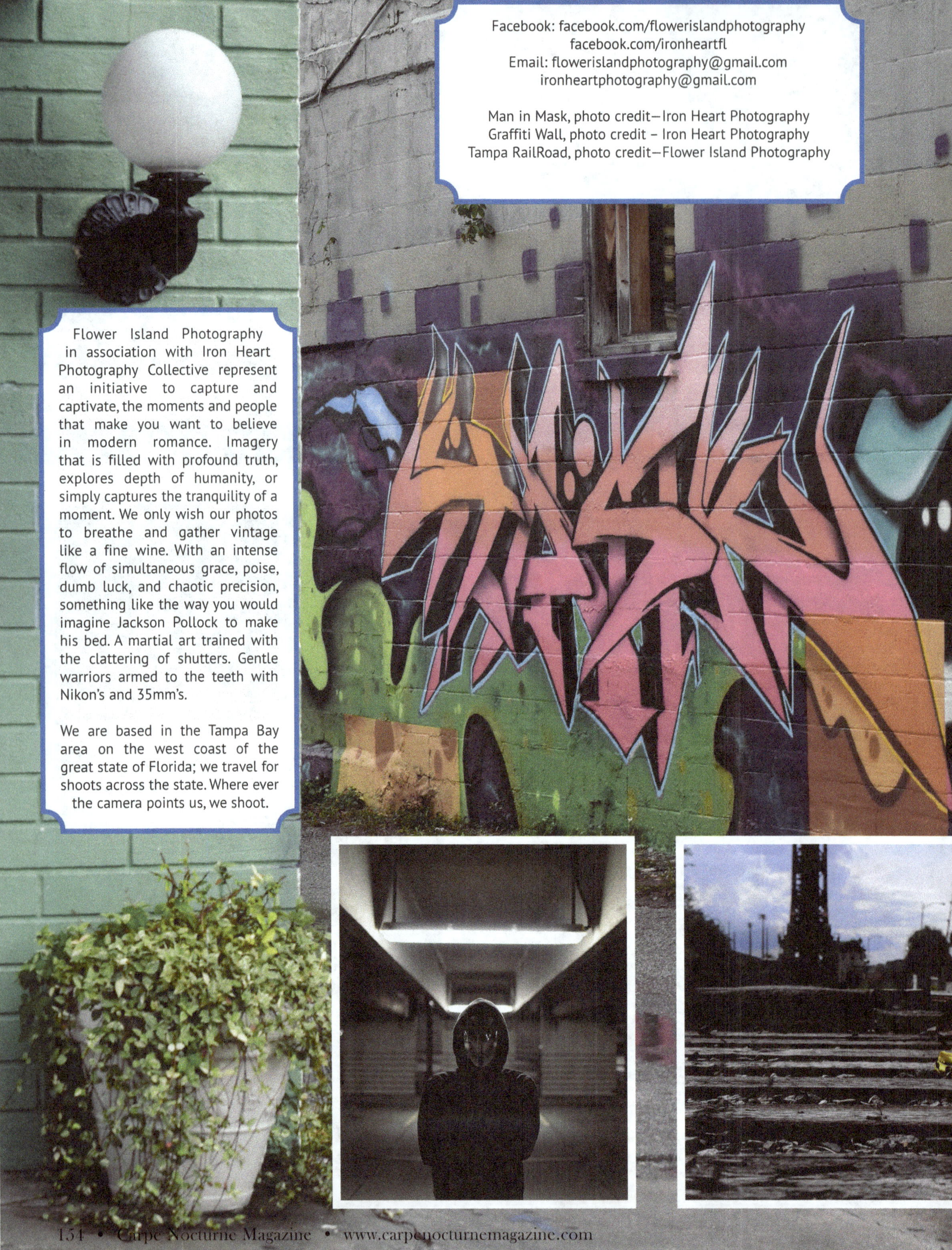

Facebook: facebook.com/flowerislandphotography
facebook.com/ironheartfl
Email: flowerislandphotography@gmail.com
ironheartphotography@gmail.com

Man in Mask, photo credit—Iron Heart Photography
Graffiti Wall, photo credit – Iron Heart Photography
Tampa RailRoad, photo credit—Flower Island Photography

Flower Island Photography in association with Iron Heart Photography Collective represent an initiative to capture and captivate, the moments and people that make you want to believe in modern romance. Imagery that is filled with profound truth, explores depth of humanity, or simply captures the tranquility of a moment. We only wish our photos to breathe and gather vintage like a fine wine. With an intense flow of simultaneous grace, poise, dumb luck, and chaotic precision, something like the way you would imagine Jackson Pollock to make his bed. A martial art trained with the clattering of shutters. Gentle warriors armed to the teeth with Nikon's and 35mm's.

We are based in the Tampa Bay area on the west coast of the great state of Florida; we travel for shoots across the state. Where ever the camera points us, we shoot.

Robert Walker

Puppet Maker

Website: fantasypuppet.com
Facebook Page: The Midsummer Knight's Dream
Location: Ocala, Florida, USA

What got you started as a puppet maker and when? I was fascinated with marionettes when I was about 12 and my interest grew as I experimented with different ideas.

Upcoming events you perform at regularly: Renaissance fairs and conventions around the USA.

Favorite Bands: I like so much music from classical to very modern like Abney Park and Panic at the Disco.

Hobbies/Interests Other than performing: I like to create all kinds of things, whatever I decide to put my hands to really.

Have you ever appeared in any other publications or on the radio? Local and a few newspapers across the country.

Are there any artists I'd like to meet? Yes but most have passed on I would have loved to meet Jim Henson.

Are there any parts of the country/world where you would rather be based and for what reasons? No I love Florida, it's a good place to travel from and come home too.

How long have you been involved in making the woodbabies? Since 1983.

Who/What inspired you to get into puppets as a living? It just sort of happened friends wanted them and then their friends wanted them and I was in business.

Do you have any schooling/training in art? Yes I have a Bachelors degree in graphic design.

Is your work compared to the work of anyone else? Yes, Jim Henson's work and Brian Froude.

Do you show your work? Yes at renaissance festivals and convention across the country.

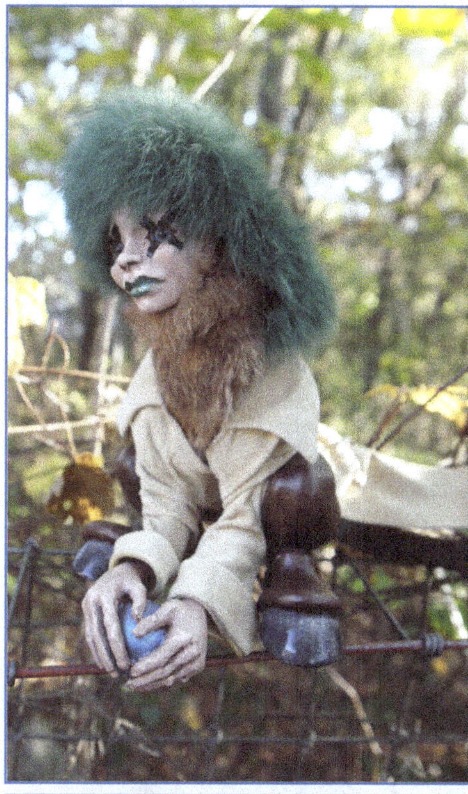

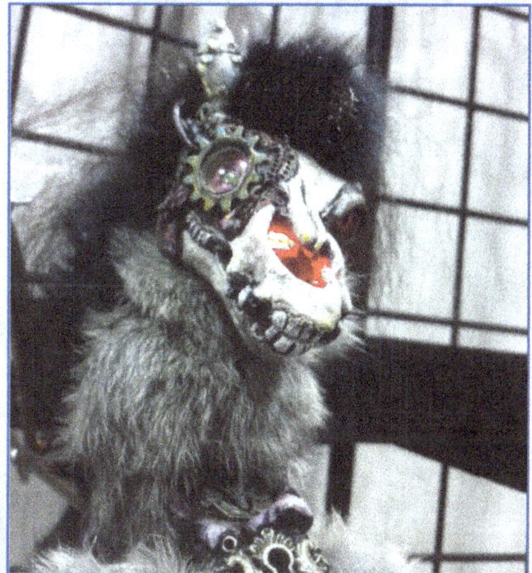

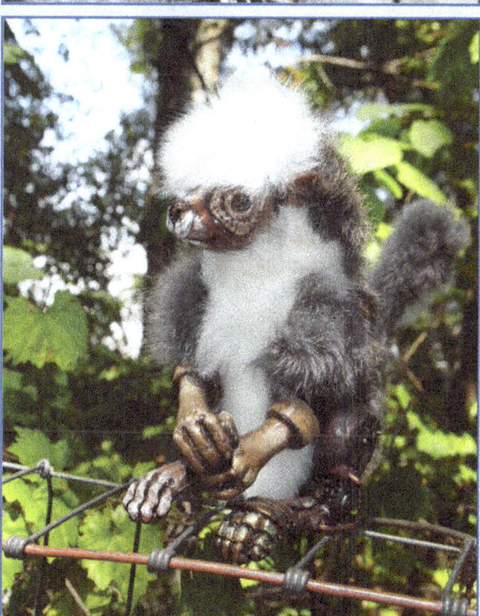

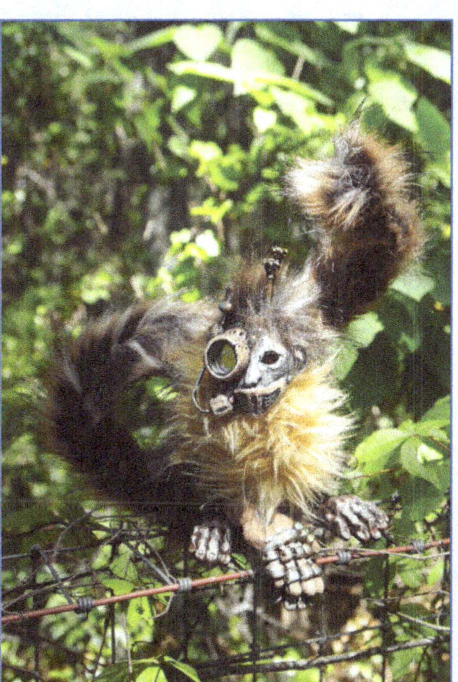

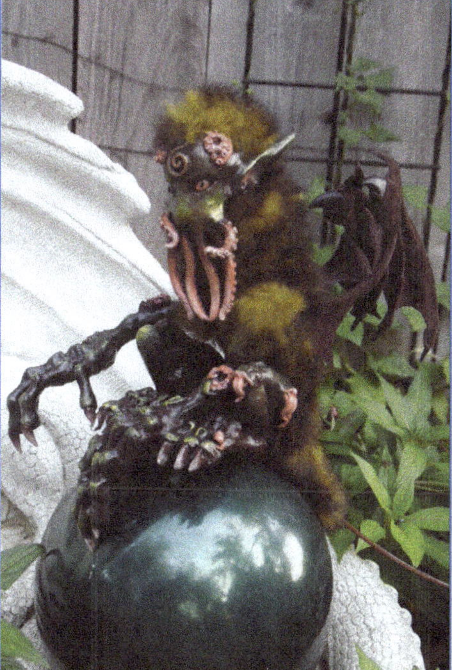

NIC NASSUET
Musician

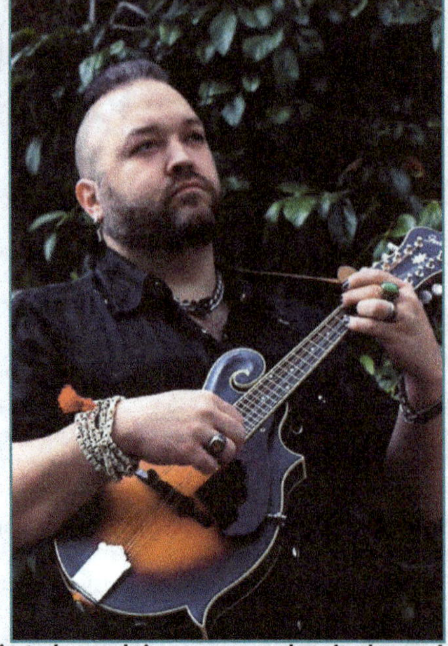

Website: www.nicnassuet.com

Facebook Page: www.facebook.com/nassuet

Location: Hollywood, CA, USA

Biographical Information: I've always been singing and writing songs, for as long as I can remember. I didn't work up the motivation to pursue it as a career until after a family tragedy.

Likes: Animals, guns, pizza.

Dislikes: Pickles, mustard.

Hobbies/Interests Other than performing: I only have two hobbies: Joining cults, and espionage.

What got you started as a musician and when? I started back in elementary school doing professional musical theater. In high school I was always in a band, or two.

Where did you learn your craft? I've been a singer, and played around with musical instruments, for my whole life. I was a professional musical actor for many years, and fronted for a few unknown bands. I suppose that would constitute my education on music and songwriting. I don't know how to read music, and I loathe the concept of songwriting classes. After a series of personal tragedies, I learned to sit and listen. What I heard was music and words, so I plunked them out on a guitar, then filled in the gaps, and had it all professionally recorded.

Do you have any preference in equipment that you use and why? I love Breedlove acoustic guitars. They have the best tone, features, and handcrafted quality for the money. For strings (mandolin, acoustic guitar, electric guitar, and acoustic bass), I use SIT strings exclusively.

What are your preferred music genres and/or are you known for a specific style? I started calling it "Gothic Folk" way back in 2000 when I was trying to do acoustic versions of music that I really liked. I didn't know what else to call it. When I moved to Hollywood, that seemed to stick with my publicist, so that's what they refer to my style as is in the blogs and magazines. It crosses over a bit into neofolk territory at times, with a hint of horror punk, and, some have said, 90s grunge, but I stick to acoustic guitars, upright basses, violins, cellos, and mandolins, so it all has a folk-rock feel to it, even though one excited promoter referred to one of my songs as "acoustic metal".

Do you get to perform at many events and, if so, where have you traveled to in the past year? We were invited to a couple of events, and traveled as far East as Nashville, but I really prefer to stick close to Hollywood, since I live there. That said, the environment in Hollywood isn't ideal for musicians. Everything is pay (a lot) to play (a little), and the market is saturated.

Do you have any favorite venues/clubs to perform at and why? I really like Boardner's/Bar Sinister in Hollywood. The back room is covered with a large canopy, so it is totally sheltered, yet people can smoke - a rare thing at concerts. The stage is deep, and framed with dark red velvet curtains, and a very large candelabra with lit candles and melting wax sits in the middle of the floor within a water fountain.

What do you feel the state of the scene is today and, in your eyes, has it changed much (and how) since you first started? You can't just say crazy shit and expect people to believe you anymore. I know that sounds kind of harsh, but back in the 90s there were a lot of people spouting a lot of crazy things, and without Google Earth, and Wikipedia, people believed what they were told. Greater access to information, and a more discerning crowd, has led to the demise of the esoteric aspect of the scene, which, in my opinion, is a good thing.

Have you ever appeared in any other publications or on the radio? Yes, I was on the cover of an indie music magazine this year, did a couple of on-air interviews, and was reviewed/interviewed in a few dozen publications recently.

Do you have any specific bands whose music you really enjoy and why? I could listen to old Misfits albums all day, until the day I die.

I imagine you've met many of the artists who inspire you. Do you have any favorites and why? My favorite band of all time is My Life With the Thrill Kill Kult. Their lead singer was really sweet the first time we met and kept trying to kiss me. Later, we hung out with him after a Leatherfest in Silverlake, and it turned into a weird situation with cops and assault charges. They have a really great sound guy who opens for them as DJ Toxic Rainbow, you should check out his stuff. I'm also a really big fan of Danzig's early work, especially with Samhain. I've been fortunate enough to meet Glenn a couple of times. I love Nine Inch Nails' older stuff, and had the chance to talk briefly with Trent Reznor on a studio lot after a screening.

Are there any artists/bands you'd like to meet? AFI (the entire band), Ogre from skinny puppy,

Are there any Venues/Clubs/Events you'd

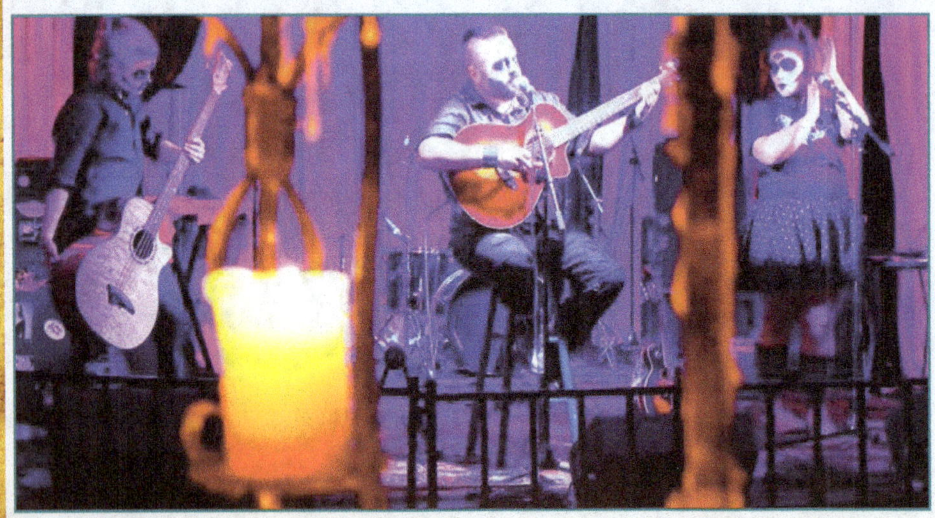

really like to perform at anywhere in the world? I would really love to perform at Superman's Fortress of Solitude, sadly it doesn't exist.

What direction do you think our "scene" is going and do you feel it's positive? It is becoming more consolidated, out of necessity. There are fewer people going to clubs, and everyone got older. I think it is positive, since change is good, but I will be honest, and say that I don't like a lot of the change I see right now. Things are getting really tame, and the PC movement is creeping into every aspect of society. People are afraid to be themselves now, and it didn't used to be that way.

Are there any parts of the country/world where you would rather be based and for what reasons? No. I love Hollywood.

What is the scene like in your area and, if you travel, how does it compare with other parts of the country/world? LA is weird. It still has some of the old standard bearers in the scene - both people, and clubs/institutions. You can have anything you want, in whatever way you want it, in LA, and you don't have to dig too far beneath the surface to find what you are looking for. I travel a lot, and I would say that the scene here in LA compares very favorably to other parts of the country/world.

Do you have any new music you are performing and how is it being received? I'm about to put out an EP of old tracks I rediscovered from a horror punk band I was in over a decade ago. Obviously, that will sound very different from the violins, cellos, and acoustic instruments on "Eleutherios". Eleutherious got some really great reviews, and was well received. I put a couple of the old horror punk tracks out to test the waters, and they were also well received, although from a very different audience.

Is your work compared to the work of anyone else? The group of artists that my work has been compared to is so diverse that it boggles my mind. I don't know how you can make comparisons to Jeff Buckley, Peter Murphy, Axl Rose, Sisters of Mercy, and Nick Cave in the same review, but some critics have done just that.

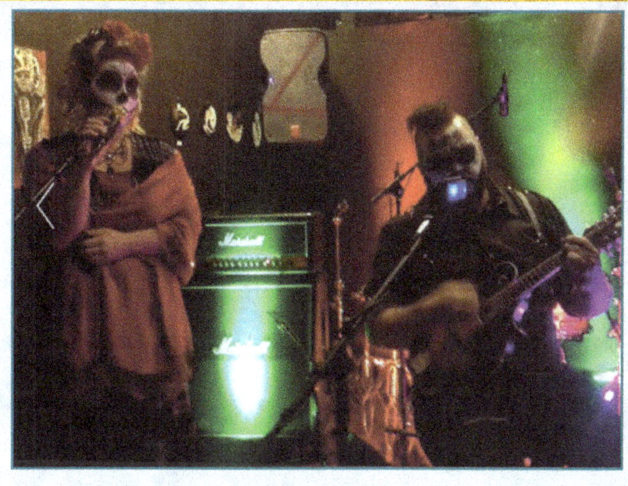

Do you show your work/cd's/merchandise? Yes. We perform all over Hollywood, and sell CDs at Amoeba records, iTunes, google play, and at shows.

Instagram: @NicNassuet
Twitter: @NicNassuet
www.nicnassuet.bandcamp.com
http://www.facebook.com/nassuet
www.nicnassuet.com

Also search for us on iTunes, Amazon, Google play, and Spotify!

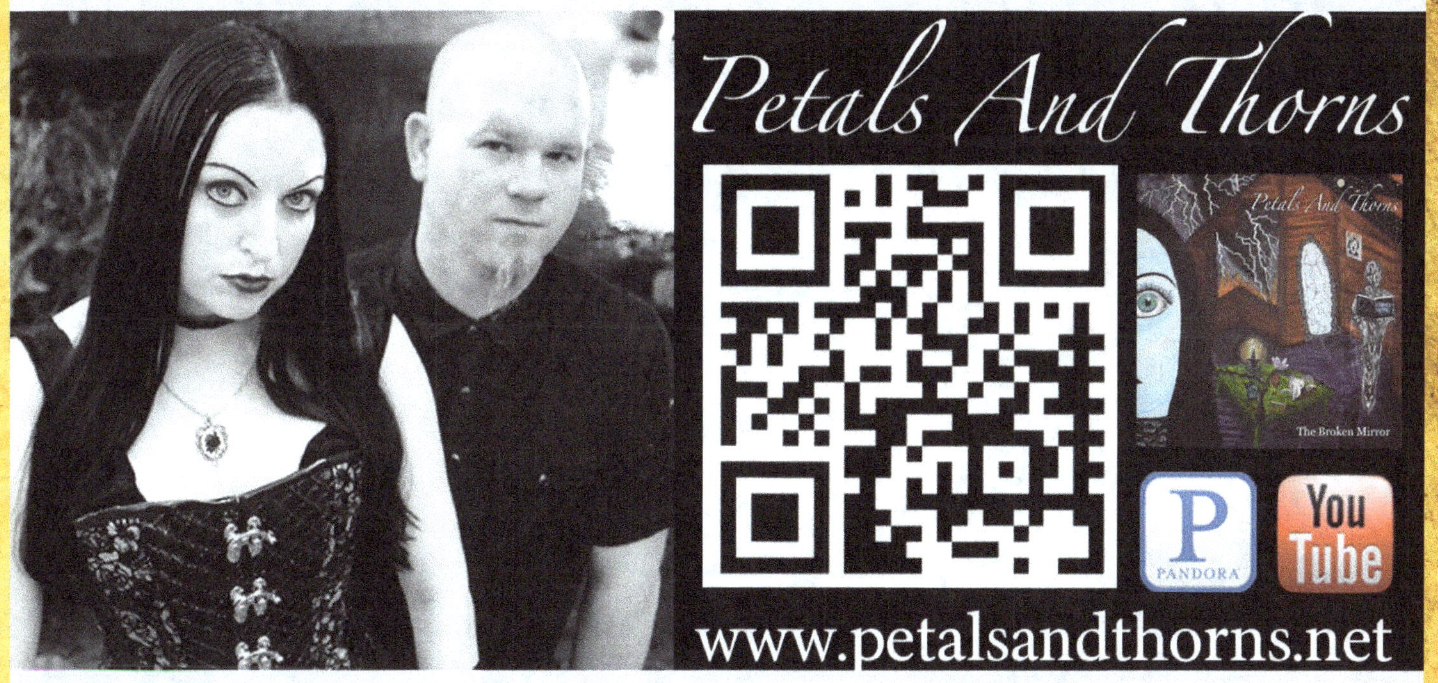

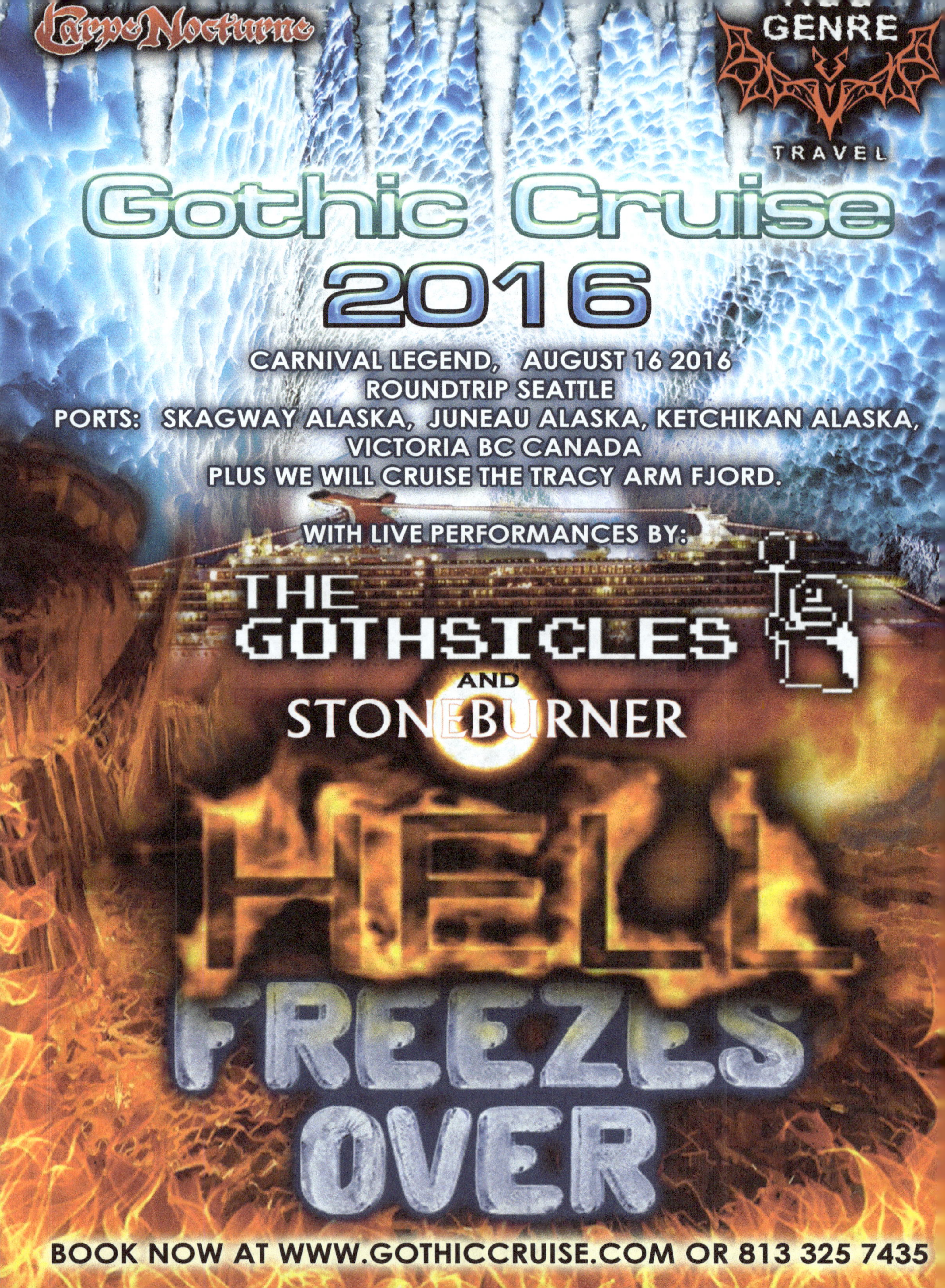
Carpe Nocturne
GENRE
TRAVEL
Gothic Cruise
2016
CARNIVAL LEGEND,   AUGUST 16 2016
ROUNDTRIP SEATTLE
PORTS: SKAGWAY ALASKA, JUNEAU ALASKA, KETCHIKAN ALASKA,
VICTORIA BC CANADA
PLUS WE WILL CRUISE THE TRACY ARM FJORD.
WITH LIVE PERFORMANCES BY:
THE GOTHSICLES
AND
STONEBURNER
HELL
FREEZES
OVER
BOOK NOW AT WWW.GOTHICCRUISE.COM OR 813 325 7435

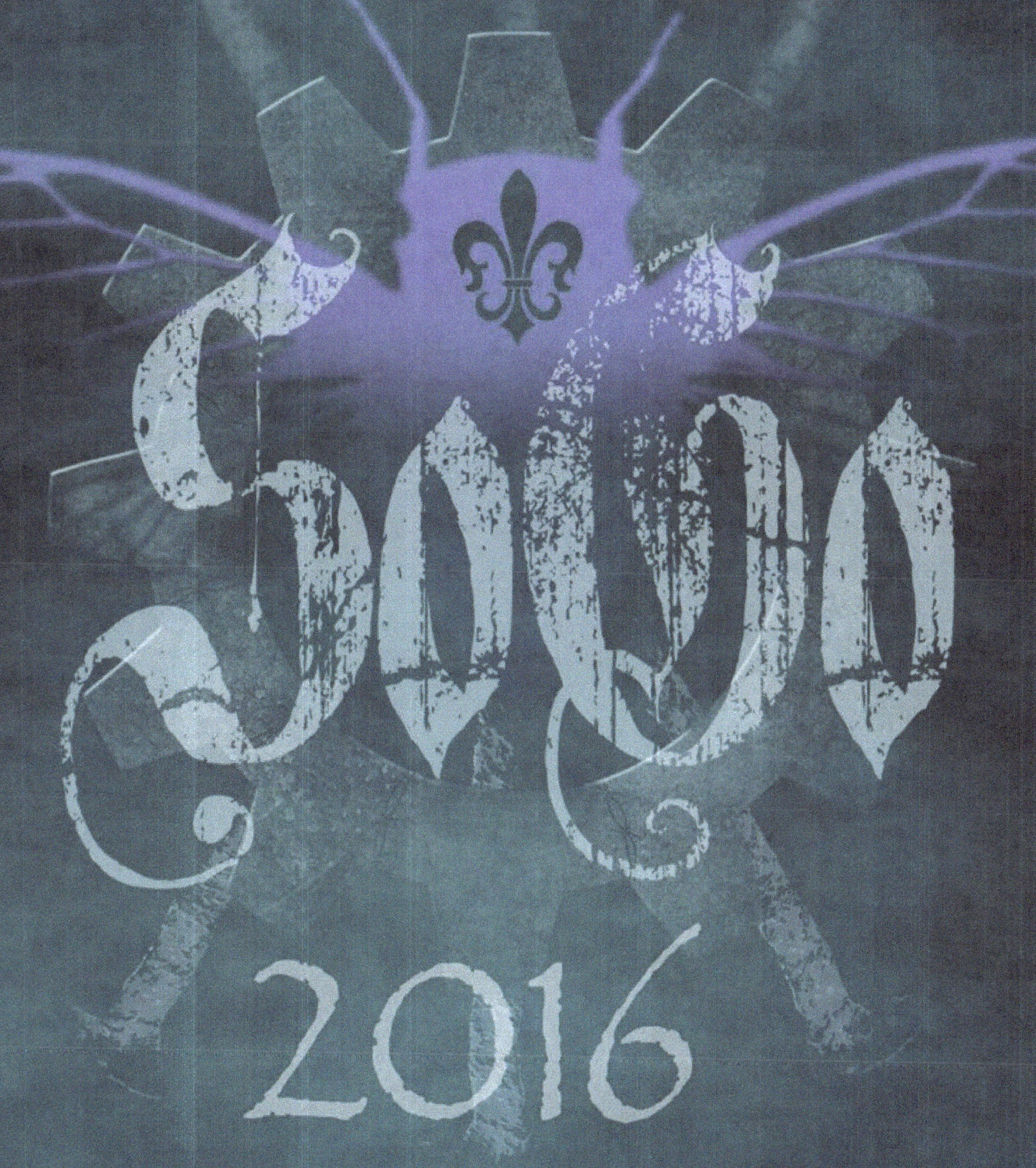

www.facebook.com/SoGoFest
SoGo
2016